CITIES

BRASÍLIA

CITIES

by

JAMES MORRIS

A HELEN AND KURT WOLFF BOOK

HARCOURT, BRACE & WORLD, INC.

New York

For
MY MOTHER
with much love
from us all

ITINERARY

ACCRA, Ghana
ADDIS ABABA, Ethiopia
ADEN, Aden Colony
ALGIERS, Algeria
AMSTERDAM, Holland
ATHENS, Greece
BAGHDAD, Iraq
BANGKOK, Siam
BEIRUT, Lebanon
BERLIN, Germany
BOGOTÁ, Colombia
BRASÍLIA, Brazil
BUENOS AIRES, Argentine
CAIRO, Egypt
CANBERRA, Australia
CAPE TOWN, South Africa
CARTAGENA, Colombia
CHESTER, England
CHICAGO, U.S.A.
CUZCO, Peru
DAMASCUS, Syria
DARWIN, Australia
DELHI, India
DUBLIN, Ireland
FORT-DE-FRANCE, Martinique

GENEVA, Switzerland
HAMBURG, Germany
HELSINKI, Finland
HIROSHIMA, Japan
HONG KONG, Hong Kong
  Colony
HONOLULU, U.S.A.
ISFAHAN, Iran
ISTANBUL, Turkey
JERUSALEM, Israel/Jordan
JOHANNESBURG, South
  Africa
KABUL, Afghanistan
KANO, Nigeria
KATMANDU, Nepal
KUWAIT, Sheikhdom of
  Kuwait
KYOTO, Japan
LA PAZ, Bolivia
LENINGRAD, U.S.S.R.
LIMA, Peru
LONDON, England
MADRID, Spain
MARIENBAD, Czechoslovakia
MELBOURNE, Australia
MONTREAL, Canada

Itinerary

MOSCOW, U.S.S.R.

MUNICH, Germany

NAPLES, Italy

NEW YORK, U.S.A.

ODESSA, U.S.S.R.

OXFORD, England

PARIS, France

PORT OF SPAIN, Trinidad

PRAGUE, Czechoslovakia

RAWALPINDI, Pakistan

REYKJAVIK, Iceland

RIO DE JANEIRO, Brazil

ROME, Italy

ROTTERDAM, Holland

SAN FRANCISCO, U.S.A.

SANTIAGO, Chile

SINGAPORE, State of Singapore

STOCKHOLM, Sweden

SYDNEY, Australia

TEL AVIV, Israel

TOKYO, Japan

TRIESTE, Italy

VENICE, Italy

WARSAW, Poland

WASHINGTON, U.S.A.

WELLINGTON, New Zealand

ILLUSTRATIONS

11

Illustrations

between pages 352 and 353

Acknowledgements are made to British European
Airways for the photographs appearing as plates
11, 19 and 20; to British Overseas Airways
Corporation for plates 1, 4, 12, 13, 22, 25, 26, 27
and 28; to the British Travel and Holidays Association for plate 18; to Camera Press Ltd. for plates
2, 5, 6, 7, 8, 9, 10, 14, 16, 17, 21 and 23.

FOREWORD

This book is a view of the urban world, as it looked, sounded and smelt to an Englishman in the fifties and sixties of the twentieth century.

The ten years of my prime, between my twenty-fifth and thirty-fifth birthdays, I spent as a wandering foreign correspondent, and this peripatetic existence gave me a precociously wide range of comparisons. 'Comparison,' George Santayana once observed, 'is the expedient of those who cannot reach the heart of the things compared': but though I happen to agree with him, nevertheless I profited from the experience, for it seemed to me that in trailing here and there about the hemispheres, without much pattern or programme, I glimpsed almost all the contemporary processes of history, reflected or embedded in the places I visited.

I sniffed the cold war, for instance, that blight of our decades, in Berlin, in Moscow or in Kabul. I sensed the resurgent energy of Europe beside the Rhine in Rotterdam, or trailing an imaginary compatriot through the streets of Paris. I observed the already ageing strength of Communism—cruelly in Marienbad, sadly in Warsaw, endearingly in Odessa, menacingly in Hong Kong. I watched the black and brown peoples emerging into responsibility among the glories of Delhi, the miseries of Johannesburg or the specious high jinks of Accra. I warmed myself wryly, in Fort-de-France or Rawalpindi, before some late embers of Empire. I mourned the old order in Chester or Addis Ababa. I felt North America hardening with power, in San Francisco or Washington, and South America uncertainly maturing among the prodigies of Brasília. I saw the nuclear shadow lying still upon the pavement of Hiroshima.

Two lessons in particular I learnt from it all. The first, a hackneyed one, concerns the intermesh of the world—which is small even for us ordinary travellers, and has always been easily spanned by great ideas and remarkable souls. Thus, in the pages of this book, you may meet Muslims in Cape Town and Anglicans in Buenos

13

Foreword

Aires, Frenchmen in Fort-de-France or Algiers, Algerians in
Reykjavik, Oscar Wilde in Isfahan, American architecture in
Holland and Arabian philosophies in northern Nigeria. The
courtesan Lola Montez turns up in Munich, Melbourne and San
Francisco. From the walls of the Escorial, on page 241, we may look
out with Philip II to the ramparts of Cartagena de los Indos, on page
95. No man is an island, and even less is any city.

My second deduction, though, is less conventional. It is this: that
for all the horrors of our time, for all the woes of our Cassandras,
for all our real forebodings and alarms, the world is perhaps in a
friendlier condition today than it has ever been before. In all these
wanderings I can recall only three or four occasions of hostility—a
stone thrown in Egypt, a dogmatic sneer in Moscow, ribaldry in
Australia or hinted gibes in New York. By and large, wherever he
goes in the world today, the traveller will encounter only kindness.
There are precious few savages to spear you or eat you. There are
not many fanatics to throw you out of their places of worship. The
ideological war, though it encumbers the nations still, scarcely
affects the ordinary individual, so that you may walk with equal
assurance through Leningrad and Chicago. Though you may still
find poverty indescribable, you may also see more people more
prosperous than ever. We are passing through a period of excitement
and discovery, a renaissance of all the sciences, such as mankind has
seldom known before: and this tremendous movement has brought
some good to almost all of us, even the poorest, even the most cynical.

So my book, though I hope it is not all sickly sentiment, is certainly
not all despondency. It is, however, necessarily a patchy collection, and
would be tedious indeed to read straight through, like a novel. Some
of its essays are set pieces, some commemorate mere episodes or aspects
of a city. Some of the places I know very well, some all too little. Some
I have visited more recently than others. Some I have probably treated
too unkindly, some too generously. Often I have, luckily for the rea-
der, forgotten all the symbolisms of history, and just enjoyed myself.

But it does at least possess two binding unities—unity of
vision, unity of time. I have seen all these cities for myself, and I
have seen them all within a single decade. If I had been born a generation earlier, I could scarcely have done it in a lifetime. If I had the
cosmos to explore, I might not bother to try. But mine is the moment
of the jets, between the steamships and the rockets, and this is how the
earth's cities seemed to me, during the last of our earthbound years.

ACKNOWLEDGEMENTS

Several generous institutions put the quicksilver in my ears, as Sancho Panza once described it, and I must especially thank those responsible at *The Guardian* (Manchester), *The Times* (London), *Life*, the *Saturday Evening Post* and the World Bank.

I am also grateful to several editors for permission to reprint essays or parts of essays. Thus Bangkok, Beirut, Cairo, Kyoto, Lima, San Francisco, Singapore and Venice were first published in *Life*; Oxford and Delhi in *Horizon* (New York); Dublin and Marienbad in *Encounter*; Istanbul in *The Queen*.

The essays on Aden, Baghdad, Cape Town, Chicago, Damascus, Honolulu, Isfahan, Jerusalem, Johannesburg, Kuwait and New York have appeared in somewhat different form in previous books of mine. Essays too numerous to mention first appeared, in part or in whole, in one shape or another, in that paragon of patronage, *The Guardian*.

ACCRA

Like splendid pickets down the West African coast stand the strongholds of the Portuguese, erected one by one, with guts, bloodshed and slavery, as the caravels of Henry the Navigator probed southwards towards the Cape. They are spacious, flamboyant, arrogant structures, given a sense of dark power by their origins, and a sense of piquancy by the tumble of exotic trees, palm shacks, long-boats and African fizz with which their gorgeous ramparts are now invested: and in their cynical old way they still contribute powerfully to the flavour of those territories, like so many country mansions left high and dry among the housing estates.

I once climbed a steep path to the most formidable of these castles, and observed from its walls the distant low confusion of a city. A handsome cheerful cripple, a sort of crystallized crooked smile, led me hobbling up the hill. A man in a blazing blue toga waved at me from a nearby hut. 'Hey, Massa!' shouted the fishermen on the beach below, sinewy black figures among their nets and lean canoes. In the village that spilled down the slope below the castle walls, like the fief hamlet huddling beneath Krak des Chevaliers, they were celebrating a local holiday: the village chief sat gaudily beneath his ceremonial umbrella, the official linguist brandished his totem of office, the drums thumped away among the mud huts. On the village notice-board it was announced that at the forthcoming obsequies of John Hackman (alias Ankam Tsia), Bishop of the 12th Apostle's Church, the chief mourners would include Prophetess Grase Thannie and Senior Prophet John Elubah Kuwesie. But I strode through them all, undeterred by their distractions, until I reached the uppermost vantage point of the fortress, and could look down the delectable palm-fringed shoreline to that distant metropolis. Only one capital on earth, I thought, could be approached through quite that combination of sensations, that amalgam of history, gusto, colour and immaturity. Only one city possesses quite such a tart hinterland, and they call it Accra: at one time or another

17

Accra

a settlement of the Portuguese, the Dutch, the Danes and the British, and now the republican capital of Ghana.

She is not beautiful, but she is inescapably exhilarating, not always for the best reasons: a jazzy, high-spirited, ever bubbly place, whose inhabitants are dressed in dazzling multi-coloured togas, and love to dance a slow, blaring shuffle known as High Life. Accra has passed through some queer and cloudy political fluctuations since Ghana attained her liberty, but for all the vagaries of statesmanship she still feels elevated by the very fact of independence, like a young man flourishing his door key still, long after his twenty-first birthday. Many of Accra's gleaming, grinning, vivacious citizens are poor people, very poor, subsisting on dried fish and stringy vegetables, living in squalid tumbledown huts, embroiled in many a mediaeval tangle of loyalty and superstition: but the city as a whole is well heeled and confident, sustained always by the price of cocoa from the immense plantations of the interior. Like Bangkok, like Rio de Janeiro, this is one of those cities that feel inherently lucky, inherently easy-going, where it is all too easy to shrug your shoulders, throw away your statistical pamphlets, and go sight-seeing.

Or more pertinently, go gossiping. Accra is not really much to look at, but she never stops talking. Education has bitten deep into her inherited mores, and since it was generally bestowed by Europeans or missionaries, its flavour is sometimes strangely incongruous. The 'youngmen' of Accra (as the Ghanaians like to call those who have ripped themselves away from the old outlooks) cannot often tell you the origins of the Golden Stool of the Ashanti, or the outcome of the battle of Amoafo, but they are often embarrassingly well informed about the House of Tudor or pragmatic sanctions, and are likely to quote Joshua, Shelley or E. M. Forster with disconcerting accuracy. The fine public library of Accra is always busy, and not only with those pallid English housewives, in Horrockses cottons and sandals, to be seen there at tea-time looking for the latest animal best-seller. The press of Accra, reckless, racy, inconsequential, spitting rivalries, ambitions and semi-private jokes, boisterous in misprint, cross-eyed with mixed metaphors, Rabelaisian in abuse and Dickensian in characterization—the indigenous press of Accra is nothing if not vital. The Supreme Court of Accra, during any big hearing, is packed with eager and well-informed enthusiasts, swathed in togas or uncomfortably sealed in reach-me-downs, their big white eyes flickering between the antagonists of a cross-

Accra

examination like tennis fans at the centre court. The National Assembly in Accra, fast discarding the old-hat conventions of Erskine May, often assumes strange beguiling manners: nothing in contemporary politics is more suggestive than the spectacle of a Ghanaian parliamentarian in the full spate of argument, rolling his eyes, waggling his forefingers, mouthing rather than just uttering his sonorous phrases, hurling cabalistic passes at his opponents like a magician about to bisect his young lady. The rich stew of life in Accra is salted always with slander and intrigue, so that any waiter or shop assistant is quite likely to admit you, with a lowering of the voice and a secretive glitter of the pupils, into the latest Cabinet disagreement, and the whole structure of affairs is subject to sudden underhand convulsions, mass arrests or awful denunciations.

Nothing is altogether commonplace in Accra. She is a city of excesses. Public commerce is dominated, physically and figuratively, by the full-blooded, brawny-armed 'mammies' of the market, women of highly tempered economic instincts who play an extraordinarily important part in the progress of Ghana, and who are astonishingly close in manners as in methods to the glorious market women of La Paz, on the other side of the earth. These *grandes dames* of Accra are flounced in primary colours and half-swamped in dried fish, rolls of dazzling cotton, mounds of murky vegetables, chickens on the claw and cards of elastic, and they are distinguished by a noble Billingsgate spaciousness. Nobody ever hoodwinked an Accra market mammy, except perhaps another one, and no wise politician ignores their interests. It is their money, too, that finances the celebrated "mammy-wagons" of Accra, perhaps the most memorable of all this city's gay folk spectacles. No form of modern transport is gayer or gaudier than these bright-painted trucks. Their average speed is bone-shakingly high, their cargoes are wonderfully jumbled, and they are emblazoned with curious slogans, some of them pungent ('A Lonely Woman Is a Man's Temptation'), some pious ('Follow the Truth and Obey the Heavens'), some merely enigmatic ('Why?' or 'You Never Can Tell'). You can easily tire of such phenomena, with their brassiness, their clashing colours, their strain of the juvenile: but they do give a kaleidoscopic momentum to the capital, and make you feel as though you are wallowing in a bottle of rather cheap pop.

Juvenile? In my reactionary moments, I cannot help thinking so. For all the real pleasures of Accra, all her boisterous kindliness and

19

Accra

intelligence, she seems to me the least adult of capital cities. She expresses all that is noisiest and least reassuring about Africa, the *mélange* of primitive or half-understood beliefs, the crossed values, the vacant frivolity. If Moscow is like an old dressing-gown, as Tolstoy thought, then Accra is a fancy-dress pom-pom. Here you feel none of the stateliness of Ethiopia, the high dignity of Kano, the blazing punch of Cairo or even the tragic talent of the Johannesburg locations. This is Africanism almost undiluted: graced by no old Semitic heritage, style of Arab or mystery of Jew, and fast swamping the remnants of imperial order. Historians like to recall that the fascinating Benin bronzes were fashioned only five hundred miles from Accra: but to me, I must confess, this steamy coast of Guinea feels frighteningly devoid of old art, deep wisdom or towering religion, and seems like a nursery shoreline, bickering, giggling and blowing tin trumpets among the gew-gaws.

There are still ju-ju murders and Senior Prophets in Accra. There are still magical agencies, seers and wizards. On the lovely bathing beach, among the surfboards and the bathing huts, you may still be shown a palm grove well known to be the domicile of a particularly powerful fetish. In the markets of the city you may still find, brooding among the motor-bikes, the snakes' heads, dried rats, chameleons and monkey-skulls of the witch-doctors. Now and then a diner of traditional instincts will still excuse himself from the restaurant of the Ambassador Hotel to pour a precautionary libation in the garden. The average scholastic standard at the University of Ghana, I am told, is higher than that of most British universities: but a fearful amount of drivel is uttered by its graduates when they emerge into the fizzle of public life. The slogan 'Freedom and Justice' is written bold across the Triumphal Arch in Accra: but it often rings sour and sorry, when yet another political discontent is shut away in silence, or yet another travesty of democracy is foisted upon an excited electorate. When three of the most prominent members of the ruling party were suddenly arrested one morning the official newspaper instantly described them as dangerous opportunists, criminal sycophants and diabolical renegades. 'Master-adventurer Adamafio and his tribalist gang, spear-headed by himself, Ako Adjei and Cofie-Crabbe, figured erroneously that they could throw dust into the eyes of the nation. This vile trio today stand condemned as the most inhuman band of lunatic power-seekers and ungrateful tribalist ruffians ever to emerge in the struggle.'

Accra

This is vivid and full-blooded stuff, and springs directly out of the Gold Coast's sanguinary past. Accra indeed is full of traditions, from castle walls to chieftaincies, but no certainty of loyalty or purpose underlies them. Adamafio and Cofie-Crabbe figure perennially in the chronicles of these parts, but the old-school abuse of the *Ghanaian Times* reflects something insecure and jejune in the state of Accra. This is partly the fault of the imperial West, with its slave trade, its sometimes misinformed convictions, its thoughtless missionary zeal: but to my mind—*pace* that delightful crippled cicerone, *pace* the friendly fishermen on the beach, *pace* the genial chief beneath his panoply and that splendid view of Accra from the ramparts of the fortress—to my diehard English mind it is mostly only Africa, lovable and terrifying old Africa, which is noble sometimes, and sometimes cruel, but feels so often like a continent playing at history.

ADDIS ABABA

A young lion vetted me in Addis Ababa one morning. He lay at ease in a compound outside the palace of the Emperor of Ethiopia, his paws neatly crossed, his tail straight behind him, and he looked me long, cold, detached and calculating in the eye. I would like to have known his views on the future of Addis, that ebony legend among capitals, but he did not encourage advances. Like the city itself, he looked back at me with an expression not exactly forbidding, and certainly not malevolent, but rather secretive or bemused, as though he had recently swallowed a dormouse, and was determined not to belch.

Addis Ababa, too, is in a digestive condition, and having some trouble with her juices, but she possesses nevertheless a certain leonine dignity. I cannot call her a handsome city. Her pattern is formless and straggled, her architecture ranges from the mud shack to the pseudo-Corbusier by way of a thousand baroque and Bauhaus aberrations. She is a city without much focus, her slums and her palaces intermingled; here the pony-tailed misses streaming out of the lycée, there the palsied beggars crawling on blistered knees through the market. She offers no shock of vicious contrast, for her separate elements are too intimately fused, but physically she is a faceless kind of place, a little blurred perhaps, a little splodgy.

She has travelled a long, long way from *Black Mischief*, still the Western world's standard handbook to her character. Among African cities today Addis Ababa is one of the cleanest, one of the least squalid, one of the calmest. This is partly politics, for she is the capital of a patriarchal autocracy not at all encouraging to effervescence and high jinks; but it is mostly geo-history. Addis Ababa compensates for what she is by where she is, and when. Around her the delightful Shoa highlands lie like a Wiltshire evocation, and groves of junipers, larches, figs and eucalyptus trees sidle into the heart of the city, like the magical forests that invest Kyoto. A glorious half-alpine climate gives a sparkle and a sting to

22

Addis Ababa

this capital, keeps it free from sludge and stinks, fructifies its shanty slums and humours the wild polychromatic abstracts painted on the walls of its newest apartment blocks. The name Addis Ababa means 'New Flower', because she was founded in the odour of hope towards the end of the last century; and to this day the city feels young and unexpectedly charming, graced alike by the superb manners and the green fingers of the Ethiopians.

Never was there a more handsome citizenry, since the days of the Assyrian bas-reliefs. I once paused to watch a merchant weighing millet in the market-place of this city. His wife sat loyally beside him, dressed in a long white gown and a string cap, and three or four labourers in ragged tunics hastened backwards and forwards with their sacks. The merchant sat on a kitchen chair as lordly as any Prester John, bowed gravely over his scales, and when he looked up at me I saw burning black eyes sunk deep between the cheekbones, a nose chiselled like granite, a mouth at once haughty and infinitely delicate, grey hair curling Homerically around the temples, a thin face cold with authority, a look marvellously salted with dry and knowing humour. He smiled when he noticed me, the thin quiver of a smile, and as he did so he slammed the lock of his scales with a gesture terribly final, as though he had ordered the instant expulsion of the Jesuits, or had just beheaded his grandfather.

Addis Ababa is full of faces just as memorable: the resigned, distant, Biblical faces of the old men who loiter, leaning lightly on their crooked sticks, outside the iron-roofed shacks of the district courts; the intelligent, wary faces of the young bloods home from Europe and America; the aloof, incurious faces of the Muslims washing their feet in the fountains of the mosque; the gentle, empty, haunting faces of the young prostitutes, in virginal white and vicarage embroidery, who wait outside their dim-lit boudoirs (sickly pink, blue, or conventionally red) along the pavements of Churchill Street. This is Africa with Semitic injections. These are not the coarse, laughing faces of Accra. Here there is something extra in the blood, something more restrained and lofty, something that suggests to me the black nobles of legend, or the Magus at the stable door.

For Addis Ababa has nobility; the nobility of a proud but gentle Christian faith, and of an immemorial self-respect. This is a city, like Bangkok, that has scarcely known the long humiliations of colonialism, and has not been obliged to wallow through the sad

23

Addis Ababa

morass of recrimination, frustration and twisted emotion that belabours the emancipation of subject capitals. Amid all the thump and hubbub of the African renaissance, Addis Ababa stands alone as the capital of an ancient and truly African State. She thus retains a trace of feudal hauteur. There is a Minister of the Pen here, and a functionary called the Mouth of the King. Lions of Judah abound in gilded effigy, and from every hotel office, every restaurant wall, every barber's mantelpiece, there gazes the image of His Imperial Majesty, the Elect of God, Conquering Lion of the Tribe of Judah, splendidly ceremonial in Court dress, austerely military in khaki. This is a traditionalism rich and lovable, but flecked with pathos. It reminds me a little of Honolulu, a city still fragrant with the frail memories of the Hawaiian monarchs, who dressed themselves in the feathers of the o-o bird, and set great store by orbs and sceptres. There are not many kings left on the earth, and it is moving still to encounter one who claims direct descent from Solomon and the Queen of Sheba.

It cannot last, this lion's style. It is fretted, frayed and mocked already. Isolation bred the grandeur of the Ethiopians, but this is a capital no longer remote or mysterious. I can think of half a dozen capitals more difficult to reach, and several more backward and obscure. There is a daily air service nowadays to Europe, and the London Sunday papers get here on Monday. Addis has all the appurtenances of a modern city, from cold-jet dentistry to espresso coffee bars. Americans from Berkeley, Germans from Frankfurt, sometimes think this an insufferably primitive capital, with its beggars and lepers and bumbling bureaucracy, but to us old hands of Empire and Bandung, us habitual waiters in anterooms and addicts of enterovioform—to wanderers like us Addis Ababa is a haven of convenience. Mr. Waugh would scarcely recognize her now. Mr. Wilfred Thesiger would hastily saddle his camels for the wasteland. Mr. Graham Greene might begin to feel at home.

For the sleazier corrosions of progress are also beginning to show, and a little of the Pan-African fizz is bubbling around the inherited certainties. The patriarchal order is doomed, and even the Emperor himself, that grand old warrior-sage, is no longer sacrosanct. Addis Ababa seethes with foreigners, Swedes and Germans and Americans and Englishmen, connecting telephones, teaching woodwork, managing hotels, building roads, squabbling and intriguing and exhorting and complaining and making money and always, night and

24

Addis Ababa

day, year after year, syllable by syllable, assuring this antique comity that its systems are wrong and its values misguided. Addis Ababa is not a passionate city, daubed with slogans and loud with demonstrations; but as this flood of alien energies pours in, as ever more young Ethiopians come home from Harvard, Bonn or Oxford, so we may expect the new hybrid culture of Africa to take root here, too, swamp the old gardens of Ethiopia with its jazzy proliferation, and reduce this still lofty metropolis to the level of our times.

But it has not happened yet. The Emperor still rules in Ethiopia, and this remains a capital of high-flown protocol. There were thirty-five other lions in the compound that morning, some young and cuddly, some majestically mature, and as I walked away I fancied the ruminative gaze of each one of them fastened steadily upon my person. They were very silent and absolutely still. It was like that moment of polite but faintly embarrassed hush when the ladies are leaving with a swish for the drawing-room, and the men are eyeing the port. Those animals did not really want me there at all, but they were cubs of the Conquering Lion, and they would not dream of showing it.

ADEN

The only European colony in the Middle East is the British bunkering station of Aden, which lies near the south-western corner of the Arabian peninsula in a situation of startling discomfort. 'To the newcomer to Aden,' says an official pamphlet, 'this famous fortress and port presents rather a forbidding aspect.' This is, I think, an understatement. At first sight Aden strikes most newcomers as unmistakably the most repellent city they have ever set eyes on. During more than a century of prosperous and sensible government Britain has not brought one single beautiful thing to her, and she stands there on her bay, blasted and despondent, as if life has become one long awful hangover. Her streets are cracked and rubbish-blown. Her buildings are drab, her shops slatternly. Her setting is infused with savage force, but there is little sense of majesty or power to the vast rambling installations that announce the faded presence of the Raj. A hang-dog, shabbily mercantile feeling permeates the geometrical streets of the colony, and only the great ships offshore, endlessly steaming in and out of the harbour, give it any sense of grace.

In the Middle East this is unusual. In those parts almost every town has some mosque of dignity, some cool, austere courtyard, some endearment of manner. Aden, though, has none of the piquancy or spice of an Arab city. Her people are a hodge-podge of races—Arabs, Somalis, Indians, Jews, Egyptians, Syrians, Persians, Chinese, Britons—and her traditional status has been a grubby and graceless one: a coaling station. She is a great merchant centre, too, an air base and a naval station; but it is all too easy to equate the place, as you stroll its blighted boulevards, with one of those desolate coke yards that lie depressingly among the purlieus of English railway stations. There are no glimpses of aristocracy to Aden, no hints of gilded excess, no swaggering princelings, no imams of unspeakable sanctity. Her vices, you may feel, are squalid ones, tucked away in smutty back streets; and her virtues, though very real, are a terrible bore.

Aden

The old part of the Aden Colony is called Crater, because it is built inside the cirque of an extinct volcano, and in this dismal place there are some archaeological remains to which the unsuspecting visitor is sure to find his way. The famous cisterns, so we are told, were probably built in the millennium before Christ for the storage of rain-water; and so important are they, *qua* cisterns, and so fresh a light do they throw upon the pre-history of Aden, and so lonely is the eminence they occupy among the sights of the city, that you will no doubt approach them with an interest not easily to be repressed. Calm yourself. Of all the archaeological remains I have ever seen, of all the unrecognizable ruins and battered bulls, the cracked water pots and lumps of lead, the bits of chariots and buttons and painted ostrich shells and rusty spears and headbands from the tombs of Bronze Age chieftains—of all these scholarly phenomena, the cisterns in the Crater at Aden are easily the dullest.

Melancholy, too, hangs heavily around the crags of this colony. If they ever talk nowadays of the Empire on which the sun never sets, they can only be thinking of Aden. She is drenched with the imperial mystique. Her climate is atrocious, her manner garrisonic, and the visitor must climb about four hundred almost perpendicular steps to sign the Governor's visitors' book. Until 1937 the colony was administered from British India, and its character today is still masked by an Anglo-Indian façade. Indian merchants and lawyers abound. Labourers are coolies here, Englishmen are sahibs, the *suk* is the bazaar. The spirit of the Indian Empire lives on, perhaps more potently than anywhere else, tattered by the decades but not yet superseded. The old fans twirl slowly in the offices of the secretariat. The sweating bank clerks, in their shirtsleeves, write slowly in big ledgers above the godowns. The public gardens sometimes announce themselves to be For Parents and Ayahs Only, and up on the hill the Union Jack still flies all but imperturbably. If you would like a sad, nostalgic reminder of the British heyday, go to the Union Bar in Aden for your sundowner; the box-wallahs will be drinking their whiskies by the bar, wearing cummerbunds and talking about the price of hides or the boorish behaviour of the brigade major; and their women will, with luck, be wearing those shapeless and respectable cottons which one used to see, labelled 'Tropical Wear', in a magical window of Robinson and Cleaver's in Regent Street; and there will be copies of *The Field* in the morning-room; and from the veranda you will be able to inspect whatever

27

Aden

spick-and-span and obsolescent cruiser happens to be showing the flag in the harbour. There is a certain sombre attraction to this spectacle, and one can only wonder at the resilience of this fusty old organism, which has creaked on through the years like a steam train on some unhurried country line, and still has the same kind of determined strength as one of those crotchety but faintly twinkling old relatives who nonplus their hopeful heirs by repeatedly refusing to die.

It is a rich old body, too. Aden is a free port, and a great entrepôt. She distributes goods to many parts of Aden and East Africa, and through her wharves there pass to the markets of the world all kinds of Eastern substances—skins, hides, coffee, mother-of-pearl—whose names on packing-cases read pungently anomalous among the warehouses. A vast oil refinery seethes across Aden's bay. More ships arrive every year to refuel, and their passengers stream ashore to buy horrible handbags, Leicas, watches, and Arab costumes for the fancy-dress ball with which the ship's captain plans, in desperation, to kill an evening on the long voyage home. Aden, for all her ramshackle manner, is vigorously prosperous still. Three or four merchant princes dominate the commercial life of the place. They sometimes have labour troubles, for the trade-union idea (spiced with a strong pinch of nationalism) has caught on famously in Aden, but they seem to be still very comfortably enthroned. The greatest of these trading houses describe themselves as general merchants, importers, exporters, government and building contractors, ship repairers, refrigeration and radio engineers. They are agents for cars, oil, engines, ropes, batteries, binoculars, dyes, citrus fruit, wire, gin, tyres, cameras, exposure meters, beer, refrigerators, fans, radios, watches, and vitamins. They own a soap factory and a large garage, and until recently they were the proprietors of the Crescent Hotel, which they used to describe with telling ambiguity as 'the only one of its kind in Aden'.

So all in all the rambling, higgledy-piggledy streets of Aden disguise reserves of unsuspected substance, and the colony's one allure is the shining chance of moneymaking. To the indigent, though, as to the transient visitor, Aden does not offer much comfort. Her aspect is, as the pamphlet said, unmistakably forbidding. One of her major sources of revenue is a narcotic called *qat*, which almost everybody chews. This not very harmful drug comes by air each day from Ethiopia, and the Government, far from banning it, taxes the

Aden

stuff instead. I once asked a man in Aden how important a part *qat* played in his life. 'Sahib,' he said, looking wildly around the peeling coffee-shop in which he spent every minute of his days, 'Sahib, without *qat I know of no reason to continue.*'

And there breathed, I felt that afternoon, the very soul of Aden. If not currency, *qat.*

ALGIERS

In 1962, for the first time since the pashaliks and the corsairs, Algiers became an independent capital, chief city of a Muslim State, and set off into history once more with a hopeful if unsteady gait. In any lexicon of our times, though, this city must stand for anxiety, because for so many years, around the troubled middle of our century, she was symbolic of the struggle between the past and the future. To the generation that matured in the years after the Second World War, she played rather the part that Spain had played in the thirties: she was a prod to the conscience of Europe, a catalyst of emotions and a running tragedy. Her headlines were always baleful, her slogans of brotherhood and fresh start nearly always trailed away in acrimony, and in her image several contemporary agonies were cruelly epitomized—inflamed nationalism, perverted pride, motives soured and dignities defiled. Of all the cities of that time, she was the most chronically chafed by misery.

Let me describe her to you as she was then, on a hot summer day in the late fifties, when the French Republic was still clinging to its African territories, the poor colons still hoped to preserve their precarious privileges, and in the Algerian hinterland a war was still being fought. There she stands above her bay, unmistakably a great port, and still unmistakably French—almost as French as Marseilles, her neighbour across the water, certainly as French as Singapore is Chinese. The big British cities of Asia have reverted to the Oriental; Quito and La Paz are fast forgetting Spain; Salisbury, Johannesburg, Cape Town and Léopoldville feel African cities already, blended to their veldt or upland; even Alexandria, that old Greek temple and observatory, is an Egyptian seaport at last; even Sydney does not always rise to 'God Save the Queen'. Almost the whole North African shoreline has torn itself away from Europe, and the Mediterranean is no longer an inland sea, let alone Mare Nostrum, but stands as a frontier between the continents. Only

Algiers

Algiers, on such a day in the nineteen-fifties, remains a city transplanted out of Europe, and feeling European still. She has survived by stubbornness and savagery against all the storms of history. Half her inhabitants are Muslims already, but she is the supreme remaining example of the colonial metropolis, and she is shot through still with the energies of the lost imperial ideal.

She stands nobly enough above the sea, her tall sombre terraces illuminated by the precipitous staircases of Pépé le Moko, and blotched by the blurred white triangle that is the Kasbah. From a fine wide amphitheatre she surveys the bay below, her harbour always busy at her feet, her great merchant houses ranged in stolid order above her promenades. Tall arcades support her sweeping corniche, like the arches of a Roman aqueduct, giving her a lofty, classical expression; and here and there among the apartment blocks you may see the domes, crescents and crenellated white walls of a mosque, reminders that for all these first appearances, Algiers already stands on the edge of an alien hinterland. The hills behind the city, running away through pine forests and delectable lush valleys, reach towards the mountains of High Atlas and the immensities of the Sahara; and though Phoenicians, Romans, Vandals, Greeks, Arabs, Spaniards and Frenchmen have all settled at this spot, nevertheless a hot breath of Africa hangs upon the air of Algiers, a scent of jasmine and a rasp of sand.

She is a desiccated, heartless city, for all her lovely gardens, and you may glimpse her character most starkly during the blazing hours of early afternoon, when an ominous calm seems to fall like a blanket upon her streets, and the whole place seems to be cherishing some dread and menacing secret—as Albert Camus's Oran, down the coast, once cherished the awful secret of the plague. Only a few desultory students sip their anisette or toy with their peanuts on the boulevards. Only a lazy ship or two plods out of the shimmering harbour. Only a few slow, fat, sleepy eaters still linger over their *bouillabaisse* in the fish restaurants beneath the arcades. The tricolour droops listlessly from the yard-arm of the Admiralty, and up in the fetid tangled lanes of the Kasbah, that legendary harbour of vice, only a few elderly harlots, horrible with kohl, beckon to you from the frayed hangings of their brothels. In the railway sidings beside the sea the snorting old steam engines clank and clatter in the sunshine, and up the winding, monotonous hillside streets the trolley-buses swing weary and half empty, as in some tedious dream.

Algiers

Algiers is a heavy city. Her architecture is mostly graceless, her manner lacks merriment. She is the least romantic of the Mediterranean seaports, without the gift of fun or ecstasy. She might have been built, as she was once governed, by the Turks.

But when the heat begins to die, and the citizens emerge into the streets again, the shops open and the trolley-buses fill, then you may feel the baleful spirit of Algiers stealing into the open, like the plague rats slinking into the gutters. There are always Muslims about in Algiers, but in the early evening the centre of the city is overwhelmingly French and *bourgeois*. It feels like some humdrum provincial capital in France, tight-laced and respectable, but behind its prosaic façade dreadful things are happening, and if it is a day of political demonstration, an anniversary or an occasion of protest, then you may see the conventions discarded, the restraints torn away, and all the passions of the place laid bare. Algiers in the fifties is obsessed with her own self, her own hopeless struggle to remain French and European, and nothing could be much more depressing than one of the great public meetings at which she expresses this tragic resolution: for haunting its every gesture is the certainty of eventual defeat, the knowledge that in his innermost heart of hearts not a soul there, from the toughest young thug of a soldier to the homeliest old body of a grandmother, really believes in its success. There is a streak of the insane to the anxiety of Algiers. '*Algérie Française*' may be the cry of the hour, beaten out on drums, on car horns, with stamped feet and clapped hands: but it already sounds weirdly threadbare and arid, like the incantations of some dying cult, a ritual of Shakers, a dogma of Dukhobors.

The big public forum, outside the Government buildings, is crammed to suffocation on such an evening, the crowd spilling away through the pleasant gardens, up and down the steps, across the neighbouring squares, and petering away on its fringes into footweary housewives at the tables of deserted cafés, and groups of leggy schoolboys playing football in the streets. There stand the grim paratroopers, the high priests of mid-century Algiers, theatrically dressed in berets and camouflage suits, festooned with tommyguns, grenades and pistols, lounging about in attitudes fearfully tough and jungly, or swapping badinage with the crowd. There are the queer bigwigs of this confused and unhealthy city, hastening up the steps to the Governorate, or briefly appearing upon some

Algiers

flowered balcony: ramrod generals in *kepis*, greasy double-breasted politicians, wild creatures of the nocturnal Right, bearded plotters or fanatic militarists. The atmosphere is at once feverish and jaded: feverish because there is violence simmering just below the surface, jaded because Algiers has seen it all before. There is a taste of *déjà vu* to all this city's torments.

But nothing is more intoxicating than mass emotion, and before long that whole vast crowd, like so many maudlin drunks outside a saloon, is caught up in histrionics, swayed to a man by the querulous, pitiful passions of Algiers. Then you may see this poor city in the raw. Endless but emotive are the platitudes now pouring from the loudspeakers, emitted by gesturing generals and interspersed with martial music. Ever more inspiring is the presence of those hefty soldiers, the waving of flags, the blowing of trumpets, the echo of old French glories in the dusk. Ever more cruel do the public grievances seem to be, as the evening wears on: ever more misused the Frenchmen of Algiers, ever more misunderstood their motives of brotherhood, ever more heady their visions of Frenchness, fraternity, unity, generosity, honour. A sickly cheer greets a delegation of Muslims, now paraded in the forum as emblems of magnanimity: spindly old men with ragged robes, boys with cropped heads, a covey of bewildered white-robed women, with a trilling of high female voices and an arabesque of reedy clarinets. A battery of floodlights blazes through the square as the dark comes down, glinting on weapons and helmets, and making that great piazza feel ever more isolated and intense, surrounded only by silent darkness. Slowly, eerily, inexorably the emotions of the invested city gather with the night, invoked by all the old gods of rhetoric and patriotism, until at last, with a roll of drums, a sting of hot tears in the eye, a stiffening of muscles and a stirring of the heart, all that huge assembly, all that rag-bag of ambitious politicians, all that puzzled and baffled citizenry, all those childish paratroopers, all that decent, ordinary *bourgeoisie* bursts into the 'Marseillaise'—and for a moment all seems clear, all seems honourable, and only duty calls. It is marvellous what that noble hymn can do, when thirty thousand Frenchmen sing it beneath a forest of flags.

But it never lasted. Even then, when the French Army still manned the Algerian barricades, such a moment of emotion was transient and forlorn. It was like the tremor of a proud smile, crossing the face

Algiers

of some shrunken old harridan on a death-bed. Algiers was withered by a sickening of the spirit, and no atavistic potion could restore her. A year or two had still to pass before she was purged: but already, when that great song ended, it was succeeded only by the rumble of the crowd dispersing, the last clicking of the amplifiers, the hoarse shouting of sergeants, and the long, low, anxious murmur of Africa.

AMSTERDAM

I was once in Amsterdam when the first snow of the winter fell. The men in the central junk market, among their stuffed birds and rusty curios from Surinam, broke up the most hopelessly lop-sided of their kitchen chairs and made bonfires of them. The young girls ran disconcertingly about in short cotton skirts over blue woollen tights. A cold wind whistled in from the North Sea, huddling the more mature housewives in their mutation minks and driving the portly burghers to the felt-covered newspaper tables of the cafés, where they meditated ponderously over their coffees like so many East India merchants considering the price of apes.

Standing on a bridge in the flurry of the snow, however, and exchanging inconclusive repartee with a juvenile bargee, I happened to notice a sleek tourist motor-boat, all glass and chromium fittings, gliding down the waterway with a warm hum of diesels. Inside it, snug behind the glass, sat five young Americans in bright open-necked shirts and jeans. They all wore side-burns, and peered through their windows with an air of vacuous, if not actually narcotic, concentration: and as they passed slowly by, inspecting me, too, as though I were a mediaeval philosopher, they emanated a powerful suggestion of allegory. They were new men in a very old world. Their identity tags flashed around their necks like ritual amulets. They seemed to me like young priests from some distant cloistered seminary, on a mission of dogmatic inquiry.

Amsterdam often throws the visitor into this kind of relief, because she herself has a fictional and withdrawn quality, as though she is an illustration to a book of antique tales. Like Venice, she is a city of canals and curious prospects, but unlike Venice, she never shows off. She is one of the great tourist centres of western Europe, but she does not feel like one. Take a boat by all means, she seems to say, and stare at me out of your plated windows, but expect no song, dance or exhibition. Amsterdam was born a merchant city, at the point

35

Amsterdam

where the dike-controlled Amstel flowed into the River Ij, and she still has a manner of profitable function. Her very name only means 'the dam on the Amstel', and the big square that is her heart, where the great stores cluster, and the Royal Palace stands, and the church where the Dutch kings and queens are crowned—even this great piazza is called, to this day, simply The Dam.

Amsterdam's allure, indeed, is of a firmly logical and commercial kind, lyricized though it has been by time and art. The canals that set the style of the place do not run higgledy-piggledy or heedless, but follow an orderly and symmetrical design—spacious but sensible, like everything about Holland in her seventeenth-century prime. At first they seem to flow with a gay inconsequence, but in fact they pursue a series of four concentric semicircles, a half-moon with rings, centred upon the Nieuwmarkt, blocked at the north-eastern end by the quays of the Ij and the huge railway station, built upon an artificial island. Nothing was left to hazard, in the grand plan of Amsterdam. Industries were banished to six man-made islands in the Ij, and the whole of the inner city was laid out with exemplary common sense. A network of lesser waterways links the big canals, splendid embankments buttress them, four hundred bridges cross them, and if you walk outwards from the centre of the city, you will find that the four arterial canals are obligingly named in alphabetical order—Heerengracht, Keizersgracht, Prinsengracht, Singelgracht.

Thus, though her appearance is lovely and her culture profound, she is not one of your rapturous cities. Her effluences are essentially homely and comfortable, and of all the cities of Europe, none remains more resolutely European. There is no self-doubt about Amsterdam, and flying here from London, that seething hodge-podge and market-place of values, is like moving directly from cocktails with a degenerate genius to tea with an ambitious bank manager above his office on early closing day. The self-service civilization, the way of the disposable napkin, the expense-account ethos, the mock-American accent—all this has not yet swamped Amsterdam, and even the city's espresso bars, those emblems of the new cosmopolitanism, feel curiously mute and sober-sided. The streets of pleasure near the Amsterdam docks are among the most blatant corridors of vice in the Western world: but there is something almost cosy about their little steamy windows, behind which the violently scented girls in pink blouses sit with crossed legs in postures not perhaps quite so maidenly as those of your Aunt Ethel at the parish council meeting, but with just the same integrity of purpose. Even the teddy-boys of Amsterdam, though they lounge about in the approved attitudes of froward decadence, are often to be found eating sticky cakes of a particularly motherly and innocent sort, and somehow the crumbs of flour and sugar around their mouths make them look less like problems of society than urchins who have been at the strawberry jam.

The shops of Amsterdam, especially along the celebrated pedestrian canyon called the Kalverstrasse, are often gay and gaudy, but the everyday colours of this city are still sombre. Church congregations, Catholic or Protestant, are rows of subdued browns, greys and blacks, only intermittently enlivened by a daring feather hat. Cars are rarely salmon-pink or scream-yellow, ties are rarely jazzy, fashions do not often bowl you over with delight. At the hobbies exhibition held in the Great Exchange building each year— one of the most characteristic events in the Amsterdam calendar —you will find multitudes of adolescent enthusiasts absorbed with an almost gloomy fervour in their collections of medal ribbons, eye-glasses or Maltese match-boxes. The contemporary hunger for dispute, speed and disillusionment has not yet overtaken Amsterdam, and the things that people seem to talk about are placidly rooted things. Who will be the next conductor of the Concertgebouw? Will Sparta win their crucial soccer match? Who wrote the editorial in *Algemeen Handelsblad* this morning? Amsterdam lost some of her fizz, I suspect, when seventy thousand of her Jews were deported or murdered by the unspeakable Nazis: but she has powerfully retained her sense of cultivated and experienced calm.

She is not an enormous city, nor is she even the official capital of Holland—Government sits at The Hague. Rotterdam is a greater port by far, and Amsterdam is, for the foreigner, rather the kind of city you spend a night in on your way to somewhere else, by courtesy of K.L.M. Nevertheless she never feels provincial. This is partly because the Dutch, though now so small a nation, have never declined into pettiness, and retain, in the power of their industries and the pride of their institutions, a flourish of historical conse-quence. It is partly because Amsterdam herself is one of the great cities of the world of art, where Rembrandt lived and worked, where the Rijksmuseum cherishes its noble collection, where one of the world's best orchestras plays—a city of bookshops, libraries, antiquarians, of scholarly men and well-read women, where you may

Amsterdam

taste the European culture at its best and gentlest, untarnished by autocracy or silly jingo pride. Holland can be an exceedingly dull little country, but Amsterdam is something more, for she is a city of diverse and adventurous origins, enlivened by relays of remarkable immigrants, and ringing still with the exploits of her old merchant-venturers, who furnished half the entire capital of the Dutch East India Company, who sent Henry Hudson to the Hudson River and Abel Tasman to discover New Zealand, and who used to navigate their vessels actually past the Rock of Gibraltar, the most ferocious bastion of an implacably hostile Spain, to catch the lucrative Italian grain market.

And most of all Amsterdam cannot feel a backwater because of her urbanity. She is a city of intense polish. There are few greater pleasures in contemporary travel than to lean over a bridge in this old place and watch the Amsterdamers passing by. Perhaps there is a thin mist on the morning air, such as Rembrandt loved, and a cool ripple or flush on the surface of the water; and behind the lime trees the grand old palaces, door to stately door, stand there like so many eminent generals, their gables rising helmet-like above the embankment, their windows, still shuttered, suggesting rich claret comforts within. Down the canal the little bridges succeed each other in demure humps, and somewhere behind you the traffic rumbles down Damrak to the station. The citizenry walks by you incuriously and unhurried, a neat, buttoned, unobtrusive kind of people, and every now and then a barge labours beneath your bridge, with an oily chug of engines and a slow grin from the giant at the wheel. The air seems to carry coffee-beans upon it, gently roasting, spiced with the smell of old masonry, water, and the diesel exhausts of the passing boats. The skyline all around you, silhouetted by the rising sun, is wonderfully elaborate and lacy, with bumps and half-arches and scallop designs, tall chimneys and whimsical embellishments, cast in and out of shadow by the movement of the inescapable trees. The whole is cemented by a powerful impression of completeness. It does not feel as though this scene will ever change. It feels immune to bulldozers, improvers or speculators, and whatever brash or seamy transactions are to be conducted after breakfast in this old city of the traders, at least, one feels confident, they will always be discreet.

Discretion: perhaps it is this quality, above all others, that keeps

Amsterdam

Amsterdam separate, almost aloof. She is the home of the diamond-cutters, she has dealt all her life in vast sums and priceless commodities, and she can always keep a secret. I recommend her wistfully to those who feel, when the thump of the transistors is particularly intrusive, that all the barriers of human reticence are down. Amsterdam has not succumbed yet, and perhaps never will. No wonder those five young men in the tourist boat, looking out upon the city so pallid and expressionless, seemed like figures of some old romance. They were the Folk From Across the Water, but here behind the Dam the City disregarded them.

ATHENS

'In former days,' says Murray's dear old *Handbook* of the Protestant cemetery in Athens, 'our countrymen were generally interred in the Temple of Theseus'—and by all the gods of high Olympus, what a falling-off is there!

Athens is a city, indeed, of former days: not only the heroic former days of classical antiquity, but the homelier lost age of the Victorians, when every gentleman considered Greece his second home, when 'any Englishman', as the book says, 'with the usual knowledge of ancient Greek will be able to read the Athenian newspapers with ease', when Austria was proudly represented in this city by a Prince, Germany by a Baron, France by a Count, Italy by a Marquis, Russia by a Court Chamberlain, Turkey by a Bey, and even the United States by a diplomat not abashed to be called an Esquire. Athens is a city always looking over her shoulder, and this habit of perpetual retrospect makes her half haunting, but half drab. Most visitors to Athens are disappointed in her, but at the core of their reactions there stands a nugget of excitement and fulfilment, just as the breathtaking relics of ancient Greece stand lonely and lofty among the modern mediocrities. Our countrymen were formerly buried in the Temple of Theseus, a fate of splendid consolation: and though this is no longer an age of mortuary privilege, nevertheless the fact that the English are now dumped, like everyone else, in a common-or-garden cemetery down the road somehow expresses the changed status of Athens herself—from capital of a way of thought, to lesser Levantine metropolis.

For Levantine she is. Gone, all gone are the clean-limbed young gods of legend, with their chiselled noses, curls and lissomness. Gone are the frank fair maidens, the Penelopes, calm of brow and composed of bosom. If there is beauty to the modern Athenians, it is beauty of a swarthy kind: sallow skins, black eyes, the merchant allure of great wealth, an olive, volatile fascination. There are burly heroes in Greece still, strapping men with mighty chests and

Athens

gargantuan appetites, but they do not often live in Athens. 'From the Jews of Thessalonica,' runs an old invocation, 'the Turks of Negropont and the Greeks of Athens, Good Lord deliver us!' The modern Athenians are a sympathetic people, but they have been moulded, like the Welsh and the Egyptians, by centuries of alien domination—and when your masters have been the cunning and ferocious Turks, your own outlook is likely to be artful indeed, and your tactics exceedingly slippery. Perhaps, in fact, the men of ancient Attica were like this, too, dark-skinned, stocky and evasive: but if they were, then a whole climate of scholarship has been misinformed, and a whole cycle of fables has misled us.

It is the centuries of foreign influence that give Athens her shabby, hang-dog flavour. In one quarter you find the last shambles of the Turkish Athens, slovenly with huts and grubby pavement restaurants. Somewhere else you breathe the stodgy, pompous but faded flavour of German Athens, the city built in the last century by Greece's German King, Otto I—dull grandiose boulevards, four-square merchant houses, tedious squares and mathematical avenues. In the daytime there is all the tumult of a Western-style industrial society, the clanging of trams, the hissing of trains, the blaring of radios: at sunset the Levant takes over, and the city seethes, intrigues and dances all night long. If you drive into Athens in the evening from your aircraft or your ship, she does not feel at all pellucid, pure or glistening—adjectives the old travellers loved to bestow on her. On the contrary, she gives you an instant dismal impression of honky-tonk intensity, a whiff of Soho, a meaner Beirut.

But always at the heart of Athens, among the messy and the middling, stand her splendours still. When you wake up in the morning, there lording it above the chimney-pots, like some cool divinity of the dawn, stands the Parthenon, white, shining and virginal. Behind the disappointment the old inspiration remains. There is the vale of Cephissus still, and there the Hill of Nymphs, and there the honey-ridge of Hymettus. You may walk as in a dream through the old Agora of the Athenians, meticulously reconstructed by the Americans, or you may listen to a twanging antique instrument as you drink your ouzo and eat your roast kid in some vine-bowered tavern on the slopes of the Acropolis. If you look beneath your feet, there always is the thin, ungenerous soil of Attica, with the limestone crags of the plain protruding through it, as Plato thought, like ribs through an emaciated body—

Athens

the spare, dry earth that fostered the Athenian genius, denying it the flabbiness of fecundity and easy living. And if you look above your head, beyond the dreary façades of the Royal Palace or the Hotel Grande Bretagne, there stands the sparkling blue bowl of the Athenian sky, the bluest and clearest sky of all, glittering with perpetual morning. Athens is a colourless city nowadays, but the gods are still above her.

You may feel their presence closest among the ruins of the Parthenon itself—not in the moonlight, as the old engravers would have it, but in the glitter of a windy spring morning, when the breeze blows gusty and stimulating off the Aegean, and flicks contemptuously through your guidebook pages, as if to scoff away all pedantry. There will be other tourists about, to be sure, chivvied in goat-like flocks by lecturing herdsmen. There will be students earnestly examining plinths, and cheerful English schoolmasters with babies in carry-cots, and indefatigable American ladies with notebooks on golden cords. But it is a big place, that supreme assembly of ruins: if you choose one of the outer porticoes, and lean against a hillside rock, you may still feel yourself all alone with Greece, as you have imagined her all your life.

There far below you lies the sea of Salamis, with the tumble of docks, jetties and riggings that is the port of the Piraeus. A steamer plods industriously out to sea, the bay is flecked with fishing-boats, and away on the horizon, infinitely suggestive, infinitely old, stand the islands of the Aegean, stealing away like magical stepping-stones towards Kithnos, Milos, Naxos and the Sea of Crete. All around you, beyond the sprawling city, lies the tawny central plain of Attica, fringed with olive groves and bounded by mauve mountains, and humped among the urban sprawl are the sister hills of Athens— Lycabettus, Pnyx, Museium, Sterfis, the chapel-crowned spur called Ayia Marina, worn smooth at one side by the generations of women who have slid down it as a remedy for sterility. The dull hubbub of the city streets seems a million miles from this high wind-swept eyrie, and all really does feel pristine, fresh and innocently urbane, as in the prime of the world.

And gloriously symbolizing it all, overwhelming in its grace all the fallen hopes of the city below, is the mound of the Acropolis itself, on whose rocky flank you are meditating. Nothing in the world feels *cleaner* than this bumpy, tumbled old rock. It feels bleached by the suns of a dozen centuries, swept of all impurities by

Athens

that heavenly breeze off the sea. Its lovely ruins, which have served in their time as churches, mosques and powder-magazines, are dazzlingly white and fragile. Its limestone surface, over which the tourists resolutely stumble, scraping their shins and clutching their cameras, looks as though it has been actually scrubbed, by the ghosts of loving savants, perhaps, or the watchful muses themselves. The memories of great men, the echoes of noble speeches seem to be all round you, and you feel yourself to be at the fount of all that is best, all that is most enduring in the civilization of the West. It sounds sententious, and it smacks of reach-me-down culture in glossy magazines, but it is still disconcertingly true. When once you have sat thus on the Acropolis, you will remember the sensation all your life, the very feel of the rock beneath your bottom, the very glint of the sunshine, the exact salt tang of the wind, the precise drift of smoke from the steamship in the bay, beating out to the Cyclades.

So the former days triumph, and you will be a dullard indeed if, when you leave Athens for regions less sublime, you remember the tramcars more vividly than the ethereal temples. All the same, things have sadly changed in Athens since the heyday of Hellenism, long since humiliated by harsher cultures. As the *Handbook* says, 'the really clever dragomen are now all either dead or superannuated', and few are the English gentlemen who can still, with a swift mental appeal to Liddell and Scott, plunge confidently into the intricacies of the morning editorial.

BAGHDAD

Bang in the blistered middle of Iraq lies the city of Baghdad—in a country of many races, a capital uncompromisingly Arab. In the Middle Ages she was known to the Muslims as the City of Peace, and she is still one of the focal points of Arab consciousness, the only rival to Cairo as the capital of the Arab world. For at least a century Baghdad sheltered the greatest conglomeration of wealth and learning on earth—she was at once the Alexandria and the Manhattan of her time—and to this day, of all the cities of Islam, she retains the most potent allure. There are few citizens of the West who will not respond, if not with yearning, at least with wonder, to the old magic of her name.

The foreigner is nearly always taken aback by his first sight of this legendary place. He has been surfeited with images of Baghdad as a caliphean boom city, a cross between Houston and the *Arabian Nights*, at once burgeoning with skyscrapers and enriched with antique romance. Alas, few fairy battlements embellish the modern skyline of Baghdad, and Rashid Street, her main business thoroughfare, must be one of the most insufferably dreary streets of all. Endless are the evenings which stretch away, from the windows of hotel bedrooms, down these shabby, peeling colonnades. A pot-holed roadway, mean and grubby shops, whining beggars, a constant oozing, hooting traffic jam: 'A fig for the caliphs!' says the new arrival, ordering a soporific whisky. 'Boom city my foot!'

But he is wrong, as new arrivals often are. Baghdad is not only a city of vast and growing wealth, not only a political capital of great significance, not only a centre of intrigue and suppressed discontent; she is also a capital of pervasive charm in which, for those who care to search, there still linger a few reminders of Scheherazade and the despots of fable. Almost everyone who lives in Baghdad for long grows to like it, and the Baghdadis, an easy-going, arm-in-arm, slightly raffish kind of people, soon endear themselves to most foreigners. Cairo is bigger and brassier, Beirut more sophisticated,

44

Baghdad

Damascus lovelier, Amman more stimulating, Riyadh nearer the mores of the desert; but for me Baghdad remains, in her sleazy old way, the most beguiling of the Arab capitals.

The river greatly helps. The Tigris flows grandly through the very centre of Baghdad, and often the quickest way to get from one part of the town to another is to take a boat. There are always a few boatmen hanging about at the ends of the alleys which run down to the water, and flowery is the competition with which they will entice your custom. The cushioned upholstery of the craft, bleached by the sun, is carefully rearranged; a plank is laid down for you; a wrinkled hand helps you on board; and as he pushes you away from the bank with his oar the ferryman murmurs some reverent invocation under his breath. The river is very wide and very solemn, swift-flowing and sometimes turbulent, and it is often cluttered with dredgers, barges, lighters or rafts, or river steamers, deep in the water, churning a passage towards Basra. The Tigris has all the condescension of a great river, as if nothing could be so impertinent as to interfere with the stately stream of its waters; but from the middle of it, leaning among the cushions, you can see how bravely the City of the Caliphs has tried to break with its past.

Downstream is a great new bridge, built by West Germans to link Rashid Street with the expanding northern suburbs. Over the rooftops you can see the handsome white block of a modern bank, clean, functional, and allegedly incorruptible—only one of a series that has toppled the lofty money-changers from their pedestals, and helped to eradicate the memory of those shrewd and subtle Jewish bankers who, until the establishment of Israel, dominated the financial life of this city. Big new roads radiate from the heart of Baghdad. Comfortable new suburbs sprout in her shadow. The marvellous old bridge of boats upstream from the city has been swept away, and a shiny new hotel, all Martinis and air-conditioning, is stealing the custom away from the old-school hostelries, fragrant with the shade of Gertrude Bell, that recline among their lawns beside the river.

But the dust wins. Baghdad remains pre-eminently a crumbly, Turkish kind of city, and here and there among the palm trees on the river bank there are fine old-fashioned houses, with charming crooked balconies over the water, all ups and downs and courtyards, date palms and wrought iron, with high rooms and

Baghdad

rickety guest chambers, and fountains in the gardens. Tucked away among the demolitions many such relics survive. It is true that the Iraq Government has no preservation department, and that if you ask for a picture postcard you will almost certainly be given one of the Rafidan Bank or the Date Marketing Board; but tradition keeps breaking through. Among the new splendours and pretensions the narrow streets still run, heavy with spiced Oriental smells, thronged with gowned Arabs, turbaned Kurds, bent-backed porters, donkeys, dogs, wasps, and ladies peering at life through the thick distorting curtains of the veil. Here are the Persian pilgrims and the visitors from the desert, and here the wandering cabaret girls, enough to 'shake the saintship of an anchorite', pile into the taxi for Teheran.

Especially in the great bazaars can you find some echoes of the old Baghdad, and even fancy (if you are of an excessively romantic turn of mind) the Commander of the Faithful wandering disguised among these rumbustious murky halls. The Baghdad *suks* are less intimate than Jerusalem's, less businesslike than Aleppo's, but they give an impression of boundless power. The big covered bazaars ramble beside the river, dense with dust, particles of food, and heady vapours. Here is the drapers' bazaar, and the alcoves are thick with bright fabrics and rolls of material—nylon slips hang in their scores on coathangers, frocks lie about in flouncy discord, the draper sits incongruously cross-legged on a wicker stool. Here is the Bazaar of the Perfumers, with the scents mysteriously bottled and an over-powering smell of eau-de-Cologne swirling through the arcades. Here are the food stalls (indigestible colours), and the leather bazaar (horse leathers and bandoleers), and the innumerable arcades of the shoemakers (ankle-straps, fluffy slippers, and enormous buckled sandals). But so hefty and muscular is the spirit of the Baghdad *suk*, and so redolent of masculine tastes, that most people remember it in terms of the Bazaar of the Coppersmiths. Brawny indeed are the backs of the smiths as they bend to their work in the heat, their long handles crashing upon the metal in a ragged unison, with a clashing of metals, a hot sizzling of coals, a glistening of sweat and molten iron, and a hover of attendant boys, all thin legs and big black eyes, holding their trays, hammers or leather gloves like acolytes at a rite. The Arab bazaar is a wonderful place, an oasis of kindliness, in which after a year or two of wandering the stranger finds himself curiously at home, whether he is in Shibam or Tripoli; and one of the best and most jovial, the most Chestertonian, is the coppersmiths' *suk* at

Baghdad

Baghdad, a full-blooded, clanging, loose-limbed kind of place.

Baghdad was the scene of the bloodiest of the mid-century revolutions, when an entire royal house was slaughtered, and fingers from the hand of the dismembered Prince Regent were hawked by touts in the shopping streets. But though I shall never forget the festering horror of the city then, nor my first chill glimpse of its wild-eyed revolutionaries, yet it is not with revulsion that I think of Baghdad. She has been a murderess in her time, but she is more a frump than a *femme fatale*.

BANGKOK

Most cities have a soul of sorts, but not many put it on public display. The soul of Bangkok is there for all to venerate, inhabiting a carved wooden pillar in the shrine called Lak Muang, and surrounded always by devotees. You walk past a petrol station to get there, across the road from the Temple of the Emerald Buddha, and around the modest little structure a perpetual bustling, jostling and merriment greets you. The lottery-men urge their tickets on you, for this is a very lucky spot. The men with wicker bird-cages invite you to buy merit by releasing a captive sparrow. The old women beckon you inside with wrinkled genial gestures. A soldier button-holes you to practise his English, a boozy mendicant seeks some more tangible form of sympathy, a throng of divine children wants to have its picture taken. All is spiced and smiling commotion at the shrine of the civic soul.

In the courtyard, to the soft beat of a drum, the jingle of bells, the clash of cymbals and the wheezing of an oboe, three or four elderly dancing girls, in all the shimmering glitter of Siamese temple costume, are performing the stylized evolutions of a dance-drama: here is the elephant, a middle-aged performer with tusks on her head, moving in a slow, high-footed, heavy-hipped prance; and here is the hero, a buxom forty, heavily rouged, grinning irrepressibly, and flourishing a sword with vim but not much menace; and there behind the stage is the band, squatting on the floor with its be-guiling instruments, tinkling and thudding and bumping and gasping, playing away with lively enthusiasm, and sometimes wink-ing at you through the melody. Nearby is a snack counter, lined with bilious bottles of beverages and preserves, and a stall where you may buy flowers, tokens, talismans, joss-sticks or infallible horoscopes; and the whole yard is crammed and cluttered with citizens—citizens

---

The photographs following are of: Accra, Algiers, Amsterdam, Bangkok, Berlin, Cairo, Damascus.

Bangkok

grand and citizens very humble, citizens in smart uniforms and citizens in almost nothing, citizens so old they look like shrivelled brown chestnuts, citizens doubled up with giggles before the stage. A pungent smell of curry and smoulder hangs upon the air, and always above the hubbub flows the dainty liquid music of the orchestra.

And there in the middle of it all, neon-lit in an alcove, is the sacred pillar itself, the spirit of Bangkok. Before it stands a collection of offerings: a pig's head on a platter, an egg upon a dish, a bowl of aromatic petals, a vase of flowers. Around it people lovingly move, kneeling with prayer rattles, burning joss-sticks, arranging flowers, murmuring, thinking or just staring. There is nothing queer or forbidding about this sanctuary. No suggestions of fear or arid superstition pervade it, no squalor enters its simple rites, there is nothing degrading, unwholesome or even pathetic to its activities. It feels the happiest and friendliest of shrines: and this is only proper, for Bangkok, as generations of observers have remarked, is the very happiest of great cities.

This is temperament, not environment. The setting of Bangkok is not immediately prepossessing, for the city lies in an alluvial swamp. Here the generous Menam Chao Phraya—Senior Lord River—flows down to the Gulf of Thailand in a soggy welter, as the Mississippi sprawls through the sultry South. The plain around Bangkok is all dampness—rice fields and water buffaloes, creeks and water reeds—and into the capital itself the wet oozes in a web of canals and back streams. In Bangkok you are never far from the water's edge. The klongs or canals of the city are its drains, its ditches, its irrigation canals, its fish-ponds, its swimming-pools, and often its highways too. Bangkok is full of the splash of swimmers, the gurgle of passing currents, the swish of oars and the chug of barges. Grandly through the city's heart strides the great river itself, thronged with sampans, ferry-boats, tourist launches daintily decorated, rafts of teak from the upland forests, deep-sea ships from the China Sea, slender grey warships and Edwardian tugs: and outside Bangkok, in the deep green purlieus of the city, the water people live in the damp woods, their houses knee-deep in muddy water, their crumbling temples strangled in wet foliage, their children born to boats and mudlarks, their morning markets assembled in flotillas of canoes, their housewives paddling easily about in conical straw hats, like marsh-insects out of the rushes. Bangkok is not, like Venice, exclusively wet-bob.

Bangkok

She has her streets and railways, her automobiles and her trolley-cars: but she still feels unmistakably subject to the Senior Lord River, and her very name means 'Water-Flower Village'.

All this makes for mosquitoes, humidity, voluptuous ease and tolerance. Bangkok, though she was founded as Thailand's capital in war and bloodshed, is an easy-going metropolis. The frequent *coups d'état* that punctuate her affairs are usually bloodless and sometimes almost unnoticed. It is true that quite recently the young King Rama VIII was found dead in Bangkok with a bullet in his forehead. It is true that until 1957 the Bangkok police, using helicopters, ran a most profitable opium racket. It is true that martial law is generally in force, and that all the members of Parliament are officially nominated. Nevertheless the flavour of life is relaxed, humorous and benign, and the shifts and vituperations of politics are regarded by ordinary citizens with benevolent detachment. There is not much hunger in Bangkok, and not much desperate hardship in a city blessed always with warmth, water and palm thatch—and so rich in nutriment that sometimes, after a heavy rain, you find edible fish splashing about in puddles. This is a city fond of animals, of fun, of company, of an evening out or a meal beside the river. Until a few years ago it was famous for its opium dens and pleasures of the flesh: and though things have tightened lately, the enterprising visitor may still enjoy, as the London clubman said of his own experiences, 'all the pleasures that mankind is heir to, excepting only the joys of child-birth'. The Thais have a second name for their capital—Krung-thep, meaning City of the Angels.

In Bangkok, almost any evening, you may stumble across a shadow play in some temple courtyard, with a multitude of children wide-eyed among the shrines and towers, and a marvellous air of innocent enjoyment. You may watch the State dancers performing, with impeccable ritual, the ancient dramas that are the glory of Thai art: the sword-fights so ferocious that the steel flashes, the monkey-figures so diabolical that the stage shakes, the heroines of exquisite long-fingered grace, the gestures and manoeuvres of infinite meaning and lofty nomenclature—'The Salutation of the Celestials', 'The Wind Sways the Tops of the Plantain Leaves', 'The Hare Admires the Moon'. You may go to a Thai boxing match, enlivened by vigorous incidental music, in which the contestants not only punch each other, but also kick, hack and trip with gusto (though it is, as one manual of the sport observes severely, 'forbidden to bite'). You

Bangkok

may eat a mild Thai curry at the water's edge, served by giggly girls in jeans, or you may penetrate the flash, flare and glare of Bangkok's Chinatown to eat a stately ten-course meal in all the rich ambiance of *la haute cuisine*. Day goes down in Bangkok with a grin of enjoyment, a rustle of salacity, a wink and a white napkin. She is a place of beautiful nights and thoughtful late mornings. There are some nasty aspects of Bangkok, from corruption to political autocracy, from noisy streets to high prices, but for the susceptible alien she remains a city of delicious stimulation: a city where—in a week, a month, a lifetime of escape—he never once feels prosaically at home. Even the hotel laundry lists quote a price for laundering either your watch-strap or your turban.

This charm of temperament is partly climatic, partly historical. It is climatic because, though Bangkok may feel sticky to the visitor from the West, her air is really kind and fructifying, blessing these fortunate people with health and reasonable prosperity. It is historical because Bangkok has never been subjected to colonial dominance, and has escaped those tortured recriminations, self-doubts and embarrassments that are the aftermath of Empire.

Both elements are instantly evident in the feel and appearance of the place. Bangkok, thirteen degrees north of the equator, is pre-eminently a tropic city, sprawling and ill co-ordinated, as though she is stretched beside the river in the shade of the palms, with a long drink in one hand and a fly-whisk in the other. She is a metropolis without a centre, shapeless and flaccid. Your taxi (a Japanese three-wheeler, neat and toy-like) bounces you breathlessly and interminably over her bumpy streets, over a hundred canals, down a thousand alleys, through a labyrinth of faceless streets, until at last, with a triumphant blast of its little exhaust and a delighted smile from the driver, it deposits you hilariously at the wrong destination. The main thoroughfares of the city seem endless and identical, extending from suburb to suburb, and only occasionally given distinction by a modernistic memorial, a bronze plumed king on horseback, a fountain or a plaza. Most of Bangkok is contained within a curve of the river, and from some vantage points you can see how her business houses, warehouses and banks cluster along the water's edge: but at street level she feels a patternless confusion, the points of the compass seem lost for ever, and you never know whether you are approaching the comfortable green districts where the embassies

51

Bangkok

reside (with their lawn-sprinklers and their monumental flagpoles), or whether you are about to topple into the muddiest of shady klongs.

Bangkok has all the trappings of Western civilization: smart hotels, television, club sandwiches, jazz, air-conditioning. She remains, though, a hot equatorial capital, a city that Conrad loved, that Somerset Maugham described in several steamy stories. A hint of the marsh, the jungle and the teak forest seeps evocatively into Bangkok, and one of the celebrated sights of the place is the Saowapha snake farm, where the cobras and banded kraits live in small white domes like igloos, coiled in loathsome intimacy, or swimming with elegant arrogance in the water-ditch that surrounds their pit. This is an Oriental capital, suggestive, exotic, with a dark orchid beauty. 'What do you call that flower?' I once heard an Englishman ask a Bangkok flower-seller, pointing to a blossom in the corner of his stall. The man smiled gravely. 'We call it the lotus flower, Master,' he replied.

To this sense of arcane excitement, the sovereignty and monarchy of a royal capital powerfully contribute. Not far from the shrine of Lak Muang stands the Grand Palace of the Thai kings, a mile square and wonderfully spectacular, with its attendant temples and its towering shrines, its City of Forbidden Women, its high fretted walls like an Eastern Kremlin, its snake-eaves and its high-pitched roofs, its shuttered living quarters and its throne halls. And down by the river, high and dry in wooden sheds, stand the royal barges— marvellous peaked craft, with dragon prows and gilded figureheads, tassels and chains, in which on ceremonial occasions, seated high on elaborate platforms and rowed by men in dreamlike liveries, the kings of Thailand and their honoured guests parade downstream in a glow of majesty. ('FORBIDDEN,' says an endearing notice beside these splendid craft. 'DO NOT TO CLIMB ON THE ROYAL BARDGES.')

The old sorcery of royalty pervades Bangkok. This has only been a capital since the eighteenth century, but everywhere there are the monuments of kings—statues or trophies, palaces or charities, a temple rebuilt or a shrine embellished. Everywhere the royal touch is apparent, in every national activity, from the race-course to the national theatre. Princely names are inescapable, for the Thai monarchy is nothing if not versatile: there are princely newspaper-men and princely composers, princely diplomats and princely

Bangkok

authors, a princely hairdresser and a princely racing motorist, princes of advanced Western views, of Oxford ties and Ivy League jackets, princes of such reticent eminence that they rarely venture from their mansions, but sit cloistered in scholarship among antique manuscripts and priceless works of art. King Rama IX himself is a clarinet player of professional standard, and his Queen is as strikingly beautiful as any slinky Paris model.

And this kingly city remains very much a capital. Men of many races live in Bangkok, but she does not feel a cosmopolitan city: she feels, for all her Westernization, overwhelmingly and unshakably Thai. She is mistress of her own land, her own culture, her own language, her own alphabet (thirty-two vowels and forty-four consonants), her own fleets and armies, her own exchequer. Thai is a member of the Western Alliance, but Bangkok is no mere puppet capital. More than most of her peers, she feels self-contained and dynastic. Like London, she has never been conquered. Like Peking, she is the heart of a civilization. Like Stockholm, she does not care for brute strength. Like Paris, she is always fun.

And like Rome, she is a city of religion. Above all it is the serene genius of Buddhism that sustains Bangkok, colouring her architecture with grace, style and delicacy, and making of her a city that few visitors can remember without affection and respect. It is not an awful or oppressive faith, the Buddhism of Bangkok. It is friendly, familiar, everyday. It is a religion still in its prime, accepted by citizens at all levels of sophistication, and so generally honoured that most young men of Bangkok, for a year or two of their lives, shave their heads, put on a saffron robe, and submit to the two hundred and twenty-seven rules of monastic discipline. The attitudes it fosters are liberal and tolerant. Foreigners are welcomed with sincerity. Women suffer no discriminations. Polygamy, though no longer common, is permitted. Christian churches have been active for years. The Chinese minority, though it endured a spate of prejudice after the war, now freely flourishes. Changes of régime are received with a shrug of the shoulders and a smile of hope. It is as though a haze of some soothing, calming substance, a miasma of gentleness, has been released from all the temples and monasteries of the capital, to linger among the back alleys like a benediction.

To sense it at its most alluring, go to the royal Temple of the Emerald Buddha, the Wat Phra Keo, on a Sunday morning, when it

Bangkok

is thrown open for public worship. This is one of the most breath-taking and beguiling of all religious buildings. It is a paradigm of everything you imagine as Siamese—all the vivacity, all the glitter, all the colour, all the charm, thrown together with such proliferation of fancy that when you walk through the outer gate and see its little world of marvels before you, all you can do is lean against a pillar and laugh with delight. There are the enchanting golden fauns, part bird, part beast, part human, that stand as archetypes of Bangkok in almost every travel poster. There are the demon sentinels, twenty feet tall, with their gigantic swords, their crested helmets and their masked but toothy faces. There are the six blunt columns that represent the planets, and all around you there are stone elephants and cows, bronze lions, painted giants and coloured monkeys, sinuous gilded serpents, pillars of wonderful elaboration, steps of delicate solemnity, with a glint of sun and a whisper of leaves and a soft entrancing clinking of wind-bells. A quaint little sculptured hermit squats upon a pedestal. A throng of country folk, gaily dressed and clutching flowers, moves across the courtyard to its devotions.

Hemmed in by all this legendary splendour stands the temple itself, with the Emerald Buddha, a small jade image, high and mysterious above the hall. Here, each Sunday morning, hundreds of citizens come to pray. Some are burning joss-sticks outside the temple door. Some are placing votive flowers in vases. Many are simply sitting in contemplative silence upon the temple floor, in twos or threes or families—reposed, contented, and so reverent that nobody would presume to stand before that divine image, and newcomers enter the sacred presence on all fours. Ceremonial drums stand beside the door, embellished with big bronze frogs; a grandfather clock beneath the Buddha was presented by Queen Victoria; the walls are gorgeous with painted battles, boats, State elephants, shrines, miracles and processions: but the atmosphere of the Temple of the Emerald Buddha is not grand at all, breathing as it does a spirit of gay, light-footed, unpretentious respect.

Such gaiety and effervescence spring, like a laugh or a song, from most of the Bangkok temples—whose fragile but gorgeous silhouettes speckle the skyline wherever you look. The Temple of the Dawn, Wat Arun, which stands in brilliant command beside the river, turns out when you approach it to be covered all over with pieces of cheap coloured china. The vast Temple of Wat Po, an untidy ramble

Bangkok

of courtyards, cloisters, refreshment stalls, gardens, crones, monks and loungers, contains the great effigy of the Reclining Buddha, a hundred and sixty feet long and indescribably serene. There is a temple shaped like a Chinese junk, and a temple on its own artificial mountain, and a temple dedicated to the art of meditation, where you may watch aspirants practising the correct rhythms of contemplative walk. Outside one temple stand the tall red pillars of a giant swing, relic of an ancient festival. Beside another rises a gigantic standing Buddha, forty feet high and made of yellow cement. Eighty life-size figures, disciples of the Buddha, stand hauntingly in the half-light of the Wat Sutat. A bone of the Buddha himself, brought from India in 1899, is preserved in the Wat Sraket.

Nothing on earth can rival the variety, fantasy and exuberance of these shrines. They make Bangkok the most constantly surprising of cities; and more important, they testify to the vision and energy of her religion. Nothing in the temples of Bangkok feels touristic, artificial or mercenary. All is enviably real.

Bangkok is a great port, a military headquarters, a university city. Her airport is busy and modern. Her Royal Palaces are air-conditioned. She has four railway stations and many cinemas, and her cars are imported from the three corners of the Western world. Yet she remains, in an obscure but persistent way, a country kind of capital. The forest lies at her back door, and in the most *soignée* part of the city—at Hyde Park Corner, say, or Fifth Avenue at 50th Street—a market assembles boisterously each weekend, with mounds of vivid victuals and peculiar vegetable stinks. Each year the streets grow and the traffic thickens, but the klongs, still intersecting the metropolis like a mesh of water, bring to its very heart a sense of rural intimacy. Bangkok is lined with green and spattered with water, and on every park bench the lovers while away their evenings in postures of classic Oriental grace, she demurely cross-legged, he leaning over her lithe and supple, like a prince in an ivory miniature.

In the northern part of the city, near the National Assembly building, there lies the Bangkok zoo, and here you may taste to perfection the civic air of sparkling inconsequence. It is a place of pools, lawns and open-air restaurants. Its bushes are clipped into cocky animal images, and its trees are festooned with fairy-lights. Two things, in particular, give this zoo a symbolic quality, and make it happily characteristic of the capital. The first is the presence

55

Bangkok

within its gardens, shackled beneath a private panoply, of the King of Thailand's white elephant: he was elevated to the peerage in 1959, under the title Phra Savet Phumiphol Pahana, and he stands there the year round, looking plump but lonely, munching hay and accepting the respectful plaudits of the populace.

The second symbolism of this menagerie is provided by its monkeys. They live in small private houses among the tree-branches, and they are free to swing upon their chains from one tree to another, sliding along loose wires. They are animals of blithe and infectious mischief, and often as you pace those pleasant walks, breathing the lotus air and fancying sweet idylls, one of these apes will suddenly swoop down his chain upon you, zooming above your head with a chatter and a grimace, and whisked away by his own momentum to the other end of the wire. It is rather unnerving the first time: but when you get to know them better those merry little animals, swinging about from tree to tree, setting the birds flying and the children in convulsions, laughing and chattering and twitching their tails in the sunshine—those jolly monkeys seem to express in their harmless, gay and rollicking agility the very essence and emanation of Bangkok. She is a city of sweet scents and laughter. A star dances all day long, above the Water-Flower Village.

BEIRUT

Beirut is the impossible city, in several senses of the adjective. She is impossible in the enchantment of her setting, where the Lebanese mountains meet the Mediterranean. She is impossible in her headiness of character, her irresponsible gaiety, her humid prevarications. She is impossible economically, incorrigibly prospering under a system condemned by many serious theorists as utterly unworkable. Just as the bumble-bee is aerodynamically incapable of flying, so Beirut, by all the rules and precedents, has no right to exist.

Yet there she stands, with a toss of her curls and a flounce of her skirts, a Carmen among the cities. She is the last of the Middle Eastern fleshpots, and she lives her life with an intensity and a frivolity almost forgotten in our earnest generation. She has inherited some of the style of Alexandria, that queen of Mediterranean ports, now relegated by history to African provincialism, and nowadays it is to Beirut that all the divinities of this haunted seaboard, the fauns and dryads and money-gods, orgiastically descend. Beirut is a tireless pleasure-drome. She is a junction of intrigue and speculation. She is a university city of old distinction. She is a harbour, a brothel, an observatory on the edge of the Arab deserts. Her origins are ancient but she burgeons with brash modernity, and she lounges upon her delectable shore, half-way between the Israelis and the Syrians, in a posture that no such city, at such a latitude, in such a moment of history, has any reasonable excuse for assuming. To the stern student of affairs Beirut is a phenomenon beguiling perhaps, but quite, quite impossible.

She is the capital of Lebanon, a small strip of hilly territory on the edge of Syria, between the sea and the deserts. She stands on no great river, commands no industrious hinterland, and all through the centuries she has been chiefly significant as a gateway and a conduit, the threshold of Damascus and the outlet of Syria. She has been a

Beirut

halting place or transit camp, through which successive civilizations have briefly tramped, leaving a stele here, a carving there, a legend in a library or a pill-box on a beach. Egyptians, Phoenicians, Assyrians, Hittites, Persians, Greeks, Romans, Arabs, Crusaders, Turks, Frenchmen, Britons, Americans—the armies or administrators of them all have passed this way, from the Pharaonic commissaries who bought their cedarwood in these parts to the United States marines who, in the nineteen-fifties, scrambled up the Beirut beaches from the ships of the Sixth Fleet. In her time Beirut has been a Giblite market, a Roman garrison town, a Phoenician metropolis, a Saracen fortress, a Crusader bishopric, an Egyptian outpost, a Turkish prefecture, a Syrian emirate, a French mandatory headquarters, a republican capital. She is a city of wide experience, but she travels light.

A stele, a legend, a pill-box—nothing much more substantial has been left behind by the conquerors, for the texture of Beirut is flaky and unretentive. Earthquakes and fires have destroyed much of her heritage, but mostly it is the character of the place that makes this a city without a visible past. Beirut tastes, but seldom absorbs. She is always contemporary, shifting and tacking to the winds of circumstance. She is the capital of a State that is half Christian, half Muslim, and she herself remains poised between the Eastern way and the Western, between the Francophile and the Afro-Asian, between the suave hotels that line her water-front and the tumbled Oriental villages spilled on the hillside above. She is not one of your schizophrenic cities: on the contrary, she has triumphantly exploited her own dichotomies, and become the smoothest and most seductive of entrepreneurs. She is a universal clearing house, and she deals in all commodities. Everything is grist to her mill: a crate of steel bolts, a letter of credit, a poem, a navigational system, a cocktail, a tone of voice, a power press, a soup. She accepts them all, processes them if necessary, and passes them on at a profit.

She lives by standing in the middle, and by the itchiest of itchy palms. She earns her keep by doing things, and there is almost nothing she will not undertake. She will pass your wheat inland to Damascus, or ship your oil westward to Hamburg. She will paint your upperworks, translate your thesis, introduce you to the Sheikh of Araby, accommodate you in pampered splendour in an air-conditioned suite beside the water. She will perform your atonal music at an open-air festival, or feed you with unreliable statistics

Beirut

about political controversies in Zagazig. She will, without a flicker of surprise, convert your Norwegian travellers' cheques into Indian rupees and Maria Theresa dollars. She has nothing of her own, no resources of iron or coal, no factories to speak of, no big battalions, but she will do almost anything you ask of her, providing you pay her properly.

No, that's unfair—it is not all for cash. Beirut is also an entrepôt of ideas, linking the bazaars with Cambridge and the Sorbonne. From the hills above this city the poet Flecker used to watch his old ships sail, 'like swans asleep . . . for Famagusta and the hidden sun': and just as those dim vessels reminded him of Grecian glories, so the cool white ships that sail today for Venice and the Piraeus seem like couriers between the cultures. Every shift of Western thought is reflected in the conversations of Beirut (which lies well to the east of Cairo and Leningrad alike), every audacity from the Left Bank or Greenwich Village is rehashed here with relish. One of the great law schools of antiquity flourished in this place, and today Beirut is still host to two of the best universities in the Middle East. She is a mongrel city, but among mongrels she is a thoroughbred: under her influence many a pair of notions has gently fused, many opposites have been reconciled. Whether a man comes from Peking or Pittsburgh, he will soon find some corner of this liberal place where, lapped in eroticism or deep in the discussion of philosophic concepts, he is sure to feel at home. There is a tang in the Beirut air, bitter-sweet but easy-going, that survives nowhere else on earth: for it is compounded of an old alliance between East and West, washed in the humanism of the ancients and bathed in the incomparable Mediterranean sunshine. It is the spirit that created old Alexandria, and it makes Beirut, for every lover of the classical mode, for every man of generous instinct, a city of nostalgic regret.

Regret always, for Beirut is a prodigy of the second class, an Alexandria *manquée*. She has enjoyed a million affairs, one feels, but has never really been in love. Her buildings are mostly undistinguished, her manners are imported. She is a sideline city, never (as the literary critics like to say) very deeply *engagée*. She stands on the rim of the Arab world, peering inside with a wry and sceptical detachment, and her conscience is rudimentary.

All this undeniably makes for fun. Glittering hotels form the breastworks of Beirut, a clutter of banks is her keep, and sooner or

Beirut

later every Middle Eastern bigwig strays her way, loud-mouthed or surreptitiously. Here you may see the political exiles, talking dark and interminable subterfuge, or the resplendent hawk-nosed sheikhs, in all the gilded refulgence of the Arab patrimony, fingering their beads and indulging in flamboyant bickerings. Here are the silken ladies of Syria, svelte and doe-eyed, Francophile to their last delicate gasp, and devoted to Bernard Buffet; and here are the waterside harlots, curled but smouldering, Semite with a touch of baroque. There are many poets in Beirut, and artists of visionary tendencies, shaggy existentialists in frayed sandals, dilettantes by the score, spies by the portfolio. Sometimes you may see Druse tribesmen in the city, out of the eastern hills, ferociously hirsute and gloriously swaggering. Sometimes the fleet puts in (British, American, French or Greek) and the water-front bars are loud with ribaldry. And when one of the perennial Middle Eastern crises erupts into the headlines, then the imperturbable hotels of Beirut are crammed again with foreign correspondents, the hall porters brush up their jargon and sniff around for tittle-tattle, and the whole city seems transformed into one sensitive, quivering antenna.

But in Beirut you are seldom in the heart of things. The firemen are always visiting, the crisis is usually somewhere else. The oil comes from Mesopotamia, the machinery is going to Syria, the dancing girls are supplied by an agent in Soho. Beirut feels a transitory place, like an exceedingly corrupt and sophisticated girls' school. Such a way of life, you feel, cannot be permanent: it is all too fickle, too fast, too make-believe and never-never. It is Alexandria without the philosophers, without the astronomers, without the Pharos, perhaps even without Cleopatra (for age does distinctly wither the *grandes dames* of Beirut, waddling with poodles and sun-glasses from salon to couturier). For all her age and history, for all her scholarly eminence, Beirut feels a rootless city—salacious but not earthy, virile but infertile. A breath of wind, it seems, a shift of fortune, and all this bright-painted fabric would be whisked away into oblivion, like the countless predecessor cities of this Phoenician shore.

Such is the nature of the place. Beirut herself would not have it otherwise, for the real purpose of this city is hedonism. The world comes here for pleasure: to live it up, to make money, to bump into friends and enemies, to water-ski or bask in moonlight ecstasies. The energies of the capital are geared to such aspirations, and even the

60

Beirut

ravishing climate conforms. No ascete could flourish in such a setting, no fervid demagogue can keep it up for long, and all the strident passions of our time, transmuted from violence or grandiloquence, are tamed here into sultry back-chat, boudoir rivalry and skull-duggery. Beirut has none of the power of Cairo, and none of the defiant derring-do that gives to little Amman, away to the south-east, some of the dusty stimulation of a frontier town. When a political climax bursts upon Beirut, it is generally a climax of the parish pump. When a limousine speeds resplendently across the Place des Martyrs, it is not usually a dictator or a lordly general hastening into cabal, but only a playboy passing by. Beirut is the small capital of an infinitesimal republic, and her events do not often feel crucial. Give it time, Beirut always whispers, don't fuss, wait and see, have a drink. You can usually find a blind eye here, a hole in the corner, the back of a hand, the underneath of a counter. This is not an earnest city. Proper Victorians would have hated it. Harvard economists or British Civil Servants, examining its improbable methods, its flibberty-gibbet charm, its blatancy and its blarney—men of sombre purpose, deposited one scented evening in Beirut, would probably pronounce her irredeemable.

But who would redeem such a place, in a world of false redemptions? Club-women and bluestockings infest our age, but the frank and lovely libertine still makes the heart lift. Such a heedless delight, such a glint in a blithe eye, is the gift of Beirut. This is a city without much soul, but with allure immeasurable, and above all it is graced by a celestial beauty of setting: beauty of a classic and timeless kind, a blue and wine-dark kind, with bewitchment such as you dream about in long damp northern evenings, as you pine for a beaker of the warm south. The city of Beirut often feels second-rate, but the setting of Beirut is superlative. 'Dream-shadow-dim' is how Flecker described this shoreline

> *Where Kings of Tyre and Kings of Tyre did rule*
> *In ancient days in endless dynasty.*
> *And all around the snowy mountains swim*
> *Like mighty swans afloat in heaven's pool.*

At this point on the Levantine coast the mountains of Lebanon stand in magnificent parallel beside the sea, so close that the citizens of Beirut may, if the wild whim takes them, ski in the morning and swim

Beirut

in the afternoon. It is the presence of these fine hills, all around the city, that elevates Beirut from the entertaining to the sublime, and provides, in its contrast between the ephemeral and the eternal, a marvellous foil to the bubbling frivolity of the metropolis.

Imagine a terrace table beside the sea in Beirut, during the brief moment of the Mediterranean twilight, when the shops are raising their shutters for the evening's business, and your restaurant rustles with the first silks and sibilances of the night. There are prawns on your table, perhaps, or red mullet from Sidon, fruit from the lush Bekaa valley, a gay white wine of Lebanon or some haughty vintage out of France. Around the bay the city rumbles, hoots and chatters: there is a clink of metal from some unseen smithy, a suggestion of spice and raw fish on the breeze, the echo of a blaring radio beyond the promenade, a distant clanging of trams—all the hot, heavy, breathless symptoms of an expiring Levantine day, like a sigh in the sunset. Below you the last of the water-skiers scuds home in a flurry of spray, showing off to the girls on the beach. Out at sea a tall elderly schooner loiters, like a ghost in the half-light, and beyond the break-water, perhaps, a graceful Italian liner steals out for Greece, with a soft tread of her turbines and a flutter of her flags. Sometimes an airliner labours in from the sea, blinking its red lights as it lands beyond the cedar groves, and sometimes a razzle-dazzle sports car, top-heavy with blondes and young muscle-men, screams and skids along the corniche towards the night clubs. All along the shore the tall white buildings stand, concrete and rectilinear, with their parasols and their lighted balconies, their dim-lit bars and their muffled music. Away over the shopping streets there flickers the radiance of the neon lights, orange and blue and scarlet, flashing through the city's glow.

Now, before the night comes, while the evening is still purple and hazy, while the velvet twilight lasts—now you may taste the impossible beauty of Beirut: for rising in strides above the capital, in serried terraces, above the skyscrapers, above the last suburbs, above the olive groves, above the foothill villages, above the winding Damascus road—there, lording it above sea and city, stand the mountains, 'afloat in heaven's pool'. A sheen of snow hovers about their high ridges, and their tawny slopes tumble away through scree and field and olive grove to the Mediterranean below. Beneath their serenity Beirut festers and celebrates: and even as you watch, sipping your wine or toying with your fish, the lights go on like star

Beirut

clusters in the villages of the hills, higher and higher up the slopes, until at last the dark falls, the end of the sunset fades, and away above Beirut only the snow of the summits remains like a dim corona in the night.

Nowhere can you find a combination more breath-taking, of sea and snow, age and vigour, history and persiflage. Only at the Levantine end of the Mediterranean could a Beirut exist, with all these undertones of antiquity, graft and tolerance. Is she really a great city, this wayward paragon? Scarcely, by the standards of Berlin or San Francisco, Tokyo or Moscow: but she is great in a different kind. She is great like a voluptuous courtesan, a shady merchant-prince, the scent of jasmine or the flash of a dazzling scandal. She has scarcely achieved greatness, nor even had it thrust upon her: but greatness has often spent a night in her arms, and a little lingers.

BERLIN

B erlin is the centre city of Europe—some might say of the world—and her heart is the stark, scarred archway called the Brandenburger Tor: not because it stands upon the last frontier of the West, the very line where Ulbricht built his Wall, but because, poised as it thus is between two overwhelming alien philosophies, it remains quintessentially German. It is a harsh and hated monument, but at least it feels real.

For though Berlin is an exciting and an ominous place, divided as she is both by masonry and by method, yet for me she feels chiefly like a queer façade. She is a stage-prop city. In the east she reads her Communist lines, in the west her libertarian, to a thump of dogmas or a tinkle of profit: but in neither rôle does she feel quite natural. Not so long ago her subject territories extended from the Atlantic to the Caucasus, and she had a brutal ideology of her own. Today she has become a kind of nightmare fair, where the two halves of the world meet to set up their pavilions. There is an emptiness and a pretence to her spirit, as though the meaning of the place had been forcibly ripped out twenty years ago, and only replaced by slogans and sealing-wax.

It is fashionable to say that she is no longer neurotic, but I cannot agree. She feels to me a terribly mixed-up metropolis, tortured by old anxieties or inhibitions, and understandably shot through with fear. That the Berliners have guts, diligence and realism nobody can deny. They have an almost cockney gaiety to them, an almost chirpy bonhomie, and they seem, on the face of things, undismayed by their ferocious ups and downs of fortune. But beneath their genial public veneer, I suspect, they cherish darker layers of emotion: cynicism, self-disgust, shattered pride, morbid resolution. Some people say the difference between East Berlin and West Berlin is the difference between light and shade. To me, though the transition from one to the other is shattering to endure, nevertheless they both feel at once dark and floodlit, like the scene of an accident.

64

Berlin

Berlin is the capital of a lost empire, and her imperial past lies like a helmeted skeleton in her cupboard. She forms on one side the capital of the Democratic Republic of East Germany, on the other a province of the Federal German Republic: but the Germanness of her survives by sufferance, by suggestion, by retrospection. In the eastern sector the placards and the exhortations, the State shops and the Khrushchev posters, the slit-eyed arrogance of Leninallee bring to the purlieus of the old Unter den Linden an oily whiff of Asia. In the west all the gallimaufry of the American world prances and preens itself: neon signs, juke boxes, *Time*, apartments by Corbusier, hotel rooms by Conrad Hilton, paper-backs, pony-tails, dry martinis and Brigitte Bardot. The old Germany lives on underground, surfacing sometimes in a splendid opera, a Schiller play, a melody or a neo-Nazi.

On the one side the East Berliners find themselves remoulded, month by month, year by year, crisis by crisis, into a new kind of people—brainwashed, as it were, *en masse* and by force of habit. On the other, the West Berliners have become walking symbols: inhabitants of a city that has no economic meaning, no geographical sense, no certainties and no security, but which is kept alive like some doomed and cadaverous magnate, just to spite the beneficiaries. Few Berliners seem to suppose that their city will ever again be the capital of a free united Germany. The East Berliners live for the hour, or the party meeting after work. The West Berliners accept what a paradoxical fortune offers them, and move blithely enough through life, like fish in a glittering goldfish bowl.

It remains, though, a single city, and there is no disguising its traumatic quality, its mingled sense of ignominy, defiance, futility and pathos. The horrible wall that bifurcates the city has not yet, not quite yet, destroyed its essential unity; every now and then somebody tunnels beneath the barrier, or vaults desperately over it, and another few years must pass before the last of the old ladies climbs her step-ladder to wave her white handkerchief forlornly to the other side. Bitterly mordant are the comments of the Berliners when they show you around their boulevards. Their jokes are coarse and often cruel, their allusions streaked with self-mockery. Caustically they tell you that each side of the Brandenburger Tor calls itself democratic—the East with a capital D, the west with a small one. Wryly they observe that the Perpetual Flame of Freedom uses an awful lot of gas. Almost apologetically they point to

Berlin

Tempelhof, still the most astonishing of the world's airports, as 'the one good job that Hitler did'. They sound resigned but secretly resentful. They know what you are thinking.

For in a way their city remains, to this day, a constant and terrible reproach against all that Germany has meant to the twentieth century. The Liberty Bell, no less than the gigantic Russian war memorial, is a reminder that in our times German values have been rotten values. Berlin, east and west, is a city built upon the ruins of Germany, watered with German tears, haunted by the shades of a million lost young men, a million lost illusions, the ghost of a dead and discredited patriotism. She is the most melancholy of cities. She has lost her soul, and is still acquiring replacements.

And for myself, I find her neuroses ever apparent: in the almost obsessive pride, for example, that Berliners have in their zoo, deposited in the very middle of the city, and famous for its shackled elephants; in the passion for flowers that blooms so eerily in this most warlike and fearful of capitals; in the bizarre assurance of the night life—the placid composure with which, for instance, comfortable burghers and their homely wives accept their beers from a man dressed up as a waitress; in the flashy extravagance of the western sectors and the dullened apathy of the east; in the inevitable, ever-growing alienation of one side from the other; in the flushed contrast between Berlin's urban preoccupations and the impeccable park-like countryside that lies outside her gates; in the absolute stunned silence with which, when I was once in the city, the cinema audience filed out from the ghastly film *Mein Kampf*, an appalling laceration of German pride and self-respect.

So it is I say that Berlin's heart is the Brandenburger Tor, with the great Quadriga restored but hardly regnant upon the top of it. Around that symbol of old pomp the real Berlin still stands: the gaping Reichstag, the ruined Wilhelmstrasse, the shells of broken cathedrals and shattered palaces, Göring's offices and Hitler's bunker, the tumbled halls of the Third Reich, the grave of a lost empire. Anything may happen to Berlin in the second half of our century; but whoever rules her, until the shades of that dreadful capital are exorcized at last, until the very memory of it is dim, all the brilliance and bluster of the new city will be sham, and its spirit will never be easy.

BOGOTÁ

Those of us given to whistling in the streets do so out of a variety of impulses. In Paris we whistle because it is expected of us, in London because it isn't. We whistle in Moscow out of self-defence, in New York out of stimulation, in Tokyo out of despair. And if we whistle our way through Bogotá, the capital of Colombia, the impulse is partly well-being, for this is a hospitable place, but partly, alas, bravado. Bogotá is a finely civilized old city, but she lacks peace of mind. She is dignified but highly strung, like an Edinburgh with twitches.

She is a blank, unprepossessing city, poised on a plateau among the eastern ridges of the Andes—which divide, as they march northward from Ecuador into Colombia, into three tremendous spurs. To the west the mountains plunge down, with ferocious waterfalls and savage ravines, into the deep tropical valley of the Magdalena, all parrots, jungle and bananas. To the east the vast Colombian plains roll away in desolate emptiness to the frontiers of Brazil and Venezuela. It is a bitter but heroic site, and grimly does Bogotá stand on her tableland, the Andes in her suburbs, four degrees north of the equator but eighty-five hundred feet above the sea.

Perhaps it is the altitude, which makes the stranger breathless and the indigene moody, that gives the city its muted manner, nervous but sedate. Shrouded often in the clouds of the high plateau, soaked often in drizzle, cursed with a climate that has no seasons, but remains perpetually loitering around a damp October, Bogotá is scarcely an exhilarating spot. She has, though, an unforgettable tang to her, a sense of rarefied individuality. Among South American capitals Bogotá is almost the farthest from the sea. She stands so high and isolated that until the aeroplane arrived a journey to the coast was a laborious expedition, and to this day she retains a tart air of seclusion and self-sufficiency, like an eccentric up-country sage.

67

Bogotá

Deposited uninformed in Bogotá you would not, I think, easily guess where you were. She might at first be almost anywhere, of a vaguely Latin cast and highland climate. The mountains look aloofly down on Bogotá, one crowned with a figure of Christ, one with a white convent, one with a cross. Around her outskirts the savannah extends green but sullen, ringed by hills on every side, and speckled with eucalyptus trees. The air smells faintly of oil, tobacco, and eau-de-Cologne, the skies are heavy, the colours of the city are browns and blacks and greys. The steamy equator seems a million miles away, and the birds in the trees are mostly sparrows.

A thicket of new skyscrapers dominates the centre of this metropolis, and the streets are clogged with hooting cars and rumbling yellow buses. There is a towering hotel in the universal American style, a bull-ring of red brick, a stadium where they play *futbol*, a *canodromo* where the greyhounds run. In the northern suburbs the houses of the *bourgeoisie* succeed each other in awful fantasy, Bauhaus beside mock-Tudor, Moorish and Gothic semi-detached. To the south something of the old town survives: an evocation of shuttered yards and beckoning staircases, the glitter of ecclesiastic baroque behind harsh brick exteriors. In one square stands the monumental Cathedral, in another the entrancing Catalan observatory, in a third the revolving wooden sails of a windmill advertise an airline.

It is not instantly arresting—rather dull, in fact: but rub your eyes and look harder, and you will see that though the passing faces may not be immediately striking, they are insidiously exotic. Sometimes you may glimpse a pure-bred Spanish beauty, a smoulder of long fingers, or a grandee of the old European school, with a big nose and grey eyebrows: but to most citizens of Bogotá there is a perceptible tinge of the Oriental—Mongol, Japanese, sometimes even Eskimo. This is, I suspect, the key to the flavour of the city: that it is infused throughout with the blood of the Chibcha Indians who inhabited this plateau before the Spaniards stormed out of the Caribbean. The conquistadores killed many of them and slept with half the rest, and the result is a society unexpectedly homogeneous, but sly with Indian reticence. Many a Bogotá gentleman will resent the inference of half-caste origins: but he will be misguided, for it is precisely his quality of slant-eyed and secretive polish that raises Bogotá from the provincial and the prosaic, and makes her a capital of beguiling pungency.

Bogotá

Athens indeed is the popular parallel. Bogotá considers herself the most enlightened of American cities, and she is in fact a place where any old-school classical humanist feels easily at home. This is a city rich in good bookshops, including one, five storeys high, whose eclectic stock I have seen rivalled only in Oxford and Helsinki. It is a city of poets—a lovely place to live in, so a Bogotá lady once told me with a sigh, because every admirer writes you a sonnet. You will not meet many crazed existentialists, nuclear disarmers or disciples of Schoenberg: but you may well encounter men with an eighteenth-century range of interest, dilettantes of immense erudition, philosophers of universal appetite. I once met a man in Bogotá who has not only translated H. L. Mencken into Spanish but also designed his own house, written books on cats, English poetry, and navigation, and compiled what must surely be the most complete collection on earth of pictures of the Annunciation.

All the punch of Bogotá comes from such men of intellect. The street life of the capital is not vivid, and its poor people often seem numb and vacant. There are Indian women in trilbies, to be sure, and men with ponchos around their shoulders. There are resplendent sentries outside the Presidential Palace wearing spiked Prussian helmets. There are donkeys about, and leather stores fragrant with saddlery, and pious shops cluttered eerily, like wax-works, with platoons of painted saints and Virgins. There is a big open-air market, muddy and shambled, where the Indian country folk lounge like gipsies among their trays of obscure root vegetables, their wicker baskets of babies, their pineapples and their tethered speckled pigs.

But nobody could really call Bogotá a picturesque city. No flaring young patricians stalk these streets, no gaudy savages clatter in from the highlands. Even sin is offered delicately: 'We have pleasure in inviting you,' says an exquisitely printed card slipped to favoured strangers in the street, 'to become acquainted with an elegant and comfortable bar, attended by beautiful señoritas, where you will enjoy a fine atmosphere'—and it is signed discreetly 'The Administration.' Superficially Bogotá is a kind and proper place. Her queues are usually orderly. Her pavement crowds are exceedingly polite. Sometimes her cars even give way to one another.

The whistler's impulse, nevertheless, is often bravado: and it is the very decorum of Bogotá that inspires him. Beneath the culture of this other Athens, behind the politesse, stark old passions undeniably survive: the dark festering resentment of Indian blood, the

Bogotá

flaming furies of Spain. Not so long ago this courteous citizenry destroyed half its own capital in a frenzy of political savagery, and even today Bogotá is brooding and humming with intrigue. You cannot long evade the tensions of the place, the posters and slogans that disfigure its walls, the squalid strikes that cripple its national university, the pervading sense of misty but menacing public malaise. The Englishman will receive nothing but kindness in Bogotá: but sometimes he may feel, as he swings off the boulevards into the hillside slums, that though the sun is high and the sparrows are cheerful, already he is whistling in the dark.

BRASÍLIA

Brasília!

Hackneyed though her name may be, she still deserves, like Venice or Jerusalem, italics and an exclamation mark. It is not, to my mind, any architectural marvel that warrants such punctuation, but simply the idea of the place: and just what Brasília means is not easily apparent until you examine South America as a whole, trace its sprawling contours on a map, and place the condition of this astonishing subcontinent within a wider historical context. The wonders of Brasília lie in the middle of a boundless wilderness, tufted with shrub, and there never was a city, old or new, more self-consciously bursting with a kind of Ozymandian symbolism.

South America is empty. That is the first thing to grasp, and the second is this: that it is inexhaustibly, unimaginably rich. A few people have scratched at the surface, nibbled at the edges of this superb territory, but all the rest lies virgin. If you journey from capital to capital of South America—Caracas, Bogotá, Quito, Lima, La Paz, Santiago, Buenos Aires, Montevideo, Brasília—you will constantly be aware how near you are to the sea. You are nearly always on the fringe of the land-mass, and constantly over your shoulder, beyond the mountains, up the river, down the ravine, lurking in tycoons' visions and politicians' promises, lies the vast, marvellous and unexploited interior. South America today is rather like the United States a century ago, before the Union Pacific, striking west from Omaha, linked the East with the embryo cities of the Pacific.

Railways do, in fact, cross the southern part of South America, and dozens of aircraft cross the Andean massif almost every day of the year. Moreover, the Amazon, plunging into the innermost forests, has been a familiar thoroughfare for so long that a generation ago the quickest way to go from Lima, on the Peruvian coast, to Iquitos, in the Peruvian interior, was to go to Liverpool and take a British

Brasília

steamer up the river. But by and large the savagery of the terrain, the lack of communications, the horror of tropical diseases and debilities, the marvellous opportunities still available along the sea-shores—all these factors kept the South Americans near the sea, and left their hinterland blank and benighted.

Four centuries after the conquistadores, times are beginning to change. History is forcing the South Americans inland: new techniques are urging them into the interior, and so is the population explosion, and so is social unrest and man's new mastery over the pestilences. On the Pacific coast they are peering at last over the Andes. On the Atlantic they are looking out of the eastern plateau into the watered and jungly plains of the centre. The Peruvians plan great things east of the mountains. The Bolivian visionaries already foresee Santa Cruz, in the inner lowlands, as their future capital. And the Brazilians, in their sweeping way, have given form to these aspirations by building themselves Brasília. Some people call this city the crazy flourish of a megalomaniac politician. Some see it as an earnest of national greatness, or an awful portent of all our futures. Some only collate it with Canberra, Washington or New Delhi as a conventional gesture of pomp. But for me it is a way-station, a camp on the Union Pacific, beckoning the pioneers belatedly away from the water-front.

The first taste Brasília left in my mouth, when I had savoured her for a couple of days, was exceedingly acrid. As an emblem of government or a place to live in she strikes me as depressing in the extreme. Some of her buildings indeed, especially those designed by Oscar Niemeyer, are altogether captivating: the Presidential Palace, with its entrancing snail-shell chapel; the airy Congress, open ramps to a sunlit roof and foundations paddling in a pool; the unfinished theatre, a hulking, crouching structure like a ziggurat in the desert; the skeleton of the Cathedral, which looks like the wire frame of a gigantic but rather arty lampshade. The artificial lake that flanks the city will be very agreeable in a few years' time, when the trout begin to rise, and the site of the capital on its low and bitter ridge is splendidly defiant.

But most of Brasília, to my taste, falls uncomfortably between the graceful and the imperial, and as a conception of things to come I do not find her comforting. Huge, anonymous, identical, rectangular, utterly functional are the blocks of steel, glass, and concrete which,

Brasília

lined up in disciplined rows like commissars at an inspection, house the Ministries of State. Expressionless as steel sheets, standard as packing cases are the towering complexes of flats, shops and playgrounds—the *superquadris*—that are Brasília's pattern for family living. The great highways are as wide as parade-grounds, and the fly-overs are so complex and so sweeping that after a few hours' plodding the poor pedestrian begins to pine for a traffic light. For Brasília will be a city, as the guide-books say, 'living under the sign of discipline, order, and logic'. In the end, I have little doubt, the unquenchable flowering genius of Brazil, the proliferation and fun and variety of it all, will overwhelm this arid intellectualism, and bring some humanity to Brasília: but today she seems to me a grim, almost a terrible kind of place, rather as though, far from starting from scratch, she were some second Hiroshima or Berlin, struggling through the haunted debris of calamity. She has no radiance. She feels starved of good red blood, laughs and gentleness.

What is more, she still disconcertingly smacks, as her critics never tire of saying, of one man's egotism. The idea of an inland capital is not new—it was first mooted in the eighteenth century—but it owes its fulfilment almost entirely to the energies of Juscelino Kubitschek de Oliveira, President of Brazil between 1956 and 1960. This vigorous statesman was so determined to get the project actually started that he forced it through at a phenomenal, some say an irresponsible, speed. Though his Treasury was bankrupt and his credit was exhausted; though every bag of nails, every sack of cement had to be taken to Brasília across roadless wildernesses; though the site itself was depressingly infertile and the political opposition fierce or derisive; against all obstacles President Kubitschek pressed on. This resolution Brasília is not allowed to forget. Almost every building seems to bear Dr. Kubitschek's name, in one context or another, and there is a sort of shrine below the Parliament building (fragrant, I swear, with incense, though its acolytes assure me it is only the smell of the stone) in which the President's association with the city is mystically recorded upon a series of marble slabs, most of them quoting at length some prophetic statement of his, some clarion call or exhortation.

All the same, if some of Brasília's philosophies are unprepossessing, at least nobility keeps breaking in. There is nobility, of course, in the

Brasília

sweep and scale of it all, the huddle of rectangular vaults on the crest of the wasteland rise, the vast twirls and loops of the highways, the supreme horizon, the marvellous clarity of the air. And above all there is the inescapable nobility of history. I strongly suspect that the architecture of Brasília will stand the test of shifting taste less resiliently than Baker's and Lutyens's New Delhi, or even L'Enfant's Washington: but that, to my mind, matters no more than the monumental extravagance of the thing, so loftily aloof to economic orthodoxies. What matters splendidly is the very existence of Brasília, this token of new times. They can never abandon her now, and even if they did some Shelley would immortalize her.

It is some five hundred and seventy miles, in a straight line, from the Atlantic to Brasília: but it is almost four times as far, as the condor flies, across the Andes to the Pacific. In South America there is room for giants.

BUENOS AIRES

Sundays have a universal way of being Sundays, and nothing in the world is more absolutely dominical than Church of England matins in a very foreign city. I once spent a winter Sunday in Buenos Aires, and the whole tone of my day was set by the singing of the last hymn but one in the pro-Cathedral of St. John. How bravely the lady choristers stood there, Canterbury caps on the backs of their heads! How insistently the gas heaters hissed down the aisles! How recklessly the congregation overcame its uncertainties and swelled the dear old theme! How diligently we obeyed the injunctions of Ancient and Modern—breathlessly *pianissimo* our inquiries (*And will man alone be dumb, Till that glorious kingdom come?*), gloriously *fortissimo* our replies (*No, the Church delights to raise, Psalms and hymns and songs of praise*)! The pillars were plastered schoolroom yellow, the sermon concerned itself with technical aspects of slavery under the Romans, and thickly around us swirled quintessential Sunday: Sunday in the singing, Sunday in the air, Sunday in blue felt hats and lavender-scented hankies, gloves on the pews and horsehair in the hassocks.

But outside, too, in the alien Argentine, Sunday had begun unerringly. Buenos Aires is not the most vital of South American capitals. She is middle-aged and a little pompous, and seems to hanker after Europe. Boulevards in the French manner intersect her right and left, curly gilded lamp standards give her a sedate Empire flourish, and above my hotel bed there hung a print of a gloomy mansion called West Clarendon Place, Surrey. B.A., as we old hands call her, does not feel a city of the New World, pulsing and irreverent, and least of all does she feel one first thing on a Sunday morning. A faintly dispirited flavour hangs about her then. The very first sound I heard that day was the wail of a ship's siren on the River Plate, but it petered away forlornly in the twilight, as though there were no air in the harmonium.

Buenos Aires

So, expecting the bleakest, at first I found it. I began after breakfast in the Plaza Britanica, where the tower presented by the British colony still stands in florid Victorian sentinel, royal crest upon its bosom. The place was almost empty, but occasionally through its spaces there wandered, desultory and vacant, those dismal groups of servicemen that are a Sunday essential anywhere on earth. Some were just kicking their heels; some were writing postcards on walls; some were dozing on the steps of the tower. The troops looked a little unkempt and dishevelled, and I felt an old urgent sympathy for them. I know how long a long weekend can seem, early on the Sunday morning.

Presently, though, the day began to liven. By ten o'clock three or four loutish but likeable youths were playing volley ball across the street in the Plaza del Congreso, hitting their balls high and hilarious across the passing traffic. By five to eleven hang-dog queues had mustered at the cinemas, and by half-past the preacher in the Church of Espiritu Santisimo was in the full spate of the most dramatic sermon I have ever experienced, a torrent of rhetorical expletives, piercing pauses and gestures of desolate remorse (B.A. is a city with a passion for the theatre). By noon, when the English were stepping into their Humbers outside St. John's, it seemed to me that the depths of the Argentine Sabbath had been plumbed, and we could come up for air.

So I picked a plush *fin-de-siècle* café for my lunch, all gilt and rubbed velvet, on the Avenida de Mayo. Around me gaggles of elderly women were sipping Cinzanos with soda water and nibbling biscuits, nuts and bits of flabby cheese: but in the dimmer recesses of the room lonely men like long-frustrated reformers were deep in the contemplation of *La Prensa*. On a wall opposite somebody had scrawled a *Viva Perón*; down the road stood the Church of Santo Domingo, long ago ravaged by Perón's young thugs, and still half-ruined; at the end of the avenue was the pink Presidential Palace, cracked by bombs during an unsuccessful revolution in 1955; and when I asked my waiter if there were many Peronistas still about he nodded darkly but wryly, with a flicker of his thumb, towards those several grey solitaries in the corners, who certainly had a brooding conspiratorial look to them, but were probably, in fact, looking through the small advertisements for second-hand canoes.

I thus left the café with an intriguing sense of political mayhem, and took the admirable civic underground to the docks. This is a city of

Buenos Aires

the sea, more intimately than the map shows. All along the eastern flank of the capital the great basins stand in salt succession, packed yard by yard with vessels, and giving such a tremendous impression of funnelled wealth, of channelled cornucopias, that I have only felt its richness rivalled at Rotterdam, where the Rhine flows out of Europe like a river of gold. The quays of Buenos Aires are open to all comers, and all among the hawsers that afternoon the families were meandering, grandmothers in Tuscany black and small boys in long white socks, like trippers at a zoo. Nobody seemed to be doing any work, I was gratified to see. The sailors were out roistering, I fondly assumed, and the rest of us were Sunday sight-seers.

Anyway, it was soon tea-time, and I walked straight from the sprawling docks to the pampered tea-room of the Plaza Hotel, the Claridge's, or perhaps the Shelbourne, of B.A. Discreetly in a balcony, like a muffled minstrel, a pianist softly lubricated the hour: and never have I seen so many delicate ladies, with such neat fastidious fingers, eating such hearty schoolboy teas—toast of delectable buttered sogginess, sticky cakes of ravishing variety, a waiter so portly and roseate himself, so instinct with jam and sponge cake that he might well have represented, in some whimsical charade, the Spirit of Four O'Clock. 'You don't eat much,' my companion said to me at this plump function, eyeing the cream slices expertly: but I told her I was saving up for a midnight feast, and she understood me perfectly.

It gets dark early in the Argentinian winter, and presently I followed those silken gourmands out of the Plaza and along the Calle Florida, the Rue Saint Honoré of South America. It may not be quite as *chic* as the Argentinians tend to think, but it really is one of the great shopping streets of the world, where you can buy anything from Polish perfume to Mr. Durrell's latest, by way of crocodile skins and Japanese telescopes. My inspection, though, was pulled up short, for half-way down the Calle I came across a shop that seemed oddly familiar. It had a proper Sunday look to it, as though its doors had been bolted by staunch Anglicans, and its windows were dressed with a kind of leisurely elegance, studied and urbane. Bless my soul, said I to myself, I've seen that shop somewhere before: and sure enough, when my eyes strayed up above the leather goods, I saw there a single and always evocative name, a whisper of Christmas and school holidays: *Harrods*.

Buenos Aires

It was my signal of dismissal. Time to move on. A and M in the morning, Knightsbridge at night. I packed my bags that evening and boarded a ship for Montevideo: and as I sat down to my dinner that night, when we were beating down-river, I hummed that old hymn-tune happily to myself, until, reaching the bit about psalms and hymns and songs of praise, and naturally honouring the prescribed *crescendo*, I caught sight of a svelte lacquered couple at the next table looking at me with distinct suspicion. But what is Sunday supper, even on a River Plate steamboat, without a hymn-tune in your head?

CAIRO

Rolling grandly northward out of the African interior, at last the noble River Nile splits into the several streams of its Egyptian delta, and creates a region so rich, so old, so deep-rooted in constancy, so sunk in the cycles of fertility and decay, that there is something almost obscene to its fecundity. At the head of this country, at the point where the river divides, there stands the city of Cairo. She is the capital of Egypt, the largest city in Africa, the metropolis of the Arab world, the intellectual centre of Islam, and for more than a millennium she has been one of the great places of the earth. Cairo straddles the Nile, and the river is at once her *raison d'être*, her life-blood, her pleasure-ground, her highway, and the thread of permanence that has bound together many centuries of fluctuating and often sanguinary history. The Nile, the sacred river of the ancients, is still the oracle of Cairo. If you look downstream from the city, there shimmers a mirage of the Mediterranean. If you look upstream, there lies Africa, brown and enigmatical. If you look away from the water, east and west, there stretch the wide deserts that have fostered the peculiar arid genius of the Arabs. The horizons of Cairo are wide, and visionary, and heavy with symbolism. She is a city half African, half Arab, Muslim with pagan undertones, softened over the generations by a sporadic soft breath of humanism playing upon her from the north. You can call her a hybrid city, or a mongrel; but she can perhaps serve as an archetype of the half-caste society of the future, a *mélange* of colours and tastes and prejudices and heritages, fused into a fitful unity, like an ingot white-hot but flickering in the furnace.

Nothing ever quite dies in Cairo, for the air is marvellously clear and dry, and the temper of the country astringently preservative. If you stand upon the Mokattam Hills, the bare-back ridge that commands the place, you can see the pyramids of Giza upon its outskirts. From here they look faintly pink and translucent, like alabaster pyramids.

Cairo

They stand upon the very edge of the desert, where the sands are abruptly disciplined by the passage of the river, and they are fearfully old, terribly mysterious and rather frightening. They do not feel, though, in the least anomalous. Years ago the traveller, trekking laboriously along a desert trail to Giza, would find these monuments lonely and brooding in the sand, with a Sphinx to keep them company and an attendant priesthood of unscrupulous dragomen. Today the city has expanded upstream, and digested a little irrigated desert too, until a line of villas, night clubs, hotels and golf courses links the capital with the Pharaohs, and the pyramids have acquired a distinctly suburban flavour. They are to Cairo what the Tivoli Gardens are, perhaps, to Copenhagen: they blend easily with the ambiance of the place, a shiny Mercedes bus takes you to them, you can have a Coca-Cola in their shadows, they are flood-lit at night, and the wiry Egyptian who guides you into the bowels of the Great Pyramid does so with much the manner of a cinema usherette, impatiently waving you into the stalls with a flurry of her torch. Cairo is a place of extraordinary continuity, with a sense of history so inescapable that all the ages seem oddly truncated and entangled. The descendants of the original Egyptians have long since been outnumbered by alien immigrants, and only occasionally will you see a face (slink-eyed, hook-nosed, haughty but haunted) that seems to spring straight from a Middle Kingdom tomb: but in Cairo ancient Egypt is still all about you, from the Sphinx itself to the suggestive ooze of the Nile, so that you may sometimes fancy an air of antique mystery to the very clang of the tramcars, or a hint of funerary ritual to the lurching silent progress of the white-sailed barges upon the river.

Another resilient layer of Cairo life is darkly mediaeval, straight-descended from the times when the Arab conquerors, storming in from their Eastern deserts, seized Egypt in the name of Islam. Look westward from your eyrie on the hill, and you will see a mottled section of the city, brownish and confused, from which there seems to exude (if you are of an imaginative turn) a vapour of age, spice and squalor. This is the Cairo of the Mamelukes. A forest of incomparable minarets springs out of the crumbled hodge-podge of its streets: one with a spiral staircase, one with a bulbous top, some single, some double, some like pepper-pots, some like hollyhocks, some elegantly simple, some assertively ornate, some phallic, some demure, rising from the huddle of houses around them like so many variegated air-

Cairo

shafts from an underground chamber. There is said to be a mosque for every day of the Cairo year, and around them there still lingers, miraculously pickled, the spirit of mediaeval Islam, just emerging from the chaos of animism and pagan superstition. Among these narrow lanes and tottering houses the Evil Eye is still potent, and a hundred taboos and incantations restrict the course of daily life. It is a place of fluttering robes, black-veiled women, noise, gaudy vegetables, bitter-sweet smells, cross-legged tailors, half-naked children, high lattice windows, iron grilles, shafts of sunlight dust-laden across courtyards, the beat of a drum, the clattering tin cups of water-sellers, the breath of the Turk, the whispering suggestion of hashish.

At one of the great gates in Saladin's city wall you may still see dirty scraps of linen and paper pinned there in supplication to some misty saint of pre-history. In the shade of the Mokattam there still sleeps the City of the Dead, a metropolis of mausoleums, its streets and squares and slums and palaces occupied only by corpses and mourners. In the filthy side-show behind the bazaars, where a fat dirty woman swallows electric light bulbs with a shimmy of buttocks and breasts and a blaze of neon, the dirt and smell and sense of animal excitement is plague-like in its intensity. When there is a festival at a mosque, and the squeaky swings are erected for the children, and an endless crowd clamours through the night around the tomb of the local holy man, then all the gallery of mediaeval characters emerges into the streets in the lamplight—the half-mad dervish, tattered and daemonic; the savage emaciated beggar, with long nails and gleaming eyes; the circumciser, preparing his instruments delicately at a trestle table; the saintly imam, bland and courteous; the comfortable merchant, distributing sweetmeats and largesse; the clowns, and pedlars, and pickpockets, and many a small company of women, identically dressed in coarse-grained black, squatting in circles at street corners, gossiping loudly or idly rapping tambourines. And if you leave these bustling thoroughfares, where life clamours on throughout the night, then you may find yourself in minor lanes so narrow, dark and ominous that you may remember with a shudder the Egyptian famine of 1162, when such unsuspecting pedestrians as yourself, wandering these back alleys, would find themselves seized with iron hooks and hauled into upstairs rooms to be cooked and eaten.

Cairo

Two or three minutes in a wild-driven bus will whisk you from
this enclave to the boulevards of modern Cairo, the power-house of
the Middle East. Westernized Cairo was born in 1798, when Napoleon arrived in Egypt with his team of savants, and she has developed since then under a series of foreign influences and interferences.
Today, truly independent at last, she is a city so well equipped and
sophisticated that beside her all the other Arab capitals—Baghdad,
Damascus, even the glittering Beirut—pale into provincialism. There
is, to be sure, a familiar sense of *plus ça change* to the place, part
constancy, part lassitude: many aspects of Cairo life have an air of
fading glory, from the railways to the libraries. Nevertheless the
modern city breathes a powerful sense of authority. The Republic of
Egypt is the self-appointed leader of the Arab world, and there is
no denying the dynamism and assurance of its capital. A company of
tall new buildings has burgeoned beside the river: two great hotels,
all glass plate and high tariffs; a tower with a revolving restaurant on
the top; vast new official buildings, immaculate outside, raggle-taggle
within; expensive apartment blocks and sprawling housing estates.
A splendid new corniche runs along the water-front, from one side
of the city to the other. A spanking new bridge spans the river. Seen
from the hills behind, Cairo's modern district looks like a prosperous,
biggish, rather dusty Middle Western business town. She is not a
stylish city, and her sense of dignity comes almost entirely from her
river and its past. Her shops are not very elegant, her citizens,
whether they wear cotton robes or drip-dry suits, are not generally
graceful or courtly of bearing. But she has great punch and power.
Her traffic moves at a desperate pace, her neon lights flash with a
particular ferocity. Businessmen from all parts of the world, East and
West, Communist and Capitalist, gratefully sip their long cool beers
in her hotel bars. In Cairo, you feel, something is always happening.
It may be some great economist flying patiently in, or a statesman
flying philosophically out, or a new *démarche* from Moscow, or a
British economic mission, or a fulmination against Israel, or a
reconciliation with Iraq, or the arrival of a Russian dam-builder, or
a meeting of the Arab League, a threat, a parade, or simply the
President of Egypt sweeping by, with a roar of his convoying motor-
cycles and a scream of sirens, in his big black bullet-proof car.

Cairo is the very opposite of a backwater. She is a fermenting city,
often bombastic, always on the move. She is a genial place, with
petulant intermissions. Not long ago the prime symbol of Cairo's

Cairo

flavour was the rioting mob, that hideous instrument of politics and discontent which used to emerge sporadically from its hovels, garlic-breathed and sweat-laden, froward and crazed, to terrorize the capital and change the course of history. Today she is a secure city, freed (for the moment anyway) from the threat of public violence, but she remains a place of elemental energies. Fielding tells the story of a blind man, asked to convey his impression of the colour red, who replied that it had always seemed to him 'somewhat like the sound of a trumpet'. Cairo is not a silvery city: but something similarly blatant and penetrating is the image that should be summoned for you, when she leaps into the headlines again.

She is a blazing place. She blazes with heat, when the merciless summer sun beats down upon her pallid buildings, her scorched gardens, the heated turmoil of her streets and the ponderous sailing ships of her waterway. She blazes with a confrontation of opposites, the clash of the modern and the traditional, aged Muslim sage beside brash agnostic officer, camel beside Cadillac, veil over lipstick—contrasts often hackneyed but always burning in implication. And above all she blazes with the glare of contemporary history. Pause on a bridge in Cairo, amid the blare of her traffic and the shove of her citizenry, and you can almost hear the balance of the powers shifting about you, as the black, brown and yellow peoples come storming into their own. In Cairo is distilled the essence of the Afro-Asian risorgimento. This is a city lashed in ideas and bold ambitions—often undistinguished, sometimes positively childish, but always intensely vigorous, brassy, combative and opportunist. Old though Cairo is, and always conscious of her past, nevertheless this is the impetus of a new world. There is a trace of black Johannesburg to her, jazzy and ebullient; there is a little of India, of a suppressed Power reviving; there is something of that sense of latent force, ill-analysed and un-developed, that gives the new China its tremendous aura. Cairo is old-young, grey-green. Her corporate tastes run to the belly-dancer, the dirty story, overeating, hearty badinage. She loves fireworks and big-bosomed singers. Her newspapers (their beautiful Arabic script dramatized in red headlines) are clever but loud-mouthed. Her cartoonists are brilliantly mordant. Her radio programmes, laced with propaganda, shriek from every coffee-house. Her variety shows are rich and fruity, her dinner-jackets white and double-breasted, her figures pronounced, her half-tone rhythms heady and insistent. Cairo

83

Cairo

is a city with an incipient fever, always swelling towards the moment when the sweat will break out on her forehead at last.

As often as not the moment of catharsis is merely pleasurable, and this hot but morbid vitality bursts out in holiday. The air is then heavy with jasmine, as the itinerant flower-sellers hawk their necklaces of blossom, and the Nile is bright with fairy-lights and crowded small boats, precariously navigated. At other times it is some State occasion that overcomes the city, the anniversary of a triumph or a tragedy, or an earnest of glories to come. Then the shops are closed and the offices shuttered, and triumphal arches are hastily erected everywhere, with flags and military symbols and crudely painted portraits. The President and his Ministers emerge to cheers and brass bands upon a saluting stand, and all the panoply of a new age, tanks and guns and jets and paratroops, sweeps across Cairo to perspiring relays of martial music.

Most often of all, though, it is some passing political climax that momentarily convulses Cairo, sets her coffee-sages talking and incites her pundits to spleen. Cairo is the political city *par excellence*. She lives, breathes, dreams, argues, eats and drinks politics. Without her perennial moments of political half-truth, the sudden squabbles and ephemeral agreements that burst so suddenly upon the sweltering city, Cairo would not be true to herself, and the place would lose its pungent stridency of spirit.

For like the emergent world she represents, Cairo is often enthusiastic but never serene. She is a half-way city—half-way between age and modernity, between East and West, between frustration and fulfilment, between peace and war, between the sublime and the ridiculous. She is constantly asserting her virility and her emancipation, just as the whole wide nebulous commonwealth of Afro-Asia, whether it is genuinely independent or only spuriously so, is always busy in self-justification. Cairo is not a widely cultured city. Her successive foreign veneers have been repeatedly rubbed off (the old French intellectual influence is wearing very thin, and the British are now only rarely to be seen in the halls where they once drank so gluttonously deep). Her periods of foreign tutelage or exploitation have left their memorials—the river barrage outside the city, the bridges, the railway, the educational system, the basic structure of administration: but now the alien polish has gone, the Albanian

Cairo

monarchy and the British Army have both long been dismissed, and we are left with the raw native substance beneath.

Cairo is a city with all the material amenities of Western life, but she never feels remotely like a Western city. Her pulse beats strongly but erratically, like a tom-tom with a leak in it. Cairo welcomes you kindly, and guides you helpfully through the streets across the square, and engages you in cordial conversation—only to do something distinctly queer at the end of the lane. Her deeper conventions are a world away from the Western experience. It is not merely that the Middle Ages live on in some parts of the city, or that many Cairenes prefer robes to trousers, and honour the social principles of Islam. It is not simply the eerie presence of Pharaonic Egypt, always peering silently across the sand. It is the particular vim and venom of Cairo that is strange to us—energies only partly harnessed, impulses only half tamed. Sometimes these things are frightening (when a mob streams down the back streets, or the great tanks rumble by); sometimes they are charming (when you share a bowl of beans with a jolly family in the park); sometimes they are baffling (when you wake one morning to learn of a totally unpredictable about-face of national policies); sometimes they are marvellously encouraging (when some young upstart politician expresses a truth so clear, so clean, so free of inherited trammels that all our horny conjectures seem out of date). The particular forces of history and conflict that have moulded our Western societies have had little share in the making of Cairo. This is a city *sui generis*, sustained by all the hopes, strengths, weaknesses and grievances of an emergent world.

Cairo is not really a rich city, any more than Egypt is a rich country. She is, though, a capital of formidable character and natural power. She stands there at the head of her teeming delta like a watchtower at the gate of a lush garden, and around her the world seems to lie supine, so that when this old city stretches its arms, its elongated shadow spreads across Asia and Africa and along the Mediterranean shores like the image of a genie. It is unlike any other city on the face of the earth: just as the greatheart Nile, passing proud but placid through the hubbub of the capital, marches down to the sea with a sad deep majesty all its own, as of a man who has watched the cavalcade of life pass by, and wonders what all the fuss is about.

CANBERRA

Sooner or later there intrudes into the progress of a nation, as into the life of a man, the conflict between reason and emotion, and nowhere will you feel it more strangely than in Australia—above all else, a *strange* country. Reason seems to decree, in this far paradise of the common man, that the splendours of State are here irrelevant: that the family home is all, that freedom is sufficient in itself, that Government is no more than an expensive labour-saving device, that the sunshine, the open bush, the fine bright air and the surf offer all that a man needs for glory. Here as everywhere, though, emotion keeps breaking in, luring the magnificent Australian divisions off to war, sustaining many a queer old strand of loyalty, and finding some tentative and dilatory expression, some hesitant intimation of pomp, in the uncompleted federal capital of Canberra.

It is fifty years now since they gave a prize to the Chicago architect Walter Burley Griffin for his Canberra plan, and when you first drive down its interminable avenues you can hardly help wondering how on earth they have taken so long to build it. The pace has been agonizingly slow, compared with Brasília or Rotterdam, and even today the public buildings are still embryonic, and the pattern of the place is only half formulated. Reason, you see, has long had the upper hand in Australia. This is not a country of flamboyant symbols or spectacular decrees, not a State that often makes the heart sing. Not only did the great depression and the war impede the progress of Canberra, but it is really only within the past few years, I am assured, that the Australians have decided that they want the thing at all. Even today the official pamphlets about Canberra have a distinctly apologetic, almost evasive air, like an extravagant daughter justifying a new dress.

So for years the project floundered in the great bowl of its plain, where the prospecting parliamentarians decided, camping out beneath the gum trees half a century ago, that the heart of this Commonwealth was one day to beat. There is something indeed

Canberra

infinitely daunting about the site, so vast, so empty, so featureless but for its low rim of hills, so changeless but for the shifting of its lovely colours with the progress of the sun. It really is like Australia in microcosm, and just as the Australians, huddled in their sea-coast cities, seem to be always overhung by the immensity of the continent behind them, so the infant Canberra feels as though she can hardly compete with the tremendous blankness of her setting. The unimaginable space of Australia dominates these structures, the immense horizons of Australia overshadow them, and so enormous is the scale that man-made verticals seem to have little meaning, and horizontals survive, like animals in the bush, only by aping the landscape around them, and blending obsequiously with its contours.

In a way this is as it should be, for all the most satisfying capitals reflect in some organic style the character of their States, whether it is Washington's marble majesty, the domed and bulbous mystery of Moscow, or the high melancholy of Madrid. It would have been possible, I suppose, for the Australians to erect their capital as a soaring clump of buildings in the centre of the plain, like the thrilling American prairie cities, or indeed like Colonel Light's admirable little capital of Adelaide: Mr. Griffin, however, held true to the Beaux-Arts tradition of dispersed symmetry, and perhaps he was right. Space is the very structure of Canberra, space implicit and space physical, space between buildings, space above rooftops: and thus she properly mirrors the Commonwealth itself, which is, and probably always will be, mostly empty space.

For by now (*pace* the pamphlets) emotion is firmly in charge at Canberra, and the National Capital Development Commission is boldly committed to all the grandeurs of Griffin's plan—suitably modified by half a century of changing taste. In making this ageing abstraction a thing of beauty they are hampered indeed by the nature of the Australian Ideal, which has swamped the outskirts of the city with hideous bungalows, some of which look actually home-made, few of which have been subject to any control of design or delicacy of taste, and all of which, lumped together in rectilinear egalitarian monotony, give to the body of the capital a drab jerry-built patina. (At Brasília, to be sure, there is a slum city tucked out of sight over the ridge: but then in Brazil reason is not often consulted in the first place.) But the planners hope that this sense of thought-less sprawl, the impression of shapelessness that is a concomitant of Canberra's size and pedigree, will be largely dispelled by the filling

Canberra

of a big semi-circular lake—here, as in Brasília, intended to provide a shapely blue focus for the place. Hitherto Canberra has been split into two distinct entities—the civic half, where the stores and espresso bars are, and the capital half, where Parliament sits: the lake handsomely links these two, filling in the bleakest of the gaps, and across it is laid the great triangle of boulevards that is the skeleton of the design. Parliament will one day deliberate at the lake's edge, and eventually, it is romantically hoped, the Governor-General will chug to his functions in a vice-regal barge.

All this will scarcely impress you at first, for Canberra still looks a bit of a mess, but the enthusiasm of the Development Commission is infectious, and as they show you their plans and charts, the huge paintings they have commissioned to inspire them, the models and the schedules, the booklets and the statistics—as they explain it all to you, so you will begin to envisage the pattern of it cohering outside your window, and feel that this huge sprawling colourless entity will one day possess a queer excitement of its own, the peculiar extra-sensory excitement that is the meaning of Australia. Already Canberra buzzes with noble intentions, making her the very antithesis of Sydney up the road, and indeed is impressive in her accomplishments, too. She is already the biggest inland city in Australia, and even has a few light industries on her periphery. Here the splendid Commonwealth Scientific and Industrial Research Organization has its libraries and laboratories. Here the magnificent new National University has been able to attract scholars of immense distinction. Here some of Australia's most beguiling new buildings have sprouted diffidently through the pomp. Up on Mount Stromlo the great seventy-four-inch telescope ticks, whirrs and photographs the sidereal hours away. Almost everything in Australia is the biggest of its kind in the southern hemisphere: but I really do doubt if you can find, anywhere below the equator, a livelier assembly of talents than is resident already among the half-cock splendours of Canberra.

For sometimes, of course, at rare moments of good fortune, reason and emotion coincide, and just as Levin achieved a reconciliation between the two, in the last gentle pages of *Anna Karenina*, so Canberra has come to demonstrate that there is sometimes solid good sense to symbolisms. I have never visited a country that so seemed to need a centripetal force as does Australia, or so cried out for something beyond the bank balance and the bungalow: for it

Canberra

is a place of endless echoing mystery and intuition, what the aborigines would call a dreamtime country, where history has no meaning unless you take a grip on it, and nothingness will beat you in the end unless you saddle up for a gesture.

CAPE TOWN

One of the world's perennial paradoxes is the genial peace of Cape Town. South Africa is a State charged with menace, suspicion, racial hatred and autocracy, where one of the most awesome of contemporary problems is lurching towards some kind of dénouement; yet its political capital, reclining in age and grace at the Cape of Good Hope, remains one of the pleasure-havens of the earth. Here the troubled visitor, haggard with the dilemmas of Johannesburg or Pretoria, may feel himself, somewhat against the proddings of his conscience, gently refreshed: for in Cape Town, if you muffle your perceptions a little, and allow your imagination to overlap your realism, you can conceive what South Africa might be like, were it not for its burdens of tragedy.

At a time of precipitous change the traveller is always discovering strange, if sometimes overworked, transitions: from the oil well to the camel caravan, the cinema to the funeral pyre, rubies to blue jeans. If you like this sort of sensation I recommend to you the contrast between the Union Parliament in Cape Town and the old public gardens that surround it. You will leave the Assembly to the hubbub of the parliamentarians behind you, proposing some maniacal new measure of segregation, flouting the United Nations or belatedly finishing off the Boer War. But the moment you are outside its doors, an idyllic charm surrounds you. Lovers talk earnestly on park benches. Squirrels scuttle across your path. Pigtailed school-girls are conducted on nature rambles in the sunshine. Eccentric vagrants eat sausage rolls out of grubby paper bags. Meditative Coloured men shuffle like poets between the elms. The long central avenue, pointing compass-like towards the mass of Table Mountain, is reserved for pedestrians, and there is no garden path in Africa more conducive to sauntering, or more instinct with the pleasures of flirtation. Amiable Dutch buildings smile between its trees, and there are fountains here and there, and exotic flower-beds, and birds, and everywhere you may sense an easy mingling of the races, black,

Cape Town

brown, white, yellow and all. This is the old vegetable garden of the original Cape settlement, long ago mellowed and beautified, and it is astonishing to consider that each morning the South African Ministers of State walk through its genial delights, past the white synagogue and the art gallery, among the early lovers and the nibbling squirrels, to enact the dour philosophies of apartheid.

Cape Town is a strangely delicate, maidenly city for a seaport and a capital, and what sense of power she has lies chiefly in her setting. She clusters most obscurely about the massif of Table Mountain, rather as Rio meanders about her bays, so that the poor stranger, already bewildered with politics and hospitality, never knows which direction he is facing, whether the sea is in front of him or behind, or which way he must walk to get home. Only the mountain stands firm, to reassure him. It sits above the city in an attitude of righteous supervision, kindly but severe, like a bewhiskered Victorian pater-familias in an antimacassared chair. If you drive down from Paarl early on a winter morning you may see its flat plateau protruding brilliantly above the clouds that envelop the city, a sudden thin sliver of rock encouched in a cushion of white. At other times, if you stand on the green slopes of the mountain, you may observe the cloud resting soft as feather-down upon its plateau, while the Cape Town people jerk their thumbs affectionately at the old thing and say: 'Well, the tablecloth's spread this morning.' A huge cleft strikes diagonally across the north face of the mountain, and offers you an easy climb to the summit. Heavenly beflowered slopes lead up to it, sprinkled with the spiky gaudy proteas, and there are pleasant little streams, and rocky grottoes, and a marvellous panorama of Table Bay below you. Little rock pools of rain-water stud the summit of this famous mountain, and give it an unexpectedly marine flavour—like the top of Ayers Rock in Australia, or perhaps some crab-scuttled Cornish beach, except that now and then a troop of swart baboons slouches moodily from one side to the other.

There is a little of San Francisco to the city that rambles so incohesively about the mountain, and a whisper of France. This is an old and lenient capital. The fine white houses of the Dutch colonists still ornament its streets, and the castle is full of lovely Dutch furniture and pictures, a most comfortable, polished, gastronomic kind of fortress. There are flower-stalls (like Nob Hill) and Oriental quarters (like Chinatown) and down by the City Hall a jolly open-air

Cape Town

market sets up its trestle tables with a swagger, and restores to the city a trace of its old nautical roll. You can buy anything under the sun there, but I remember chiefly thousands of obscure workshop tools and innumerable cluttered collections of second-hand books. The crowd that oozes among the stalls is relaxed and friendly, and there are many of those absorbed shabby old men, *habitués* of markets everywhere, who seem to devote their old age to the adoration of musty volumes, and who are to be seen there any morning ritually buried in memoirs and mezzotints. Sometimes you may come across a soap-box orator in Cape Town, frothing a little at the mouth, spitting profusely and throwing himself about with stiff ungainly movements as he hoarsely declaims: 'Why, the Lord God, my friends, He knows, my friends, knows the innermost unspoken intimate thinkings and cogitations of your souls. My friends, He knows the ultimate machinations and considerations, my friends, of your ultimate beings, and He calls on you, calls on you now, my friends, calls on you before the Awful Day comes to think again, my friends, think again and cogitate and meditate and Repent!' I was once asked by a Coloured man outside the City Hall if I would care to buy a copy of *Lorna Doone*, and I once saw the guest conductor of the Cape Town Symphony Orchestra striding through that market-place like a mogul, wearing an imperial beard and a check tweed boiler-suit of his own design.

For Cape Town is an inconclusive, unregimented, individualist city, at least by the cramped standards of South Africa. She makes allowances for mannerisms and minorities. Now and then, to prove the point, you may see a woman in a filmy blue dress and a veil sidling through the back streets with a piquant suggestion of the arabesque. The Malays of Cape Town, descendants of slaves, bring a Muslim magic to the city and provide a soft Asiatic balm for its activities. On the doorsteps of their modest quarter you may see their doe-eyed children playing, squeaky but always graceful; and there are little mosques with fairy-lights, and proud old sages sitting in chairs in open doorways, and wafts of modest billowing ladies, enshrouded in scent and fragile sensibility. There is nothing gorgeously picturesque about the Malay quarter, nothing so bold and vivid as the big African locations on Cape Town's outskirts, or so teemingly vigorous as the tenements of the Coloured half-castes: but if you wander through these little streets, up and down these threadbare alleys, you will find yourself savouring the very breath of

Cape Town

Islam, compounded of dust, incense and red pepper, and spiced with serenity.

It is partly sheer age that gives Cape Town such undertones of ease, and partly a sense of maturity. In this city there are pleasant clubs overlooking squares, beside whose bars you may even, if you are lucky, bump into a professional actor (there are perhaps only four places in the entire African continent where you may have this unexpected pleasure). There is an eminent and courageous university. There are bookshops innumerable, staffed by that particular kind of droopy-eyed lady often to be found in staunchly Democratic book-shops in the United States. There are espresso coffee-shops, and gently prosperous suburbs, and a hotel called the Mount Nelson which is marvellously decorated with portraits of old English worthies, and seems to be inhabited exclusively by dowagers and Admirals of the White.

In short, I like Cape Town. Perhaps I have exaggerated her pleasures a little, and minimized her squalors, and touched up her colours a trifle, and rubbed away her smuts. You will probably not meet those actors in those bars. The guest conductor has long since gone home to Europe. The baboons of Table Mountain are almost extinct, and the perfumes of the Malayan ladies are, to be frank, apocryphal. Year by year the acid of apartheid is souring the city's spirit, and upsetting its careful equilibrium. Still, in a nation curdled Cape Town has retained some sweetness: at a cynical moment of history, she cherishes some kind illusions.

CARTAGENA
DE LOS INDOS

The most lovably rumbustious city of the Americas is Cartagena of the Indies, the pride of the old Spanish Main on the Caribbean shore of Colombia. The tone of this famous place is instantly and unforgettably set by a statue of Blas de Lezo, one of the legendary heroes of Spanish America, which, glowering from its pedestal outside the city walls, stops the unsuspecting visitor trembling in his tracks. It is more than two centuries since this greatheart repelled, against all the omens and all the odds, an assault on Cartagena launched by Sir Edward Vernon with twenty-seven thousand men, three thousand guns and the largest fleet that had ever crossed the Atlantic. His image today, though, looks as bursting with indomitable pugnacity as ever it was on the battlements long ago. There he stands in vivacious bronze, looking marvellously ferocious: one-eyed, one-armed, one-legged, waving his sword above his head, as battered an old general as you could wish to see, and patently invincible. His tricorn hat hangs nonchalantly on the corner of his plinth, and engraved around it are facsimiles of the medals foolishly struck by Admiral Vernon before he left England. 'The Spanish Pride Pulled Down!' cries one, and a second wanly claims that 'True British Heroes Took Cartagena, April 1747.'

Cartagena did not always win: she would be a much less interesting city if she had. She had her ups and downs of history, her ignominies as well as her storied triumphs, her weaklings beside her paladins. But she remains triumphantly the city of old de Lezo, instinct to this day with that forbidden but still delicious excitement, the pomp and panoply of war. She was built at the mouth of the Magdalena River to receive the flow of treasures extracted from the interior by the conquistadores, and to ship them home in her galleons to Spain. Born to such a purpose, and blessed with the

Cartagena de los Indos

finest harbour in South America, it was scarcely surprising that she became, for two gunsmoke centuries, the ultimate target of piracy and maraud. Every self-respecting buccaneer had his eye on Cartagena: Morgan sacked her, and so did Drake, and Hawkins bombarded her, and a succession of audacious Frenchmen filled their holds with the gold, emeralds, indigo, tobacco and cacao of her legendary warehouses. She was always in the wars. The Spaniards made her the most powerful of all their American strongholds, erecting fortifications so elaborate that King Philip II is said to have looked out of his window in the Escorial to catch a glimpse of them, assuming that since they cost so much they must be visible from Madrid. It was only in the nineteenth century, after the final bloody achievement of Colombian independence, that the guns of Cartagena were spiked at last, and her fortress gates unlocked.

It takes more than a few generations of peace to efface such a past from a city's character, and Cartagena still feels warily, if a little rheumatically, on guard, as though she is half expecting another blackguardly onslaught, or thinking about oiling her arquebuses. Her immense ramparts are still formidable: fretted and peeling with the corrosion of an equatorial climate, but still scowling grandly seawards, a vast pinkish agglomeration of forts, castles, watchposts and gun platforms, with ramparts so wide that you can drive a bus along them, and gloomy old dungeons still fetid and barred beneath the battlements. There are still warships brooding off Cartagena— the severe Swedish-built destroyers of the Colombian Navy, forlornly attended by the hulk of a frigate scuttled by its commander, it is said, to evade investigation of the wardroom accounts. There are still guns on the high breastworks of San Felipe. The direct channel into the harbour, the Boca Grande, is still blocked by the defensive breakwater built there two centuries ago, now to be seen like the rubble of some faerie castle beneath the glistening green surface of the bay.

Behind those mighty walls, too—seventy feet thick in places— Cartagena feels bravely ready, like some grizzled blue-eyed pensioner hopefully awaiting mobilization. This city was built·as a strong-box, sealed within layer upon layer of defence: the sea itself, the breastworks, the cross-firing fortresses, the inner walls, the very houses themselves, each a little citadel, with its own water supply, its own lookouts, its own barricaded courtyard. The old city of Cartagena is exceedingly intricate, Moorish in flavour, crooked and secretive. Tall

Cartagena de los Indos

proud churches loom over its little squares. Massive wooden doors, exquisitely carved, guard the lush gardens to be glimpsed tantalizingly through swinging gates, cracks or keyholes. The great city gateway is gracious and serene, with its whitewashed steeple, its big clock and its weathervane, but inside its portals all feels plate-mailed and introspective. Sometimes the lanes are so narrow that you can touch each wall with your outstretched finger-tips. Often the high wooden balconies of houses, protruding from upper floors, plunge a whole alleyway in shadow. It is a crowded, cheek-by-jowl, fretted kind of place, haunted by the shades of soldiers, slaves, martyrs, poets and pirates, by memories of rapine and ransom, miracles and phantoms, trumpet-calls, curses and groans. It is a stifling, claustrophobic entity, a mixture too rich for comfort, and it comes as a sudden gleam of freedom to look through some crumbling gateway in its walls and see the cool, calm sea beyond.

Floridly cosmopolitan is Cartagena, as any old seaport should be, especially one founded upon treasure chests, blood and thunder. The architecture of the place is Andalusian, by conquistador out of Islam; the sharp-snouted fishing-boats from the islands are lateen-rigged, like dhows or feluccas; the Magdalena river-boats, off-loading coffee at the wharves, are glorious old stern-wheelers, superannuated from the Mississippi, ornate with scrolls, whirligigs and tall black funnels; the citizenry is hilariously hybrid, ranging from lofty Spanish grandee to frayed miscegenated beach-comber, and infused always with the rhythmic energy of the Negro, that conquering slave of the Indies. Cartagena has always sheltered foreigners—Dutch engineers, Italian architects, English naval officers, long-transplanted Scotsmen with names like Guillermo MacGregor or Zoraida Atkinson de Llach. There are Chinese about the place, and Americans from the naval base, and a few Sikhs, and up at the Convent of La Popa, proudly surveying the bay, the caretaker is a Jamaican—'Born beneath the same flag, sir!' he reminds his English visitors happily, as he welcomes them to his improbable bailiwick.

The markets of Cartagena are uproariously bold and pungent: here a gigantic Negress butcher, heaving in pink cotton as she hacks at the beef, here a slant-eyed Indian beldame smoking a cigar, haggling mulattoes with straw hats and streaky moustaches, jovial poulterers brandishing dried chickens, gutted and flattened until they look like so many dead flying-foxes. Big black sailors swagger

Cartagena de los Indos

through the stalls, abetted by flouncy paramours. Emaciated country-women stalk by with trays of vivid vegetables on their heads. There are men selling coconuts, horoscopes, charcoal, prawns, lottery tickets, mounds of frilly petticoats, tinsel trinkets by the ton, amulets, crabs, outboard motors, and, for children with a centavo to spare, the cheap thrill of an electric shock. And when some rumba rhythm emerges from a hidden radio, all around you the market seems to twitch, with a kick of an ankle at one corner, a shimmy of buttocks at the next, a soft bare-footed shuffle among the radishes, a giggling *pas de deux* behind the coffee-stall.

A bombastic city, but always engaging, like one of those crusty, half-crazed, infinitely appealing old military men that Tolstoy loved to portray. That figure of Blas de Lezo rightly honours the flamboyant gusto of Cartagena, but another monument down the road better epitomizes the gentler side of her allure. Long ago somebody said of this marvellous city that one loved her 'in the way one loves a pair of old boots'. The municipality took the remark to heart, and erected outside the eastern gate a memorial properly peculiar to the place: two huge old well-creased boots of bronze, one upright, one on its side, the kind of boots that do become friends to a man, when he has worn them through love and bloodshed, toil and ecstasy, and only kicks them off at last when he is warm by the fire at home. A pair of beloved boots, a one-eyed, one-armed, one-legged old tyrant of a general: such are the emblems of Cartagena.

CHESTER

Once a year on the Roodee race-course they run, as they have since 1540, the Chester Races. Then the traditional race week buskers come to town, sharpening their wits and their badinage. The traditional race week fair churns and screams and blazes down by the Dee. The traditional race week Cheshire cheese awaits the winner of the traditional Chester Cup. Historical continuity is the stock-in-trade of Chester, once the garrison town of the 20th Legion, and in race week especially the air of the place is staunch with loyalty and old custom and honoured memory. It is one of the most enthralling cities in England, and the high jinks and ceremony of it all would be the greatest fun imaginable, were it not for one nagging and uncomfortable thing: the fact that few places in our hemisphere, in my experience anyway, reflect more poignantly the bewilderment, the indecision, the dislocation of Western civilization.

A pretentious claim, for a smallish country capital on the edge of Wales, but consider: England feels the predicament more sharply than any other nation, for she has suffered most deeply from the changing times, without the catastrophe of military defeat to brace or numb her for the shock: and Chester is peculiarly a paradigm of our age, for she is an ancient cathedral city, a Barchester, tauntingly situated at the back door to Liverpool. To the north you may see where the industrial revolution was born, among the mills of Yorkshire. Here, more than a century later, you may still observe its aftermath. Few sporting events seem more confident of perpetuity than the race for the Chester Cup, but look inside the city wall, and the odds are on uncertainty.

For a city wall there is, partly Roman, mostly mediaeval, and its lofty old progress around the centre of Chester contributes boldly to the civic sense of unbroken, organic development. It is as though the genius of the place has been sheltered or buttressed down the

Chester

centuries, from Romans to Saxons to Normans to us, so that all Chester's history overlaps and interlocks. The prosperous shops are still clustered in the Rows, quaint timbered galleries like the poops of old sailing vessels. The main manufactured product is still chemicals, as it was at the end of the eighteenth century. The china department of one store inhabits a thirteenth-century crypt, the smoke-room of one pub is the council chamber of a mediaeval guild. The fire station is built in elaborate mock-Tudor. The Music Hall Cinema has been, in its time, the Theatre Royal, the Wool Hall, and the Chapel of St. Nicholas. Scarcely a garden of the inner city does not cherish some relics of Rome, and hardly a cheese factor or a warehouseman, white-coated among sawdust and old beams in dim fragrant chambers, is not instantly suggestive of mediaeval gourmandcy.

Antique titles, ranks and dignities encrust the city. The arms of the Ancient Earls of Chester and the Barons of the Court of Hugh Lupus shine in dim heraldry from a Cathedral wall: Ranulf and Blundeville, Malpas and Dunham, Hawarden and John Scott. The Sheriff stands in direct descent from Robert Fitsjames and Adam Venator, who shared his office in 1257. The Dean has succeeded Richard, Monk of Bec, first Abbot of St. Werburgh's Abbey. The Mayor is still dubbed Admiral of the Dee, a survival from Chester's seagoing days, and everywhere you may find reminders of the dukely house of Westminster, reputedly descended from Chester's Norman earls, and still a power in these territories: Grosvenor Bridge, Grosvenor Park, the Grosvenor Museum and the Grosvenor Hotel, Grosvenor Street and Road and Place and Crescent. Chester was a fiercely royalist town in the Civil War, and since 1254 the Earldom of Chester has almost always been held by the heir apparent to the English throne.

Down on the Dee the professional salmon-fishermen still tar their nets and caulk their boats—thirty-one families are licensed today by hereditary privilege. Up in Goss Street the Chester Goldsmiths' Company still stamps precious metals with the Chester hall-mark. Across the river the flag still flies above a military headquarters, where once Julius Agricola commanded. Beyond Grosvenor Bridge two elderly couples still occupy the little house mysteriously called, since time immemorial, Nowhere, and Chester Castle is still, by some hoary paradox, excluded from the civic authority to form a barren county parish of its own. In the Cheshire Regiment's museum they still preserve the white marble throne of the Amir of Sind—that principality immortalized, when Napier conquered it for the Queen, by the triumphant but fictional telegram 'Peccavi.' Twenty-three of the twenty-five Chester guilds are still existent, and have recently acquired a disused church to be their Guild-hall. In the red sandstone Cathedral, a building of such soft and lucent material that it seems to be always aglow, a well-rubbed inscription shows where two generations of Cestrians have pointed to the name of Jack Cornwell, the boy hero who won his posthumous V.C. on the light cruiser *Chester* at Jutland. An extension to Chester Infirmary has been built on the very same field in which they used to bury the victims of the plague.

Chester still feels like a border city, where you may hear Welsh voices exotically in the coffee-shops, and a market city, mouth-watering with cheeses and shellfish. Above all, she feels always and inescapably *old*. It is as though for two thousand years the life of the place, scarcely interrupted by common wars or vulgar revolutions, rolled on placidly, gently, benignly, graciously, gathering sediments of lore and experience like some rock of the sea-bed, encrusted with the limpets and seaweeds of a million tides.

But suddenly, or so it seems, this comfortable stroll through time has been shatteringly interrupted. Far from feeling assured today, Chester seems to me painfully confused, torn between the old and the new, the familiar and the enterprising, the backward and the forward, the alien and the home-grown. Somewhere in the core of the place stand the Bishop and the Dean, the Sheriff and the Admiral of the Dee, the museum curators and the racing stewards, the colonel of the Cheshire Regiment, the fine old bookseller in Watergate Street, the jolly fishermen of Handbridge, the exquisite fur buyer in the posh department store, the warehousemen and the cheese factors, the schoolmasters and the genial young art dealer of Lower Bridge Street—somewhere in the heart of Chester the old culture survives, with its roots in country society, the humanities, Church, Crown, King and Country: but flooding heedless all around it, murky but tireless, is the tide of our brave new world.

Leeds and Huddersfield never knew the *ancien régime*, and in such towns of the north there remains a sense of brawny and un-troubled confidence, as though they understand our times, and know how to cope. For much of southern England, though, Chester can stand exemplar, and painful it is to see such a place caught in the anxieties of change. On the crudest level of analysis, Chester has been invaded by ignorant barbarians. Nowhere in a life of constant travel have I seen young people so instantly and altogether unprepossessing as those who infest these mellowed streets: stoop-shouldered and greasy-haired, loud-mouthed and loutish, physically pitiful and mentally apparently half daft, slouching through alleys, chalking rude inanities on walls, misbehaving in the shadows of the Rows, retching outside pubs. One Saturday morning in race week I saw a young mother, heavily lipsticked and violently dressed, directing her small son to relieve himself against the wall of the Grosvenor Hotel, in the very centre of the city; and on Saturday evenings the city walls are haunted by couples of horribly blotched and vacuous intensity.

By this gallimaufry, by all the pressures of an industrial age, by the proximity of Birkenhead and Manchester, old Chester feels overwhelmed. The Goblin Tower, to which the visitor is directed by every guide-book, turns out to be littered with cigarette packages, matches, fag-ends and bits of newspaper. The river is silting up, driving the fishermen ever farther downstream. Even the pool in the Cathedral cloisters, when I looked in it one day, had a scum of rubbish floating upon its surface. A paralysing stream of traffic clogs the old thoroughfares of the place; vandalism is rampant; the show at the Royalty Theatre, when I was last there, was a strip-tease spectacle, succinctly described by the management as 'the saucy, sporty race week Revuesical Musical: Girls—Giggles—Glamour'.

All this, perhaps, is irrelevant. It is not the challenge that is disturbing, it is the response. There have always been louts and thugs in England, and most people like an occasional taste of girls, giggles, or at least glamour. Until now, it seems, the old culture has easily held its own and sustained its mastery, and what is frightening about the Chesters of today is their apparently new inability to stop the rot—their hesitations, their lack of conviction or virility, their loss of standards. They feel, more than anything, leaderless. The gentry has mostly faded: nothing is more pitiful than a county function in Chester today, with its phoney accents or its shrivelled authority, the one false, the other fated. The Church fights on dauntless but evidently baffled, unsure how Barchester can best be modernized. All that is new in Chester seems to be alien, and often nasty: take-over bids for family firms, London money for develop-

Chester

ment schemes, espresso bars, hot dogs, American magazines, Elvis Presley haircuts. The indigenes seem to have lost their sap or their purpose, and are either immured in the contemplation of tradition, or unconvincingly pretending they like the new ways really. As a wise old citizen observed to me one day, Chester is not actually hostile to modernity—*'but she doesn't know how to use it'*.

She doesn't know how to use it. She doesn't know how to keep up. She can't get into step. I dare say at the grammar schools of Chester, or away at the universities, a generation is growing up that will redefine the purpose of the city. I admit that some of the city's unwholesomeness is unavoidable, and stems from technical advances that have made such old country centres obsolescent. I accept the truth that as the population grows, so there are more of all kinds of us—more good as well as more bad, more delinquents and more honest men, too. I do not doubt that they will still be running the Chester Cup five centuries from now, down on the Roodee, between the gasworks and the Grosvenor Bridge.

But when I read of a Russian rocket or an African celebration, a Chinese bomb or a Japanese tanker, I often think of Chester, all the same, remember the Dean and the Dee and the teddy-boys, and keep my fingers crossed.

CHICAGO

The summit of the American Middle West (if one can use the word of a region so uniformly flat), its crown and symbol, the prime product of its energies, the pride of its heart, is the city of Chicago, on the shores of Lake Michigan. I first approached this place by train, and since there is perhaps no city in the world more readily and universally preconceived, I looked out of the windows of my sleeper to glimpse some token of its vigour or catch the distant staccato flashes of its guns. I was prepared for almost anything in Chicago. Was not one nineteenth-century traveller informed, as he rode on *his* train into the city: 'Sir, Chicago ain't no sissy town'? Had I not been told by Middle Westerners everywhere of the unsurpassable blast, bustle and energy of Chicago, her boundless intentions, her sprawling size, her self-confidence, her incomparable resources of brawn and muscle? Did not Carl Sandburg, poet of the Middle West, describe her (with a perfectly straight face) as 'Laughing the stormy, husky, brawling laughter of Youth, half-naked, sweating'? Even Bismarck, whom one somehow does not instinctively associate with Illinois, once remarked wistfully to an American visitor: 'I wish I could go to America, if only to see that Chicago.'

On my first evening in Chicago I was taken down to the water-front to see the lights of the city. Behind us the lake was a dark and wonderful void, speckled with the lights of steamers bringing iron ore from Duluth or newsprint from Canada. Until you have been to Chicago—crossing half a continent to reach her—it is difficult to realize that she is virtually a seaside city. She has her sea storms and her rolling waves, her sunny bathing beaches, her docks; you can board a ship for Europe in Chicago, and see the flags of many nations at her quays. So wide is this Lake Michigan, and so oceanic in aspect, that more than once I have been compelled to walk down to its edge and reassure myself that it really contains fresh water, not salt.

So, with this queer land-locked sea behind us, we looked that

Chicago

evening at the city lights. The lake-front is the best façade in
America; more regular and uniform than New York's, so that it
presents a less jumbled and tangled mass of structures; bigger and
grander than Miami's, which shines with a beckoning gaiety across
the water of Biscayne Bay; less brassy and frontierlike than the
waterside aspect of Seattle. Its glittering row of big buildings extends
for miles along the lake, brilliantly lit—some of its skyscrapers clean
and clear-cut, some surmounted by innumerable pinnacles, turrets
and spires, so that the generally functional effect is tempered by a
few touches of the baroque. Beside this magnificent row there sweeps
a great highway, following the line of the lake, and along it scurries a
constant swift stream of lights, with scarcely a pause and scarcely
a hesitation, except when some poor unacclimatized woman stalls
her engine or loses her way, and is deafened by a blast of protest
from behind; then the line of lights wavers for a brief moment, until
with a roar of engines and a spinning of wheels the traffic diverts
itself and races away, leaving the poor lost soul behind, biting her
lower lip and having a terrible time with the gears.

For in many ways Chicago is still a heartless city. The incom-
petent will meet few courtesies in her streets; the flustered will be
offered no cooling counsel; it is necessary in life to get places, and to
get there fast. Between the buildings that stand like rows of hefty
sentinels above the lake, you may see numbers of narrow canyons
leading covertly into shadier places behind. The façade of Chicago is
supported by no depth of splendour; hidden by its two or three
streets of dazzle is a jungle of slums and drab suburbs, a hodge-
podge of races and morals.

In the daylight, indeed, the bright glamour even of the business
district is not quite so irresistible, if only because of the din and the
congestion. This must surely be the noisiest place on earth. The cars
roar; the elevated railway rumbles; the policemen blow their strange
two-toned whistles, like sea birds lost in a metropolis; the hooters
shriek; the horns hoot; the typists, on their way back from coffee,
swap their gossip at the tops of their tinny voices. Across the crowded
intersections scurry the flocks of shoppers, like showers of sheep,
while the policemen wave them irritably on and the cars wait to be
unleashed. The tempo of Chicago is terrible, and the overcrowding
desperate. Just as each new plan to improve the life of the Egyptian
peasant is overtaken and swamped by the inexorable march of the
birth-rate, so in Chicago every new parking place is obliterated, every

Chicago

new freeway blackened, by the constantly growing flood of motor-cars. Each morning the highways into the city are thick with un-wearying cars, pounding along head to tail, pouring in by every channel, racing and blaring and roaring their way along, until you think it will be impossible to cram one more car in, so bulging and swelling is the place, so thickly cluttered its streets, so strangled the movement of its traffic. It is good business in Chicago to knock down offices and turn them into parking lots. And it is decidedly unwise for the nervous or overconsiderate driver to venture into the turmoil of these streets, for in this respect, as in others, Chicago still ain't no sissy town.

Crime and corruption are still powerful influences here, although in recent years there has been a striking decrease in crimes of vio-lence. The Syndicate, the shadowy central office of vice, is still busy, and is said to have its agents in both local political parties. There have been many hundreds of unsolved murders since the days of Al Capone, but most citizens prefer to let such matters slide. People have too much to lose to meddle. The big man may lose a contract, the little man the dubious co-operation of his local police chief or petty boss. Extortion, on many levels, is still a commonplace in Chicago. A policeman wrote to the *Chicago Tribune* some years ago complaining about the word 'cop', which he said was derogatory. The letter brought a blistering and revealing reply from a Chicago citizen. 'How do you address a you-know-what,' he asked in a series of such rhetorical demands, 'when he stops you without cause and questions you or searches you or your property? How do you address a you-know-what when you've been looking for one of them a long time and finally find one mooching free drinks in a saloon? How do you address a you-know-what when one comes around to your place of business soliciting funds you don't dare refuse to give?' Everyone knows that a five-dollar bill slipped to your examiner may well help you along with your driving test. Everyone knows too, if only by reading his papers, that murders are still terribly frequent; but when I once talked to a senior Chicago police officer on the subject, he adroitly ducked away to the twin topics (for they seem to go arm in arm) of traffic congestion and prostitution.

All this sordid unhealthiness would be less intrusive if the city itself were spacious and wholesome of appearance. But despite the illusory grandeur of her lake-front, Chicago is a festering place.

Chicago

From the windows of the elevated railway, which clangs its elderly way through the city with rather the detached hauteur of a Bath chair, you can look down upon its disagreeable hinterland. The different sectors of slumland each have their national character— Italian, Chinese, Puerto Rican, Lithuanian—but externally they merge and mingle in a desolate expanse of depression. Here is a brown brick building, crumbling at its corners, its windows cracked or shattered, its door crooked on its hinges, with a Negro woman in a frayed and messy blouse leaning from an upstairs window with a comb in her hand. Here an old Italian with long moustaches squats on the steps of a rickety wooden tenement, its weatherboards a grubby white, its balcony railings sagging and broken. Slums are slums anywhere in the world, and there are probably areas just as blighted in Paris or Glasgow; but here the misery of it all is given added poignancy by the circumstances of the citizenry, people of a score of races who came to America to be rich, and have stayed on to live like unpampered animals.

Such a climate of existence has inevitably eaten away like a corrosive at the old blithe and regardless self-confidence of Chicago. Not so long ago Chicagoans were convinced that their city would soon be the greatest and most famous on earth, outranking New York, London and Paris, the centre of a new world, the boss city of the universe. During the period of its fabulous nineteenth-century growth, when millionaires were two a penny and the treasures of the continent were being summoned to Chicago, it was not unnatural for such an eager and unsophisticated community to suppose that the centre of territorial gravity was fast shifting to the Middle West. In a sense, I suppose it has; the railway tracks, the sprawling stock-yards, the factories of Chicago and her sister cities are the sinews of the United States, and so of half the world. But the blindest lover of Chicago would not claim for the place the status of a universal metropolis. Too much of the old grand assertiveness has been lost. Nobody pretends that Chicago has overtaken New York; instead there is a provincial acceptance of inferiority, a resignation, coupled with a mild regret for the old days of brag and beef. For one reason and another, the stream of events generally passes Chicago by. Even the Chicago theatre, once a lively institution, has fallen into dull days, making do with the second run of Broadway productions, and a few mildewed and monotonous burlesques. Despite the tumult and the pressure, Chicago sometimes feels like a backwater.

Chicago

The impression is only partly accurate, for there are many wonderful and exciting things in Chicago. There are magnificent art galleries—one of the best modern French collections in existence—and splendid libraries. There is a plethora of universities, of varying degrees of academic distinction. There is an excellent symphony orchestra (hampered though it has often been by the determinedly fashionable character of its audience, which has apparently restricted some of its conductors, so intricate are the channels of snobbery, in their choice of programmes). The huge marshalling yards lie lounging over the countryside, littered with trains. The bridges over the Chicago River open with a fascinating and relentless ease to let the great freighters through. The *Chicago Tribune*, which calls itself the World's Greatest Newspaper, is certainly among the sprightliest. There are brave schemes of expansion and improvement —plans to run a new highway bang through the heart of the place, to build a new suburb on an island in the lake, to erect a huge new office building astride the elevated railway, so that the trains will rattle through its open legs. It was for Chicago that Frank Lloyd Wright conceived his last marvellous effrontery, a skyscraper a mile high. It was in a Chicago squash court that Enrico Fermi and his associates achieved the first nuclear chain reaction.

But such driving activity no longer represents the spiritual temper of the city. Chicagoans are still pursued by the demon of progress and haunted by the vision of possible failure, so that the pressure of their existence is relentless; but the strain of it all, and the persistent rottenness of the place, have blunted some of their old intensity and lavishness of purpose. They have accepted their station in life, no longer swaggering through the years with the endearing braggadocio of their tradition, but more resigned, more passive, even (perhaps) a little disillusioned. Chicago is certainly not a has-been; but she could be described as a might-have-been.

CUZCO

Out of a Peruvian mountain fifteen llamas sway down an ancient road, silently pursued by a man in a poncho and knee breeches and a woman wearing a white straw hat, a blazing flurry of petticoats, and a baby-hammock on her back. The man is chewing an opiate wad of the coca leaf, the woman is planning to request the intercession of the Lord of the Earthquakes, whose miraculous figure in the town below is known to sweat in sympathy and weep real tears of compassion. To the north an elderly American locomotive, with a cow-catcher and an old wail of a whistle, is plunging zig-zag into the valley with a string of cattle-trucks. From the south a clanging of cracked bells rings out of a florid campanile. And as those travellers swing round the last dusty corner, with a soft shuffle of bare feet and padded cameloid hoofs, there below them they see, clear-cut in that alpine sunshine, the capital of the Land of the Four Quarters.

It could only be Cuzco, a little city of such supreme interest and historical symbolism, of such variety and punch, that in the South American context she combines the compulsions of a Stonehenge, a small Seville, and a Katmandu. She lies at eleven thousand feet in the Peruvian altiplano, and to reach her from Lima you fly breathtakingly across the Andes in an unpressurized aircraft, nibbling an oxygen tube like a hookah: but her valley is green, the hills around her are as fresh and springy as English downland, and only the testy pumping of your heart at night, and the celestial supervision of the snow peaks, remind you that on the other side of the world the ski-slopes of Saint-Moritz are five thousand feet lower than your hotel.

Five centuries ago this remote and barricaded place, somewhere between Lake Titicaca and the dreadful Amazon jungle, was the capital of the Inca empire, a brilliant but baleful organism, part refulgent aristocracy, part deadening discipline, that extended its power over most of the Andean territories, commanding an area as large as France, Switzerland, Italy, Belgium, Holland, and Luxem-

Cuzco

bourg all reluctantly put together. Here the mummified Inca emperors, all entrails sucked out, sat flicked by fly-whisks down the decades in the glittering Temple of the Sun. Here the Chosen Women span their incomparable textiles in imperial virginity, here the ferocious Inca generals marshalled their armies, here the diviners interpreted the intestines of their guinea-pigs, the priests prepared their intoxicated victims for the sacrifice, the marvellous Inca surgeons performed their prodigies of trepanning, amputation and excision. In the fifteenth century, when we in England were just beginning to be ourselves, Cuzco was the heart of a civilization so strange, precise and rarefied that nothing remotely like it has ever been seen again.

Cuzco was the core of it all—the very name means 'navel'—and everywhere in the town you can still feel the presence of the Incas. Often it is vulgarized in tourism and profit, in Incaland souvenirs, costume jewellery of weird exoticism, schoolgirl vestals with lamps and improbable headdresses at folklore festivals. More essentially, though, it is perpetuated in the massive masonry that still forms, to this very day, the ground layer of Cuzco: vast and impeccably chiselled stonework, like the craft of meticulous giants, with queer unexpected angles and corners of daunting exactitude—the whole looking so new and so contrived that it reminds me of the building material known in England as 'reconstructed stone'. The basis of the Temple of the Sun remains, marvellously rounded beneath a church, and so does the wall of the House of the Chosen Women. There are sacred Inca snakes still above a doorway, and sacred Inca sanctuaries still in a cloister, and brooding above the city, like a gargantuan Maiden Castle of limestone, stands the enigmatic fortress called Sacsahuaman, incorporating some of the largest chunks of stone ever raised into dubious utility by the ingenuity of man.

But all this terrifying structure Pizarro toppled, with few other weapons but guts, greed and a little gunpowder: and on the prostrate capital of the Incas, *sans* Emperor, *sans* Chosen Women, *sans* soothsayers and all, the Spaniards built themselves a second city, dedicated to a very different version of the Sun God. Gilded, ornate, candle-flickering, snobbish, radiant with Christian miracles and the titles of grandees, with arches and bell-towers and graceful plazas, with songs from Andalusia and Moorish doors and sizzling coquettes and silver tabernacles—there the Spaniards' Cuzco stands today, triumphant still above the Inca engineers. They called her

Cuzco

'The Very Noble and Great City of Cuzco, the Most Principal and Head of the Kingdoms of Peru': and deep among the canyons of the Peruvian Andes, she remains a paradoxical memorial to the virility of Europe.

Returned to her origins, she might not be remarkable, but in this utterly alien setting, high on the continental divide, Spanish Cuzco really smacks, as her old divines would wish it, of the miraculous. Fretted, solemn and domineering are the churches that stand around the Plaza de Armas—the dark but glistening Cathedral, the arrogant Church of the Jesuits, the gloomy shrine of Jesus and Mary beside the hall of the Inquisition, the aloof Church of the Triumph from which, in 1536, Our Lady emerged with the Christ Child in her arms to disconcert an Indian rebellion. Elaborate and delectable are the mansions of the old magnificos, with their dazzling gardens glimpsed through crooked doorways, their dripping pitchers of flowers, their crests and carved balconies and suggestions of silken solace. Nearly every church has its specimen of the Cuzco School, a sickly but compelling seventeenth-century style of painting that specialized in the cherubic, the wide-eyed and the rosy-cheeked. Nearly every corner has its hint of Spanish pride: as one of the local guide-books apostrophizes the city: 'We, your sons, who proudly bear you in our hearts alive with the fiery flood of your blood, do know well that the beating of your heart is still latent under the embers of the years.'

But the Spaniards do not dominate Cuzco today, for all the flourish of their architecture. Nor do the vanished Incas. Stonehenge and Seville she may represent, but for me she is, above all, a Peruvian Katmandu. Here you stand always among the mountains, and from here the ancient roads stride out to the trekking country of the Andes and the glorious snow summits. Cuzco today is mostly run by mestizos, half-castes of Spanish and Indian cross, but all its living colour and verve is provided by the fuller-blooded Quechua Indians of the countryside. Sometimes they look like gipsies; sometimes, in their trailing skirts, like Navajo Indians from Arizona; sometimes, with their tall white hats and shawls, like ladies out of Borrow's wilder Wales; but to me they usually seem, and sound, and smell, and move like Sherpas of the Himalaya—less carefree perhaps, less hearty certainly, but still instinct with dung-fires and potatoes, smoky dark interiors, sweat, untanned leather, back-breaking labour, poverty, superstition, resilience, and the viscous alcohol that is brewed in these parts by fermenting maize in women's saliva.

Cuzco

They are all over Cuzco, prostrate before the Lord of the Earthquakes like Tibetans in a tinkling temple, or hastening barefoot through the night, down the shadows of a cobbled alley, bent double with loads of straw. Away in the desolate expanses of the altiplano the Indians of Peru are usually demoralized, I am assured, often destitute, sometimes actually starving; but you would not know it in Cuzco. Their presence there is possibly a little wan, but still earthy. Their children are so adorable that I would happily adopt half a dozen myself. Their women, strolling thick-set through the tumbled market in their rakish hats and flounces, spinning their wool as they walk, look to me as though only an ounce of opportunity, only a dram of education, only a year of square meals, would release resources of wonderful strength and character. Their menfolk, half doped as they are by coca, malnutrition and the degradation of centuries, look as though nothing on earth, from a hostile omen to the most atrocious of hangovers, could deter them from the endless dull drudgery of their lives.

Undoubtedly the Indians win, in this Most Principal and Head of the Kingdoms of Peru. Beside them the half-castes look upstart, and the Lima gentry doomed. It will be a long, long time before they come into their own again—if indeed they ever do: but when I run my mind's eye back over the Cuzco scene, away from the snakes above the doorway, away from the smoke-darkened Lord of the Earthquakes, past the campaniles and the fortress on the hill and the puffing wailing train, in the end it rests again upon those distant figures of the Inca road, the fifteen lolloping llamas, the man with the plug of coca in his cheek, the barefoot woman in the bright but dusty petticoats, and the infinitesimal baby Quechua on her back, so swaddled in textiles that only one brown pondering eye shows through the muffles, jogging eternally out of the Andes.

DAMASCUS

Quivering in the expanses of the Syrian desert is Paul's city, Damascus, where runs the Street called Straight. She is a metropolis of the wastelands, facing the East and the Bedouin country, and her atmosphere is bird-like and inconsequential, like the minds of those who spend their lives in empty places. The rioting students, you may be sure, will be demonstrating for some quite different end tomorrow. The kidnapping blazoned in the newspapers has probably never taken place, or if it has, the victim is happily sipping sherbet in some silky country house. The gendarme who chivvies you so irritably will, if you treat him nicely, happily pose to have his picture taken. In Damascus, keep calm. It will probably never happen.

For though the reputation of this city is violent indeed, she always seems to me less menacing than quixotic. If nothing feels very serious, certainly nothing feels very predictable. Not so long ago political events here had the profoundest effect upon affairs in the surrounding Arab regions. Damascus was the obvious capital for the Arab Kingdom projected in 1918, just as she had been the headquarters of all Turkish power in the Middle East. Nowadays, though, she has a stringy back-street flavour, and her opinions are unlikely to have any decisive bearing on those of Amman, Baghdad, or even Beirut. This is because there is little original political thought in modern Syria. Beirut is a conduit of the world's ideas. Cairo is a showplace of Afro-Asianism. Baghdad has the weight of oil behind her. But Damascus, the oldest of the Arab capitals, is a light-weight, fluctuating eccentrically from year to year, whisked here and there by the breezes of opportunity, now adhering enthusiastically to the United Arab Republic, now plunged in prickly repudiation.

Such historical continuity as she has is principally religious. For a thousand years she was the starting-place for the greatest of the pilgrimage convoys to Mecca, and her links with the sacred centres of Arabia remain living and intimate. It was in the plain to the

Damascus

south of the city that Doughty joined his pilgrims' caravan; there was, he said characteristically, 'a new stirring of this goodly Oriental city in the days before the Haj'. Later the Medina railway was built, a pompous station was erected in the centre of Damascus, and at the season of the pilgrimage thousands upon thousands of pilgrims thronged its narrow platforms and pressed into the stuffy confines of its carriages. The trains still run from Damascus, though since the First World War the railway has never been restored to Medina—funny little trains they are, with prim, brass-cluttered engines, and they move ponderously with grinding and snorting noises. Nowadays few pilgrims travel directly from Damascus to the Holy Place, except by air, but a good many set off in buses and cars to join a pilgrim ship at the head of the Gulf of Aqaba. They travel by the old routes still, down the traditional highway of the Haj, and at the season of the pilgrimage Damascus is still especially busy and bustling, though the craftsmen at work are the garage men, the welders, and the menders of tyres.

Linked by such passages of terrain and of history, Damascus is never far in spirit from the Holy Places of the Hejaz. Of the more advanced Arab capitals, she is the most fanatical in her religion, and she herself boasts all kinds of spiritual merits. Abraham, we are told, was born here. Abel was killed here. Moses, Lot, Job, and Jesus prayed here. Mohammed lived here with his mother. At least 70,000 prophets and martyrs are buried on one hill outside the city. To be sure, there are plenty of young men drinking alcohol in the bars and restaurants, and many a worthy whose Islamic observances are more ostentatious than sincere; but the touchy, effervescent, almost whimsical political temper of Damascus is still closely linked with the prejudices of Islam.

She has none of the sense of power of Cairo, nor the raciness of Beirut, but she has a special charm of her own, at once fizzy, bitter, and mellow. She lies rather grandly among her sparse hills, projecting her roads into the deserts, surrounded by the lush green gardens of her oasis; and since you can never be altogether sure of what may be going to happen on any given day, nor who will be in power tomorrow, nor what particular ideology is fermenting in the bazaars that morning, a sense of uncertainty stimulates the activities of the city. The suburbs, stretching away up the hillsides, look trim but cautiously shuttered. The centre of the capital, speared with minarets and towers and criss-crossed with alleyways, is a place of lingering romance. And the shiftless nature of Damascus is the best conserver of her character; for nothing ever seems to last long enough to alter the place very profoundly, and temperamentally she is still much the same as she was in the eighteenth century.

The *suks*, for example, are still very beguiling. Little that is remarkable is made in Damascus nowadays (the decline in artistic craftsmanship began when Tamerlane took away the best workers to his new capital of Samarkand); but the shops are gay enough still, and full of daggers and silks and carpets and perfumes, so that if you stroll about peering at the windows through half-closed eyes you may easily fancy yourself back in the scented heyday of the caliphs. The streets are jumbled, narrow and winding, and picturesque old men obligingly wander out of archways, and there are donkeys silhouetted in alleyways, and veiled women, and fat businessmen in tarbooshes. Sometimes the dark-roofed bustle of a bazaar, crowded and clamorous, suddenly blossoms into a Roman arcade, decorated with splendid columns and sculptured blocks. Sometimes you wander down a narrow Biblical back street to find yourself abruptly out of the shadows and on the threshold of a golden mosque, its courtyard inviting you through the gates like a fresh field seen through the crooked doorway of a barn.

Most wonderfully of all, you may find yourself stumbling in this way through the gateway of the Great Mosque of the Omayyads, the noblest thing in Syria and, to my mind, one of the two or three most fascinating buildings in the world. Of all the sensations I have ever experienced from proximity to architecture, the most compelling of all is the feeling I have when I emerge from the shade of the Damascus cloth bazaar to find myself at the doorway of this marvellous structure. It is a potpourri of styles and periods, an amalgam of varying tastes, but it has the manner of some calm, unshakeable organism, or perhaps a clipper ship, or a great mountain. In Damascus, of all cities, its rock-like serenity is wonderful to encounter.

Like nearly all mosques, it consists of space surrounded by structures. Its predominant elements are air, light, and a combination of wisdom and freshness. The Great Mosque also has a tinge of the eccentric, as befits a Damascene monument. Its principal minaret, for instance, is a peculiar affair with a covered veranda and a big round bobble on its summit. Poles and yard-arms and loudspeakers protrude elaborately from its walls, and it stands there with the

Damascus

clouds scudding behind it for all the world like the superstructure of a warship in that glorious period of naval architecture that spanned the transition from sail to steam.

On the other side of the great courtyard is the Basilica, based on a Christian structure. It crowns a monumental prayer hall, dim-lit and murmurous, with a shrine supposed to contain the head of John the Baptist, and a graceful forest of pillars. There is always a hum of life and worship in this cavernous building. Sometimes you may see a whole country family at prayer in the shadows, the woman demure and respectful, the children awed, the bearded father rocking slightly on his heels as he chants the prayers in a languorous, sweet tone from a holy book held very close to his eyes. I like to sit on the floor of this hall and watch the worshippers passing by. There is great sanctity to the place (no spider ever weaves its web there, so the faithful say, and the prophet Jesus will come to the mosque on the Day of Judgement); but there is also, as nowhere else in Damascus, a sense of tolerance. Outside in the bazaars you may meet suspicion and unfriendliness. Here in the Great Mosque nobody will question the presence of a Christian, and if you like you may even open your airmail *Times* and see who has got engaged without incurring the displeasure of those passers-by.

And the courtyard itself! It is pale and flagged and exceedingly old. There are two strange little structures in the middle of it—one a treasure house, one a library—but its character is essentially one of venerable space. Pigeons fly about it, and Muslims wander here or there, praying or talking or simply thinking. High-vaulted arcades give it shade, if you prefer to withdraw from the bright yellow dazzle of the Damascus sun, and at the eastern end there is a series of bright mosaics, towns and trees and rivers and mountains, of infinitely surprising skill and humour. I have only to see a glimpse of yellowish sunlight, or remember for a moment the slow serenity of those worshippers, to be transported instantly to the Great Mosque at Damascus, and spend half an hour lapped vicariously in its charm.

Alas, it is not typical of the Damascus scene. Ask any ill-informed Londoner for his impressions of the Arab world and he will at once enumerate for you, with a pitying smile, all the characteristics of this lovely city: flightiness, prevarication, political *naïveté*, stubbornness, instability. Here it all comes true. Mingle these sorry ingredients

Damascus

thoroughly, add a flash of humour and a basinful of charm, flavour with brave memories and a trace of ineffectual nobility, soothe with a glimpse of magnificent architecture, and you have the essence of Damascus.

DARWIN

When you arrive at Darwin, your landfall in Australia, you are given a form to complete for the Customs, and satisfyingly bush-whacking are its demands. Have you any dangerous weapons, like spring-blade knives, daggers, bludgeons, coshes, knuckle-dusters or swordsticks? Are you carrying any saddles, bridles or horse rugs? Are there horns or hoofs in your baggage, dried blood, feathers, germ cultures or microbes? Are you accompanied by 'insects in any stage of development'?

Thus you are pre-conditioned to Darwin, for this is a town that prides itself upon its frontier manners, its horse-rug flavour, its traditions of bludgeon, horn and hoof, the weird animal life that leaps and wallows about it, kangaroo to buffalo, crocodile to dingo. Never did a town greet its visitors more boisterously. Never did the beer flow quite so fast. Nowhere is the traveller treated with such an easy, lolloping, happy-go-lucky, careless and gregarious courtesy. As an introduction to Australia, Darwin is a work of art, for here, carefully fashioned by climate, custom and inclination, is a mosaic of all the reputed Australian virtues, from the instant accessibility of the biggest swell to the determined golden faces of the barmaids. ('But don't judge it all by this place,' its genial citizenry will assure you. 'There's nowhere else in the whole bloody continent like the Top End.')

The Top End: Darwin stands at the very extremity of Australia's Northern Territory, on the shore of the Timor Sea, scarcely a gunshot from Indonesia and linked with the distant south only by the long, lonely road to Alice Springs—'The Track', as they fondly call it, or 'The Bitumen'. Immediately behind Darwin there begins one of the world's most fearful wildernesses, all desert and dry scrub from here to Adelaide. It is almost exactly a thousand miles to Alice, the next town of any size. Even the railway peters out three hundred miles to the south, and the Darwin telephone district is bounded east and west by areas that have, as the directory blandly tells you, no

Darwin

telephones at all. This is an isolated tropical town, twelve degrees south of the equator, blazing and humid in the Australian summer, caressingly warm in July. It is all on its own at the Top End, very fond indeed of its own company, but sometimes uncomfortably aware that several hundred million Asians live in crowded indigence just across the water.

You must not envisage it a Pacific paradise, all palm-fringed and zephyr-blown. Arnhem Land, this bump in the forehead of Australia, is a tough and unlovely place, clad in scrub jungle, with mangrove swamps at the water's edge and a flat monotonous bushland all around. Thirty years ago, I am told, this was a whole-hog frontier port, gambling dens, molls, Chinatown and all. Today it is much more respectable. Its principal purpose is Government, for it is the administrative centre of the Northern Territory, and some sixty per cent of its people are civil servants. They live in trim uniform Government houses, they honour all the hierarchical rules of Civil Servants everywhere, and they multiply, so the locals say, faster than jack-rabbits. The chief import of Darwin, according to a local proverb, is Civil Servants: the chief export is empty beer bottles.

But if sixty per cent of the people are conventional enough, the other forty per cent are marvellously free-and-easy. If Darwin has her self-service stores, espresso bars and used-car lots, she also retains some spirited echoes of her roistering days, and many reminders that down the road there still stands an empty continent. The saloon bars are full of handsome sprawling young men in shorts; prickly longshoremen with beer on their breath still lounge around the docks; sometimes a splendid rangy cattleman strides into the Darwin Hotel, with his wide-brimmed hat and his patrician air; and just occasionally you may see in a store one of those tight-lipped taciturn women, in faded floral prints and curlers, who are traditionally the helpmeets of pioneers.

With one eye always cocked towards Asia, Darwin has long since outgrown her racial prejudices. You may observe her tolerant proliferation best on Saturday evening, during the interval at the Smith Street picture house, when the audience pours out to its cokes and ice-creams in the neighbouring milk bars. This is a people of astonishing variety: black, brown and yellow, Italianate and Chinese, gleaming aborigines, half-castes, women who look like Californians and men who look like gigantic Dutchmen. Up here the notion of White Australia seems ludicrous indeed, and there is nothing strait-

Darwin

laced or loftily Nordic in the air. The illegitimacy rate is extremely high, miscegenation is as old as Arnhem Land, and Smith Street on such an evening fizzes with an almost Brazilian gusto.

Binding all this community together, though, stamping its character, providing the cast for the crucible, is the Australian as we have always thought of him, still recognizably British, and one of the very best and most likeable men on the face of the earth. Here you may see him at his most confident, on the edge of the great Outback. He may be of any age, this 'dinkum Aussie', descended from convicts or new-arrived from Newcastle. He may be a humdrum bank clerk, or a prospector driven wildly in from his shack in the wilderness, to squander his money on drink and loose living—'riding the vaudeville', as an old fossicker once described the process to me. Whoever he is, he is magnificent to meet: as free a spirit as you can find in the world today, shackled by no inhibition of class or disadvantage, with little sense of thrift and still less of decorum, no agonizing reserve, no envy, no contempt, no meanness. He is like some splendid English working-man relieved of the burden of the centuries, strengthened and cleansed by the southern sun, and allowed to begin history all over again.

Of course there are blemishes to such a reincarnation, at least to a visitor out of Oxfordshire. The brewery jokes soon stale, and the beeriness of life itself sometimes borders upon the bestial. For myself, I find those steely golden barmaids something less than alluring, and I resent the laboured bandying of my Christian name—'Nice to know you, Jim'—as though I were participating in a television quiz show. There is a certain air of middlingness to the place, like a boom town without a boom, or perhaps an army without any officers. Darwin does not feel to me a place of spectacular promise, an embryo San Francisco: she is growing all the time, but she remains, after many a long decade of settlement, and many a million gallons of beer down her collective throat, still a small and undistinguished town.

Nevertheless she is a fine introduction to Australia—something fresh, and new, and crackling. She is always alive, always laughing, always full of tall stories and improbable characters, always drinking, always ready to help. The visiting Englishman can scarcely help feeling a dude in such a setting, but for myself I respond all too easily to these tolerant and spendthrift philosophies. Perhaps it is some hereditary instinct in the blood, that makes me feel at home and

Darwin

at ease in this wide unfamiliar landscape. Perhaps it is the old yearning of the islander for horizons less cramped, skies less smoky. Whatever it is, it is exceedingly potent. It may not seem likely, when you hear my effete voice diffidently requesting a second pineapple juice across the bar, but by golly, give me a four-wheel drive and a good bush-woman, and I may well go walk-about myself.

DELHI

Some cities give an instant impression of provinciality, however urbane they are, however cultivated: such are Stockholm, San Francisco, Brussels, Karachi. Some, though, strike you the moment you arrive with the pulse and posture of history: and such a one is Delhi. Before your aircraft even lands you know you are moving into the big time, for few capitals await you with an air of such solemn distinction, sprawling vast, brown and mottled among its desiccated plains, the sand lapping at its suburbs and curling around its ruined redoubts. Such a setting is this, so infinitely far from the sea, so invested by all the immensities of Asia, so lost in everything big, and crowded, and old, and gnarled with legend, and scarred with tragedy, and hazed with uncertainty, and tinged with nostalgia—such a setting is this, where everything is larger and more intense than life, that when you land in Delhi you feel you are setting foot in some ultimate headquarters, far behind the lines, where the marshals meet to deploy their armies. Only Moscow offers quite the same sensation of inner power; and it is no coincidence that only Russia and India, among the big nations of the earth, are known to their peoples as Mother.

Delhi has been a metropolis for longer than history remembers, and eminence comes easily to her. Here, before the Muslim conquerors stormed across India, the blurred monarchs of Hindu tradition built the city of Indraprastha. Here the Slave Kings erected the stupendous tower of victory called the Kutb Minar, still standing talismanic in the southern outskirts. The successive capitals of Siri, Tughlakabad, Jahanapahan and Firozabad, the fifth, sixth, seventh and eighth cities of Delhi, were all built on this tremendous site; the Tughlak dynasty flourished and waned here, and the Sayyid, and the Lodi; and when the Moguls established their empire in Hindustan, it was in Delhi that Shah Jehan built the Red Fort, home of the Peacock Throne, one of the great fortresses of the earth, and one of the most perpetually haunting. The centuries

Delhi

have never left Delhi alone. Nadir Shah the Persian captured her in 1739, Ahmed Shah Durrani the Afghan in 1757, Mahdo Rao Scindia the Mahratta in 1771, General Lake of His Majesty's Army in 1803, the blood-crazed sepoys of the Indian Mutiny in 1857; and when in the nineteen-hundreds the regnant British cast around for a new Imperial capital, it was to the plains of Delhi that they sent Lutyens and Baker, commissioned to erect the greatest of all monuments to that diligent, blazing but ephemeral Raj. Seventy kings, two queens and a president have all ruled in Delhi. Empires one after the other have tumbled through her chronicles. Cultures have fused here, styles have succeeded one another, the pride of one era has given way to the pretensions of the next. As Murray's *Handbook* put it a century ago, this is the Rome of Asia.

Every stone of Delhi is thus soaked in the essence of history, but it is not really the past that fosters her sense of towering significance. Delhi is awe-inspiring today because she is the scene of a supreme experiment. Like almost every country on earth, the Republic of India has recognized that the way to national self-esteem, if not actually to survival, is industrialization. Like England two centuries ago, like the United States in the nineteenth century, like Soviet Russia since the revolution, like China today, like Egypt with one thing in mind, and Siam with another—like all the rest of the world, India has launched her industrial revolution, destined to transform her from an agricultural, subsistence economy into the kind of society that lives by buying and selling, by making things and putting things together. In the past such fundamental social convulsions have seldom been achieved without compulsion, overt or implicit. In Huddersfield and Halifax the English achieved it by the brutal exploitation of ignorant peasants—cruelly long hours in the mills, child labour underground, methods so ruthless that you may still recognize their legacies in the bandy legs and wizened frames of elderly North Countrymen. The Americans achieved it, scarcely less insensitively, by harnessing those millions of poor immigrants who would endure almost any hardship, work almost any hours for a chance of eventual dignity and security. The Russians have achieved it by brute force—sometimes, indeed, by nothing less than mass murder. The Chinese are achieving it by absolute despotism, at the cost of individual self-respect.

But Delhi is trying to do it without coercion, threat or exploitation. She is mounting an industrial revolution within a free society,

Delhi

on a scale staggering to conceive, among a community of peoples traditionally and endemically centrifugal, disputatious, caste-ridden, proud and superstitious. Such a portentous adventure has never been risked before. It is this that makes Delhi a city of such daunting import, and fosters her paradoxical affinities to Moscow, on the other side of the Asian divide. She is not just the capital of the largest of all democracies, 432 million strong and not a gauleiter among them. She is also a champion and a pioneer. In Moscow they are proving, year by year, that a people can be whipped into greatness. In Delhi they are trying to show that greatness can be voted into office, if applied for in triplicate, through the proper channels.

The first impact of democracy, in such a climate, at such a moment of history, is exceedingly slovenly. Delhi is two cities, the old walled part, the monumental new: and the shabby confusion of the older districts is anything but lovely. Up the road in Rawalpindi the Pakistanis, standing at a similar historical staging-post, have used the instruments of benevolent autocracy to fashion a capital very spanking, trim and orderly. Here, where Government is only by will of the people, things look much messier. The boulevards of Old Delhi are cracked, crumbled and rubbish-strewn. The thirteen-gated city walls look villainous and neglected. The tired tongas have lost their varnish, their bright paint and their nodding horse-plumes. The scrambled bazaars have little sense of craftsmanship or dedication, and the street bands always wandering through the Chandni Chauk, with their faded drooping epaulettes, their grubby white breeches and their tarnished tubas, look demoralized by the discordant monotony of their own art. The traffic of Delhi is dented and ill organized, and the policemen, in uniforms slightly frayed, boots slightly worn, and belts that often need a polish, are sometimes to be seen, to the horror of visiting Englishmen, smoking drooping cigarettes on point duty.

Even in New Delhi, the grandiose geometrical capital of the Republic, wherever the people are, there is muddle. It is rather as though a million gipsies have been let loose within the purlieus of Capitol Hill. The shops of Connaught Place, the Place Vendôme of Delhi, have little elegance or panache, but are mostly frumpish and down-at-heel, forlornly preserving some dying sense of horse-leather and English tweed, or frankly subsiding into lassitude—dusty books in heedless tumble, fabrics in bilious disharmony, comical signs in

Delhi

misspelt English or scratched toys that nobody can find the key to. Into the crevices among the palaces of State all the welter of India has penetrated, like brambles overgrowing a gazebo: wherever there is a space there is a crooked ill-printed notice, a tangle of barbed wire, a ramshackle hut or a covey of old men cooking something on a fire. Behind each grand façade, there is a hint of disorder. It may be a ping-pong table in a lofty courtyard, or a dirty cup on a counter. It may be the rusty squeak of an ornamental gate, or the incipient beard of an official, or the dead-beat, dog-eared procrastination of Indian bureaucracy. It may be the general emanation of imprecision and unpunctuality. It may be the atrophy of inefficiency. Whatever it is, it feels raggety and flaccid. Any dictator would dislike Delhi. Any posturing twopenny despot would feel impelled to take her in hand, clean up her litter, put her clocks right and dust down her venerable pants.

But people of a gentler vision will see more than just the muddle, as a perceptive schoolmaster can detect, beneath the incurable untidiness of a gifted boy, other and more essential talents. The infatuated visitor, indeed, may find the moral of Delhi in her very dishevelment: for without tolerance, without a blind eye, without profusion and variety this would be quite a different kind of city, occupying an altogether different niche in history. Delhi is a cemetery of petty tyrants, and stands above the primping and window displays of autocracy. Everywhere in this city you feel the easy benediction of *noblesse oblige*—just as you do, come to think of it, in the best Romany encampments. It is true that often, out of the halls of Government, you may hear a waspish buzz or the rattling of vulgar sabres—when the armies of non-violence march upon a Goa, for example, or the spokesmen of Gandhian love hiss an imprecation towards some distant antagonist. But the spirit of the city itself is seldom resentful. Delhi does not harbour recriminations, and takes the transient world as it comes. She is, for all her unkempt illiterate veneer, a cultivated city, a sophisticated city in the oldest sense. She is full of cultured men, scholarly or avid to understand. She is rich with immemorial experience. She pushes nothing down your throat, and seldom says, 'I told you so.' She accepts each facet of her history, heroic or humiliating, and blends it carefully and sadly into the fabric of her presence. Her environs are littered with the relics of a dozen kingdoms, crumbled mosques or broken pavilions, stumps of columns and dust-heaps of forts. Her slums are pierced by the noble mosques

Delhi

of the Muslims, calm and commanding still in this Hindu capital. The queer Iron Pillar of the Guptas still stands venerated in its enclosure, as it has for nearly a millennium. Beside the Kashmir Gate the white Church of St. James is as gleaming today as it was when Colonel James Skinner, drawing ten thousand pounds from his bank account, erected it in thanksgiving for his own survival in battle.

Most of all will you feel this bigness, this sense of generosity, inside the Red Fort, sprawling in red sandstone above the city walls. This has been many things in its time, Imperial court to British Army barracks, but today it stands to the Republic of India precisely as the Kremlin stands to the Union of Soviet Socialist Republics. It is more than just a tourist sight. It has a savour almost religious, so ark-like does it embody all the convictions of national independence. Physically it has not much changed since the days of the Raj. The little shops of the covered bazaar, the entrance to the fort, are still spiced and dim-lit. The sentries still stand with fixed bayonet at the gate. The Diwan-i-Khas still faintly reflects the opulence of the Peacock Throne, embellished once with a thousand sapphires, pearls and rubies, guarded by two dazzlingly jewelled peacocks and a parrot carved from a single emerald. Beneath the walls the lumbering Himalayan bears still enact their clumsy boxing matches, staggering and cuffing one another in the dust, while their masters beat time on muffled drums or scurry to catch the tourists' tossed rupees. The guides still quote, with a lyrical quiver, the famous Persian distich carved above an archway—'If Paradise there be on earth, it is here, it is here, it is here!' Physically nothing much has altered: but in the feeling of the crowds that wander through this old fortress you will sense something altogether new, something unique to the world in our time, and inspiriting to contemplate.

What incomparable crowds they are! What variety of face, costume, gesture, language, tone of voice! What proliferation of styles and costumes, dazzling yellow toga beside pin-stripe reach-me-down, slinky sari after bouffant skirt! Here is a man from the northern frontiers, squat and Mongoloid, swarthy and slant-eyed, wearing an amulet around his neck and smelling of sweat and musk. Here, in the shadow of the Lion Tower, two Muslim women stand breathing heavily, shrouded from head to foot in suffocating cloth, and peering out at the world through a tight-meshed grille about the eyes. Here are dark-skinned people from the south, from Madras and the Coromandel Coast, and here are gigantic Sikhs, whiskered

Delhi

and turbaned, and here are stunted shrivelled folk from the central flatlands. Here are pilgrims from Assam and Kerala, Mysore and West Bengal, from the buffer States of Nepal and Bhutan, from the distant island dependencies of Minicoy and Nicobar. A group of young soldiers clatters laughing by, their shirts emblazoned with military symbolisms, their ammunition boots striking sparks on the steps of the Pearl Mosque. An Indian patrician of the old school consults his guide-book beside the Royal Baths, wearing a jacket of impeccable cut and leaning gently on a shooting-stick. Perhaps a Buddhist priest stalks by, rake-thin in flowing saffron, or perhaps you hear behind your back a barked succession of irritable commands, and down the pathway a young man chivvies, like a shepherd with his silly sheep, a flock of Rajasthani women, chattering squeakily among themselves, hastening with a jerky barefoot motion, aflutter with orange cotton, and so hung about with ivory bracelets, silver bangles, necklaces, anklets, belts, charms and ear-pendants that they overtake you like a jiggling, tinkling orchestra, fading away towards the Delhi Gate in a long exotic diminuendo.

For this is an imperial city indeed, ruling a dizzy variety of peoples and provinces—Kutch to the Naga Hills, Arabian Sea to Chinese frontier. The sight-seers at the Red Fort are responding, like the Kremlin crowds, to all the pride of common ownership, to the slow swell of patriotism in a nation of a million diverse loyalties. But the distinction of Delhi is this: that these people are masters of their own contemplations. They have not come to the Red Fort in tagged and regimented groups, hectored by a State-trained educator. Nobody is going to brainwash them, or send them away for reorientation, or even tell them which mosaic to examine. To any autocracy, even the grandest, there is a second-rate, next-best, parochial feeling, whether you are sensing it among the squabbling military juntas of today or the endless gossiping soirées of the Tolstoyan yesterday. This sensation will never nag you in Delhi. She is the capital of one of the poorest, most backward, most problem-ridden of all nations: but she is free, and she has style.

Lastly you must look at New Delhi, for there in the seat of Government you will glimpse the grandeur of the Indian experiment—not its intimacy, nor even its pathos, but its sweep, scale, risk and possibility. The British built New Delhi, and it remains the greatest memorial to an Empire that was mostly metaphysical—the only

Delhi

British relic, outside London, that has the tremor of power to it, like Baalbek in Lebanon, the pyramids of the Egyptians, the fearful jungle cities of the Aztecs and the Incas, or the Roman aqueducts lording it across Provence. New Delhi has the strut of inherited confidence, just beginning to sour, perhaps, into the flatulence of doubt. Here the British dismissed, for once, their rooted instinct for the rolling way, the crooked way, and abandoned themselves almost sensually to symmetry, size and splendour. There is undeniable glory to New Delhi: the very wealth, pride and energy that could build such a place has majesty. There is beauty to it, for of all the planned capitals, from Washington to Brasília, this is perhaps the most successful. There is nostalgia: gone, gone are the plumed English satraps of this city, the Viceroy among his attendant Indian gentlemen, the Etonian cavalry colonels at the garden parties, and today only King George V is left, all alone and slightly elongated, beneath the tall cupola of his memorial. And there is a tinge of gentle irony to the place: 'Liberty will not descend to a people,' says an aphorism above one gate of Government, 'a people must raise themselves to liberty.'

But today the British shades of New Delhi, quietly retreating into the past, are only incidental to the fascination of the city. Today, if you stand on Raisina Hill, you will feel only a native grandeur, for in two short decades of independence this has become one of the pilot-capitals of the world. Look to the west, and you will see the enclaves of the foreign ambassadors, brilliant evidence of this Republic's sudden importance—the American Embassy resplendent in its moat, the British High Commission a huge compound of offices, villas and apartment blocks. Look to the east, and there arise the big new offices of Government, four-square and functional, filling in the gaps of Lutyens's grand design—for already this vast State has outgrown the imperial capital, as it leaps from one phase of history into another. Look behind you, and there stand the splendid lancers of the Presidential guard, languid but commanding, lofty but alert. Look in front, and there rolls away into the sandy distance the immense ceremonial mall, along which, on occasions of State festivity, the splendid troops of India march, horsemen gorgeously caparisoned, infantry lithe out of the northern hills.

And look to your left, and you will see the laboratory that is the real heart of Delhi—more vital than any desert reactor, nobler than any rocket workshop. There, in its pillared rotunda, half a mile

Delhi

round, sits the Parliament of India. It is the only properly democratic assembly between Athens and Tokyo, and one of the earth's political poles. It is a body often testy, often childish, sometimes arrogant, occasionally hypocritical. Sometimes its disputations make the Jeffersonians squirm and the eager sceptics scoff. But it is the very point and purpose of Delhi, and makes her a far greater capital today than she has ever been before, in all her incarnations. If her immense experiment succeeds—social revolution within a free but half-stunted society—then the whole democratic world can breathe more proudly and more confidently. If it fails, the grimmer philosophy of Communism, sweeping down from Russia and China like an energy of Tartars, will eventually master all Asia, and possibly all the world.

No wonder Delhi leaves you solemn, respectful and a little scared. She carries a millstone of history on her back, and she bears herself like a statesman of terrible responsibility, or an Atlas groaning beneath the hemispheres.

DUBLIN

When I was in Dublin one day, for the first time in my life, I took a stroll along the extended breakwater, bleached in sun and sea-wind, that protects the mouth of the Liffey from the exuberance of the Irish Sea; and passing the drab remains of Pigeon House Fort, and raising my hat to the crew of the pilot-boat, lazing offshore, and gazing about me pleasurably to the sunny hill of Howth and the distant derricks of Dun Laoghaire, presently I saw before me, implanted across the causeway, the club-house of the Half Moon Swimming Club. Around it, on the pebbly beaches, various lonely bathers were doing things with bits of equipment, goggles and pipes and flippers, and fiddling about with small brown boxes such as might contain, in another environment, rail-waymen's lunches: and immediately beside the door of the building there was a bench, facing directly down the mole, as though in judgement. Even from a distance I could see that four or five heavy pinkish figures occupied this seat, motionless but glistening in the sun, like Buddhas, and I could feel their eyes steadily focused upon me as I approached them down the causeway: until at last, reaching the purlieus of the club, I raised my own eyes modestly to meet those divinities face to face. Five old, fat, gleaming Dubliners looked back at me, severely: and they were all entirely nude.

I walked past them hastily towards the distant lighthouse of Poolbeg, but already their plump gingerish faces had comforted me. The stranger in a great city, if he takes his travelling at all seriously, is constantly suppressing his preconceptions and adjusting his pre-judices—'Ah, but you must remember, New York isn't America,' or 'That's what every blerry visitor thinks, when he's had half an hour in the Union,' or 'I suppose, Mr. Morris, like all our English visitors, you fondly suppose that the secret police are following you laboriously about our city?' He is always secretly hoping, though, that his pre-conceptions will prove true: and when they do, the warm glow of recognition is both soothing and stimulating. The five fat naked men

Dublin

of the Half Moon Swimming Club perfectly fulfilled my notions of Irish life: and in their rheumy but relentless gaze, I felt, were distilled all those essences of leisure, inconsequence, eccentricity, outrage, detachment and beery excess that every traveller surely cherishes, when he crosses the Irish Sea for the first time, and finds himself in Dublin.

I needed their reassurance badly, for many of my Dublin dreams had already been shattered by the time I took my promenade along the mole. 'Dublin,' one of my guide-books had told me, 'is the most uniformly elegant of the western European capitals': but it certainly does not show, when you step from the airline bus into O'Connell Street, fighting off the covey of sticky, raggety small boys who want to carry your bags for you, and setting off towards the river. O'Connell Street is, so Dubliners say, without much conviction, the widest street in the British Isles, and is the principal thoroughfare of Dublin: but it has long since sunk into squalor and mediocrity, and smells of tobacco, old beer and stuffiness. A succession of sad cafés lines this once splendid boulevard, ringed with the hot heavy miasma of cabbage, with a drooping commissionaire at each door, and the jangle of a juke box, and a plate of wilting cakes in each window, and a procession of dowdy provincials, in felt feathered hats and shapeless trousers, making their way towards the viscous coffee of the Snackery. Here and there stands a huge but unglittering emporium, all balconies and flannel nighties; outside the Gresham Hotel a wedding party, emanating scent and cigar-smoke, offers a brief but overwhelming impression of rhinestone finery; the streets of dull shops that run away from Nelson's Pillar look like slices of a shabbier down-town Boston; and when at last you reach the river, and feel the bold exhilarating wind from the sea sweeping beneath its bridges, you discover no splendid monuments, no antique curiosities, no fine memorials, but only a fusty succession of pubs, dim bookshops and neglected auction-rooms, lining the embankments of that celebrated stream like so many dispirited spinsters.

This is the stranger's welcome to Dublin, the city of Wilde, and Shaw, and Yeats, and Lady Gregory, and Joyce, and all those numberless anonymous wits who have (so legend constantly assures us) made this the liveliest, sprightliest and most irreverent of cities. Dublin still has her corners of grace, relics of the Protestant Ascendancy or tributes to the export trade: the linens, tweeds, cut glass and whimsy leprechauns of Grafton Street; the glorious conservatism of

Dublin

the Shelbourne Hotel, where the lifts ascend as stately as Cunarders, and the page-boys' cries have a peculiar hereditary intonation all their own, like the calls of immemorial reptiles; the space and splendour of the great Georgian squares, and the noble symmetry of the Custom House, and the calm of Trinity College. ('Ah, and there's been some fellows educated there! What a clever lot of fellows!') By and large, though, she seems to me an unconscionably shabby, down-at-heel kind of capital, as though all the festivity of our time had passed her by, and left her to grow crotchety in an attic.

This is nothing to do with her design or situation. Seldom was a city so blessed with air, light, freshness. From her broad streets (preserved by the Dublin Wide Street Commission, established in 1757) you can see the green mountains of the countryside. On her perimeter stands the magnificent Phoenix Park, as big as Hyde Park, St. James's Park, Green Park, Regent's Park, Kensington Gardens, Primrose Hill, Parliament Hill and Hampstead Heath all put together. A perpetual vigour of the sea sweeps into the city up the Liffey, and the air is so sharp and salt, the light so pellucid, that sometimes you are reminded of a spring in Venice, and sometimes of crystal sea-cities in Japan. You can indeed imagine Dublin, painted and revived, as the brightest of capitals; you can see, in the mind's eye, her lovely squares bright at midnight with satin and soda-siphons; you can almost hear the sparkle of her poets and playwrights behind the heavy brocade curtains of her drawing-rooms. Dublin seems made for charm, comfort and easy-going affluence.

But it is not there. The few squares that retain their urbanity are dominated by offices and embassies. The wonderful library of Trinity is musty, cluttered and unpolished. Shabby brown buildings blur the grand vistas of the place. Above all, there stretches across Dublin, to an extent almost forgotten in most of western Europe, the dingy blight of poverty. 'You should have seen the place ten years ago,' nearly every Irishman replied, when I mentioned the slums and beggars and penury of Dublin: but Dublin will still give you a shock, if you happen to have spent much time in the twentieth century. The urchins who weave their irrepressible way, clad in rags and confidence, among the traffic of Gardiner Street or Mountjoy Square, or who scamper so endearingly barefoot through the shadowy aisles of the pro-Cathedral—those small Dubliners are Dickensian urchins, long vanished from the streets of London, but still the familiars of this backwater capital. The old ladies still to be found, muffled in

131

Dublin

black shawls, begging sixpences in the small hours upon the quays, are, to the English visitor, images of a dead past, like coelacanths from the deep. Cracked are the window-panes, sordid the halls, broken the railings, unwashed the crones and children who hang around the front doors of Dublin's Georgian slums. Through each beautifully proportioned window you may see a jumble of unmade bedding, brass bed-posts, tumbled clothes and broken trinkets: and the voices that echo raucously down the staircases are filtered through layers of slops and slovenliness. In the magistrates' court behind Inns Quay the crowd that huddles upon the spectators' benches might have sprung direct from a Cruikshank plate, so instinct are its attitudes with whisky and dirt and threadbare comity. The public places of Dublin are mostly frowsty and peeling, and through the greenery of St. Stephen's Green, beneath the windows of the Shelbourne, there wander platoons of old men in frayed greatcoats, spindly children outgrowing their pants, down-and-outs and hairy mendicants. Dublin still has her corners of style, her fine restaurants and pampered *salons*: but to the English stranger it comes as a shock to realize that within the perimeters of our common islands there stands the poorest and most stagnant capital of western Europe.

For at a moment when the Western world rings with wealth and progress Dublin seems stuck in a forlorn but stubborn rut. Ireland has become the lost soul of Europe, without resources, without backers, without (one is almost tempted to say) purpose. The gusto of capitalism, the surge of Communism are both absent from Dublin, which is left waving a little green flag and looking towards Lourdes. Compared with this city, Reykjavik feels go-ahead, Oslo feels luxurious, even Prague feels almost hopeful. Bismarck, I am told, once suggested that as a solution to the Irish Problem the inhabitants of Ireland should change places with the inhabitants of Holland: the Dutch, with their diligence and skill, would soon make Ireland rich, and the Irish, with their genius for cheerful fecklessness, would soon let the dikes rot and drown themselves. Modern Dublin seems, at least to the stranger, to support this mystic thesis. Nearly all that is beautiful there was left behind by the English: and there are moments, when you trail through the drab back streets of this city, when it feels as though the Irish have already opened their own floodgates, and are slowly expiring in Guinness (on a Gradual Payments Plan, to crib the Dublin euphemism for hire purchase). They will tell

Dublin

you that the Irish actually *prefer* to be poor; that it is not their fault anyway; that the crime rate in Dublin is so low that the prisons are languishing for lack of convicts; that Ireland is the one country where the individual still successfully defies the State. Perhaps. Nevertheless there is a strong streak of the ironic to this kind of nationhood, which sends its bored and penniless thousands to London or New York, and says its prayers in Gaelic. ('Dublin?' said my Irish charwoman, when I returned to England. 'I wouldn't go back there if they were to pay my fare, really I wouldn't: Ireland's on its last legs, and I have no intention of subsiding with it.')

Nor has poverty plus independence, which sounds a heady kind of mixture, bred genius. Dublin, that old home of poetry and paradox, feels a sterile city. At the Gate Theatre, while I was there, they were performing *While the Sun Shines*. At the Abbey (playing, since its theatre was burnt, in borrowed premises) there was a half-baked comedy-drama, relying heavily upon Ould Irish Jokes, and drawing a great deal of embarrassing laughter from those tourists in the audience who still supposed that anything delivered in an Irish accent was meant to be funny. If there are first-class Irish novelists writing in English today, or first-class Irish painters painting, they are not readily apparent in Dublin, where the National Gallery is still dominated by Nathaniel Hone, and the admirable Municipal Gallery is rich in foreign moderns, but poor in what they fondly call The Irish School. *Dublin Opinion,* the *Punch* or *New Yorker* of Dublin, is, as somebody observed to me, 'just the thing to read on top of a tram'. Dublin contemporary architecture is very difficult to find, there being very few new buildings at all. That old Catholic Grundy, the Irish censor, is still active. Irish humour these days seems to lean heavily towards the chamber-pot and the bathroom door, and Irish design wanders feyly through the hinterland of folklore, bog, tweed and Little People. I looked and listened vainly for those brilliant Irish talkers, half sozzled but pyrotechnic, whose exchanges I had so often heard in imagination across the bars of Dublin: even Mr. Brendan Behan had packed his bags and bottles, and gone away to London. Dublin—I hesitate to use the phrase, with so many formidable shades to read it—Dublin is dull.

This is perhaps because the Irish War of Independence has, with reservations, been won. It is true that the Six Counties up the road still bask blatantly in the sunshine of the Welfare State, anointed

Dublin

with Protestant lotions: but nowadays the squabble with Britain seems pitifully unconvincing, like the last fading grumbles of a nagging wife, when her husband has actually done the washing-up, and she is tucked up in bed in her curlers. The fanaticism has long since died, the heroics are over: many Dubliners will tell you that only the obduracy of Belfast prevents a closer association between Ireland and England. Nobody appears to resent the Foreign Office's bland definition of Ireland as a 'non-foreign country', or denigrates those myriad Irishmen who leave for England to work, vote, go a-soldiering or have their tonsils out. Royal prefixes are still common-place in Dublin, from the Royal Hibernian Society to the Powers Royal Hotel, and nobody has ever had the heart to knock down Nelson from his column. The Dublin bookshops are still full of revolutionary narratives, rather baffling to those innocent aliens who can't quite remember what the Easter Rising was, and confuse a Black-and-Tan with a Mild-and-Bitter: but in general the fight is o'er, and the old quarrels are only sustained artificially by middle-aged patriots of nostalgic yearnings (like that pitiful class of Englishmen, plunged in banks and solicitors' offices, who are still in fancy leading their troops through Libya, or being intermittently heroic upon the Normandy beaches).

This absence of fiery conflict unquestionably contributes to the vacuous atmosphere of Dublin. National independence has, by an unkind paradox, turned the Dubliners into provincials. In the old days this citizenry was invigorated by all the passion of frustrated liberty, keeping Dublin constantly in the world's headlines, breeding poets, martyrs, Heaven-guided orators. Now all this fury has been spent, and Dublin has retreated into the obscurity of a medium-sized city in a predominantly agricultural island, somewhere to the west of England. Here and there indeed you may detect, beneath the kindly dinner-table badinage of an intellectual, a buried spiky streak of Anglo-phobia: in the tobacconists' there are still many journals, rather of the crack-pot breed, declaiming against the British Occupation of the Six Counties, and lurid with atrocities. But the fizz has left Irish Nationalism, and the flaming Irish patriot finds that, like Othello, his occupation's gone. There is anticlimax and disillusion in the air. There can be few sillier street signs than the one which directs the visitor, in handsome Gaelic script, towards the 'Aerphort': and never did I hear a more convincing *cri de coeur* than that of the down-and-out whose midnight company I enjoyed during a long stroll up

Dublin

Grafton Street, and who told me as we parted: 'I'll tell you the truth, sir, God bless you, I've lived in Ireland every minute of my life, and the more I see of the place, the less I understand its intentions.'

They are, though, unmistakably honourable. Ireland is a very nice country, and Dublin, for all her dowdy disappointment, is a very agreeable capital. This is because the Dubliners, through all their fluctuating fortunes, remain at once highly intelligent and delightfully unsophisticated. The faces of Dublin are not striking. Irish features are seldom clear-cut or arresting, and look a little blurred, as though you are seeing them through the frosted glass of a saloon (the Anglo-Irish gentry, when you observe them in their suedes, checks and pleated skirts, look highly chiselled in comparison): but the Dublin eye, seldom dimmed by National Health spectacles, is still irresistibly blithe, and few cities on earth give you so smiling a welcome. Hardly anybody is grumpy in Ireland. The Dubliner is often, as they say, a queer fellow, and his reactions are tempered by centuries of foreign rule and exploitation, so that he seldom openly disagrees with you, but answers your questions obliquely, as a perceptive fish might nuzzle a fly: but despite (or perhaps because of) this almost Oriental sense of camouflage and elusion, he remains wonderfully fluent and entertaining. The Dublin accent remains, to the Englishman, perennially fascinating: and the Dublin vocabulary is not only vivid, but also splendidly precise, and never trails away, like the Londoner's, into a train of confused syntax and ill-remembered words. The Dublin girls rely heavily upon fresh Irish charm and laughing eyes, but are undeniably pretty; Dublin offices seem to be organized with exemplary good sense; Dublin policemen, who often look like genial parodies of Irish-American cops, have managed to retain their courtesy; and nobody at all in this city will snub you, however irritating your questions, brash your criticisms, or patronizing your approval.

I do not myself believe that you will find much more individualism in Dublin than you will in Rome, New York, or even dear old Manchester: but there is still a pleasing undercurrent of easy-going eccentricity to life in this declining city. When they take you to the site of the old Abbey, and remind you as you stand there of all its legendary triumphs, its idols and its hilarities, its flops and its world-beaters—as you linger in that evocative side-street it is all too easy to feel the presence of Dublin's pungent old celebrities, glib and facile and brilliant and sometimes profound, talking the hind legs off any passing donkey, and ignoring with a fine Celtic flourish all the petty demands of convention. In the Church of Michan, where the guide invites you to shake hands with a mummified Crusader in a vault, you may fancy a fleeting gleam of irony in your cicerone's eye, as he tells you that the organ-loft was carved by the well-known firm of Grinling and Gibbons—'The harp is there, d'you see, the trumpet is there, the drum is there, the violin is there, all done to perfection, d'you see, by that well-known firm.' An endearing flicker, too, crosses the salesgirl's face as she offers you a salad bowl engraved, upon demand, with your family crest—O'Boyland or O'Boyle, O'Fogarty or O'Heffernan, O'Griffy, O'Tools or MacDonell of the Glens (there is a choice of two hundred and fifty-two). Sometimes, as the barman laboriously removes the froth of your draught Guinness with a wooden board, you may hear an odd snatch of conversation, from across the next partition, so wryly hilarious, so bitter with pith, that it sets you chuckling as you stand there waiting, and the barman looks up and laughs, too, and removes the last drip of froth from your stout, and says proudly: 'Oh, we get some comical fellows in here, you've no idea!' And if, one cold evening, you succumb to the lure of the neon signs along the quays, and descend into a basement for a Bingo session, there before the familiar trestle tables of Housey-Housey will be a vision of your vicarious Ireland, wreathed in tobacco smoke, its faces at once jolly and intent, with a wealth of whiskers and brogues and old-fashioned hats and aprons and homely witticisms, as though the whole reputation of a city were to be seized, given a glass of beer and bundled into the basement.

When I had passed those elderly nudists at the Half Moon Swimming Club (looking surreptitiously out of the corner of my eye, to observe the expressions of their faces, which were exceedingly haughty), I thought I heard one of them speak to another, as I continued my progress, slightly shaken, along the wind-swept mole. I cannot be sure, but what I *think* I heard the old gentleman say was this: 'That fellow there, the one with the clothes on—surely he can't be a member here, can he?'

But I walked on disregarding, for I knew it was only a bluff: and when I passed back that way, all those five fat old men had gone, leaving only the damp impression of their being upon the faded blue boards of the bench.

FORT-DE-FRANCE

When I was dining one night in the Restaurant de l'Europe, which opens on to the main esplanade of Fort-de-France in Martinique, an extraordinary girl burst into the dining-room and began dancing a kind of ferocious screeching rumba to the music of the radio. She wore an enormous straw tricorn hat and a red swimsuit, and when the management objected to her presence she instantly threw herself into a spectacularly flamboyant tantrum. She screamed, shouted, sang ear-splitting snatches of songs, threw plates about, dropped her hat, made savage faces at the customers, knocked tables over, and reduced the whole room to helpless laughter; until at last, to crown a splendid entertainment, somebody dialled the wrong number and obtained, instead of the police, the fire brigade, whose clanking red engines skidded to a halt outside our windows and whose helmeted officers, trailing axes and hoses, stared in bewilderment through the open door at the hilarious chaos inside.

'It was magnificent!' was the general verdict as, wiping our eyes and resuming our victuals, we watched that uninhibited performer withdraw; and we might have added, such was the gaiety and licence and spontaneity of this farcical scene: 'It was France!' Martinique is a department of France, and the spirit of that astonishing country is deeply ingrained here, in a tropical volcanic island on the other side of the earth. There are many places in the West Indies more advanced and more splendid than Fort-de-France, in many ways a slatternly little town. The offices are plusher in San Juan, the hotels are infinitely grander in Montego Bay, life blazes much more brilliantly in Port of Spain or Havana. But I venture to guess that in all the wide Antilles there is hardly a town more civilized than Fort-de-France, or a community that feels more hauntingly and oddly akin to our cherished European values.

Its colours and crystal lights are Caribbean enough, and so are its peasant costumes. Every kind of straw hat flops and nods through

137

Fort-de-France

its streets, from tall conical goblinesque things to the sort of wide Mexican hats sometimes worn by duchesses at fancy-dress extravaganzas. The wrinkled old women of the markets are gorgeous in long draped cottons, subtly inclining towards the Directoire, with bright bandannas scrunched mysteriously on their heads and inflexibly mercantile expressions on their faces. On their wide trestle tables are spread the exotic edibles of the island, as in some wild harvest festival: marvellously green and yellow and orange, pineapples piled with carrots, oranges with mangoes, huge bananas and melons and breadfruit and squashy red fruits like dissolute apples. Down the creek that runs through the town, smelling rather Venetian, the long-prowed fishing-boats splash away to sea, dazzling in blues and reds; and out in the bay a sailing-boat or two rides invitingly on the tide, like a promise of love, or a raised eyebrow.

But through all these tropical excitements there permeates, gently but inescapably, the Frenchness of Fort-de-France. In the centre of the park outside my restaurant, in an honouring circle of tremendous royal palms, stands a rather maternal figure of the Empress Josephine, most celebrated of the islanders; and wherever you walk there are the statues and memorials, the old guns and cannon-balls and flag-staffs and ramparts that testify to the fine martial conceit of France (though, by Jingo, it was from this very harbour that de Grasse sailed into defeat at the Battle of the Saints). A trim little French warship lies beneath the fort. There are *kepis* and pom-poms in the cafés. The Préfecture is embedded in impeccable gardens, and above a building up the road an immense tricolour pennant, streaming in the breeze, assures us of the probity of Le Crédit Martiniquais.

In a hundred subtler ways, too, you can feel the French presence. There is a natural ease and courtesy of manner to the groups of men in greasy trousers who drink their rums and white wines beside the water-front. There is fricassée of crab and Camembert in the little Restaurant de l'Europe. Elderly men at corner tables exude faint pleasant suggestions of high collars and buttoned suits, and look as though they are members of archaeological societies. In the Cathedral (which has a metal lattice-work steeple, like an obsolete American battleship) a young man runs his eye earnestly, but not very hope-fully, through the film lists to see if Miss Brigitte Bardot's latest has gained the approval of the hierarchy. The local magazine is full of the consecrations and cultures and symbolisms and aphorisms so characteristic of the higher French journalism. And sometimes you

Fort-de-France

may observe, raising her fork or driving her Citroen, choosing a mango or gossiping on the benches beside the war memorial, one of those inexplicable Frenchwomen who contrive to seem, in spite of moderate figures and ordinary brains and only a reasonable amount of money, almost unattainably elegant and intelligent.

The open drains of this bustling little town are incongruously balanced by delicate verandas, wrought ironwork, steep red roofs and small secluded gardens. When the shops shut up for the night they fortify themselves like private Carcassonnes, with a splendid profusion of bars, shutters, chains, and heavy old padlocks. You can buy a Beaujolais in Fort-de-France, or a Diorissima, and when the shopgirls hasten home they pause to look at the 'Marie-Claire' patterns in the windows of the department store. Sometimes there are even mountain-climbers in the park, actually preparing an expedition to Mont Pelée, but instantly reminiscent of the square outside the post office in Chamonix.

All these French signs and symbols, earthy, graceful, or ornate, enrich the flavour of life in Fort-de-France, and often whisk you in memory or intent back to their originals in Europe. But here is the miracle of the place: French though its manners may be, and European many of its values, there are very few people in the streets of Fort-de-France who could confidently be classed as pure white. Some of that cool enviable woman's ancestors came from Dahomey or Ashanti. Those endearing archaeologists are, to use an old-school phrase, as black as your hat. Many a cheerful half-caste face grins from beneath its *kepi*, and when we laughed at that wonderful girl and her baffled attendant fire brigade, Africa was in our smiles. So long ago were the pigments confused in Martinique, so warming is the touch of French tolerance, that the wretched question of colour simply does not arise. The Martiniquais is a Caribbean Frenchman, and in Fort-de-France the concept of a colour-bar seems as absurd and discredited as a flat earth or a steam-omnibus.

In this, Martinique is not alone among the islands of the Caribbean. Puerto Rico is also free of this particular curse. Jamaica is ostensibly so. Cuba, Haiti, and the Dominican Republic are all more concerned with power rivalries than colour prejudices. But in Martinique racial equality has been combined, to a remarkable degree, with a sense of dignity, tradition and self-respect. The island is poor enough, and has its problems and its squalors, Heaven knows, but at least it is no razzle-dazzle wilderness of politics and pin-tables.

Fort-de-France

'Is there any anti-French feeling in Fort-de-France?' I asked a man one morning. He looked at me blankly. How could they be anti-French, he said, scratching his curly head, when they were French themselves?

There are some places in our contemporary world where, observing a ruined village or a shattered family, one has smiled a sad sceptical smile at the civilizing mission of France. In others *la présence française* remains what it ought to be: a noble force for good, for gaiety, for sanity and fricassée of crab. How agreeable to come across it here, on the rim of the Monroe Doctrine! And how we shall regret its passing, if ever it is lost to the world!

GENEVA

One way to judge Geneva—harsh, perhaps, but telling— is to drive into the city from France on New Year's Day. On the French side of the frontier, when you roll down from Haute Savoie, all is bibulous good cheer. Wine hangs merrily on the gendarmes' breath, as they examine your papers with winks, sighs and badinage: their chins look a little prickly, they wear their cloaks with a special celebratory flourish, and when you drive away through the barrier they stand there for a moment looking affectionately after you, tilting their *kepis* and waving to the children.

No such holiday relaxation welcomes you to Geneva, down the road. The policemen are as briskly courteous as ever. The man in the office grants you the standard regulation smile. When you wish the cloak-room attendant a happy New Year, you are returned no more than a tolerant inclination of the head, as though you are being humoured. Geneva is simply not a festive sort of city, and her merry-making is always of a decorous and mercantile nature, the kind that goes with guilds and aldermen. Her eye is never bleary, her lenient formalities are seldom skimped, and if ever she wore a swaggering blue cloak she would zip it meticulously up the front.

I would be ungrateful to deny that I have, on many a wan occasion, arrived in Geneva as to a comforting haven. Marvellously bright did her lights seem, marvellously warm her embrace, when I first pottered into this neutral refuge out of a war-shattered Italy. Delectable has her cherry jam often tasted, ambrosian her crisp white bread, when I have stepped haggard off the night train from Paris. Many a marvellous cheese have I eaten in the little restaurant under the Tour de l'Île. Many a good brisk walk have I taken through the agreeable lakeside gardens of the place. Many a supremely cosseted night I have spent in this metropolis of the hoteliers. There is almost nothing *nasty* about Geneva. Almost nobody will be rude to you, or cheat you, or reproach you with irrelevant political grievances, or displease you with cigarette smoke and chipped cups. Even the

141

Geneva

scrawled *graffiti* in the public lavatories, though they may take you by surprise, are quite tastefully executed. Even the frontier police, though they seldom slap you on the back, hardly ever open your suitcases.

But of all the big cities of Europe, Geneva is perhaps the most boring: the most pallid, the most unprovocative, the most suburban, the most Swiss. This is odd, because in fact she has long been a great metropolis, frequented by great men and bolstered by a long tradition of autonomy. For several centuries Geneva was independent, ruled by her own counts and bishops, and when Calvin stormed into town on the wings of Reformation she became a blazing theocracy, one of the pacemakers of Europe, the Protestant Rome. Her Catholic neighbours viewed her with such suspicion that for two hundred years they refused her admission to the Swiss Confederation, and it was only after many perilous fluctuations of fortune, including a brief annexation to Napoleonic France, that they relented and let her in. She is like a plump pigeon nowadays, but in history she stands as something much more aquiline and ruffled.

She has summoned to her presence, too, many a fine mind and radiant notion. John Knox was a refugee in Geneva, and so in a manner of speaking was Voltaire, who here indulged himself in the greatest of all his pleasures—acting in a play of his own composition in his own private theatre. Here J. J. Rousseau lived, and here Dr. Zamenhof invented Esperanto. Keats, idly imagining an ideal home, said he would like its windows to open upon Geneva's lake— 'and there I'd sit and read all day like the picture of somebody reading'. Ruskin honoured Geneva as 'a centre of thought and learning', and in 1898 the Empress Elizabeth of Austria was assassinated while admiring the view from the Quai du Mont Blanc. In the past Geneva has seldom been a backwater. Here the Red Cross was founded; the International Committee still consists of twenty-five Geneva citizens. Here the protracted *Alabama* dispute, which nearly brought Britain and the United States to war, was settled in 1872— an agreement still commemorated in the Alabama Room at the Hôtel de Ville. Here many a dark exiled conspirator came to plot the overthrow of the Tsars, and Allen Dulles organized his network of agents in Nazi Germany. Here the International Labour Office was born, and here, when the poor League of Nations cast about for hospitality, the Palais des Nations set up its pillars and its principles.

And perhaps it is the fate of that sad institution that gives Geneva

Geneva

her present air of reconciled mediocrity. The palace is still there, enshrouded in shrubbery and initials, still the home of a few lesser instruments of salvation, still a great place for inconclusive subsidiary negotiations: but it survives only by sufferance and cheese-paring, and stands in relation to the glittering skyscraper on the East River as the most withered of spinster cousins stands to some sensational Riviera heiress. Geneva is very much the same. She is a city without much zing. Zurich and Basle are both bigger, and both livelier, and though fifty years ago a writer could say of the Geneva architecture that its modernism produced 'a blinding glare', today nobody need shield his eyes as he enters this city, for she has no dazzle left. The Swiss seldom make anything actually ugly, but in Geneva they have almost succeeded in making nothing actually beautiful either.

Here and there you may find exceptions. The old city of Geneva, clambering steeply away from the south bank of the Rhône, has a certain curious charm. The gigantic fountain of Eaux-Vives, squirting two hundred feet out of the lake surface, is both gay and spectacular. The big new lake-front hotel is very striking. The lake itself, when the light is right, can still look romantic and even remote. The celebrated panorama of Mont Blanc, which so fatally absorbed the Empress Elizabeth, really is breath-taking. The wide promenade along the water-front, if colourless, at least has a noble sweep to it, and the six bridges across the Rhône look, when the evening traffic rush has begun, agreeably animated. The flower market is lovely. The post office is grand.

But you have to try hard. I read somewhere that only dullards find Geneva dull, but if so I am not alone. Even the most sycophantic of guidebooks devote only four or five pages to this city, and one great expert on ecclesiastical architecture has described Geneva Cathedral, in a backhander of cruel subtlety, as 'an excellent example of a small cathedral of its own style and plan'. The mountains that overlook Geneva from the west are the Juras, the drabbest in Europe. The Eaux-Vives fountain only spouts, so the guide-books despondently say, 'now and again, on Sundays and holidays'. Joseph Conrad, who must have been temperamentally allergic to everything Swiss, once described the Geneva setting as possessing 'all the marvellous banality of the picturesque made of painted cardboard', and he detected in the little Île Rousseau, beside the Pont du Mont Blanc, 'something of naïve, odious and inane simplicity'. No towering

Geneva

romantic, no deep-sea man, no Cape Horner could really enjoy Geneva. She is a mill-pond city, with ornamental quays.

Well, the Genevois will say, what more do you demand of us? Don't we honour our own principles? Indeed they do, and no transient visitor, awaking in his exquisite bed to a cup of the best coffee in Europe, has any real right to complain. Every city has its function, and Geneva is a kind of civic nursing home. But the day I find I prefer that calm, impeccable routine at the Swiss customs post to the unpredictable and sometimes ill-tempered fizzle at the French—the day I enter Geneva with relief, I shall know I am getting old.

HAMBURG

On the top floor of the Hamburg Historical Museum there runs, four times daily through the year, the most elaborate model railway in Europe. Its locomotives are perfect replicas, its operations are marvellously complex, but for my money the most interesting part of it is the man who makes it go. He stands in a small glass cabin above the layout, earnestly fiddling with switches and delivering a running commentary into a microphone: and so solemn does he look up there, so dedicated in his attitudes, so conscientiously does he abandon his own voice, now and then, to impersonate the station announcer on a platform beneath—so *respectful* is his manner of controlling that prodigious toy, that you might think its trains were performing some symbolic ritual, and that he was only acolyte to its mysteries.

Hamburg is not a gullible town. She mostly escapes the dread innocence that gives Munich and Berlin their undertones of wide-eyed menace. As German cities go today, she is argumentative, even sceptical—'*Hei lucht!*—He's a liar!' Hamburgers sometimes like to shout, when the tourist guide has reached some pinnacle of hyperbole, and they have a little grog inside them. She nevertheless possesses, beneath her dazzlingly affluent new veneer, an old-fashioned air of wonder, as though the world is still worth gaping at. The marvels of technique, so casually accepted in Frankfurt or Düsseldorf, here still provoke gasps of admiration, as the talking doll talks, the shipyard crane hoists, or the jet takes off for Idlewild. The economic miracle of Germany, elsewhere a little tarnished by time, still seems divine and pristine to the Hamburgers. A little of the magic of foreign places has rubbed off on to Hamburg, a seaport for a thousand years, and this is a city whose character has not yet been smoothed out, deprived of its bumps and wrinkles, and tight-laced in superhighways. Most of Hamburg's legendary gabled houses were destroyed in the war, but somehow it does not seem to matter: she is an ancient port, gilded by centuries of foreign trade, and that

145

Hamburg

is still exactly what she feels like. It takes more than a war or two, the collapse of a civilization and the reshaping of a continent to expunge the signature of the merchant venturers.

For this is a dyed-in-the-wool merchant city, sabled and aldermanic, like Bristol in England, or Genoa in the south. It is also, in tradition and in political fact, a Free City—one of the eleven constituent *Länder* of the German Federal Republic. Hamburg, sò the official guide-books like to say, 'is one of the larger among the small States of Europe'—larger than Andorra, Liechtenstein, San Marino or Monaco, and big enough to contain several thousand Vatican Cities. For several centuries Hamburg, champion of the Hanseatic League, was one of the Powers of the world, and though Germany has progressed from chaos to confederation, from Empire to Federal Republic, from Zollverein to The Six, still Hamburg thinks of herself as a State apart, bigger than Liechtenstein, the place where the great ships are built and the traders come home from the east—the gateway, the dockyard, the dour open end of Germany.

She is one of those cities, devastated though she has been by fire and war, whose personality assaults you the moment you arrive. The five great spires of Hamburg stand above the twin lakes of the Alster in almost stylized comity, like a foreshortened old engraving, embellished with curly horsemen, or a poster whose landmarks are scrunched together for impact. The tremendous port of Hamburg, surveyed by towering shipyards, patrolled by fleets of tugs and ferries, with the ceaseless flash of its welders and the high white shapes of its liners in dry dock—the port of Hamburg looks for all the world like one wide animated Kokoschka, so bold but smudged are its effects, so muscular and functional its patterns. The *Fleets* of Hamburg, the meshwork of narrow old canals that link the Alster lakes with the Elbe, still seem at once secretive and diligent, though most of their old warehouses have vanished and the fur-bales are no longer piled along their crumbled quays. Hamburg still feels a city of the Baltic north, sister to Lübeck, Visby and Novgorod, tempered by the long gloom of the northern winter—a city of furs and scarves and fattening cakes and pudgy, buttoned, hurrying, humourless people. She feels spacious but also money-grubbing, cosmopolitan but also mean. She is the greatest city of West Germany, Berlin apart, but she feels far from the centre of things: though she has her fine opera house and her celebrated newspapers, her millionaires and her

Hamburg

shipyards, she is still unmistakably provincial. Germany is a country without a convincing capital, and Hamburg, for all her two million people, never feels properly metropolitan.

In some ways she is cramped and crabbed. Her aristocracy, a caste of cultivated merchant princes, is notoriously snooty and clannish. Her manners are often brusque, her attitudes often curmudgeonly—she speaks the Low German dialect, *Plattdeutsch*, which, mumbled testily under the breath, has fine powers of petulant invective. She displays towards the rest of Germany, not altogether in fun, a lofty and sometimes contemptuous façade. She is obsessively, even comically, self-engrossed, buttressed by her own history and fortified always by favourable statistics: that historical museum, train and all, is really one enormous monument of civic conceit, beautifully arranged, meticulously planned, and instinct in its every showcase with the assurance that everything about Hamburg is biggest, best and unbeatable. To the world at large the reputation of Hamburg is essentially genial: but Germans from other regions often loathe her, and find her too pleased with herself by half.

This may partly be because Hamburg, though self-satisfied, has never been violently nationalist, and has seldom shared the inner passions of Germany. The hunger for *Lebensraum* has never meant so much to Hamburg, with the world's expanse beyond her breakwaters, as it has to the inland German cities, circumscribed by fears and frontiers. Hamburg has always looked outwards, down the Elbe to the North Sea and the Atlantic, Africa and the Americas. The tall boat-prowed Chilehaus is a symbol of Hamburg's foreign enterprise, and so is the Hamburg-America Line, whose ships not only sail from this port, but were often built here, too. Hamburg is a city of the sea, and around her core of parochial complacency there are encrusted rich layers of experience, like geological evidence. Her streets are laced with salt and spice. If you wander down to one of her stuffy little water-front restaurants, their windows steamed up with fug and black tobacco, you may eat one of the great seamen's dishes of Europe—eel soup, flavoured with prunes, herbs and onions and washed down with beer-and-schnapps. If you walk up the Reeperbahn after dark you may inspect one of the most raucous of all sailors'· pleasure quarters, the stews and cabarets of St. Pauli, where the show-girls ride their bare-backed camels, the female wrestlers grunt in the small hours, and through the eerie silence of the prostitutes' alley, sealed off from the streets by high wooden

Hamburg

walls, the harlots gaze from their windows pink-lit and grotesquely painted.

Hamburg is full of foreigners, wandering Levantines and African students, shashlik in the all-night cafés, Persian mosques and Scandinavian churches and Japanese ships and English bankers (successors to those who, in the prime of the British Empire, acted as intermediaries between German industry and the vast markets of the Raj). Two Englishmen built the first Hamburg water-works, many French refugees contributed to the skills of the Free City, the Church of St. Nicolai was once restored by Giles Gilbert Scott, and half the Swiss merchant fleet is based on this port. There are fifty-three consulates in Hamburg, more than anywhere else except New York, and at the marine gateway of Schulau ships of all nationalities are played into port with their own national anthems, boomed over loudspeakers from the shore. Hamburg knows far more about the world than most of Germany does: within her narrow limits are concentrated the maritime and mercantile skills of a vast, mostly landlocked, and endlessly ingenious nation.

Hamburgers like to think that all this has made them more broadminded than most Germans. They often voted against the Nazis, they have often had a Socialist Government, and they seem less guiltridden by memories of war than the Bavarians, say, or the sinister Berliners. They may not be a very *soigné* citizenry, but at least they do not resent independence of view. They have never cringed to the central Government in Bonn: Ministers of the Hamburg *Land* Government are even forbidden to accept Federal honours. The English, old friends of the Hamburgers, are apparently well liked still, and several English wives lived unmolested in Hamburg while the Royal Air Force was bashing the city into rubble. Some of Germany's most liberal newspapers and magazines are published in Hamburg, and some of Germany's liveliest young artists work there. Hamburg was never a viciously militarist city, by German standards. She is scarcely open-hearted, let alone open-fisted, but she was never one of the screaming jack-boot communities, neurotic with grievance.

How could she be? She has been scoured by too many salt breezes, has swapped bills of exchange with too many distant customers, and has been kept awake at night, down too many generations, by the high jinks of the seamen.

But if it is hard to conjure up the shades of the Nazis in Hamburg,

Hamburg

or to imagine the Jews dragged from their beds, only twenty years ago, in this plump *bourgeois* seaport, it is scarcely less difficult to envisage the city fitting comfortably into the new Europe—so steely, so hard, so uniform. Already, as this new entity develops, Hamburg feels a little ill at ease. As the growing power and responsibility of the United States of America has whittled away the blithe sparkle of San Francisco, so the emergence of a United States of Europe is likely to leave Hamburg high and half dry. Her great days, one senses, are passing. She is one of the greatest of European cities still, the most productive place in Germany, the fourth port of the world: but the times, one feels, are catching up with her.

What will her function be, when Europe coalesces at last, and the frontiers of Germany dissolve? The German Customs Union made her rich, but the union of Europe may well enervate her. Soon the ports of Germany will range from Venice on the Adriatic to Antwerp and Rotterdam on the North Sea, and the German industrialists will have the choice of a hundred efficient outlets. Then Hamburg's principal *raison d'être* will fade. She is a northern port, built for the cold-water routes, designed to handle the trade of a Germany that looked, willy-nilly, northwards: but today the impetus of Europe is moving southwards, and the centre of German gravity is shifting towards friendlier climes and warmer seas. Like Trieste, Hamburg is losing her hinterland. Like London, she is suffering from a shrinkage of geography.

But hers will be a long, slow, stubborn decline, caused not by the end of an Empire, or even the devastation of a war, but only by more ponderously organic processes of history. Hamburg is a very substantial sort of pageant, not easily faded, and many a big tanker must yet slide down her slipways, many a breathy assignation emanate from the table-telephones of her night clubs, many a clickety-click of wheels vibrate the layout of the most elaborate model railway in Europe. She is not exactly bland, nor even urbane, but she has something heavily imperturbable about her—the stolid, simple, almost fatalistic spirit, I suppose, that sustained her so resolutely through the nightmares of war. I was once standing at the entrance of that whores' alley, beneath the flickering neon-sky of the Reeperbahn, when an unexpected figure passed through its portals, weaving a bustling, purposeful, businesslike way among the pallid lechers loitering inside. It was a waiter from a neighbouring café, nattily dressed in white, and carrying a cup of coffee neatly on his polished

Hamburg

tray, with two lumps of sugar hygienically wrapped. He made his way dexterously to one of the brothel windows, and peering into the gloom to pick his customer from the row of ghoul-like prostitutes inside—dim, apparently phosphorescent images of flesh, paint and pink nylon—he handed her the tray with a polite little bow, and returned to the world outside.

HELSINKI

Liberal though you may be, and broad-minded, and looking for the best in everybody, nevertheless leaving the grey purlieus of Communism constitutes a festivity: an airy, lacy celebration, like having your first swim of the season, or falling in love. They check your baggage very carefully in Leningrad, and thumb laboriously through your manuscripts, and visibly brighten when they come across a chart of the Seven-Year Plan, and send you off to your aircraft feeling obscurely chastened, as though the headmaster is not precisely angry with you, only just a little disappointed. But a brief hour in a bumbling Ilyushin, alone with the wistful stewardess (wearing her brown fur-collared coat over her uniform), and at Helsinki you tumble into the other half of the world. The man at the desk merely says 'Passport, please': but bells ring, birds sing, and somewhere a bottle pops.

Here are the things that overjoyed me most, when that kindly man, with a barely perceptible examination of my passport, sent me whistling into Finland, guided by an exquisite airline hostess: Finnish airline hostesses first, for their reviving breath of elegance; clean, glistening architecture second, for its whisper of liberty; nice little houses in a row; Esso and International Harvester, for their welcoming gleam of profit; cars of all nations, driven at a proper pace (in Russia they never seem to exceed thirty, even in the howling spaces); the rosy cheeks of plump burghers, and children playing in their own gardens; shop windows gracefully dressed, well-cut suits, a quayside that anyone can walk along, a jolly polished steam train beside the docks, Simplicity patterns, *My Fair Lady* in Swedish, coffee-pots whose lids, you may be confident, will not fall off with a dismal splash into the coffee-cup.

Even after Leningrad, that loveliest wraith among cities, Helsinki feels marvellously free, easy, and undaunted, and down her comfortable streets all the breezes of the West sweep like a cocktail of elixirs. A visit to the city's most famous bookshop, which claims to be

Helsinki

the largest in Europe and is bursting with the books of a dozen languages, is like a shot in the arm and a sniff of salts after the drab, dutiful, brownish bookshelves of the Soviet Union. A stroll beside the harbour, where the patient ice-breakers (when they are not on strike) potter stolidly backwards and forwards down the shipping lanes, is wonderfully exhilarating: the wind off a Russian sea feels like a death in the family, but when it blows out of the Gulf of Finland it is only a tingle in the cheek. An hour in a sauna, the Finnish steam bath, where you are slapped periodically with birch twigs and plunged deliciously from agonizingly hot to shivering cold, is enough to scour the very miasma of Russia from your person and leave you as clean, brisk, and spanking as a magazine advertisement.

After the stocky, buttoned Russians, the people of Helsinki seem marvellously lithe and light-footed, big but agile, jovial at *smorgasbords* or loping and sloping across their snow-fields like Tibetan holy men. Their children, slithering about with ice-hockey sticks, give the heartening impression that they came into the world on skis and have not just put them on in the interests of some ideological demonstration. Their wives are as neat as pins, and gossip sharply in expensive coffee-shops. Their hotels are either delectably modern, all pale wood and sliding glass, or fragrantly Edwardian, with murals and cigar-smoked panelling. Their suburbs are posh with provincial snobbery, and they are a people that nobody in the world, not even the heart-throb marching progressive, could possibly feel sorry for. They are as tough as nails, and twice as spiky.

In Helsinki, only an hour from the Winter Palace, you can do exactly what you like. You can take a ride in a sleigh across the frozen harbour, unimpeded by suspicious policemen and pulled by a bleary kind of pony. You can build yourself a little hut on the ice and fish for your dinner through a hole. You can drink mystical liqueurs from the forests, made of berries, pine cones and arctic brambles. You can eat, stifling a sentimental tear, smoked reindeer tongue with salad, or guzzle your way through a fish cock—pork stuffed with fresh-water herring, and baked peculiarly into a loaf. You can go to a French film or an American play, and read the English papers with a flourish outside the Presidential Palace (a pleasant minor mansion of the kind described by estate agents as being 'suitable for conversion').

All these many pleasures and stimulants greet you as your taxi

152

Helsinki

skids genially into Helsinki; and all the fun and freedom of the West welcomes you, and all the vitamins and calories are there to bolster your wasted stamina. Most people, when they leave the potato world behind the Curtain, seem to pine for some fresh or virile victual—a lettuce or a pineapple, a cucumber or a pickled egg. My own craving, when I flew into Finland out of eastern Europe, was for raw carrots, and when I arrived in Helsinki I went straight to a grocer, ordered half a pound, washed them in my hotel bathroom, and ate them luxuriously with a glass of schnapps.

But here is an odd and provoking fact: I ate those rich red vegetables with delight, and I wallowed like an emperor in all the milky pleasure of capitalism; but when, later that day, I wanted something to read with my dinner some unexpected instinct guided my choice, a kind of reluctant nostalgia, a niggling trace of respect and affection, and when I sat down to my pig's trotters I found myself dining with Turgenev. (And all that well-dressed little capital, I felt, all that brave and courteous citizenry, could not offer me quite such company.)

HIROSHIMA

Poised in the estuary of the Ota River, where a covey of islands meanders into the mists of the Inland Sea, lies the city of Hiroshima. She is a seaport, an industrial town, an old military base, a market centre: but for many years her life has revolved around a catastrophe, and to this day she lives and breathes and talks and thinks the atomic bomb that exploded over her on August 6, 1945. The city has long been rebuilt, and a new population has flooded in to replace the victims of the holocaust: but for all the bright new buildings and the broad boulevards, no Pompeii is more surely frozen in its attitude of disaster, and no Mont Pelée more permanently scarred.

Above the city ('on the rim', as they will tell you, 'of the radiation area, and two miles from the epicentre')—from the hillside above the city you can see how horribly plump and passive a target Hiroshima offered. She lies compactly in a funnel among the hills, where the Ota flows pleasantly into the sea: because she is built on a group of islands, she is criss-crossed by channels of water, and in her very centre is the T-shaped bridge that was the bomb-aimer's objective. Today she has all been reconstructed. The usual straggly houses of urban Japan run away to the sea, and in the business district there stands a group of tall buildings such as you may often see, an earnest of commerce and hospitality, silhouetted upon the American horizon. A ship or two stands offshore. Traffic flows fairly thickly down the streets. Loudly striped advertising balloons loiter above the City Hall, and a homely hum of activity hangs on the soft, damp air. It all looks normal enough from the hillside: even beautiful, with the city lying there so new and shining, and the deep blue of the high ground behind, and the placid island-speckled expanse of sea sweeping away to Miyajima and the Pacific.

A few days in Hiroshima, though, and you begin to feel oppressed by the hideous abnormality of the place. The soul was ripped out of this city: and though the taxi-cabs may scurry about you, and the

Hiroshima

street-cars clang, and the neon lights blaze merrily enough, and the girls in the kimonos bow you seductively into the night clubs, yet it somehow feels an empty city still. There is something obscurely pallid and muffled about it, for all the world as though the tall new buildings are not there at all, and the islands of the Ota delta are still blackened and smoking. Assured indeed must be the visitor who has not, just for a fleeting foolish moment, wondered if the stones of Hiroshima were still radioactive, or eyed the running water thoughtfully.

This inescapable presence of dread is partly artificial. The horror of the atomic explosion has been deliberately cherished in Hiroshima, and the memory is purposefully sustained. Piety, politics, and hard-headedness have all contributed to this policy. Piety, because many people believe that the agony of Hiroshima can be turned to good ends, and that the city can stand as a token of peace and a prod to the world's conscience; politics, because many a Communist, dupe, or muzzy liberal wishes to preserve its torments as an indictment of American barbarism; hard-headedness, because in the decade since the explosion Hiroshima has been turned into one of the great tourist spectacles of Japan, whence the ghastly photographs and the atomized tiles are carried to the ends of the earth, like camel-saddles or Lincoln Imps.

In the centre of Hiroshima you are trapped within this tragic but morbid cage. Outside the windows of your grand new hotel stands the Peace Memorial Museum, partly an exhibition of nuclear science, most compellingly a chamber of horrors, dominated by a huge circular model of the devastated Hiroshima, and ornamented with terrible photographs. From the cultural centre across the way there emerge at hourly intervals the saccharine harmonies of adagio hymn tunes, played with lush vibrato on a recorded carillon. There are shrines all about you, the Children's Memorial and the inter-denominational shrine, and the celebrated Shadow on the steps of the bank, and the noble epitaph on the central memorial: 'Rest in peace, for the error shall not be repeated.' You must be pathologically callous or world-weary beyond cure to remain unmoved by the re-minders of Hiroshima: but staying in the city today, nevertheless, is like spending a nightmare weekend in one of Mr. Evelyn Waugh's California cemeteries, where the dignities of death were honoured with such sickly and cosmetic fulsomeness.

One could stomach it the more easily if this were a catastrophe of

Hiroshima

the distant past, but there are many people in Hiroshima still directly suffering from the effects of the atomic explosion. There are the unfortunates so hideously disfigured that they seldom emerge from their houses. There are the patients still, to this very day, in hospital. There are the sufferers from leukemia. There are the mothers whose children, in the womb at the time of the attack, were born with terrible handicaps and distortions. And there are those who experienced the thing, but were not injured by it, and who now seem like hollow men, haunted and devitalized, with something sucked out of them—'Always tired,' as one man said to me, 'I seem to have been tired ever since.'

Most pitiable of all, there are those many young people who are afraid of the genetic effects of the bomb. They are too young to remember the explosion, but they cannot stifle the thought that the smear of radiation may prove to be hereditary, and that their sons or grandchildren may be cursed with some unsuspected abnormality, to be passed down the generations like haemophilia or colour-blindness. Cruelly cynical has been the exploitation of this foreboding, by press and by politicians; wild and heartless have been the rumours of two-headed babies and strangely endowed goldfish, and a kind of eerie stockade has been erected about the young people of the place. Men look for their brides elsewhere. Girls try to hide their origins. Cruel reporters sniff about for horrors.

Up on the hill a team of American scientists, with Japanese help, is trying to discover the truth about it all. They have proved that the first post-atomic generation—that is to say, children conceived after the explosion by parents who experienced it—is perfectly normal; and they have apparently shown that the admitted abnormalities of children in the womb in August 1945 were such as might have been caused by any violent explosion. But they naturally cannot be dogmatic about hereditary possibilities, and their caution is recklessly exploited by their enemies in Japan. Thousands of ordinary people in Hiroshima have helped the Americans with their researches: but all too often you will hear the suggestion that theirs is a propaganda mission, that their task is to 'play down' the terrors of the bomb, that you cannot trust their reassurances—'First they drop the bomb on us,' say the critics waspishly, 'then they come and tell us it's good for our health.'

Of course, there is no love lost for the Americans in Hiroshima:

Hiroshima

but if the postures of the publicists and the propagandists are disagreeable to observe, one finds only kindness and common sense from the average citizen. The girl with the hideously disfigured face looks you straight and sweetly in the eye. The Man with the Bomb Story tells it with about the same wry relish as his opposite numbers in Bristol or Berlin. Everybody I asked agreed that Hiroshima was at least a legitimate military target (she was a military headquarters and a port for the invasion fleets), and said that the Japanese would certainly have dropped an atomic bomb if they had made one first.

Nor did they seem to think that dropping it in Tokyo Bay, for example, would have had the same military effect. In 1945 many Japanese were still convinced of the God-ordained certainty of victory, and it was partly the indescribable shock of Hiroshima's destruction that jolted them out of this delusion. Hiroshima seems to accept this as truth, and except on the level of the newspapers and the museums appears to harbour astonishingly little recrimination. This is partly, a Japanese clergyman told me, because these people are accustomed to violent catastrophes of nature; partly because of an inbred fatalism; and partly because the Japanese are a hard-working and down-to-earth nation, too busy for brooding.

So the skull-like emptiness of Hiroshima seems to be something organic—as though through all the reviving human activity some grim nuclear influences still permeate. I cannot describe the feeling of Hiroshima: but it is as though some indefinable essential element has been withdrawn from the ambiance of the place—not colour, nor smell, nor sound, but something else, something which gives meaning and warmth to a city, like salt with your victuals, or eyes in a beautiful face.

HONG KONG

More people live in Hong Kong than in all the rest of the world put together, and they make more noise than a million electric drills, and they work like automation: and their babies are beyond computation, and their machinery chitter-chatters away for twenty-five hours every day: and in their markets they sell every fish that was ever caught, and every shrimp that ever wriggled, and every crab that ever pinched: and their excellent shirts cost fourpence-ha'penny apiece: and there are five million Chinese for every European in the city, each one of them more energetic than a power station: and all these unbelievable paradoxes of prolixity and profusion are a lesson in the impermanence of power and the mutability of history.

Just over a hundred years ago the British seized Hong Kong from an addled China, and were conceded sovereignty over it 'in perpetuity'. The island was almost uninhabited, but they made of it a tremendous port and a gunboat station supreme, where British merchants could command the China trade beneath the guns of the Royal Navy. Hong Kong became one of the greatest of free ports and entrepôts, and a brilliant symbol of European superiority. Here the techniques of the Western world were applied to the corrupt and ramshackle structure of China. The merchant princes lived in splendour on the eminence of the Peak, while across the hills in China the impotent Asians squabbled and cheated each other and carved the ivory ornaments that would one day look so pretty upon the mantelpiece in Epsom.

Today the British are still in Hong Kong, and the rich merchants roll down from the Peak each morning in their big black ponderous limousines. The great banks and merchant houses are still magnificently bustling, the company flags fly bravely beside the Union Jack. But you cannot spend a day in Hong Kong without realizing that she lives by the courtesy, and at the mercy, of the new China.

Hong Kong

Times have changed with an imperial vengeance. The long grey warships that still lie in the harbour (successors to *Aphis* and *Mantis* and the elegant old river gunboats) no longer fool anybody, least of all the hard-headed British. Hong Kong is indefensible, militarily and economically, and she lives half on trust and half on cynicism.

Consider her geographical situation. If you stand on a high place on Hong Kong Island you can see virtually the whole of the Colony. Below you is Hong Kong herself, for ever England, and beyond it is the glorious sweep of the harbour, crammed with the steamers and junks and ferryboats and launches of free enterprise, never silent, never motionless, one of the great mercantile waterways of the world. But in the middle distance are the mountains of China proper, and most of the land in between—the essential hinterland of Hong Kong —does not belong to Britain, but is only held on a lease that expires towards the end of this century (if international leases have any meaning by then). Not only is China ominously close. In her own back yard British Hong Kong has only the precarious rights of tenancy.

Or move, for another view, to an economic vantage point. At West Point on Hong Kong Island there is a wharf where the junks arrive from Pearl River and Canton, in Communist China. It makes no bones about its affiliations. In the tumbledown eating-house, where the labourers stoically consume their rice and villainous fish, a huge poster proclaims the industrial potential of Communist China, and the tugboat outside carries on its superstructure a series of slogans about people's rights and imperialist aggression and that kind of thing. Somewhere in an attic above your head a lonely but determined flautist plays a Communist propaganda melody, and the ducks that are off-loaded in their thousands from the rickety junks, crammed in huge wicker baskets and carried by relays of cheerful and courteous coolies—even the ducks are brainwashed Khaki Campbells. Without this traffic from China, without its ducks and hens and vegetables, Hong Kong probably could not long survive. The Communists know that when the lease of that hinterland expires in 1998, Hong Kong will be theirs for the plucking: but they also know that if need be they could squeeze her into submission long before then. All the cards are theirs. They can take the place by force, if they are willing to risk a world war. They can starve it out. Or they can simply wait for another few decades, a mere flicker of time among the Chinese centuries.

Hong Kong

With so plump and once cocky a mouse between its claws, it is perhaps understandable that the Chinese cat enjoys playing with its victim with that strange mixture of the purr and the snarl that usually accompanies such kitchen-corner exercises. There is an element of sadism to the attitude of Peking to Hong Kong. The Communist propagandists are blatantly active in the city, flaunting their huge posters and their red flags, selling their books and their magazines and their newspapers, infiltrating the schools and threatening the unions. But if the Hong Kong Government allows itself a mild riposte, closing a school, expelling a subversive educationist, or tearing down a flag or two, swift and menacing is the protest from Peking. 'I once brought a message to the Governor from Peking,' a strikingly slimy Communist told me in Hong Kong, 'after some riots in Kowloon. It was simply this: "Don't let it happen again, Your Excellency." '

Because of all this, because of the overwhelming strength of the new China, people sometimes say cleverly that Hong Kong is in effect Chinese already. This is no more than a quarter truth. Hong Kong is, of course, a Chinese city in the racial sense, and it is obviously humiliating to the British to endure these political degradations. But the Britishness of the place, for all its insecurity, is still staunch and admirable. Everywhere there are great new public projects—huge housing schemes, hospitals, airport runways, roads, dams, land reclamations—some of the biggest of them in the New Territories themselves. The administration is still by all accounts excellent, and since Hong Kong remains pre-eminently a place of business there is not much pressure for legislative reform, and almost none at all for self-government. What is more the British are still, to this awkward day, reaping rewards from Hong Kong. Practically the whole cost of the administration comes from local revenues, and Hong Kong earns a lot of dollars, offers a flourishing market for British goods, and sustains a number of great British merchant houses. She is a valuable intelligence outpost on the edge of Asia, and she provides a lavish example—too lavish, many Englishmen might think—of the capitalist system with all its thrusting, barging, shoving, no-holds-barred stimulation.

She is also a haven. Hong Kong is jammed full of refugees and

The photographs following are of: Delhi, Hong Kong, Isfahan, Istanbul, Johannesburg, Kano, Katmandu.

Hong Kong

deportees and émigrés from Communist China. Some of them have come here because it is a fine place to make money, with its low taxes, its splendid port, its cheap labour and its stable government. Many others have come, as Chinese have through all Hong Kong's history, to escape the hardships or the dangers of life in China. The Hong Kong Government has done its best to help and assimilate these people, and to my mind this is a duty that is satisfying beyond political pin-pricks, and not to be abandoned without dishonour. Greed, self-interest, pride and morality all contribute to the flavour of the British presence in Hong Kong: and Heaven knows they have met each other before.

But though the British are not doing badly in Hong Kong, and are performing some good for the world, too, nevertheless the moral of the Colony's situation is a daunting one. The Communist Chinese tolerate its independence partly because they have bigger things to think about, and partly because they don't want to arouse new issues needlessly; partly because they need bargaining counters, and partly because they themselves find the economic services of Hong Kong useful (the tallest building on the Hong Kong water-front is the Bank of China, an invaluable clearing house of foreign exchange for Peking). The capitalists of Hong Kong thrive because they do not believe the Communists will move before 1998, at the earliest, thus leaving them time to make a quick new fortune or embellish an old one. The simple people get what benefit they can from good government and economic opportunity, and try not to think about the future. But above all these several attitudes, the place is haunted by a sense of the hugeness and fertility and brute strength of Asia. Not so long ago a writer could observe that England had cut a notch in China as a woodsman cuts a tree—'to mark it for felling at a convenient opportunity'. In Hong Kong today, with Asia already flooding through Queen Victoria Street and Waterloo Road, and with six hundred million more Chinese over there across the hills, and with the whole place a tumult of Asian energy and noise, and constantly threatened by Asian power, and riddled with Asian ideologies—here in Hong Kong you cannot help wondering how ambitious a woodsman China will be when she reaches the summit of her power, and how many of us old elms she is going to notch for firewood.

In the central market of Hong Kong the edible frogs are tied to-

Hong Kong

gether in bundles while they are still alive, a string of straw binding them around their stomachs. They thus present a multi-limbed symmetrical appearance, and one pair of little legs is constantly jumping to the left, and another pair kicking out to the right, in a very erratic and unpredictable conflict of impulses. This, though clearly uncomfortable for the poor frogs, is not altogether unfunny to watch: and when I saw it for the first time, my goodness, said I to myself, how are we to compete with this extraordinary people, when even their frogs have twelve legs apiece, and lunge about with such comic and irresistible vigour?

HONOLULU

The day I arrived in Honolulu a legislative inquiry was being held in the Iolani Palace. The prison administration had been accused of namby-pamby attitudes towards its convicts, and there in the shadowy cluttered hall was all the paraphernalia of American official investigation: the microphones, the reporters, the lounging shirtsleeved witnesses, the interrogators stern-faced at their tribunal, the sweating gossipy audience crowding at the door. It was a cameo of Americana, and a middle-aged lady even introduced herself to me as the wife of the prison psychiatrist—most indignant she was, too, at the very impertinent thought of an inquiry.

Just twenty feet away, though, in the other half of the same building (a sort of little ginger-bread Blenheim) there stood all but deserted the throne room of the Hawaiian royal dynasties, still preserved in all its feathered splendours. I was pursued by the drone of the inquisitors as I entered this elaborate chamber, but inside all was flamboyantly royalist, and all around me were the gorgeous gewgaws, the regal portraits, the thrones and escutcheons that supported the precarious dignity of the Hawaiian monarchy until its overthrow by the Americans in 1893. I could all but hear the sonorous decrees of those vanished Polynesian kings—'The Law of the Splintered Paddle' was one of the most celebrated. I could almost see them sitting there, clutching their imported sceptres and smothered from head to foot in robes made from the tufted feathers of the o-o bird.

Think of it! Seventy years ago, in our grandfathers' time, Hawaii was an independent kingdom: yet by the time I got there she was quite happily debating whether to call herself the Sugar State, the Pineapple State, or the State of the Golden Welcome. There are people alive today who can remember when Her Majesty Queen Lydia Liliuokalani, 'The Salt Air of Heaven', still ruled the speckled islands of the Hawaiian chain, united under one flag by her two-fisted predecessor Kamehameha the Great (whose countenance was truly savage, wrote Thomas Manby in 1793, 'as all his foreteeth are

Honolulu

out'). There are citizens still about who coyly admit, tidying up their back hair, that the blood royal of the islands runs in their veins. Yet the world has forgotten the very existence of those lost monarchs, and thinks of Honolulu as the nadir and epitome of honky-tonk Americanism.

The Americanization of Honolulu has not been a sudden phenomenon. It happened in fits, starts and accidents. An Englishman, Captain Cook, was the first white man to set foot in Hawaii, and the first to die there (his head was given to Kahuopeonu, his legs went to Kalaniopuu, and his heart was eaten in error by a man who found it hanging on a tree and mistook it for pig's offal). Nor was it any bold Yankee empire-builder who first raised Old Glory in these parts, but a strait-laced group of evangelical missionaries, blown in by the trade winds from New England. They arrived in the eighteen-twenties, and long before Washington assumed political power in the islands, they had snatched the easy-going Hawaiians out of paganism, invented an alphabet for them, schooled them and offered them salvation, taught them the elements of hygiene and modern government, and even dressed them more properly (for they went in for grass skirts and bare bosoms) in long-skirted dresses, called *muumuus* and *holokus*, that were adaptations of respectable female attire back home in Massachusetts.

In Honolulu the traces of those high-minded old zealots are still everywhere apparent: in the roll of island names, for instance— Bishops, Richards, Binghams, Judds, Spaldings, Doles; in the enveloping flowered *muumuus* still to be seen in every draper's window; in the strong strain of evangelism still stoutly surviving; in the handsome old Kawaiahao Church, on the corner of King and Punchbowl Streets, where squeaky Hawaiian songs still emerge from the schoolroom, and where a memorial tablet to the Queen Regent Kaahumanu says of her that 'although naturally proud and haughty, she humbly accepted Jesus as her saviour'.

Since then many another kind of American has landed in Honolulu, from the rip-roaring whalers of the eighteen-hundreds to the bush-bearded Stanton Dole, who led a republican revolution in 1893, deposed the last of the feathered monarchs, and prepared the way for American annexation. Today in this fabled city, half-way between Tokyo and San Francisco, you may experience almost the whole gamut of the American way, set paradoxically against a back-

Honolulu

drop of volcanoes, glistening rainbows, succulent expanses of fruit, phosphorescent surf and delectable tropical flowers (of the 1,700 botanical varieties found in Hawaii when the white man arrived, nearly 1,600 were unique to the islands—as were 90 per cent of the 3,750 insect species). Mark Twain called Hawaii 'the loveliest fleet of islands that lies anchored in any ocean'; and since his day the Americans, with their talent for fun and their resolute idealism, have made this a paradise all their own. Some of it is, as the world assumes, tinsel and money-mad, and makes the old American residents of Honolulu sad in contemplation. Here through the floodlit night, just as in Omaha or Cedar Rapids, the endless gleaming acres of used cars await their buyers—there is a car in Honolulu for every two and a half inhabitants. Here you may see Miss Wiggles performing nightly in the Forbidden City Burlesque Revue, described in the advertisements as 'sexy but nice'. Here you may wander bemused through the dim exotic labyrinths that have become a requisite of American holiday hotels, or you may biliously suck a Banan-a-Dip—frozen banana dipped in a stew of chocolate and walnuts—as you wander towards Mr. Henry Kaiser's Authentic Hawaiian Village. You may attend the Honolulu Den luncheon of the Lions, you may have medicated honey applied to your sun-tanned shoulders, you may eat hot dogs at the corner drugstore, shop at the inevitable air-conditioned supermarket for the inescapable processed foods, join the evening hula classes at your hotel, or even buy yourself, if your puritan instincts are wearing thin, a 'shortie' *muumuu*, less ladylike by far than those demure New Englanders ever conceived, and showing a distinct reversion to tropical type. There are a dozen radio stations in Honolulu, and there is a television set in eight out of every ten homes. The word *aloha* is an ancient Hawaiian synonym for love, greetings, farewell or welcome: but to hear it exuded breathily by the switchboard girl at the Surfrider Hotel, you would think it had been a publicity slogan all its life.

But America, that Janus, has brought many nobler things, too. There is a universally literate population in Honolulu. There is a fine art gallery, a symphony orchestra, a distinguished university (graced, as it happens, by the greatest living authority on British naval history in the first quarter of this century). In the very middle of the city's tourist frenzies there is a delightful bookshop, open until midnight, supervised by an elderly lady who whiles away the night hours

Honolulu

painting surrealist landscapes. Admirable roads radiate from the capital, and a mesh of air routes links it with the sixteen airports of the island group. Honolulu is full of nice, quiet Americans, and even the tourists, especially in the less fashionable months, can be unexpectedly engaging—they have often saved up for years to live it up just once on Waikiki beach, and their pleasure is irresistibly infectious.

A sense of power, too, makes Honolulu much more than a Pacific holiday camp. Hawaii lies slap in the middle of the Pacific Ocean, where the trade routes cross and the Western outposts of the United States look towards Asia. Midway, scene of the greatest of all naval battles, lies in the north-west of the Hawaiian group, and at Pearl Harbour, a few miles up the road from Honolulu, the funnel of the doomed battleship *Arizona* still protrudes from the water as a terrible memorial to 1941. This city is a bastion still, the headquarters of all American naval forces in the Pacific—a command covering an area of eighty million square miles. The streets of Honolulu are full of willowy American sailors in virginal white. The skies of Honolulu are busy with aircraft—a streak of fighters across the mountains, a flow of airliners from the west coast, Australia and Japan (only reduced now that the great jets stream clean across the Pacific from one shore to the other). If you look between the warehouses of the docks, where the white tourist ships come in to a shimmy of hula girls and a flurry of garlands, as likely as not you will see a great grey carrier brooding there offshore, or the shark-shape of a nuclear submarine.

Most agreeably of all, Honolulu remains resiliently Hawaiian. Americans sometimes talk of Hawaii rather as the Russians talk of Kazakhstan, but in fact the environment is coming out on top. I do not mean the hula girls and the Royal Hawaiian Band, or the surfboard men riding in like princes at Waikiki. I mean the very atmosphere and temperament of the place, which has miraculously survived war, vulgarity, and all the bounce and thrust of commercialism. Honolulu remains in many ways an Oriental city. Nearly half her population is Japanese by stock, and another quarter is Chinese. Seven per cent are original Hawaiians, or thereabouts, and there are sizeable communities of Filipinos, Puerto Ricans and Koreans. In 1960 one of Hawaii's three Congressmen was Chinese by origin and another was Japanese: one recent Miss Hawaii was part English, part Chinese, part Japanese, part German, part Irish, part Scottish and

Honolulu

part Polynesian. All this has happened, over decades of immigration, with scarcely a trace of racial friction, and for this we must thank the easy-going benevolence of the indigenous Hawaiians, which still imbues everything in this capital, from the mission halls to the milk bars, with a graceful and indolent charm. They seem to me the very sweetest of people, even if they did eat Captain Cook. At first you think their smiles and friendliness must be the mercenary kind, picked up at long range from the practitioners of Madison Avenue: but no, it is the real thing, and it is inescapable. Wanderers of every kind have settled in these islands: whaling-men and speculators, paunchy hoteliers, rugged Scottish traders, a Prussian royal band-master and an English court butler, and all that lounging riff-raff that is washed up with the driftwood of tropical seas. Yet through it all, surviving all the ups and downs of historical fortune, the old Hawaiian magic—Rupert Brooke's dark scents whispering, dim waves creeping—has triumphantly, hauntingly survived. One immigrant from the mainland told me, as we sat beneath a banyan tree beside the murmuring sea, that during sixteen years' residence in Honolulu he had only six times heard a car horn hooted in anger.

The State motto of Hawaii is *Ua-Mau-Ke-Ea-O-Ka-Aina-I-Ka-Pono*, which means 'The Life of the Land Is Preserved in Righteousness,' and for once such a declamation rings true. A stone's throw from the holiday madhouses of Waikiki there stands a row of rickety tables beside the sea, shaded by straw matting, where elderly Honolulu citizens while away their Sunday mornings with chess, chequers and inexplicable card games. I was sitting there in reverie one morning, happily lost in the sun and the salt breeze, when a prickly old gentleman on the bench beside me tapped me on the shoulder. 'You look kinda melancholy, son,' said he kindly. 'Aincha read the proclamation?'—and he pointed to the notice painted on a weatherboard above us. 'This Is a Public Park,' it said. 'Have Fun!'

ISFAHAN

And on from thence to Isfahan,
The golden garden of the sun,
Whence the long dusty caravan
Brings cedar and vermilion.

Abruptly the east-bound aircraft, crossing into Persia out of the Gulf, enters the Zagros Mountains, and begins to bump. The man in the next seat clutches your arm for support, the more elderly Muslims around you invoke the protection of Allah and prepare their paper bags. The aircraft is probably not young, and its American pilot is both skilful and daredevil, so your passage through that unfriendly range is, if you like that kind of thing, hilarious: but this is your way to the imperial city of Isfahan, Wilde's golden garden of the sun.

It is an Eastern world across the mountains, with a taste of Asia to it, and a flicker of India, and the potent radiation of Islam permeates Isfahan and flavours her very air. Like Damascus, she is an oasis. The desert that surrounds her is moonlike and mysterious, punctuated by small pimply hills; the landscape is alive with constantly shifting colours; and Isfahan stands amid the aridity, domed and pinnacled, in a posture of elaborate welcome. She is one of the most famous and most beautiful cities on earth, but she is graced also with a marvellously beguiling eccentricity.

At first you will be struck only by the astonishing beauty of the place. Isfahan is a planned city, laid out by Shah Abbas at the end of the sixteenth century and retaining an orderly perfection of form. There are some textile factories scattered about the perimeter of the place, and the suburbs are beginning to straggle into the surrounding desert; but the centre of Isfahan remains very much the same as Shah Abbas left it, and it is easy to accept the legend that this fabulous Oriental city, glimpsed by the ambassadors and couriers of the seventeenth century, was the inspiration of the Champs-Elysées.

Isfahan

The gorgeous heart of Isfahan is Imperial Square, which the Persians sometimes claim, though they are by no means a boastful people, to be the biggest square on earth. In this great space, called in Persian 'The Design of the World', the glittering court of the Safavid monarchs played its polo and mounted its magnificent military parades. At one side of it is the Shah's own pavilion, a high grand-stand directly related to Ascot or Churchill Downs, where even now a grey top hat or a flouncy parasol would not seem out of place. Opposite is the delectable mosque of Lutfallah; to the north the bustling entrance to the bazaars; to the south the unbelievable Blue Mosque—a structure as blue and calm as an Eastern sea, grand and delicate at the same time, a kaleidoscope of pools, tiles, and shining Islamic script.

So genuinely magnificent is this spectacle, so vast and almost Kremlinesque in concept, so grandiose but graceful in style, so wide and airy, that it might well be unpleasantly pompous. But such is the temperament of Persia that it is redeemed by a singular circumstance: it is crooked. Not only is Imperial Square 'out of true', so to speak, with the rest of Isfahan, so that it is not parallel with the two great thoroughfares that intersect the city; it is also asymmetrical in itself, because the great Blue Mosque is twisted towards the south-east so as to be in the correct relationship with Mecca. If you therefore stand at the entrance to the bazaars and survey the square before you, there stands the Shah's pavilion, dominating one side neatly enough; and there is Lutfallah's mosque, opposite; and tidy, symmetrical gardens lie in the centre, where the polo ground used to be; but the masterpiece at the other end is all askew, its gateway facing one way and its great *iwan* another, so that it looks like one of those quixotic attempts, by architectural draughtsmen of the eighteenth century, to draw buildings in two perspectives at the same time.

The Arabs across the mountains, with their flair for formality in architecture, would never have countenanced this quirk of design; but Persia makes her own rules. There was never such a tortuous, inside-out, back-to-front way of thinking as the Persian way; never such a fascinating, will-o'-the-wisp, unpredictable community of peoples; nowhere buildings so inexpressibly lovely as these dreams of Isfahan; nowhere a landscape more peculiar than the wide plain around her, sometimes bleak beyond description, sometimes warm and multi-coloured, often queerly criss-crossed with the big round

Isfahan

craters that mark the passage of underground water channels. In Isfahan you are never far from expressions of oddity. Not far from the Blue Mosque there is another building which the people of Isfahan regard with almost equal favour. It is called, I think, the Quivering Mosque, and its claim to fame is that if you stand inside one of its two little minarets and shake it with your shoulders, the other minaret quivers, too. Earnest and determined is the expression on the face of the caretaker as he performs this curious duty. Ponderously he climbs to the roof, past the tomb of the fourteenth-century divine who is buried in the mosque, and worms his way inside the minaret. You stand in the sunshine expectantly; and presently there is a sound of heaving, squirming, heavy breathing and grunting, as the caretaker, now jammed hard inside the tower, sets the phenomenon in motion. At first nothing at all seems to happen; but after a moment or two, sure enough, a faint but just perceptible rocking movement overcomes the roof, and if you concentrate very hard you can see those two little minarets swaying together in queasy parallel. When you climb downstairs again there stands the caretaker's wife, rubbing her palms on her skirt, to tell you with an air of ineffable astonishment that, miracle of miracles, while you were up there on the roof the tomb of the fourteenth-century divine began to quiver, too!

It is impossible to escape the pleasant suspicion that she thinks this rather funny. Life in Isfahan is largely governed by a sense of humour, and depends for its continuity upon a series of *non sequiturs*; so that affairs there progress bumpily but soothingly, like an opiate with grits in it. It has long been so, for through centuries of despotism the Persian has erected around himself an indefinable screen of humour, slipperiness and oddness, a smoke-screen or camouflage, a false trail, a tear gas, behind which he can dive when trouble approaches him, to the bewildered chagrin of his tormentors. It was so in the great days of the Persian imperial dynasties, when a monarch might decapitate you at the drop of a hat, and if anything it is probably more so now. Everywhere among the glories of Isfahan you meet quiddities and irrelevancy. When I was once visiting the Palace of the Forty Pillars they were repairing the roof of its great audience chamber. On the floor, among the frescoes and glass cases, all was solemn and in earnest; but high above us a workman on a scaffolding was clowning away in the shadows, with dances and funny faces and quaint mimicry, for the amusement of his fellow craftsmen. (The palace really has only twenty pillars, but the Persians, who like high-sounding titles, include the reflections in the great pool outside.) On the opposite side of the road there is a photographer's shop, in which you may expect to see the usual faded display of outdated picture postcards. You will be agreeably surprised, for the *pièce de résistance* of that respectable window is a series of brownish photographs of local criminals at the moment of apprehension. Wonderfully bestial are the faces that peer at you from behind the dusty glass, and proud and stern the looks in the eyes of the successful constables, who have generally clamped an enormous chain around the neck of the criminal, shackled his hands and feet, and caused him to sit on the ground in front of them like some ugly ill-bred dog.

Three fine bridges cross the river at Isfahan, and the best of them is almost Florentine in splendour. When I was first taken to see this structure my guide told me that Shah Abbas, its builder, had taken a particular interest in its design. There had to be a rest room for tired travellers, comfortably furnished; and a retreat for holy men; and rooms where jugglers and singers could entertain the travelling public; and a place reserved for wedding festivities. 'And the strange thing is,' my informant added seriously, 'that it is also exactly right for the washing of buses!' I looked over the edge as we approached the bridge, and indeed, two rickety buses had been driven beneath the inner arches, where the water was shallow, and were being energetically washed; the bridge might have been made for them, so exactly did they fit. Why did the buses have to go under the bridge to be washed? In case it rained, of course.

In the bazaars this tang of Isfahan is very potent. Of all the splendid bazaars of the Middle East, I enjoy these most. They are winding and rambling and mysterious, lit by shafts of sunshine streaming through the roof, full of fabrics and carpets and jewellery and vegetables, with exotic turbaned figures wandering through them, and a constant pushing and tumbling and shouting and bargaining—the whole conducted in a series of vaulted corridors of faintly ecclesiastical character. Women get short shrift in this Islamic mart, being pushed out of the way with donkeys or sworn at mercilessly, and sometimes the vivid gusto of the place evolves into the macabre or the eerie. I was once walking through the bazaars when a young man fell off his bicycle; a package fastened to the carrier rack came undone, and on to the pavement rolled the

Isfahan

complete head of a horned sheep, its eyes glassy and protruding, a thin trickle of blood oozing from its neck. No less disturbing is the antique camel mill which still works in a kind of dungeon near the entrance to the bazaars. You enter it down a flight of worn steps, and find yourself standing in a windowless, subterranean cavern. There in the middle of this awful place two aged camels, their eyes covered, lope round and round a grinding mill in the half-light, with a smell of dung, hair, straw and burning wood, and the flicker of a flame from a distant corner where three old camel-men in rags are cooking themselves an improbable meal.

In such places you can clearly hear the beat of the Persian heart—old, shuttered, wily, erratic. There is an edgy feeling to the crowds that shuffle and barge through these draughty arcades, and in the Persian's eye, though he has a gaudy streak of the buffoon in his make-up, there is always a look of deep and calculating introspection. You never feel remote from the desert in Isfahan; you are never divorced from Islam; there are many reminders that the city stands on the brink of wild, unworldly territories, inhabited by roaming bands of tribesmen and coloured by many a lingering taboo and superstition. This is the home of the Zoroastrians and the great Persian mystics, and the nurturing-place of the fragile Persian poets of antiquity. To this day, up more than one winding and rickety staircase in the bazaars, in the dust and the sweet smoke of the hubble-bubbles, you will find the miniaturists still at work, squatting cross-legged on their benches with their pupils around them.

Isfahan is both bitter and perfumed; and if you are ever lulled into sentimentality by the charm of it all, there will soon come swaggering by some figure of glorious insouciance, dressed in turban, cloak, fur hat, sheepskin boots, cummerbund, limpid gown or tight-belted jerkin, the very personification of the perennial Persia. His astringent image haunts the golden garden, and breathes a spiced breath upon all its affairs.

ISTANBUL

Two celebrated waterways divide southern Asia from its neighbours. One is the Suez Canal, and on it stand the tawdry tenement towns of Suez and Port Said. The other is the Bosporus, and on its banks lies Istanbul, one of the supreme cities of the world. She has inherited the glories of Byzantium and the mixed reputations of Constantinople; she is scarred by the hazards of an unusually variable fortune; she has suffered a thousand degradations; and she lies there now wallowing in age, a city of dourness, melancholy and lavish high-flown beauty.

She is dour because of her inhabitants. Istanbul is a strong and stocky city, like the Turks themselves. 'Why did Constantinople get the works?' asks a popular song, and shrewdly answers itself: 'That's nobody's business but the Turks'!' The Turks do not easily tolerate meddlers, for they are a dogged, self-sufficient race. An hour or two in Istanbul will demonstrate to you how formidable a people they are, strong-jawed and granite-faced, like animated obelisks: crowded stoically in their trams, clattering along the quaysides in their heavy ammunition boots, teeming in earnest resolution down their precipitous hilly streets. They are lacking in vivacity and humour, and seem as far removed from the graces of Greece and the Mediterranean as Genghis Khan from Giorgione; but if ever you ask a policeman the way, or present your currency problems frankly to the tram conductor, you will perceive beneath a somewhat steely exterior an intermittently genial heart. They are not a Dickensian people, the Turks: but they make daunting enemies and loyal friends, if angered or asked nicely.

Istanbul is melancholy because she is an imperial capital without an empire, an older London, perhaps, or a less buoyant Vienna. This is a place streaked with nostalgia and high memories. Constantinople was created as capital of the Eastern Empire—the new Rome—and for several centuries she was the grandest and richest city in Europe. Besieged and battered, now triumphant now disgraced, raped by

173

Istanbul

Crusaders, bombarded by Muslims, crammed with treasures or viciously sacked, coloured by excesses and degeneracies and tragedies, Constantinople strode through history like a tasselled potentate. Her period of supremacy was tumultuous and very long. The city was founded in the fourth century: but sixteen centuries later it still seemed of such vital importance to the British that they launched their unhappy assault upon the Dardanelles, believing that the fall of Turkey would mean victory in Europe. Few cities have played so florid or significant a part in the processes of history, or enjoyed so many generations of eminence.

No wonder you may sense sadness or cynicism in the air, as you wander the streets of Istanbul. The Sick Man's dominion of the Ottoman Empire has vanished, Turkey is a minor Power, and Ankara is its capital. The old horrors and glories have gone, and if there were marauding Venetians still about, with their eyes open for golden horses and relics, Istanbul might seem scarcely worth the plundering. At many a crumbling street corner the imaginative Englishman may fancy an echoing India Office or an emasculated Admiralty, or sense the presence of a complacent Victorian sultan, or see a Byzantine Nelson hoist his sails in the Bosporus. Like us, the Turks have lost an empire, and for all her resilience Istanbul sometimes feels strangely wizened and inverted. Othello's occupation's gone.

The beauty of the place remains, however, all the more haunting because of its poignancy. There are people who loathe Istanbul, who hate her damp, her noise, her stagnancy, the cobbled ugliness of her modern quarters: but nobody has ever disputed her monumental grandeur. To grasp her space and dignity you should climb one of the hills that overlook the Bosporus from the Asian side, and see the whole city reclining there below you with an ironic combination of the drab and the magnificent. Away to the north runs the Bosporus, a watery by-pass edged with green, overlooked by villas and terraced restaurants. Down to the south lies the Sea of Marmara, sprinkled with dim blue islands. And directly below you, tumbled and infinitely grand, lies Istanbul herself. This is one of the classic views of Europe. The horizon is immensely wide. The air around you is mountain-clear, and only a thin mauve haze hangs around the domes and spires of the city. Istanbul is built upon hills and surrounded by water, and everywhere you look there is space: seas, open country-side, hills, and that splendid arm of the Bosporus called the Golden Horn.

Istanbul

The Golden Horn! One of the great names of romance, and still among the most marvellous of waterways, bisecting Istanbul like a wide bustling frontier. 'You are accustomed,' wrote Kinglake, 'to the gondolas that glide among the palaces of St. Mark, but here at Stamboul it is a hundred-and-twenty-gun ship that meets you in the street.' Istanbul remains a city of shipping. If you stand on the Galata Bridge across the Golden Horn, a dove-infested mosque in front of you, a crowded clamorous hill behind, you will find ships all about you: a fermentation of shipping, ferry-boats and rowing-boats and fishing-boats and tumbledown old men's boats; bright-canvassed deep-sea sailing-boats, with occasional gay and graceful caiques; liners standing haughtily offshore; warships and motor-launches and rafts and indefinable general-purpose jack-of-all-trade skiffs. The Golden Horn is alive with boats and business, and with the constant ebb-and-flow of the pigeons beside the mosque, the thick stream of pedestrians, the clanging of the trams behind you, the sunshine on the water and the pungent mingling of smells that emanate from those quaysides, there is no more memorable loitering-place in the world than the sidewalk of Galata Bridge.

The shores of the Golden Horn are slatternly and rubbish-blown, but the horizon beyond is magnificent with domes and the silhouettes of monuments. This is the heart of Byzantium, the stomach of the Ottoman Empire. Here is the great basilica of St. Sophia, one of the most famous of all buildings: a squat, brooding Byzantine dome, like a meditating elephant, leavened by the minarets that commemorate its conversion to Islam. There are many such splendid structures of the Eastern Empire upon this hill, a forum, an aqueduct, a sprawling city wall, several gaunt cathedral-mosques: and there are also the covered bazaars—what is left of them—to remind us that part of Istanbul also faces east, towards Aleppo and Damascus and Isfahan. Two empires and two ways of life meet up there on the hill, and the spaces between their memorials are crammed with those ordinary things that transcend the dynasties, crooked streets, poor houses, sudden city gardens and stalls of gaudy Asiatic vegetables.

And among it all, perhaps the most evocative of Istanbul's myriad curiosities, there stands the Seraglio, a little town of its own. This was the Sublime Porte itself, the centre of Ottoman power and pleasure, and in its endless variegated halls there linger the traces of many an old ambition and salacity. In its heyday it housed five thousand people, all devoted to the well-being or advancement

175

Istanbul

of the Sultan, not to speak of thirteen mosques and more than two thousand horses. Here was the treasury, and the mint, and the high Divan, and here also was the Harem. You cannot wander through the silent courtyards of the Seraglio without envisaging the great shuttered organization that satisfied the appetites of those antique despots: the Corps of Eunuchs, often thrusting and powerful; the ornate formalities of the inner court; the jealousies, intolerable boredoms, frustrations and sadnesses of the Harem; the romances of Roxelana and Aimée Dubucq de Rivery, 'the French Sultana'. The Seraglio is a maze of yards and halls and buildings, some of them serene, some of them exhaustingly rococo: and its atmosphere, too, is a confused and heady *mélange*.

Perhaps it may stand, among all its remarkable peers, as representative of Istanbul: for like the city itself it is a jumble of the beautiful and the squalid, the lavish, the kind and the cruel (only a century ago faithless women of the Harem used to be executed by drowning in the Bosporus, tied in sacks and pushed under with oars). You may leave the Seraglio chilled by its memories, or depressed by its manner of forgotten power: but as you walk back across the bridge, look over your shoulder up the hill, and there you will see, glittering nobly in the sun, the most magnificent of European skylines. The great domes stand there like rocks; the minarets rise aristocratically; and the grey buildings of Stamboul, here a pleasure-house, there a mosque, tumble down the hillside to the Golden Horn, where that multitude of craft plays beneath the bridges, and the pigeons strut along the shabby water-front.

A sad, severe, gorgeous city, like an old proud emperor, or a retired eunuch of distinction.

JERUSALEM

O f all the cities of the earth, the most tragic is the city of Jerusalem, because she is divided against herself. The frontier between Jordan and Israel, established in war, runs miserably through the place with a tangle of barbed wire and a dingy strip of no man's land: on one side live the Arabs, on the other the Jews. She is one city for the Jews, another for the Gentiles, for though all of her is sacred to Hebrews, Muslims and Christians alike, nevertheless to most Jews nowadays Jerusalem means the new city outside the walls, while to all Arabs it means the fortified mediaeval city around the Dome of the Rock.

To me the strange sad flavour of this incomparable place pervades all of it, spick-and-span on the one side, dusty on the other; but the heart of the city remains, inevitably, the Old City of Jerusalem, now in the hands of the Arabs, where the Church of the Sepulchre stands, and the Dome of the Rock, and the site of Calvary, and the Wailing Wall too. Israeli Jerusalem has her wonders indeed, but the most glorious and tantalizing view in all Israel remains the view across no man's land, over a patch of tawny grass and a huddle of derelict houses, to where the walls of Old Jerusalem stand like a dream of Saladin beyond the frontier.

Only one narrow roadway crosses from the new Jerusalem into this ancient prodigy, infested with barricades and watchposts. It is called the Mandelbaum Gate, after an otherwise unknown merchant who once had a house nearby, and who thus joins St. Stephen, Herod, the cities of Jaffa and Damascus and the shining metaphysic of Zion in bequeathing a name to a gate of Jerusalem. Traffic along this road is not heavy. Officials of the United Nations pass through it, and diplomats, parties of tourists, journalists, and the bodies of those who are killed in frontier forays, crossing this drab and heartless portal to be buried in their own countries. It is only a few yards long: but when you wave good-bye to the Israeli sentry at one end, stumble down the silent sunlit street, and hand your passport

Jerusalem

to the Jordanian at the other, you may feel that with a proper circumspection are you approaching the walls of this heart-rending and holy place.

The antipathies of Jerusalem thus hang all around, but somehow within the Old City itself they do not feel anomalous. This has always been a scene of bloodshed and bitterness, and it does not come as any surprise, if you are wandering through the shuttered streets of Old Jerusalem, to be reminded that a watchful enemy is only a few yards away. Despite it all, this remains a golden city. It is still the holiest of holy sites, still a magnificent capital, still a place of pilgrimage. If you climb to the Mount of Olives in the evening you will find that its buildings, though scarred and battered by the fighting, still look beautifully mellow and serene; and through the shadowy, tortuous streets of the *suk* there still move the pilgrims and priests, the Bedouin and bootblacks, the coffee-sellers and gowned merchants of its tradition. There are Armenian clerics, ominously hooded, and Greeks in tall conical hats. There are Muslim women behind impenetrable veils, and leathery Bedouin tribesmen, and splendidly swaggering fat grandees. Parties of American pilgrims kneel at the Stations of the Cross in their cotton frocks and sun-glasses; and there are enchanting muddy-faced children about, and grave hurrying monks, and bent-back porters grunting hoarse warnings to the passers-by. Wars may come and go, but Old Jerusalem remains miraculously the same, and the innumerable pious orders and institutions which function within its walls do so now as they have done, through all the wild vicissitudes of Palestinian history, since the beginnings of Christianity and Islam. Only the Jews have vanished.

The people of this fortress-city have long been hardened to danger and hatred. I climbed one night with a Polish nun to the roof of Dom Polski's, a little hostel for pilgrims in the very heart of the Old City. Jerusalem lay below us, softly illuminated, cobbles and high windows and a bright moon. From the bazaars arose the hum of the butchers and shoemakers and sellers of souvenirs; above the topsy-turvy jumble of rooftops the dome of the Church of the Holy Sepulchre stood in solemnity. To the east the moonlight glistened on the Dome of the Rock, in the Haram ash-Sherif, rivalled only by the Great Mosque at Damascus in its delicate solemnity. 'Look!' said the nun, 'the soldiers are practising on the walls!' As she spoke, the white of

178

Jerusalem

her habit gleaming in the moonlight, I heard the familiar clink of a rifle butt, the clatter of ammunition boxes, a muffled order from the battlements above the great Damascus Gate: the Arabs, with an enemy literally at the gates of the city, were manning the walls of Jerusalem. This was an invested fortress, and the pettiest tomfoolery—an accidental rifle shot, a stone tossed across the line in fun or bravado—could bring a storm of machine-gun fire and mortar shells over those high ramparts. The nun sighed, but not, apparently, from fear or despair. 'Poor soldiers,' she said, 'they look so young, and they work so late.'

For to this protracted emergency, as to countless others, the Old City of Jerusalem has readily adapted itself. As somebody once remarked to me over lunch in the shadow of the walls, things were much worse in A.D. 70, when Titus was at the gates. The spirit of Jerusalem has withdrawn from the grand new suburbs, now in Israel, into the walled city. The streets are clean and seem prosperous. The marvellous Dome has been regilded. Big American cars are driven precariously up ramps and along ancient stepped alleyways. The Armenian postcard-seller outside the citadel wears a new pair of shoes. An advertisement for an hotel announces spryly: 'The Day, the Night, or as Long as you like. Your Room is Spacious and Airy. The Cosy Bar a Delight.' To some degree this blithe spirit is whistling in the dark, for the whole of Jordan is suspended over economic and political ignominy, and Jerusalem depends to a dangerous degree upon the demands of tourism and piety. It is also, though, a reflection of the abnormally tough fibre of this city, where deaths and battles, hardships and privations, are perennial normalities.

Of course this sprightly commercialism pervades the holy things of Jerusalem, too, and repels some of the pilgrims who come to the city in their innocence, expecting all things bright and beautiful. The postcard man will certainly accost you outside the Garden of Gethsemane, and someone may well offer you a fragment of the True Cross, or a corner of St. Veronica's veil; but for myself, I do not feel that these activities tarnish the sanctity or delight of the city.

The Church of the Holy Sepulchre has been infested for centuries by sectarian squabbles and commercial appetites; within it the various churches protect their respective rights of property and possession with a devotion that often seems to verge upon the vicious; and the

179

Jerusalem

building itself, constantly altered and extended, and propped up, since the 1927 earthquake, with a scaffolding of hideous iron girders, possesses something less than ethereal beauty. Yet even for the sceptic or the unbeliever, there remains an incomparable magic to the church. In its great porch is the soft-carpeted divan on which the hereditary Muslim guardians of the fane recline away the infidel days. Inside, the priests and pilgrims of a dozen different persuasions conduct their devotions. Here down a dim-lit aisle comes a procession of Franciscans: cultured voices and Gregorian chants, and a reverent visiting English priest, and a stream of pilgrims carrying lighted tapers, with two small boys at the back shuffling their feet. Hard on their heels come the Greeks. Harsh, grating and discordant is their music, and their cassocks are rough and hairy. There are five or six young acolytes, their voices half-way between childhood and maturity, and hemmed in closely among them is an aged bishop, so enshrouded in his vestments that only his spectacles and a few white hairs can be glimpsed beneath his hood in the gloom, and he looks for a frightening moment as if he has no face at all, but is made of crumpled surplices. In every corner, in every secluded chapel, there are serious monks and whispering tourists, and guides whose rasping urgent murmurings echo among the gilded candlesticks. A family of Italians kneels to kiss the Stone of Unction (over the centuries such fervent kisses have worn away three stones already); and it is agreeable to observe the faces of visitors, cluttered with their cameras and guide-books and lighted tapers, when they climb to a little upper chapel and realize suddenly, with awe or ecstasy, that they are standing upon the site of Calvary.

Spurious relics and grasping guides cannot spoil this place of sanctity. I think they throw into relief the extraordinary magnetism of the place, which draws so perpetual a stream of pilgrims through every kind of danger and disturbance. I always remember the Church of the Holy Sepulchre as a place of pleasure. I once saw an old woman, horribly crippled, struggling down the last steps of the Chapel of St. Helena, a faintly illuminated crypt. Her progress was agonizingly slow, but she was determined to reach the altar by herself. Painfully she shuffled down the stone steps. Her two sticks tapped and squeaked, and prayers were mingled with her heavy breathing. Each step was a torment. When at last she reached the bottom, though, and I peered into the dimness to watch her, she abruptly leaned down and placed her two sticks beside her on the

Jerusalem

ground. Then, straightening herself as far as her old crooked frame would allow her, she raised her arms above her head in triumph and exuberance, more like some whip-cord young athlete at the moment of victory than a poor old woman, distorted and arthritic, who would soon have to face the steps again.

One other moment I remember with rapture from the Church of the Holy Sepulchre, a building of constantly shifting aspects and unbelievable architectural complexity. The site of the sepulchre itself is maintained by the Greeks, and directly behind it there is a little chapel shrouded in black curtains. One morning, during a lull in the ceaseless round of the church's life, I found myself all alone beside this shrine; and as I stood there in the silence I thought I heard a faint ticking noise from inside. For a moment I stood hesitantly, thinking it might be the clicking of a perpetual censer, worked by some system of silver weights, or perhaps the swinging of an ornate lantern on its chain. But it was so regular and so insistent that I pulled the heavy curtains aside and looked in. There on the altar, all among the ikons and candlesticks, a red, moon-faced kitchen clock ticked away robustly, for all the world as if it were timing the eggs.

I laughed with pleasure at this unexpected discovery, and there was an answering chuckle behind me. Standing among the tall pillars of the rotunda, all but hidden in the shadows, there stood a gigantic Abyssinian priest in an attitude of serene meditation. When I turned to look at him, a white gleam in the darkness testified to the smile upon his black, bearded face.

No other city lingers quite so tremendously in the memory. She is, to my mind, the greatest of them all, the supreme capital—Jerusalem, for so many millions of souls, through so many centuries of history, the ultimate sanctuary of pilgrimage and desire. 'Next year in Jerusalem,' the Jews cry every Passover: and Muslims and Christians, too, each in their own style, echo this symbolic aspiration. When once you have entered the gates of Jerusalem, you are never quite the same person again: and thus, though there is a fearful sadness to that cruel dividing frontier, though it feels actually degrading to pass between armed sentries from the Old Jerusalem to the New, nevertheless when you are back in Israel, and glimpse through the windows of your smart hotel the legendary walls and pinnacles of the place, so wise and old and beautiful—then you do not feel only pathos or regret, but also a certain triumph.

JOHANNESBURG

It is sad but fitting that the northern gateway of South Africa, that pariah among the nations, should be the swollen mining camp of Johannesburg, for she is the most miasmal of African cities. Greedy, harsh and angular, she stands on the bleak uplands of the high veldt like an emblem of materialism, an unfailing confirmation of the traveller's preconceptions. You expect the worst of the Union, and sure enough, as your aircraft flies in from the genial north, the grim landscape of the Witwatersrand lies there below you with an air of degraded melancholy, the least welcoming, the least jovial, the least heart-warming of countrysides.

Perhaps it is early morning when you arrive above the Rand, and a pall of mist, smoke and pale cloud hangs low over the country. Then there is an austere and bitter seduction to the scene. Far away over the veldt this vaporous carpet spreads, sullen and clammy; but protruding through its whiteness, giving an unworldly grandeur to the scene, stand the mine workings of the Transvaal goldfields. The vast yellow mine dumps, flat-topped ziggurats, glisten a little in the early sunshine, the mist lapping their flanks. The big wheels of the mine shafts revolve as the early shifts plummet to the gold galleries below. A solitary tall chimney smokes away on the horizon. In a sudden clearing in the vapour you may glimpse a train chugging through the suburbs to Boksburg or Springs: and away to the east, swirled and swathed in mist, there stand the cold tall buildings of Johannesburg. There is a dank beauty to this landscape, so sprawling and inhuman, a country nourished on gold: but there is nothing soft or affectionate about it, and nothing at all to calm your forebodings.

Nor is the city, when at last you arrive in your Volkswagen bus among its truncated skyscrapers, an immediately exhilarating place. It lies nearly six thousand feet up, so that the guide-book warns you not to be alarmed if you puff unduly on the stairs; and because it stands over a many-layered warren of mining tunnels it is sometimes gently shaken by earth tremors, the belly-rumbles of the Rand. But

Johannesburg

it has surprisingly little sense of pace or astringency. The publicists
often speak of Johannesburg as a little New York, but here there is
none of the sparkle, the dazzling colour, the sophisticated gusto of
Manhattan. Jo'burg (as even her inhabitants call her) is more like
one of the medium cities of the American Middle West, perhaps
Omaha or Grand Rapids, except that the shops are not so good. She
sometimes feels painfully raw and new. Seventy-five years ago she
simply did not exist, and until 1947 a familiar habitué of Pritchard
Street, one of the principal streets of the metropolis, was the Mr.
Pritchard it was named after.

Oddly enough, although Johannesburg is the world's greatest
gold city and a business centre of incalculable importance, there is
something rather haphazard to her arrangements. Her streets are
geometrical and orderly of design, but there is a peculiar tatter-
demalion feeling to her traffic and wandering crowds. The white
people feel shiftless and shabby, and the myriad blacks lounging
among the back streets, sauntering among the shops, or riding their
bicycles with such precarious indecision, clothe the place in a
sort of crumbling black patina. Everyday life in Johannesburg is
often snarled with unexpected petty difficulties. In the coffee-shop
there seem to be too many waiters all looking for the sugar. At the
bank there is likely to be some confusion about your draft. The post
office hasn't got the right form. The young man who tells you the
way to the City Hall does so with endless imprecisions and circum-
locutions. Bite and decision are strangely lacking from the Johannesburg atmosphere, for all the cutting winter winds that howl down
her canyons, for all the calculating generations of skill that have
secured her prosperity.

Gold is her life-blood, and even in the centre of the city you
cannot escape the presence of the mines. Sometimes you may see,
gazing blankly into a haberdasher's window, a black miner still
wearing his mining helmet, like a soldier fresh from the trenches: and
as you wander about the streets you will often glimpse the alien
mass of a mine dump, a yellowish mountain of waste, blocking a
thoroughfare or looming over the warehouses. Sometimes the colours
of these dumps shift subtly in the sunshine; sometimes they glitter
suddenly, as if minute particles of gold still embellished them, like
rhinestones on a dowdy frock; but mostly they look cool, aloof and
neglected, with a massive Pharaonic beauty. There are a few gold-
rush buildings in Jo'burg, too, ornate pillared stores or rambling

Johannesburg

hostelries, with a hint of the hitching-post and the frontier moll; and downtown there stand in blank grandeur the offices of the Anglo-American Corporation, the greatest mining corporation on earth. No sign relieves the severe magnificence of these offices, or softens their monolithic effect: only the magical words '40 Main Street' stand there as an imperial motto, the *Ich Dien* of gold mining. Gold keeps Jo'burg alive, and the paving stones of her streets are, so the analysts swear, literally impregnated with gold dust.

Hard-headed British and Jewish financiers dominate the finances of this place, and few cities are more intimately adapted to the amassing of money. In its boom periods the whole white population follows the stock markets as keenly and as knowledgeably as ever a Londoner followed a Test Match. Johannesburg has a determined social life, a host of charitable organizations, a good deal of private talent and some vestigial public culture. Generally, though, she is frank enough about her aspirations. There is a compelling fascination to her steely hardness, something complete and functional, and there are perhaps no suburbs in the world more brazenly luxurious than the white highlands on the northern edge of the city. They say the white South African has higher living standards than anyone else, and if you take an aeroplane over these wealth-sodden dormitories you will see the swimming-pools glittering there below you in their hundreds, among the pampered lawns, the tailored trees, the occasional bashful mock-Tudor and the grand modernistic flats. Less than a century ago there was not a single tree upon the site of Johannesburg: today the city is encouched in the gardens and greeneries of these fortunate suburbs. A swift procession of American cars sweeps along their avenues. At St. John's School, when the lunch bell rings, the small boys come streaming out in caps and shorts like an army of juvenile stockbrokers, as richly English as a five-pound note but for some indefinably South African fore-shortening of their features. The Bishop of Johannesburg stands bravely in his purple cassock in a world of sprinkled grass and cocktail olives. Conversation is often excellent, for the rich people of Johannesburg are, by and large, an intelligent and perceptive lot: and now and then you may even meet one of the liberal celebrities of this tortured country, standing there amidst the scented wealth like a cormorant among puffins.

There is a parallel element of gaunt power to Jo'burg. From any ridge outside the city you can see her buildings elevated above the

Johannesburg

desert of the mine dumps with a squat and ugly force. There is little elegance or delicacy to the place—even the big stores smack heavily of the provincial draper, so that the dreariest of nightdresses stand in flat-chested modesty in the windows, and you almost expect the change to churn overhead in an antique aerial cylinder. But a streak of brutal virility enlivens the city. The great railway station sprawls across the heart of the place, an enormous splodge among the office blocks. The City Hall flaunts smoky, swing-door suggestions of Tammany or Boss Pendergast, and when there is a rugby match at a big stadium half white South Africa seems to be there, shouting its head off angrily.

The poorer Europeans sometimes reflect in their persons and manners a little of this stubby toughness. In the shabby white quarters that meander in and out of the mine dumps you may see them sitting on their stoeps, a leathery, open-necked kind of people. Some are British by origin, some Afrikaner, but when they talk English they share the peculiar flattened, twisted diction that is the hall-mark of all South Africans. In some cities it is architecture that strikes the senses most forcibly, in others faces, but nothing can recall me more abruptly to Johannesburg than the memory of one of those pallid sentences, sing-song and hollow, heard wafted across a drawing-room or eddying through a bus.

On my very first night in Johannesburg one such remark found its way into my notebook. I was eating a depressed fried-egg sandwich in a snack bar in President Street. The night was cold, the street gloomily empty, and I was alone with the three middle-aged white-coated women who administered the shop. So violently distorted were their accents, and so bemused was I by the impact of the city, that I could scarcely understand a word they were saying to me: but one phrase did strike home. 'Man,' said one of those ladies, sliding the salt across the counter, 'I can see by your face, you'll like Jo'burg so well you'll never want to go home again.' It did not seem probable to me, that draughty African evening, that her prediction would come true: but I confess to a sneaking, shamefaced affection for the Golden City, and a certain reluctant response to her magnetism.

She is, though, a city chilled always by tension. White Johannesburg is lapped by another metropolis, the vast housing estates and slums of the segregated black locations; and every breath of her air is thick with the broodings of apartheid. Hate and suspicion are integral

185

Johannesburg

elements of the civic atmosphere. With that resentful African proletariat brooding all around her, Johannesburg sometimes feels like an invested fortress—except that each morning, very early, thousands upon thousands of black besiegers pour meekly into the city to work. You are apart from the black men, and yet they are among you; you are afraid of them, but you need them on your pay-roll; you despise them, but you welcome their good hard cash in your till. Johannesburg is a schizophrenic city, for everyone knows that in those locations beyond the mine dumps terrible things happen when the sun goes down: the young tsotsi thugs go looking for adventure with their razor blades and loud ties; sozzled Africans brawl in illegal drinking houses; there are gang wars and desperate tribal clashes and police raids and murders innumerable. A huge alien black world is on the move out there, just out of range of the neon lights.

This is a disturbing thought, even for the confident burghers of Johannesburg, and domestic life in the city is distorted by it. You must never leave your child, say the Jo'burg matrons, alone with an African. At night you must shutter and bar your windows, set your burglar alarm and say your prayers with conviction. If you are especially resolute of chastity you may place a tear-gas bomb beside your face-cream on the dressing-table. If you are a millionaire in a penthouse flat you will prime the booby-trap in your safe. After dark this city locks itself up, like a mediaeval stronghold dropping its portcullis, or a frightened Cairo merchant barricading himself against the plague. In winter especially an eerie semi-silence falls upon the Jo'burg night. A curfew keeps the Africans at home. Few cars travel the streets, and there are hardly any of those loitering loving couples or late-night buses that give a homely geniality to the London midnight. Only the raggle-taggle black watchmen sit in their shop doorways, sometimes shouting unintelligibly to one another, or singing a sudden snatch of song, or laughing throatily, or spitting; and sometimes there are the sounds of a brief echoing struggle in an alleyway, pantings and choking imprecations, though when you reach the window in your pyjamas only the watchmen are still sitting there placidly, muffled in old army greatcoats and tattered balaclavas. Johannesburg never feels sound asleep: not because she is dancing, or loving, or putting the world to rights, but because her sleeping-pills have lost their potency.

For this great city is a paradigm of the racial dilemma. Here,

Johannesburg

better than anywhere else, you can pertinently ask the question: Should the black man be Westernized, or should he be encouraged to cherish his old African ways? Not only is Johannesburg a showplace of apartheid, the place where, above all, the new urbanized African is confronted by the entrenched privileges of the white man: she is also an intelligent city, where keen minds (and kindly ones, too) are constantly pondering the problem and searching for solutions. Somewhere among her money-bags there lies a conscience, and it is partly a sense of guilt that keeps her awake at night. In the grey classical buildings of Witwatersrand University, on a ridge outside the city, are to be found some of the least befuddled liberal thinkers in South Africa. The broad-minded Institute of Race Relations lives in Johannesburg; there are many Jo'burg Jews of progressive inclinations; the *Star* is the best and most urbane newspaper in Africa; and in Commissioner Street are the offices of the magazine *Drum*, owned and edited by white men, but dedicated to the interests of the Westernized African. Johannesburg is a big city, with room for deviations, and she is the crucible of the new Africa, where the ingots burn their fiercest.

No wonder she is tense. There is an endemic revolutionary situation in Johannesburg, and from time to time it erupts into violence. Sometimes the African workers boycott the buses as a gesture of their discontent, and come streaming into the city on foot, in tumbledown second-class taxis, or in the cars of white sympathizers. Sometimes there is a half-cock attempt at a general strike, and you will find the hotels short of bell-boys, and only half the factory chimneys smoking, and an odd sense of desertion in the streets. The English-language newspapers are full of the awfulness of it all, and outside the City Hall you may sometimes observe a few young liberal zealots, frowsy-looking girls and stark young men, distributing pamphlets of protest. The police of Johannesburg have a reputation for brutality; the courts are full of Africans arrested for failing to carry their passes or ignoring the curfew or procuring alcohol; and it is impossible to escape, in a conversation or a breakfast in bed with the papers or even a quiet stroll through the Sunday streets, the appalling antipathies of South Africa.

There used to be Africans living in Johannesburg proper, but the Nationalist Government has forced its black subjects ever farther from the Golden City, away from the swimming-pools and grand hotels into the harsh plateau of the veldt. The black townships

Johannesburg

around the city's perimeter, Meadowlands and Sophiatown, Orlando, Moroka, Pimville and Jabavu, are the saddest places under the sun. Some are modern planned locations, some haphazard slums of hideous jumbled complexity, riddled with disease and squalor, and they lie there vast, numb and torpid, with a terrible impersonality. I know of few more dispiriting experiences than trying to find someone in a Johannesburg location at dusk: the roads bumpy and untarred; the constant fear of rude questioning policemen; the endless rows of dark identical houses, with numbers running up into the tens of thousands; the all-pervading sense of insecurity and mistrust; the vicious upland wind; the lights of Jo'burg shining mockingly in the distance; and the final moment of despair when at last you find the house, and knock at the door, and there emerges some demoralized sot in a stained shirt and slippers, brandy on his breath, a flow of facetious speech tumbling over his tongue, and in the darkness of the parlour behind a blaring wireless and a giggle.

Poor African! Snatched from his loyalties, his savageries and his tribal lands, deposited in helotry at 3647 North Kruger Road, he spends half his life in recrimination, and the other half trying to be funny. He is one of the most deliberately downtrodden men on earth, but he is also one of the most cheerful. His culture is a jazzy, mock-American, slangy kind of affair, but he is often talented and sometimes deeply impressive. At first, indeed, the Westernized inhabitants of the Johannesburg locations may seem to you as remote and incomprehensible as any queer laughing creature in a menagerie. Their English is a strange muddle of Americanisms, Afrikaner idioms and racy appendages of their own, but their manners are defiantly African. Sometimes they are grave and courteous, and you are reminded of Ethiopian chieftains or great men of the Congo; sometimes they treat you with such bubbling flippancy that you think for a moment they are teasing you; sometimes a flash of malice enters their eyes, or something gives them such inexplicable amusement that they burst into a tumult of infectious laughter, or dance a little jazzy jig upon the pavement. When they talk, they do so with explosive animation, but when they listen, the whole of their being supplements their hearing, they become one great ear, and their white eyes, their tense bodies, their eager fingers and their yellow-striped socks all wait upon the speaker's words. Then, suddenly, they become all too human. There can be no kinder listener in the world than the Johannesburg African; however dull your story,

Johannesburg

those big patient eyes will be fixed upon you with a gaze of infinite appetite and encouragement.

The locations are dreadful indeed, but full of life at its most intense—full of violence, fun, variety, secret jokes and gregarious music. In the white heart of Johannesburg it is sometimes difficult to remember that they are there at all, ringing the city with their black multitudes: but for an effective reminder of their perpetual presence, and a pastiche of all that this city means to the world today, go and look at the central bus station in the evening, when the stores have closed and the factory hands are hastening into the dusk. Then all the poor black workers of the place, forbidden to live within the city precincts, rush for the buses that will take them to the slums or sprawling estates of the Western Areas. As the dusk falls a vast tattered queue moves in raggety parade towards the depot. It encircles the entire square outside the Drill Hall, so that the tail of the queue meets its own head, as thousands and thousands of Africans shuffle their slow way in double file towards the buses. It is the longest and most miserable queue I have ever seen. An air of unutterable degradation haunts the evening, so heartless and machine-like is the progress of the Africans, as the white folk hurry off in their cars to their welcoming suburbs, and the lights glitter in the windows of the department stores, and these poor lost souls are crammed into their shabby buses and packed off to their distant ill-lit townships. Many of them are ill-fed. Most of them are terrified of robbery and violence when they step off the buses into the dark streets of the locations. Half of them spend almost all their leisure hours travelling between the city and the cruel reaches of high veldt in which they are obliged by law to live. You can hardly watch such a Jo'burg scene, and ponder its implications, without the stirring of some crusading instinct in you, some Byronic impulse, perhaps, or at least a stab of pity.

But when you get back to your hotel again, and are drowning the memory in a Riesling from the Cape, perhaps you will hear some tinny twangs of music from the street outside: and there beneath the arcades of President Street some solitary black man will be lounging by, in a crumpled brown hat and blue dungarees, plucking away at a guitar as he walks, humming a high-toned melody, and expressing in his every gesture, in the very swing of his shoulders, the spirit of blithe indolence.

KABUL

High to the north-west of the Indus River lies the country of the Great Game. Here some of the cruellest territory on earth separates the Russians from their opponents across the Asian divide—in the old days the British in India, today the Americans and their Eastern allies. Captain Arthur Connolly dubbed it the Great Game in 1840, just two years before he was decapitated by the Khan of Bokhara, and ever since then the essence of the sport has remained almost comically undiluted. Both sides have advanced their frontiers, the Russians becoming masters of Turkestan, their antagonists advancing to the Khyber and Northern Baluchistan: but the central arena of the dispute, now as in the eighteen-forties, remains the kingdom of Afghanistan, sprawling in tumultuous grandeur around its capital of Kabul.

Kabul has been, my old Britannica says, 'a city of vast importance for countless ages'. She stands, protected by her wild hinterland, as insulation between two sizzling and puissant energies, the archetypal buffer capital. To her south, east and west stand Pakistan and Persia, American allies both; to her north, along seven hundred miles of savage frontier, is Russia; and at one inaccessible map reference to her north-east—'Within the ken of no living creature except the Pamir eagle', as a frontier commission loftily put it in 1897—the easternmost point of the Afghan kingdom meets the westernmost point of China. Into Kabul debouch the Hindu Kush passes, the immemorial trade routes out of Central Asia. Through Kabul many grim old paladins have passed, on their way to more tempting destinations—Alexander and Genghis Khan, Baber and Ahmad Shah, Greeks and Mongols, Buddhists, Muslims and whiskered Christians. Kabul is one of the keys to India, but nobody has ever conquered her for long—of the British Army that took her in 1845, only one solitary officer escaped unscathed to Jellalabad, and he was a Scotsman. She is the most evasive and elusive of capitals, a quick-sand city, and trying to understand her is like juggling with a

Kabul

weighted ball, or teaching a fox to beg. She cherishes all the traditional attributes of Asiatic guile: the gifts of bluff and prevarication, the dash and reckless courage, the ingrained xenophobia, the Islamic fire, the egoism, equivocation and sudden charm. I once asked an old man of Kabul what would happen if another enemy attacked this capital, as the British attacked it in 1845. Would they be exterminated, too? He gave an angry tug at his beard and threw me a look of piercing and bloodshot intensity. 'The same!' he hissed. 'The same again!'

Kabul perfectly fits these smouldering preoccupations. She is an Islamic city of the old sort, the kind that Burton liked to steal into, disguised as a mad dervish. She is a place picturesque but baleful, hemmed in by bald arid hills, with the Kabul River tumbling slate-grey and stone-strewn among her bazaars. Her history is streaked with bloodshed, bigotry and jealousy, and though her people are usually kindly enough nowadays, she can feel a frightening city still. She is scarcely beautiful, except for her lovely gardens and orchards: her buildings are mostly low and shabby, and even the great fortress called the Bala Hissar, dominating the capital from a spur of the hills, looks drab and down-at-heel. She is, however, wonderfully pungent—even other-worldly, in a sly and stunted way.

Her people are dizzily variegated, slit-eyed or shaggily bearded, smooth like conkers or layered like pine-cones, huge strapping frontiersmen or slinking mountaineers, Pathans and Uzbegs, Persians and Sikhs—men in every degree of social maturity, from the mediaevally austere to the padded-shouldered progressive. Most of the women of Kabul still sidle eerily about in heavy ankle-length veils, lit only by a grille about the eyes, and sometimes on the outskirts of the city, so I am credibly assured, you may encounter a citizen who, for hazy motives of dogma or penitence, prefers to go through life stark naked. In the fast-flowing river the fishermen stand brawny to their waists in the water, and all over the city bright-painted traps clip-clop beside the bazaars, gay with tassels, bobbing velvet balls and head-plumes. Kabul has some tentative and unconvincing emblems of modernism—a State hotel of violent expense, a boulevard or two, an international telephone exchange, even a Parliament building. *Au fond* she is, though, astonishingly, sometimes excruciatingly, archaic. She is one of the most backward of all the capitals. Somebody recently said of her that she was 'leaping into the thirteenth century', and one American resident of

Kabul

the city, asking his gardener why he had taken the wheel off the wheelbarrow, was told that it was easier to carry without.

This weird detachment is not casual, but deliberate. It is partly geographical, but mostly religious or political. Everywhere in Kabul you may sense not only suspicion and wariness, but also a resolution to keep clear, stand aloof, play off one side against the other. Here the Great Game, or the Cold War, is reduced to a parochial temper, and sometimes offers elements of knock-about farce. If you get up very early at the Ariana Hotel, one of the less pretentious of the city's hostelries, you may catch a glimpse of Kabul's Russians, current favourites in the tournament. They are sleeping four to a room, their iron bedsteads hugger-mugger, and they are moving about sluggishly and sleepily in very baggy pyjamas. One man is gargling from a chipped mug, another is massaging his broad but flabby chest, a third is up to his jowls in greyish soap lather. They look as though they have never laughed in their lives, except at obscure technical badinage, and long before you arrive downstairs they will have left the premises in swart high-axled jeeps, to return like stowaways only when the sun has dropped. But as the Russians set out to work, down the road the Americans are similarly stirring. Their air-conditioning hums, their fin-tailed convertibles await them, their mouthwash is antiseptically prepared, and Junior is already playing with his plastic moon-station. In Kabul the Ivanovs and the Rileys are in direct and visual competition, each pouring money, skill and sickly good will into Afghanistan with the single intention of thwarting the other. They are like rival sugar-daddies hovering around a blonde: and just as the blonde is sometimes not so silly as she looks, so it sometimes crosses the Kabul mind, I suspect, that there's one born every minute.

For so far, after twelve decades of conflict, the only winner in the Great Game has been Kabul herself. She has accepted all, and given nothing. Her streets have been metalled by the Russians. Her university is a gift from the Americans. Moscow provided her civic bakery. Washington has taught her to run her airport. Hundreds of millions of roubles and dollars have poured into her coffers, and up and down her streets scurry the glassy cars and stubby lorries, some from Detroit, some from Kiev, that are the harbingers of fortune. If the Great Game was played correctly, wrote Connolly in the eighteen-forties, the destinies of the native peoples would be changed 'from turmoil, violence, ignorance and poverty, to peace, enlighten-

Kabul

ment and varied happiness'. So, with some less altruistic undertones, say all the Afghans. There is every sign that the subtle rulers of Kabul, far from succumbing to the blandishments of one side or the other, only wish to keep the ball in play.

Theirs is a city of cynical and subtle resolution, not at all tempted towards subservience, as you will instantly grasp if you ever see a battalion of the garrison come marching by—stocky, slant-eyed, dusty small men of ferocious bearing, led with drawn sabre by an officer on a prancing black horse, hoarsely chivvied on all sides by angry outriders. There is nothing ingenuous about Kabul. She enjoys a masterly command of camouflage and double-talk, and the most telling of all her historical monuments is the old British gun, rusting and toppled on its carriage, which stands on a ridge above the capital: once it must have commanded the city, from the sprawling fortress to the tangled bazaar, but now it looks forlornly towards Jellalabad, along the road down which three successive British armies, extracting themselves from the Kabul morass, have trudged in weary resignation back to India.

She is a tense, shifty, nervous capital, and edgiest of all at night, when the street-lights are dimmed, the brilliant Asian stars come up above the hills, and only a few shrouded watchmen are left brooding on the doorsteps. Then the whole place feels sleepless and dry-eyed, like some insomniac conspirator. Sometimes a shot rings dead on the night, and sometimes a distant shout, and when a donkey pads softly by you can hear the two men upon its back, nebulous in white robes, murmuring to each other in low sporadic undertones.

KANO

As the traveller wanders across the breadth of Africa, through the welter of animisms and tribal faiths, the witch-doctors and sacred stones and fetishes, the gimcrack Christian deviations, the struggling missions and occasional messiahs—as he journeys through this cauldron of devotions he finds himself upon the outer fringes of Islam; and at once the stately order of that marvellous religion brings a fresh dignity to society, and tinges the air with its ornate magic. Such an outpost of the Muslims is Kano, the principal city of northern Nigeria, where the Emir of Kano lives in state in a splendid rambling palace, and the piles of ground-nuts stand like white pyramids outside the walls.

One of the sad results of the Western mission in Africa has been the vulgarization of the continent. Millions of Africans have been weaned from their precarious inherited mores and stuffed with a heady smattering of education and Christianity. It is entertaining, for a week or two, to observe the frothing and the bubbling, the jazzy effervescence that is often the product of this diet: the irreverent gaiety of slogans and posters, the brassy rhythms of High Life jazz in Accra, the unkempt and often scurrilous newspapers, the earnest schoolmasters discussing Sedgemoor or Voltaire, the perky black barristers in their wigs, the fundamentalist preachers, playing upon trumpets and foaming at the mouth. There is tremendous vigour to Westernized Africa, especially along the shorelines of Nigeria and Ghana, and a bottomless reservoir of fun.

After a while, though, you begin to feel the pathos of it all, and to realize that these are temporarily rootless peoples, racked by sensations of inadequacy, unfulfilment or frustration, and deprived of the often scratchy cultures that gave them pride of history. It is probably no more than a sorry but inevitable stage in the development of black Africa, and certainly it is balanced by all manner of material blessings, from polio vaccines to pink chiffon: but stroll through the slums of Lagos one day and consider this sad miscegena-

Kano

tion of manners, and you may murmur to yourself, as you pass from the dried monkey heads to the blaring radios: 'God help us, what a mess we've got them into!' Stretched between the tribal devils and the deep blue sea of progress, between the old religions and the new, the chieftain's council and Erskine May, many a poor African is a muddle of instincts and aspirations, whistling tunelessly in the dark.

But when you walk through the gates of Kano, with her grassy ramparts running away to the horizon like Mississippi levees, all this vanishes in a trice. Outside the walled city there are communities of Ibos and Yorubas from the south, pagans and Christians of diverse sects, among whom you may often see a young man in a cowboy hat, or hear the thump of rag-time, or even be conducted around a piggery: inside all is Muslim, the throaty quarter-tones of an African muezzin echo from a minaret, and there is a sense of style and latent pageantry. The three provinces of Nigeria have long been federated in independence, but Kano feels a different country still, her people have ancient and deeply rooted loyalties of their own, and on ceremonial occasions (or travel posters) the Emir's bodyguard wears chain mail and visors, like the Muslim warriors of antiquity.

From the great white mosque near the palace you can catch the pulse of this romantic and remarkable city. A few cheerful convicts, wearing spotless white numbered smocks, lounge in its courtyards vacuously, and on his platform beside the gate the muezzin, black and beturbaned, arranges his robes rather nervously before beginning the descent of his ladder. It is not always easy to gain access to the minaret of the mosque, for there has been a small commotion about the numbers of unbelievers who have been climbing its staircase; but after a few moments of breathy negotiation a retainer swathed from head to foot in bright red textiles, like a painted mummy or an indigestible Swiss roll, unlocks the door for you and ushers you upstairs.

The city sprawls below you festooned in heat and dignity. Somewhere across the horizon lies the Sahara, and this is a place like Isfahan or Damascus, subtly impregnated with desert ways, with an echo of caravanserai, slave trade and pilgrimage. An enormous higgledy-piggledy market straddles a rivulet in the middle of the city: a wonderful affair, with all the colour of black Africa but little of that fetid smell, compounded of dried fish and obscure medicinals, that brings a touch of the jungle to the great marts of Ibadan and the coast. Across the dusty plains radiate the trade routes that still link this ancient place with the Mediterranean, the Red Sea and Mecca itself. Below you lie the palaces of the great Fulani notables, still the aristocratic rulers of this city. Kano looks exceedingly old from that high eyrie, exceedingly assured, exceedingly grand.

But calm and silent though it may seem, in fact the winds of progress, like the horns of Elfland, are faintly blowing through these walls. The British, in half a century of generally wise suzerainty, broadened the basis of princely rule, but by no means abolished it. Nor has the Federal Government of independent Nigeria. The Emir and his fellows maintain many of their privileges, but inevitably the people are beginning to look around them. Many of them know the Sudan; thousands have been to Saudi Arabia on pilgrimage; there are old links with North Africa; and there is, as among all Muslims and speakers of Arabic, a deep interest in the doings of Egypt, at once the patriarch and the showboy of Islam. In the end, I do not doubt, the emergence of Nigeria as a free nation will whittle away the character and the traditional stability of Kano, for this city is not quite as serene as it looks. The distrust of the northerner for the southerner is still stubborn, and vice versa. The Ibos and Yorubas outside the walls, with their clerkly attainments and school certificates, are anathema to the aloof Hausas and Fulanis of Kano; and in return the southerners turn up their educated noses at a people so incorrigibly sunk in mediaeval heritage. No great depth of security supports the grandeurs of the place. Like all such survivals of more spacious times, it lies at the mercy of common sense.

Still, for the moment there is no lack of confidence to Kano's muffled dignitaries, with their amber prayer-beads and their pieties, and no waning assurance to the earnest thumbs-up greeting with which Kano citizens often salute a passing foreigner. It is at the great international airport of Kano that many a traveller boards his aircraft to be swept away to Europe. As he flies northwards to the Mediterranean he will be wise to steal a last valedictory glimpse of this antique city, criss-cross between its grassy walls, like Samarra beside its Tigris or some lofty market town of Persia. What a farewell to Africa! And what a far-flung triumph, against all the odds of the jazz age and the hucksters, for the old philosophies of Arabia!

KATMANDU

'Katmandu?' Few destinations nowadays can raise the travel agent's eyebrows, but this lovely, limpid name, rolled casually off the tongue in Piccadilly or Fifth Avenue, may still summon some of the old wonder. A last haze of romance still surrounds the capital of Nepal, a last suggestion of the secret and the arcane; and though there is a road there now, and the Rolls-Royces of the Maharajahs are no longer carried up from India wheelless on the backs of coolies—though you can drive a jeep there these days, or book yourself a seat on a twice-weekly aircraft, nevertheless it still feels faintly adventurous to be going there at all.

Colour, sparkle and clarity are the first essentials of the place. Katmandu is not very high, but above her stand the celestial Himalayas, and she feels more alpine than she is. The heavenly green of the Bagmati valley is flecked with flowers and bright vegetables, and through it the river flows cold but placid, blue water over grey shingle, running away out of town to the plains of India far below. To the north you can see the firs, pines and larches of the foothills, forests of rhododendron and aromatic juniper, and when-ever the day is clear there high above you, higher than you conceive to be possible, far higher than you dare to expect, more like clouds than snow-peaks, nearer Heaven than Katmandu—there stand the mountains, kind but icy.

In this Arcadian setting Katmandu stands assured enough, but suspicious. Architecturally she is a magnificent mongrel. She is ennobled by intricate temples, Buddhist and Hindu: gilded stupas with painted accusatory eyes, towering pagodas, armies of teak-carved Hindu images—rats and bears and monkeys and elephants, legendary giants, grimacing warriors and dancing Jezebels, wrestlers, cabalistic symbols, antique kings and gods with many arms. Her back streets are tortuous, shadowy and disturbing, suggestive of plague processions, slave marts or heretics blazing at the stake. Her narrow bazaars are shambled and slovenly, and the palace of the

Katmandu

Kings of Nepal, in which the monarchs of this kingdom still assume the fabulous feathers and helmets of their ceremonial dress, stands in plaster-deep splendour among green but dusty gardens. High above the undisciplined rooftops a tall white tower honours the memory of some dead sovereign, and out on the green *maidan* the young patricians ride their ponies with unorthodox grace.

Upon this aged fabric the fall-out of modernity is settling. History has humbled the great family of the Ranas, which used not only to provide the monarchs of Nepal, but also the Prime Ministers, Ministers of State and Generals. All the paraphernalia of intermittent democracy has flooded into the capital, and with it the first trappings of a modern society. The shutters are down. The first enterprising tourists are in. Several cinemas prosper in Katmandu, and in the shops you can buy almost anything Western man can want, from toothpaste to Scotch to seamless stockings. Some of the great palaces still serve traditional purposes. ('One house,' a nice young English lady reported inaccurately upon her return to India, 'is set aside for the accommodation of the owner's porcupines.') Others have been debased by the times, into banks, merchant houses or hotels. A hostelry I once stayed at was still brave with the bric-a-brac of grander days—stuffed tigers locked in inconclusive combat, pictures of Nepali grandees in dramatic uniforms, mats bearing emblazoned slogans like 'Bless This House' or 'East West, Home's Best'; in the great courtyard strutted the chickens later to appear in sad regularity upon the dinner-table, in the bar a jazz band played raucously, its double-bass player an elegant Nepali woman in horn-rimmed spectacles. There is even a public zoo in Katmandu, half-heartedly maintained by the municipality. When I visited it, everything was weedy and overgrown. The lions were heavy with boredom. The tigers were moulting. The biggest python had escaped. The pelican flapped grotesquely up and down the lawns with a laborious beating of his clipped wings. On one cage I saw a notice saying 'Gibbon': but inside there was only a solitary moribund parrot, and as I approached there vanished into the recesses of the cage, with a furtive scurrying and sliding, a troop of small brown rats, which had been clinging to the meshwork examining that unhappy bird.

The spirit of Katmandu is well reflected in that institution, for this is still a queer place, introspective and pernickity. Along its boulevards and murky alleyways moves one of the more extraordinary of the world's populations. Here are the motley Nepalese:

Katmandu

some in the white gnomish caps and narrow trousers of the prosperous; some in swathed ethereal rags; some swaggering in khaki, with all the martial swank of the Gurkhas; some blazoned with mysterious orders, in liveries of gorgeous ostentation. Sometimes you may see a lean European mountaineer buying mugs or tinned pineapple for an expedition. Sometimes a Nepalese dignitary, snooty by right of blood or authority, scatters the languid crowd with his burnished Chevrolet. Sometimes an itinerant holy man stalks by in ominous meditation; or a line of emaciated porters stumbles half naked towards the hills, loaded with bundles and packing-cases for some distant corner of the kingdom; or a group of Tibetans, with long black hair and dangling amulets, squats beside the road chatting; or a beggar crouched upon the pavement intones his stylized whimpering appeal.

In the high Buddhist shrine of Shambu-nath hundreds of monkeys clamber horribly about, reaching their skinny hairy arms through the windows to snatch a trinket or tap some shuddering visitor creepily upon the shoulder. In the settlement clustered below solitary albinos stare at you with lifeless eyes. The ghastly god Kala-Bhairab glares reproachfully across the main square of the capital, and from the lintel of the Exchange, where you go to collect the heavy silver coins that are the country currency of Nepal, four prancing monsters, claws raised and ears aprick, seem only waiting to savage you. There is often a curfew in Katmandu, and secret passwords are passed about in the lamplight on grubby bits of paper. There is often a crisis under way, and the streets are heavy with the threat of rioting, or acrid still with yesterday's bomb. There is an undercurrent of chicanery and ambiguity, and a raggle-taggle assortment of foreigners spices an already pungent city—bland do-gooders and earthy engineers, Swiss merchants and American agriculturists, shady Germans and stylish White Russians, one of whom I once heard welcomed, as he stepped off the aeroplane from Patna, with the intriguing greeting: 'Darling, the cook has run away and one of your pandas is dead.'

The shopkeepers of Katmandu are disconcertingly lethargic and reluctant, lounging on their wooden steps or lying like drugged men among their bales of stuff, and this veiled torpor is powerfully reminiscent of Katmandu in her palmy isolated days, when she lay lonely and mysterious behind her barrier of mountains, only occasionally invigorated by an imperialist war or an appalling

Katmandu

massacre (like the one when stout Queen Kot threw fifty of her courtiers down a well). The travel agent is right, to flicker his eyelid as he takes your order. Katmandu remains a capital of curious foibles. Some visitors may be struck most by the glories of her architecture, her exquisite woodwork or her prodigies of symbolism. Others may be overwhelmed by the awful squalor of her slums, the spindly pathos of her poor people, the citizens squatting in excretion beside her crystal river. For me, though, it is the peculiarity of the place that tells: the hush of the Himalayan evening on those ferocious temple images, the kites swinging above the *maidan*, monkey-arms and bloodless faces, the huge helmets and scimitars of the Nepalese kings, and the cold dead look in the eye of the merchant, as he grudgingly consents to sell you, against the better judgement of a thousand years, a yard of best elastic.

KUWAIT

I first went to Kuwait in the company of a sheikhly hawking party, who had been down to the Trucial Coast of Arabia to practise their sport. Splendid were the caparisons of those haughty Arab sportsmen, and their eyes were cold and heavy-lidded. They wore magnificent flowered gowns, and crossed bandoleers, and daggers, and spotless head-dresses, and gilded swords; and big black lackeys carried their peregrine falcons, hooded upon their pedestals; and a brass band puffed away upon the airfield at Kuwait when this gorgeous crew, looking slightly airsick, staggered on to the ancestral soil.

It was not an altogether misleading introduction. Kuwait is by far the richest place, *per capita*, on earth. She consists simply of a seaport, a desert hinterland, and the most generous of oilfields, and the dollars are packed so tightly into this enclave that they burst its frontiers and spill out into the stock markets of the world. The Sheikh of Kuwait is, I believe, the richest of all men. He is the most important single provider of new money for the London investment market. His income has increased twentyfold in ten years. When he once paid a visit to Paris, I am told, he gave his two new Cadillacs to his French chauffeur when he left. He earns more money every hour than most British Cabinet Ministers do in a year. If you laid his bank accounts end to end . . . but there, no hyperbole can do justice to the fabulous resources of this Arabian sheikh, whose grandfather was responsible for the mud wall that surrounds the city of Kuwait, a protection against marauding tribesmen.

All this wealth has permeated Kuwait, and greatly changed her character. Once she was the most Arab of the big Gulf ports. Today she is a strident hybrid—an independent State indeed, but crossed between the Eastern, ruminative way, and the Western rat-race. Along the water-front they still build the high-prowed ungainly dhows of Arab tradition, observing the immemorial taboos and shibboleths of the Gulf shipwrights. Within the city there is still a

Kuwait

big, rambling, jumbled old quarter, where many a desert custom is still upheld, and many a poor woman is held in purdah so strict that she may not even climb to the rooftop to enjoy the view. If you stroll along the seashore in the evening, when a smell of wood and oil and fish hangs on the air, and a murmurous Arabic hubbub arises from the coffee-shops, then you may still imagine the Kuwait of three decades ago, when she was little more than a petty sheikhdom, living on pearls, shipbuilding and the entrepôt trade, and supported, believe it or not, by a small British subsidy.

But most of Kuwait is now bold and noisy. The old flowery courtesies are dying fast, and of all the cities of the Middle East this is now perhaps the rudest. Huge and thoughtless are the cars that speed through the rackety streets of the place, themselves a turmoil of demolition and reconstruction. There is an air of get-rich-quick to every corner of the city. The shops are cluttered with expensive things, thrown in the windows willy-nilly, or stacked in trays like toys at Woolworth's. The names of a few big Kuwaiti merchants crop up in almost every conversation, and around the fringes of these Arab magnates there hovers an unprepossessing company of foreigners, obsequious as any pasha's eunuchs. I know of few cities more impregnated with venality, and the steely impatience of the Kuwait *suks* is a nasty thing to experience.

This is a change of values as complete and as significant as any contemporary social transition, even including the metamorphosis of Communism, for the old social structure of the Arabian desert was something very stable, powerful and serene, and fostered a particular kind of man, with standards of judgement all his own. In Kuwait today all is shattered: but though the process is often distressing to watch, nevertheless good is coming from it, as well as evil. Not all the Kuwaiti public moneys are being squandered, and the presence of oil in this city-State gives it hope and energy, besides this squalid new commercialism. There are fine new schools. There is an excellent free health service. There is an exciting sense of power and momentum. Everything is moving in Kuwait, and moving fast. There are ships always standing offshore, and aircraft always on the tarmac, and great new roads spilling into the desert, and everywhere the red flag of Kuwait flies bravely in the Red Sea breeze. Kuwait has all the attractions of a genuine boom town: gusto, vivacity, shifting wary relationships, new faces, enterprises galore, and a sometimes invigorating sense of no-holds-barred. It is a young man's town,

Kuwait

brash and scurrilous. If you stand on one of the sixty-seven towers of the city wall and look across the variegated rooftops of the place, the grasping vitality of Kuwait hits you like a slap in the face—unless, of course, it is the heat of high afternoon, when the boom town goes to sleep like any other Arab city.

It is easy to sneer at the Coca-Colonization of such a society, which is indeed ugly to observe: but it is difficult to carp at the advent of new pleasures for a people whose lot has been, in the past, not without monotony. Many a Kuwaiti housewife now has piped water—something, until a few years ago, outside the range of her imagination, let alone her aspiration. For the first time she is being prised free, bit by bit, from the tyranny of the veil, so muffling that even today many Kuwaiti women cannot even sew, but while away their cloistered lives in desultory gossip and childbirth. The ill-mannered young Kuwaiti at the cinema is certainly less agreeable to meet than his forebear, courteous and hospitable in his goat-hair tent; but it must be a fearful bore to be a Bedu for long, and who would begrudge such a youth his evening among the cowboys?

There is doubtless less honour in this city than there used to be, less beauty, less moral certainty, less sense of glory and decorum: but for the local inhabitants there is certainly more comfort, and there may well be more fun. If you agree with Jefferson that education is the first duty of government, and believe that any widening of horizons is, *per se*, desirable, then you must regretfully reconcile yourself to the phenomena of the new Kuwait. (Though for myself, loyal Jeffersonian though I am, and doubtful though I was about the absolute probity of those princely falconers, nevertheless I cannot help preferring the goat-hair to the chromium-plate.)

KYOTO

Kyoto means Capital City. For a thousand years this famous place, encouched in mountains upon the Kamo River, was the capital of Japan and the emblem of Japanese civilization: and even today she remains to the Japanese something special among their cities, far more than just an elderly provincial metropolis in the central hills. She reigns still as the supreme repository of their ancient traditions, their culture and their custom, their religion and their high-flown patriotism, their golden heritage and their resilient pride. She is a shrine, a palace, a memorial, a talisman, a poem, a picture. She is, to ninety million Japanese, the very soul and melody of Nippon.

To the foreigner, though, bouncing in by bus from Osaka, she seems at first sight something less than lovely: for though her setting is magnificent and her pose perennially imperial, yet the face she shows to the world is sadly coarsened. The frenzy of the new Japan has fallen upon Kyoto, too, cramming her streets with wild-driven traffic, tainting her old wisdom with doubt and disillusion. Kyoto was spared the worst tragedies of war, but she shares with the rest of Japan a sense of causes lost and ideals soured, of warped emotions and passions suppressed. The shape of this town was decreed by the Emperor Kammu eleven centuries ago, when he laid out his capital in the classical Chinese manner, four-square and impeccable: but though you can still recognize this grand design, nevertheless Kyoto has long since lost her symmetry and pattern, and seems to lie there, as your bus lurches through the faceless streets, floundering and inelegant, a city of lost style.

Both views are right: the impassioned Japanese, the disappointed alien. Kyoto as a whole is a plain place, shabby and shanty-like: but like others of the world's great cities—like Oxford, like Florence— she is a place of reticent enchantment, a private place, a place behind walls, a place whose beauties you must search out, and whose meanings, like the exquisite subtleties of the Japanese tea ceremony,

Kyoto

are hidden beneath layers of innuendo. Kyoto is the most conservative of Japanese cities, still half living in her gilded heyday, when her monarchs and shoguns luxuriated in cultivated splendour, and the four great sects of Japanese Buddhism settled beneath her hills in ritual and meditation. This is a nostalgic, introspective city, where many an old conviction, like many a delectable garden, lies silent but cherished behind a haughty rampart. The patricians of Kyoto are aloof and lofty still. The ultimate treasures of the place are jealously guarded. The tourists may click their shutters, the traffic may rage, the radios deafen: but away beyond the tawdry façade, even beyond the temples and the incomparable gardens, the spirit of this deep city lies inviolate and unruffled, like a carp in a sacred pool.

Temporal consequence abandoned Kyoto a century ago, when the emperors left her. Today she is poorer than Nagoya, smaller than Osaka, quieter than Yokohama, infinitely less virile than the *parvenu* Tokyo. No pounding steel mills give her force or energy, no ferocious chimneys belch away among her suburbs, no cameras, cars, radios or computers stream from her assembly lines: all she makes is silk, porcelain, lacquer ware, adorable dolls and nice little novelties for the tourists. Modern history has passed her by. Even her writers scuttle away to Tokyo, where the publishers live, and her old universities, distinguished though they are, lack the fire and sparkle of their contemporaries in the capital. Economically Kyoto is dominated by her gigantic seaport neighbours, Osaka and Kobe. Intellectually she is revered but fuddy-duddy. In all too many ways she is no more than a museum, or a memory.

Yet for all her faded majesty, she feels unmistakably a great city still, a city of lingering power and paramountcy, and sometimes even of menace. All that is most deep-rooted in the Japanese character persists in this introvert community: some of it enchanting, some of it hideous, some of it alarming, some of it delicate and fastidious beyond compare, some of it (to Western minds) perfectly inexplicable. In Kyoto you may observe, still extant and vigorous, an advanced and elaborate form of society that has no real contact with the ways of the West. She has her department stores and her television studios, her airline offices and her air-conditioned hotels; yet she remains at heart among the most Oriental of cities, looking at the world slant-eyed and cross-legged, like some heavy-lidded potentate peering across the fun-fairs from a high window of his castle.

Kyoto

A myriad shrines, temples and mansions powerfully fortify this sense of hidden strength and exclusivity. They are scattered across the city like gems in mud, unexpectedly at the ends of culs-de-sac, magnificently among pine groves on hillocks, splendidly in flamboyant courtyards. In Kyoto there are nearly two thousand Buddhist temples, Shinto shrines and palaces of importance, giving to every corner of the metropolis oblique suggestions of sanctity, delicacy and wisdom. Some are vast and portentous, their steep cypress-bark roofs (fuzzy with moss) rising high in grandeur above the houses, their ceremonial gongs gigantic beneath their wooden shelters, their spotless passages meandering interminably through gilded screens, painted anterooms, gardens of infinite sophistication, tea-houses of faultless proportion. Some are no bigger than garden chalets, flickering small shrines of contemplation, reclining in rotting silence beneath high garden walls, or balanced beside rushing rivulets. Some are the empty palaces of the emperors and the shoguns, soaked in grandeur and symbolism: their wonderful gardens representative of the ocean, or the Inland Sea, or peace, or Paradise, or a fleet of treasure-ships, or the cosmos, their chambers rich with painted tigers, bamboo groves, sea birds, turtles. Some are the great prayer-houses of monks and holy men, mysterious with candles and slow movement, the tinkle of bells, the fluttering of sacred papers, the fragrance of incense, the murmured incantations that will bring the Jodo brethren, in their after-life, infallibly to the Western Paradise.

Some are the storehouses of mighty treasures, like the thousand images of the goddess Kannon in the Temple of Sanju-sangendo—a fabulous phalanx of glistening golden figures, silent, many-armed, sad-eyed, accusatory, each one stuffed with Buddhist scripts, rank upon rank, eye upon eye, attended by the Gods of Thunder and Wind, the Spirit of Merciful Maternity, the Spirit of Devotion, the Spirit of Exorcism. Some are airy gems of lucidity, like the little golden pavilion called Kinkakuji, which was once burnt down by a mad monk, but now stands again in featherweight lucidity above its lake, with one room reserved for poetry-reading and incense parties, and a rustle of conifers all around. Some are shrines of awful solemnity, poised upon high places, approached by tall breathtaking steps, with pagodas lonely among the larches and mountain streams rushing by below. The great buildings of Kyoto are inexhaustible and inescapable. It would take weeks only to glimpse them all, and because they are distributed through every ward and

Kyoto

every suburb, they give the city dignity in depth, and clamp its drab sprawling fabric powerfully together.

The quiddities and idiosyncrasies of the Japanese tradition, surviving here more potently than anywhere else, contribute no less to the intensity of Kyoto. This is a knobbly, enigmatic kind of entity, a city for initiates, streaked with eccentricity. Its calendar is crimson with festivals, when vast toppling chariots are wheeled in precarious splendour down the highways, when a man riding a bull prays in an unknown archaic language before the Koryuji temple, when a parade of youths in voluptuous women's clothes totters through the darkened lanes with huge candle-lanterns fastened eerily to their heads: odd, shadowy, complex, sometimes uncanny rites, handed down from the recesses of the Japanese identity, charged sometimes with antique delight, sometimes with a queer significance, sometimes with a trace of arrogance.

Kyoto is a city of whimsical grace-notes. Jammed beneath the eaves of one great temple you may see an old umbrella, dropped there aeons ago by a divine personage, and preserved there for ever as a sign of holy favour. In another you may admire a painting of Fujiyama whose perspective falls into accuracy only if you kneel before the canvas. In a third you may hear the floor-boards, squeaking beneath your tread, 'emitting a sound' (as the guide-book says) 'resembling the song of a Japanese bush warbler'. You may walk the soft paths of a garden clothed entirely in moss, a padded shadowy retreat for contemplatives; or you may hear the hollow rhythmic clatter of a deer-scarer, a hinged wooden tube animated by the passing water of a stream; you may wonder at the great chains hanging down the rooftops of the Imperial Palace—placed there for the convenience of fire-fighters, but 'also forming', says the guide hopefully, 'a kind of ornament'; or you may have your fortune tactfully told and beguilingly translated ('Lucky Spring comes with happiness on a mountain and field. . . . Your wants would be able to accomplish. . . . You would have many treasures of child'). If you are specially privileged you may even catch sight of the slightly improper mediaeval picture which, wrapped in innumerable silks and stored in impenetrable caskets, is regarded as so precious a possession that only twenty people are allowed to view it each year.

The rice-paper windows of the Kyoto palaces are often pierced, by children's fingers or the beaks of inquisitive birds, but they are mended characteristically: over each hole a small piece of paper is

Kyoto

meticulously glued, cut by eager fingers into entrancing flower patterns, every petal of perfect symmetry.

Everyday life in Kyoto is patched with similar fastidious grace. Of all the big Japanese cities, this remains nearest to the water-colour Japan, the Japan of the print-makers and the flower-makers. The main streets are dreadfully banal, but beyond them are alleys of seduction. Here the butterfly kimono, the white stocking, the cloven boot and the flowered kerchief may be seen down any back street, and the fringes of the city are full of brawny country folk, brown as goblins and wreathed in grins. The fishermen of Kyoto grapple with the river torrent with marvellous sinewy skill, like images from a Hokusai print, and the sages you sometimes meet in rambling temple courtyards look like archaic hermits or astrologers. Often you will hear, as you pass beneath some towering wall, the shrill whistling of strange flutes, or the pad of a Japanese drum. Possibly you will encounter, on the grassy sunlit verge of the river, a wandering monk in a grey robe and a bulbous basket-work hat, begging his way to immortality. You may go to a Noh or a Kabuki play in Kyoto, and sit chilled or stimulated by the formalities of those immemorial arts, or you may watch them dipping the dyed silks into the waters of the Kamo as they have in this valley for a millennium and more. All around the city, on the high mountain skyline, the pine trees stand in willow-pattern silhouette, and sometimes you may catch the local students, in their peaked caps and drab serge uniforms, entreating a Shinto shrine for good marks in their examinations.

Kyoto is *par excellence* the home of the geishas, where those talented performers (part artists, part courtesans) are trained to an apogee of perfection, to perform their elaborate dances deliciously in many a lacquered *salon*, and bring contentment to many a paunchy protector. Half close your eyes one evening among the narrow streets of the geisha quarter, and you might almost be back in feudal Kyoto, before the razzle-dazzle West arrived. The lanes are gay with tea-houses and restaurants, dainty screens masking their entrances, soft slippers paraded invitingly at their doors. Hundreds of globular lanterns light the district, bathing it in orange radiance, and high above your head there floats an advertiser's balloon, flaunting illuminated letters on its tail. Now and then between the houses you may glimpse the Kamo River, wide and gurgling, with a glitter of lights and gaiety on the opposite bank, and the dim moonlit hump of

Kyoto

the hills beyond. From the terraces beside the water you may hear the clink of cups, the murmur of liquid, the whisper of evening ecstasies. A blind beggar stands mumbling among the shadows; an old crone looks testily out of a doorway, a platter of fish in her hand; two or three young men go rolling noisily pleasure-bound; and suddenly there emerges from some unexpected alley a vision of the legendary Japan—a geisha in all her plastered glory, moving fast and purposeful towards an assignation. Immensely tall is her mound of hair, jet black and shiny; her face is vivid with white and scarlet; her costume is gorgeous with silks, sashes, the gaudiest of clashing colours and the floridest of patterns; and as she hastens awkwardly down the street, embellished from head to foot with paint and brocade, she feels less like a living woman than some fabulous toy, some last masterpiece by Fabergé, enamelled like a queenly trinket, animated by the ultimate refinements of clockwork.

Everything delicate thrives in the soil of Kyoto. A divine simplicity informs the shop displays of the city. A sort of ascetic *chic* graces the little gardens, with their ineffable arrangements of stones and shrubs, and their air of mischievous meaning. When they serve you a dish in a famous Kyoto restaurant, poised above the river rapids, perhaps, with fish-pools in the garden outside and feathery branches tickling the veranda—when they bring you your prawns, your quails' eggs, your lily bulbs, your eels or your red seaweed, you will find each small victual arranged with bewitching artistry upon your plate, like an abstract miniature of marvellous sensibility. Kyoto is a city of cool calm interiors, gossamer screens, rooms of geometrical precision, women of porcelain fragility. She is a place of cherished animals: little white Spitz dogs and affectionately collared cats, the neat oxen that pull her country carts, the cranes, pheasants, ducks, geese, squirrels that bask among her decorations. Away from the motor-cycle thoroughfares, her air is full of crickets, frogs, bells, birds, the sliding of finger-tip doors, the clip-clop of clogs, the slither of slippers. She is a city of a million souls, yet you never feel far from the countryside: all around are the woodlands, sliding down towards the town, and the whole place seems inlaid with beautiful timber, aromatic planks, woods of lovely grain and dedicated workmanship.

The Kyoto zoo is poised delightfully above a river, and beneath its cages you may see men in floppy hats fishing for their dinner. The industrial area of Kyoto, in the ramshackle quarter called Nishinjin,

Kyoto

hums and clanks intriguingly with the energies of twenty thousand family looms, tucked away in every house, in every back yard, in every attic. In the indoor markets of Kyoto, vivid with sea vegetables and succulent fruits, countless tiny electric fans whirr away above each stall like so many busy humming-birds hovering above the oranges. And underneath the arches of the Kamo-Ohashi bridge a penniless old vagrant has built for his own delectation the most endearing of all stone gardens, one pebble balanced miraculously upon another with flawless finesse.

For Kyoto is still a capital, despite the rebuffs of history: within these old walls, behind these dainty shutters, up these temple stairs, hidden in these perfumed gardens, along these green river boulevards, in the silence of these tea-houses and honoured libraries, high on the mountains or lost among the moss—infused into the very texture of Kyoto is the essence, the fragrance, the pith of Japan.

All this is true, and it is the continuity of Kyoto life that gives this place its sense of power. No less real, though, are those corroded aspects of modern Kyoto that affront the foreign visitor like a juke box in an abbey; and it is the harsh juxtaposition of the near-sublime and the almost unbearable that gives the city its pungency and piquancy of character, its sting and its bitter after-taste. Kyoto does not leave every visitor soothed or elevated: there is something disturbing to her quality, some hint of the morbid or the unhealthy. In some ways she is a dead city, rotting among her mementoes, but in others she is, like the rest of Japan, pulsing and proliferating with hybrid life, part ordered familiar past, part groping present. She is not serene, no longer Heian-kyo—the City of Peace.

Hardly anywhere in Kyoto is ever empty, except the cloistered family gardens or the remoter forest glades. Down every street the citizenry pushes with a babel of horns and a gallimaufry of styles, from the immaculate *obi* to the jeans and sweaters of rip-roaring adolescence. Through every brooding temple the Japanese tourists noisily pour—schoolchildren by the multitude, festooned in satchels and luncheon bags, honeymooners ceaselessly photographing each other, businessmen gravely bowing one another out of the sightseeing bus. At every holy portal the souvenir-sellers raucously greet you, brandishing their postcards or dangling their toy birds, and the mendicant ex-soldiers, in parade-ground travesty, salute you with a hook hand or stand their wooden legs to attention. The trains, those

Kyoto

unavoidable essentials of the Japanese scene, rumble through the night beside the river, and the taxis career maniacally among the rattling trams. Sometimes you may see a bride in kimono, but just as often you will see her in a hired Paris copy, with her bridegroom pin-striped and wing-collared, and her father displaying the unmistakable satisfaction of a man who is going to charge it all on his expense account. Kyoto has escaped the worst excesses of modern Japanese night life, which make Tokyo the brassiest of all capitals, but even here you will find your mock-Tudor saloons, your echoes of rock-'n'-roll, your long-haired delinquents, your Hi-Fi Jazz Coffee Tophat Bar. They play baseball in the shadow of Kyoto's shrines. They practise athletics around the wall of the Imperial Palace. In Kyoto today you can never be quite sure whether some picturesque bauble is an object of Shinto veneration or an advertising notion. She is a two-faced city: one head a phoenix, one a jackdaw.

Is she a ferocious city, too? Do there linger yet, among these symbols and sanctities, some old savageries of the Japanese spirit? Does a sword glint sometimes, up on the hill? Perhaps. Kyoto, for all her enclaves of perfection, feels a troubled place. Even the most fulsome of tourists may sometimes sense, as she passes from temple calm to highway frenzy, some buried malaise in the flavour of this great city. Kyoto is the soul of Japan, a microcosm of the inner nation. You may taste all the fascination of this astonishing country as you wander among Kyoto's marvels—the Sparrow Chamber or the Wild Geese Chamber, the Silver Pavilion or the Hall of a Thousand Mats, the paintings of the Thirty-Six Famous Poets, the effigy lacquered with the ashes of the sage Shinran, the Veranda of the Archery Contest, the immortal garden of Ryuanji: but you may feel obscurely ill at ease in the Hall of the Imperial Visits, and all too likely the blare of a loudspeaker or the vicious hooting of a taxi horn will drown the sound resembling the song of a Japanese bush warbler.

LA PAZ

Southwards from the glistening steel-blue Titicaca runs the highway through the Bolivian altiplano, leaving the Peruvian highlands behind. To the east stand the splendours of the Andean cordillera, rank upon rank of noble snow-peaks, but the road passes through a landscape more lunar than celestial, an arid, drear, friendless kind of country, fourteen thousand feet above the sea. It is littered with the poor mud huts of the Aymara Indians, and the piles of stones they have scraped and scrabbled from their miserable soil, and sometimes you meet a peasant with his donkeys or his llamas, and sometimes you set the dust flying in an adobe village, and sometimes you see far away across the wilderness some solitary Indian woman, like a huddled witch on a moor, hastening bent-back across the rubble.

For sixty miles the road plods on through this monotony, and then it falls over a precipice. Suddenly it crosses the lip of the high plateau and tumbles helter-skelter, lickety-split into a chasm: and as you slither down the horse-shoe bends you see in the ravine below you, secreted in a fold of the massif, the city of La Paz. Her red roofs and mud huts pile up against the canyon walls and spill away into the river valley below. All around her is the immensity of the altiplano, and high above her to the south meditates the lovely white mountain called Illimani, where the royal condor of Inca legend folded its great wings in sleep. La Paz is the highest of the world's big cities, at twelve thousand feet. She is a tumultuous, feverish, often maddening, generally harum-scarum kind of place: but nobody with an eye to country or a taste for drama could fail to respond to her excitements, or resist the superb improbability of her situation.

After such an approach, in such an environment, you might reasonably expect to find, like the old voyagers, men with three eyes, or heads slung beneath their shoulders. Well, La Paz does her best. Consider a few simple facts about the city. Her atmosphere is so

La Paz

rarefied that virtually the only purpose of the single municipal fire engine is to squirt indelibly coloured water at political demonstrators. One of her liveliest institutions is a smugglers' trade union, the Syndicate of Frontier Merchants, and by far her best shopping centre is the *mercado negro*, a vast open-air emporium of illegally imported goods in which I once ran into a very respectable Customs official happily buying himself some illicit gramophone records. Half the women of this city wear bowler hats, reverently removing them when they enter a church, and among the old-fashioned cottage remedies readily available are foetus of llama, skin of cat, and horn of armadillo. La Paz has known 179 coups and revolutions since Bolivia became independent in 1825, and her currency is such that when I emptied my pockets there one day I found myself in possession of 683,700 bolivianos (I needed a million odd to pay my hotel bill, plus a few thousand, of course, for the bell-boy).

There, I am laughing at her, but only with wry affection, for I have seldom found a city more enthralling. She is anything but comic, beneath the veneer. She is pathetic, tragic, stimulating and menacing, and she still retains some of the savage glare and glitter that the Spaniards brought when they founded her four centuries ago. She is not in herself a beautiful place. Her few old buildings are swamped in half-hearted modernism, and all around her in the bowl of her canyon the Indians have built their terraced streets of mud and corrugated iron; but she possesses nevertheless, to an almost eccentric degree, the quality of individualism. She is a brittle metropolis. There is nowhere else much like her on the face of the earth, but if I had to find an analogy I would suggest some quivering desert city, Amman, say, or Kairouan, miraculously transplanted to a declivity in the Tibetan plateau.

She is a city of the Andes, and it is the swarming Andean Indians who nowadays set her style. The men are sometimes striking enough, with their ear-flapped woollen hats and Inca faces; but the women are fascinating beyond description. With their rakishly cocked bowler hats, their blinding blouses and skirts, their foaming flounces of petticoats, the babies like infant potentates upon their backs and the sandals made of old tyres upon their feet—gorgeously accoutred and endlessly industrious, plumed often with a handsome dignity and assurance, they give to La Paz a flavour part gipsy, part coster, and all pungency. There are, I swear it, no more magnificent ladies in the world than the market-women of La Paz. Bowlers cockily atilt,

La Paz

like bookies', they sit high on trestle tables in the covered market,
their bosoms grandly heaving beneath white overalls, their faces at
once lofty, cunning, all-observant and condescending; and they are
invested so closely by all their wares, so heaped about with pineapples and bananas, so wallowing in papayas, mandarins, nuts and
flowers, that they put old Marvell quite in the shade, in the luscious
sensuality of the lives they lead.

It is an Indian, highland turbulence that keeps this city tense and
wary, and makes the midnight curfew more the rule than the
exception. In the halls of Congress, beneath the painted scrutiny of
Bolívar and Murillo, they are mostly Spanish faces, declaiming Latin
polemics; but high in the balcony above the debate, peering silently
over the railing, are the dark, attentive, enigmatic eyes of the
Aymaras. In La Paz you feel everywhere the rising awareness of the
Indian people, together with the smouldering of latent violence. It is
a city of rumours and echoes. Sometimes the tin miners of Catavi are
about to march upon the capital, dragging their hostages behind
them. Sometimes, before daybreak, you may hear the tread of
marching feet and the singing of slogans outside your window.
Sometimes masked carabinieri, slung about with tommy-guns, ran-
sack your car for arms, and sometimes you find a chain slung across
the city gate on the hilltop, and a civilian with a rifle vigilantly beside
it. Fifteen years ago the mob of La Paz hung the mutilated body of
their President from a lamp-post in the Plaza Murillo, and today the
old square is stiff with soldiers, in German steel helmets and thick
high-collared jackets, self-consciously ceremonial on little platforms
outside the Presidency, unobtrusively watchful upon the roof of the
Cathedral.

All this passion, all this energy, thumps through the city night
and day, sharpened into something knife-like and tremulous by the
breathless clarity of the altitude. You can feel it on the promenade of
the Prado at weekends, when the wide-eyed girls and men with small
moustaches chatter with a gay intensity at the tables of the Copacabana. You can hear it in the conversations of the place, dark with
plots but humorous with tall stories, cynical but often secretive. You
can see it in the slogans daubed on almost every wall, with their
baffling permutations of political initials and the paint that drips
down in frenzied blobs from their exhortations. You can even see it
reflected in the smiling, bustling and wagging of the city's enchant-

La Paz

ing Carpaccio dogs. The marvellous glacial air of La Paz, which sends the tourists puffing and dizzy to their beds, makes for fizz, bounce, and heady enthusiasm, and the isolation of this queer city, mountain metropolis of a land-locked State, gives it a sense of introvert obsession.

And most of all you will know the pressure of La Paz if you visit the high Indian quarters after dark. They tumble and straggle dustily upon the hillside, dim-lit and padlocked, but at night they are tumultuous with activity. It is not a noisy sort of energy—it has a padded, hushed insinuation to it—but it is tremendously purposeful and intent. Crouching along every alley are the indefatigable street sellers, huddled about some hissing brazier, or sprawling, a confusion of skirts, shawls and babies, behind their stalls of mandarins. Hundreds of candles illuminate the pavement counters; beneath a multitude of canvas awnings, like the market restaurants of Singapore, the Indians eat their thick stews or sip their coca tea; outside each dark and balconied courtyard, the caravanserai of La Paz, the lorries are preparing for the dawn journey—down to the steaming Yungas for tropical fruits and jungle vegetables, across the altiplano for the fabulous rainbow trout of Titicaca.

The scene is shadowy and cluttered, and you cannot always make out the detail as you push through the crowd; but the impression it leaves is one of ceaseless, tireless energy, a blur of strange faces and sinewy limbs, a haze of ill-understood intentions, a laugh from a small Mongol in dungarees, a sudden stink from an open drain, a cavalcade of tilted bowlers in the candlelight—and above it all, so clear, so close that you confuse the galaxies with the street lamps, the wide blue bowl of the Bolivian sky and the brilliant, cloudless stars of the south.

But here's an odd thing. When you come to La Paz from the north, over the escarpment, she seems a very prodigy among cities; but if you drive away from her towards Illimani and the south, looking back over your shoulder as you cross the last ridge, why, all the magic has drained from her, all the colour has faded, all that taut neurosis seems an illusion, and she looks like some drab old mining camp, sluttish among the tailings.

LENINGRAD

I first flew into Leningrad out of the wintry womb of Russia, and she seemed to me that morning like a city of light.

Peter the Great called her his 'window on the West', and she remains a look-out still, watchfully Western in style and manner, a magnificent artifact of Europe at the gateway to Asia. They have tamed Leningrad and harnessed her, driven away her emperors, turned her palaces into museums and her academies for young ladies into political offices—coarsened her exquisite restaurants, exiled her fan-makers and her riding-masters, swamped her bookshops with dialectical materialism, deconsecrated her cathedrals, humbled her hierarchies, stifled her frivolities, left her great avenues peeling and pining. Yet she rides above her fate like the queen she is, and seemed to me that day, as I flew out of the horny Ukraine, still a Cleopatra among cities.

Leningrad is more than just a geometrical, but actually an astronomical metropolis: for Moskovsky Prospekt, the southern entry to the place, is not only six miles long and dead straight, but runs along the meridian from the Pulkovo Observatory on the southern heights. Calm, precise, and elegant seemed the city that morning as I drove along this celestial boulevard: a thoroughbred still, balanced and proportioned, with no uncanny Mongolesque skyscrapers to mar the skyline, only a serenity of classical colonnades, baroque mansions, domes and gilded steeples. Sea-light and snow-light filtered perpetually through the structures and shone icily from the broad frozen stream of the Neva, scattered with islands, lined with impeccable architecture, and running away between the quaysides to the Gulf of Finland and points west.

Dazzled, the scales of the Ukraine still in my eyes, I wandered through all this lucidity. Across the river the sunshine gleamed miraculously upon the golden finger-spire of St. Peter and St. Paul, slim as a stiletto above its ramparts. In the upstairs galleries of the

Leningrad

Hermitage, flooded in sunshine and surveying a brilliant landscape of white, gold, and baroque, the great Renoirs, Gauguins, Monets, and blue Matisses stood there in gorgeous vivacity, to be inhaled like a fragrance or gulped like a draught of some exalting wine. Russia in winter is a dread and dreary country, clogged alike with sludge and dogma; but fly into Leningrad as I did, and your very glands will be rejuvenated.

For all her shrines of materialist revolution, her thumping industrial fringe, the atomic submarines upon her slipyards—for all these signs of the times Leningrad retains, like an ageless courtesan, many an inessential charm. I bought a batter-wrapped sausage that morning from a solemn woman in a white overall at a street-corner stand. I found a 1905 Baedeker Russia in the jumble of an old-school bookshop, inscribed in a spindly German hand in the ink of long ago. I strolled among the hidden statues of the Summer Garden, each one locked away for the winter, like a wayward nymph in a rock, inside its own little wooden house. I wondered at the profusion of fresh flowers on the tomb of Peter the Great, and I gazed from the balcony of St. Isaac's Cathedral upon the glinting steeple of the Admiralty, like a Buddhist stupa above the ice, and the fabulous immensities of the Winter Palace, where the Tsars lived in immeasurable splendour and the revolutionaries stormed their way into history. In Moscow it is difficult not to feel a kind of snob; in Leningrad you are a serf in untanned thigh-boots, gaping at the carriages and climaxes of the past.

For this is a city with the gift of timelessness. Elsewhere most Russians seem so unalluring that it is a mystery to me how the reproduction of the species is maintained. Here there are still girls of a haunting and nostalgic beauty, such as you meet in the pages of the immortal novelists, and men of a natural elegance beyond class or era. Forgotten Western echoes, too, linger suggestively on. I observed two young diplomatists in my hotel, wearing heavy coats and high fur hats, whose immemorial English faces and languid long-limbed attitudes at the reception desk made them look like thrusting fur traders from Eastcheap, awaiting a concession from the Empress. I drank my morning coffee in a shop that might have sprung from Imperial Vienna, and I listened to jazz so brassily honky-tonk that I might have been in some forgotten burlesque of the Loop, thirty years ago in Chicago.

Leningrad

Leningrad is a humorous city. The cloak-room attendant puts your hat on your head with a delightful parody of courtly excess. Even the official guides are slyly amused by the presence in the Anti-God Museum (the museum, that is, of the History of Religion and Atheism) of a section reverently devoted to the adulation of Lenin. The young people of Leningrad, often rakishly and sometimes brazenly dressed, preserve a sense of bubbly fun: traces of taste, style, and delicacy have survived the convulsion, and there are still a few citizens whose clothes fit and whose eyes are lit with a glint of gaiety.

There are modernistic trams in Leningrad—devices I had hitherto regarded as a contradiction in terms. There are polite and mercifully unobtrusive policemen. There is a mosque like something out of Isfahan, a square in which practically every building is a theatre, a house once inhabited by the inventor of the aeroplane (twenty years, I need hardly say, before the Wrights), a Wedding Palace for the white weddings now officially encouraged in Russia, a mammoth in a museum, a vase weighing nineteen tons and twenty-five Rembrandts. Even the snow-ploughs do their work with a special kind of symmetry, moving around Palace Square in lumpish ever-decreasing circles, like old-fashioned reapers, until at last they can revolve no more, and a squad of cheerful women with brooms and shovels leaps through their clouds of exhaust to remove the last central pile of snow, where the hare should be.

I went to a children's puppet theatre in the afternoon and watched its entrancing fooleries among an audience so enthusiastically disorganized that it made the end-of-term play at an English village school feel like Order in opposition to Chaos. And in the evening I saw *Die Fledermaus*, staged with a genuine rollicking panache, and so instinct with the magic of the waltz, the whirl of white skirts and the flick of tail-coats, that when I inspected the faces of the women about me, Soviet proletarians every one, I found them glazed with a true suburban enchantment.

They gave me champagne at dinner, placing a neatly folded napkin like a white cone over the bottle-top, and very late that night, with the fizz still in me, I slithered down the river bank beside the Admiralty, and crunched a path across the frozen Neva. The sky above me was a deep cold blue. The lights of the city shone dimly off the ice, like phosphorescence. The golden steeple of the Admiralty was floodlit and resplendent, an archangel's wand in the night, and

Leningrad

beneath the bridge I could just make out the three tall funnels of the old cruiser *Aurora*, and the speckled lights of her portholes. Leningrad lay lucent still, even at midnight, and seemed to me like an exemplar, a paradigm, an obituary of the European ideal.

Next morning a fog fell upon the city, and you could not see across the river from one side to the other.

LIMA

Four and a quarter centuries ago Francisco Pizarro the conquistador founded the city of Lima, and to this day he dominates it.

He was an illiterate adventurer, a swashbuckler whose savage but indomitable energies had contemptuously toppled the Incas from their golden thrones, and it was against all the augurs that he chose this place for the Spanish capital of Peru. The site was suggested to him, so tradition says, by resentful Indians convinced that its rotting vapours and humidity would soon kill all the Spaniards off. To north and south stretched a desiccated wasteland, to the west lay the unknown Pacific, from the east the dry Andean foothills slouched down to the sea. Beyond the mountains brooded the wildest of hinterlands, tangled with steaming forests, patrolled by weird tribes, frequented by tapirs, anacondas and creatures of unsuspected fantasy. Earthquakes repeatedly ravaged the area, rain scarcely fell there, and throughout the winter a damp, dank vapour hung low over the place, blanketing the narrow plain like smoke in a saucer. Yet Pizarro's city flourished, flaunted itself, and grew prodigiously in consequence. Lima became the headquarters of a Spanish viceroy, the seat of a powerful bishopric, and eventually the capital of the Peruvian Republic. For several generations she was the greatest city in South America, and legends of perfumed allure surrounded her name. In culture, in elegance, in wealth, in reputation she stood alone among the cities of the New World—'the fairest gem', as the historian Prescott wrote, 'on the shores of the Pacific'. She was called the City of the Kings, because her site was selected upon the Feast of the Epiphany: but she was really the city of Pizarro.

Even now, four centuries later, the spirit of that old freebooter dominates the Peruvian capital. His lofty splendour glimmers down its boulevards, his opulence fructifies its suburbs, his cruelty still corrupts its attitudes. Like man, like city. Pizarro was a character of fascinating bestiality, and Lima is a metropolis of heartless charm.

Lima

Beside the Plaza de Armas, the heart of the place, an equestrian statue of the conquistador stands in lordly sentinel: his sword is fiercely and permanently drawn, and this is both apposite and inevitable, for by a quirk very characteristic of his great city, the sculptor has neglected to give him a scabbard.

Lima is the city aristocratic. She is to the manner born. She lies only twelve degrees south of the equator, on a line with Angola and Madagascar, but beside her coastline there flows the cool stream of the Humboldt Current, where the Antarctic whales court and whelp, and beneath her bridges there leaps out of the mountains the boulder-strewn River Rimac (which has given its name, clumsily mispronounced by the conquerors, to the city itself). Lima is no sweaty equatorial market-place, as the map might suggest. On the contrary, she has a quality icy, aloof and self-possessed, like a grandee in a Velázquez canvas, or a high-bred filly in the ring. Even her neighbouring deserts feel like chaperons, sheltering a sensitive charge against vulgarity. Even the winter smog seems to veil the city in a gentlemanly indolence, and indeed the fond citizens of Lima prefer to call it their *niebla perlada*—'pearly haze'. It is true that Lima is no longer a conventionally beautiful city. Generations of philistines have done their worst to her, demolishing old treasures willy-nilly and swamping her in mediocrity. Her distinction, though, is not physical, nor even animal, but pre-eminently atmospheric, a matter of suggestions and evocations, the shifting shadow of a tree on a rococo façade, the squeak of an elderly tram beneath your window, clattering hoofs and trumpet calls at breakfast, sweet shrill street cries, the smell of incense and laundered surplices, legends of courtesans and magnificos, repercussions of old arrogance.

The heart of Lima is the Plaza de Armas, the finest square in South America. Pizarro laid it out himself, and here more than anywhere else you may sense how powerfully his imperial hauteur still colours the capital. Through this place the whole of Peruvian history has marched, in endless parade of triumph and bloodshed— shootings and garrottings, feuds and reconciliations, the last ignominies of condemned revolutionaries, the ultimate glories of patriots. Look around you, and you may feel the very air heavy with the past. There stands the superb Cathedral, whose first beam, so legend says, was carried across the threshold on Pizarro's own hefty shoulders: a frowning, echoing, twilit edifice, haunted by pilgrims

Lima

and high memories, with the Captain-General's mummified corpse, strangely shrunken with the centuries, displayed in a glass case in a corner chapel. There beside it is the Archbishop's Palace, elaborate with balconies, sculptured scrolls, lions' heads and obelisks, from which generations of crimson divines exerted their authority— mighty men with flamboyant names, like Santo Toribo de Mogrejezo or Jeronimo de Loayza, sometimes gifted with such powers of command that they were not only archbishops, but Viceroys of Peru at the same time. There is the City Hall, grandly arcaded, with the ensign of the Republic nobly billowing above its roofs, built upon the very spot where, until the Spaniards stormed this way, a local satrap of the Incas held his feathered court. And there on the north side, gay but grandiose, stands the big white Presidential Palace, among its palms and courtyards: in that same place Pizarro lived and ruled, and there his enemies fell upon him at last, leaving him to trace the sign of the cross in his own dying blood upon the floor.

Among the great fountain in the centre of the Plaza sixteen stubby bronze monsters, crouching grotesquely pick-a-back, have been spouting water without a pause for three and a half centuries. Outside the Palace gates a squad of Peruvian dragoons stands in perpetual sentry-go, squat hunched men with Indian faces, wearing plumed brass helmets, spurs, boots, huge epaulettes, swords and white gloves, and looking at once elegant, suspicious and formidable. Across the way a tramways man diligently shifts the streetcar points with an iron poker. Nearby, on an alley corner, a public weighing-machine stands like a severe confessor, for night and day, year after year, its mechanisms nag and prod the passer-by, with flashings and winkings and clicking noises, and out of its recesses there oscillates a placard with the searching challenge *YA se pesó HOY?*—as if to demand of every transient Christian if he has weighed his sins that day in the balance. Structurally the Plaza de Armas has often been rebuilt. Spiritually it has taken the explosive centuries as they have come, and blandly removed their detonators.

All around this famous centre-piece sprawls the City of the Kings, and though the rich Limenians have long moved out to the palatial suburbs, and a certain blight of tourism and neglect has settled upon the city centre, nevertheless it is still the crowded, antique streets around the Cathedral that set the character of Lima, and sustain her pungency. Sometimes they are spacious enough, sometimes they

Lima

are so awkward that a tram with a list to port and a bus inclining starboard can pose insoluble problems of navigation: but whatever their design, they have a crooked flavour. This is a subtle sort of city, alive with quibbles, fancies, private jokes and nicknames—Avenida Nicolas de Pierola is the proper name of the street that runs across the Plaza San Martín, but for donkey's years everyone in Lima has called it *La Colmena*, The Beehive. It is a metropolis of grace-notes and allusions, with an Eastern sense of the picaresque, and a crab-apple astringency.

Innumerable small churches, set in minute *piazuelas* among the hurly-burly, give to this part of the city an inescapable twinkle of surprise. Each has some curious marvel of its own: in one a miraculous image, in another the relic of some gentle saint, in a third the tomb of Don Ambrosio O'Higgins, Irishman, Marquis of Osorno, Captain-General of Chile and Grand Marshal of Peru. In the Church of San Agustín there stands a figure of Death, armed and skeletonic, so horrific that its own sculptor, chancing to enter the vestry one evening, is said to have died of fright when he saw it grinning at him through the shadows. On a wall of the Church of Las Nazarenas is the holy image called the Lord of the Miracles, found among the debris of an earthquake in 1687, and now the talisman of a fervent processional cult. In the cloisters of Santo Domingo the canaries of the monastic aviary nibble their corn-cob among the mosaics. Beneath the floor of San Francisco lie, in a musty labyrinth of catacombs, the tumbled skulls and skeletons of a thousand dead monks, tied together like asparagus in anatomical bundles, displayed in ornamental arrangements of ribs, or still seated in cowls and cassocks in rickety kitchen chairs. In the Sanctuary of Santa Rosa, the patron saint of the Americas, you may see the garden in which bloomed the first of all American rose-bushes, and the well into which the virgin threw the keys of the agonizing chains she had locked around her own waist (the garden is open to everyone once a year, but Santa Rosa's chapel may be visited only by the President of Peru himself). The Convent of La Merced was founded by Fray Miguel de Orens, 'an enthusiastic monk', so the guide-book says, 'who arrived in Peru at the age of 110'. The mosaics of San Francisco were made by a man who took refuge in those cloisters after committing a *crime passionnel*. Everywhere you trip over such details of piquancy, sometimes refulgent with sanctity, sometimes dark with intolerance, always rich in a kind of easy eccentricity, a liberty of

Lima

style that sprang from a society very sure of itself, its privileges, its opportunities and its God.

Indolent individualism infuses, too, the old palaces of Lima, now mostly decayed into commercialism or crumbled into disuse. Sometimes news-stands or trinket stalls occupy their pompous portals, and their courtyards are stacked with bales of cloth or ironmongery, like Syrian caravanserai. Sometimes they have been divided among a dozen poor families, and are bursting with washing, animals and cheerful children, like the Tsarist town houses of Odessa. But usually they bear themselves like great mansions still, for all the erosions of time. Tall and gaunt are their peeling walls, austere but condescending their staircases, florid but melancholy their patios, wonderfully cool their *salons*, and high above the streets there still project, like harem peepholes above the traffic lights, the shuttered wooden balconies, the famous *miradors* of Lima, from which the ladies of the household used to spy upon the lusty world below.

The Peruvian Foreign Office occupies one such house, a former Prime Minister owns another, but the best-loved of them all is linked only with the name of a woman of fortune—La Perricholi, 'The Half-Caste Bitch', who turned the head of every Peruvian grandee as lesser ladies twist the handle of a corkscrew. It lies on the northern outskirts of the city, almost on the desert's edge, and it is supremely evocative of Lima's languorous heyday. Its gardens are soft and exotically scented, its bowers are deliciously secluded, its gazebos are delicately light-hearted, fresh little streams run through its flower-beds, and even the fact that it is now partly occupied by a school of military music, so that in any dainty summer-house you may find a trumpeter earnestly practising his fanfares, or a trombonist exercising his wrists—even the queer thumpings and *glissandi* of Peruvian Sousa cannot dispel its shades of old flirtation, or drown the ghostly rustle of its silks.

Most of all the essence of this old Lima is crystallized in Union Street, one of the great urban thoroughfares of the Americas, which strides lively but peremptory through the centre of the colonial city. This is a street of idiosyncrasies, with an air of tight self-sufficiency, like Bond Street in London fifty years ago, the sedater parts of the Kalverstraat in Amsterdam, or the once-glittering Sharia Sharif Pasha in Alexandria. Some of its shops have polished brass rails affixed to their façades, for the support of tottering window-shoppers, and they boast a baroque variety of names—Pinky,

Lima

Oxford, Casa Persia, Le Chic Parisien, René, Grand Bon Marché de Lima, and even, like a faithful hen among those phoenixes, Sears, Roebuck of Chicago. One bookshop is frequented by a little tame ape, one cinema claims to be the only anonymous movie-house on earth—they removed its name during a renovation, and never bothered to put it back. A wild range of Peruviana stares out from the shop-fronts of this street, from Inca jugs and aboriginal masks to stuffed llamas, vicuña wools, turkeys in beaten silver, alpaca slippers and decorative gourds. A splendid cross-section of Lima's citizenry saunters or staggers along its pavements: policemen in white tropical topees, looming quixotically through the pearly haze; stooped Indian women, in felt hats and tousled blouses, with babies shrouded upon their backs, and festoons of bags and bundles attached to their persons; newspaper-boys no bigger than monkeys themselves, and pavement vendors with polychromatic arrays of combs and toothbrushes laid out with infinite precision upon the side-walk; flighty girls arm in arm, each with an ornamental hair-clip at the side of her head, as though she has inadvertently left a curler in; soldiers, too, in coarse high-buttoned tunics or elaborate gold braid, and bawling lottery-sellers, and nuns in huge white waving coifs, like the wings of early flying machines, and eager tourists disguised in ponchos, and beldames in black crossing themselves outside La Merced, and pomaded bigwigs bowing to each other with smiling formality, like old-school Japanese, outside the Aereo Club, and many a poor blistered beggar, palms uppermost and eyes downcast, slinking from door to door or statuesque beside an intersection. Union Street is traditional Lima in microcosm. Its jumbled and fretted beguilement, tarnished by a tinsel commercialism, exactly expresses the rather faded, slightly seedy, elderly fund of style bequeathed to this metropolis by its fiery progenitors, and never quite exhausted.

They were men of greed, Pizarro and his men-at-arms, who made incalculable fortunes in Peru, and demanded as ransom from one poor Inca emperor enough gold to fill his cell of captivity from floor to ceiling. Lima remains an ostentatious city, instinct with ingots and goblets, with a gourmet's palate and a playboy's gaiety. Nowhere on the Pacific coast of the Americas, not even in San Francisco, can the rich man of taste enjoy himself more, feed himself better, house himself more luxuriously, surround himself with lovelier women or more exquisite possessions. Some of the finest private art collections on earth are locked away behind the garden walls and manservants of Lima, and one or two of the city's clubs are reputed to be the most expensive in all South America.

A swathe of affluence rings the gnarled core of inner Lima. Away to the south spread the golden suburbs, flowered and air-conditioned, running away through olive groves and gardens to the heavenly Pacific shore, where the penguins meditate offshore and the speedboats scud from one delight to another. Mellow but impeccable are these fortunate quarters, and marvellously rich in foliage— bougainvillaea spilling down its trellises, jasmines and jacaranda, yellow frangipani and flaming poinsettias, plumbago and hibiscus, and one mysterious shrub whose blossoms change colour as the sun goes down, the blue dying as the white unfolds its petals. This is the world of little black dresses and starched nursemaids, Chanel and country club, diffused in the misty sunshine elegantly, like the haughtier purlieus of Los Angeles. It has its race-courses and its night clubs, its golf courses and its polo field. It even has, tucked away improbably between the Avenida Antonio M. Quesada and the Avenida del Ejercito, its own imperturbable cricket club. Here the Ambassadors live, and the Peruvian millionaires. One house contains a collection of forty-five thousand pieces of ancient pottery, every single one dug up within the area of the owner's own country estate. Another houses the richest private assembly of arms in the world. A third is so excessively seignorial, so magnificent in porticoes, terraces and colonnades, that a simple Indian is said to have rung the doorbell one day and asked for a confessor, assuming it to be the Cathedral. These are suburbs in the grand manner, boudoirs and pleasure-houses for a City of Kings.

Sybaritic, too, are the pleasures this capital offers its visitors, high in new skyscraper eyries, or discreetly dim-lit among the courtyards and sculpted cherubs of old mansions. You may drink Pisco sour, most delicately biting of cocktails, made of Peruvian grape brandy, sugar syrup, lime, bitters and egg-white. You may eat succulent sea things out of the Humboldt Current, or noble meats from the *haciendas* of the interior, or fabulous rainbow trout from Titicaca, where they grow to thirty pounds in waters 12,500 feet above the sea, or spiced creole dishes out of the Peruvian past—beef chunks soused in vinegar and chili sauce, doughnuts made of yuccas, eggs and syrup of molasses. You may roister away the night

Lima

hours at Ed's Bar, the Bagatelle, the Black Out or the Rancho. You may struggle with chopsticks and abalone in Chinatown, or dance till dawn beside the Pacific breakers. Lima is a city of luscious escapism, where the oil-men of the deserts come to wash it off and live it up, where the befurred, doll-like, neat-ankled women of the city eat gargantuan quantities of cream cakes among the potted palms of the Bolívar Hotel, and where many a rip-roaring adventurer, jumping ship at Callao or bumming down from California, can still throw his money away with carefree and uncensured extravagance.

She is not a very cultured city nowadays. Her theatre is vestigial, her newspapers are unremarkable, her poets, writers and thinkers not often distinguished. But she is a city that knows to a nicety how to please herself, a sensual city, a city where money counts and the window table nearly always has, so the waiter informs you with a sniff, already been reserved.

From all this fun and privilege, cruelty springs. Cruelty haunts this moneyed city, as it distorted the energies of the conquering gold-hunters, and makes the last taste of Lima acrid in the mouth. The best vantage point in the capital is the hill of San Cristobal, which rises steep and pyramidical within sight of the Presidential Palace, covered with ash-like dust and crowned with a cross of pilgrimage (first placed there, as it happens, by Pizarro himself, in gratitude for the humiliating failure of an Indian revolt). From here you may survey the whole panorama of the City of the Kings, from the drab wilderness of its attendant deserts to the ineffable blue sheen of the Pacific. The pale prosperous suburbs lie in a splurge of gardens. The brave new office blocks tower above the business streets. Lima of the Viceroys lies there intricate and higgledy-piggledy, a meshwork of greys, browns and duns. It is a splendid prospect, a famous one, with the Andes behind you and the ocean horizon in front.

Look below your feet, though, over the crest of the hill, and there lies misery: for straggling up towards the summit, clinging to San Cristobal like some nightmare belvedere, squats a slum so bestial, so filthy, so congested, so empty of light, fun, colour, health or comfort, so littered with excrement and garbage, so swarming with bare-foot children, so reeking with pitiful squalor that just the breath of it, borne on the fresh sea wind, makes you retch into your handkerchief. From these unspeakable hovels and rubbish-piles a stench of degradation rises: it veils the City of the Kings in a kind of

Lima

haze, and it even eddies around Pizarro's cross of thanksgiving, high on the top of the hill. Lima is a pleasure-drome indeed, but only for the few. When once you have climbed San Cristobal, you will never quite enjoy her Pisco sours again. Her garden delights will curdle in your mind, and all her style and pride and history will only stick in your gullet.

For all around her lie these dreadful slums, the notorious *barriaras* of Peru, in which 250,000 people live like gutter-creatures in the dirt, and they give to Lima the reproach of a guilty conscience. Wherever you go among her pleasures, the stink of the *barriaras* hangs over your shoulder, and already their presence intrudes uncomfortably, like the nagging insistence of the weighing-machine, into the equanimity of the city. Already the beggars shuffle through Union Street like scouts of Barbary, scare-crow mothers with pinched babies, shifty unshaven vagrants, an epileptic lop-sidedly staggering from door to door, a hunchback in the alley shadows. Already, when the comfortable citizens roll past this pitiable motley, on their way to clubs, fitting-rooms or mahogany desks, you may feel history rolling up its sleeves: and when the window of a car slides down, and some passing burgher tosses out a bank-note to the whimpering mendicants on the sidewalk—when such a man's limousine sweeps by, it does not need second sight to imagine tragedy crouching there in the back seat.

This is a city virtually without a middle class. There is almost nobody between the very rich and the cruelly poor. In Lima you can never forget that of every hundred baby Indians born alive in Peru, seventy die in infancy. There are few nice little, trim little houses in this city. You do not often hear the tidy hum of second-hand lawn-mowers on Sunday afternoons, or see the proudly polished family cars setting off for the seaside with pop and picnic baskets. This is, to a classic degree of symbolism, a revolutionary capital. It is run by a polished, cultivated oligarchy, but it is invested by the grievances of the poor. Injustice stalks its streets, and through its affairs runs constantly an undertone of apprehension, a shiver of expiring time. The ancient University of San Marcos, the oldest in the New World, is addled with the protests of young discontent, and the city is littered with the offices of the politicians, always plotting and arguing, always at each other's throats, with their strong-arm minions and their high-flown manifestos, their banners and their big drums. Lima is not essentially an energetic city—her attitudes are

Lima

languid, easy-going, often a little foppish: but into her froward politics, fed by unfairness and debasement, many a burning passion is poured. You cannot ignore the selfishness and rising anger of Lima, or evade her ghastly desolations, just as, when you read with admiring wonder about Pizarro's rumbustious courage, you cannot skip the bigotry and arrogance that scarred his record with evil.

(And if you are a hedonist born, and think you can easily stomach it all, try revisiting the *barriara* of San Cristobal in the early evening: for then, in the mist of the Peruvian dusk, you may sometimes descry the shapes of small children and brown pigs, side by side, snuffling about together in the garbage.)

So Lima is not a happy city. 'Woe and desolation', says Prescott, were brought by Pizarro and his followers to the devoted land of the Incas: and even now the pleasures of his capital soon turn sour. In many cities the determined visitor can dismiss the seamier realities from his mind, as he laughs his way from Gothic apse to cabaret. In Lima it cannot be done. You can blur the truth with alcohol, perhaps, drug yourself with bullfights and cloisters, swamp your sensibilities with seashore orgies or Titicaca trout. The most effective way to get the slum-taste off your tongue, though, if only for an afternoon, is to take a car to the archaeological museum, among the villas of San Isidro: for there you may retreat to the Peru that thrived before the Spaniards came, the dim legendary Peru of the Incas. You may marvel at the incomparable textiles of Cuzco, wonder at many a gorgeous mask and trinket, sense the unearthly majesty of the Sacsahuaman masonry, stumble dream-like through a menagerie of *huacos*—pots like llamas, pots like dragons, pots like old men, pots like spotted dogs, pots like fish, like cats, like skeletons, like pumas, like monkeys, like drooping but inscrutable owls.

Only there in that long-lost world, among the eerie Inca echoes, can you escape, till tea-time anyway, the sneer of Pizarro.

LONDON

Sometimes London still seems monumentally, almost excessively, herself—and especially at those affairs of State or pageantry that are tacitly intended to proclaim the continuity of this ancient capital. If it is reassurance you want, or a shot in your weary arm, or simply one of the supremely interesting experiences in contemporary travel, then you cannot do better than to walk down to the Mall on the day of the Trooping, and watch the Queen ride by.

All is there still, on such a day, all the swank, all the *noblesse oblige*, all the arcane symbolism. The sky is doubtless grey, the park across the way is delectably lush. The people around you are mostly jolly chars and housewives, fustily dressed in browns, greys and felt hats, but instinct with an air of happy collusion, as though they all know one another, and are linked in one long line of neighbourly acquaintance from Admiralty Arch to the Palace. The troops lining the street look fresh-faced and rather touching, the policemen are properly genial, the children seem to be enacting parts in a dramatized version of A. A. Milne, and presently you will see, undulating strangely above the crowd, the head of the Queen of England, in a tricorn hat. You can hardly see her horse for the people, but high above the soldiers and the policemen, as she paces grandly by, you may study her pale face—a sad, antique face, it seems at such a moment, young but tired, half commanding, half embarrassed, half person, half idea —a face, you may remember with mystic satisfaction, lined with the blood-heritage of Alfred the Great, William the Conqueror, Charlemagne, Roderigo the Cid, Barbarossa and Victoria the Queen-Empress.

Behind her there ride the captains of her guard, bent wizened old men, dressed up in bright uniforms like waxworks, or tall young aristocrats whose faces peer, small triangles of ruddy flesh, through the great straps of their helmets and bearskins. A blur of military consequence follows her down the Mall, a dazzle of harsh scarlet and

London

towering fur, scrubbed young faces, strutting subalterns, a beat and a blare of bands, the splendid swagger of drum-majors, clattering hoofs and jingling accoutrements and white plumes flying—and so she disappears, that talisman of London, like the painted image of a saint in another city's rituals, swaying and bobbing above the crowds, until her head is hidden behind a forest of bayonets, bearskins and polished helmets, the drums are only a muffled thudding in the distance, and the deep incessant roar of London floods in behind the trumpets.

So the old essence of London lurches by, on its way to a ceremony, and nothing seems to have changed. This still seems, at such a moment, the deepest and steadiest of all the capitals, still grey but vivid, still stabbed with pomp and sustained by old loyalties, still imperturbably addicted to foibles of style and tradition. Wait a few moments, though, till the glow has worn off. Wait till the magic has subsided, and you will find yourself nagged by second thoughts. Was that image of the Mall true or false? Did it properly represent this city still, or was it merely the last wan display of a dying society, or a kind of glorified leg-show? Was it pride, or was it pathos? Should you be stirred or saddened? Is it only the veneer that survives, or only the heart, or neither? London is a congenitally deceptive city, where nothing is quite explicit: and one of the most baffling historical puzzles of our time concerns the condition of this vast old body, whether she is still as stout as ever, or whether she is sickening, year by year, parade by parade, towards an ignominious obscurity.

The *idea* of London is immensely powerful—in a Proustian way, so that the very whirring of the mechanism that introduces the boom of Big Ben, heard on some distant crackling radio, can instantly evoke the smells, sounds and glowering light of this city. London possesses a power of instant recall, and she still feels immeasurably grand, a capital that stands beyond ordinary civic standards, and has some universal or microcosmic quality—the Great Wen, whose variety will interest you longer than life itself, from whose bridges, when her mighty heart lies still at last, you may feel that earth has nothing to show more fair. London still emanates tolerance, experience, caution, passive optimism—an almost Arab conviction, fostered by generations of Micawbers, that things are going to work out all right in the end. Asquith's 'Wait and see' might almost be her motto still,

London

so deeply instinctive is this city's lingering preference for delibera-
tion and reserve, so darkly, almost slyly, does it guard its own
convictions from the stranger. It is no coincidence that this is the
world's prime insurance market, for though the surface of London
life can often seem heedless, expressed in the gay badinage of the
bus conductor or the soda-siphon hilarities of the debs—though it
often appears reckless, beneath the gambler's bonhomie there lie
locked reserves of security, the family comradeships of the East End,
the calculated aspirations of the young gad-abouts, the frequent
ruthlessness of this exceedingly polite metropolis. London has
muddled through many a crisis, of war or of economics: but just as
few of her citizens really supposed that she could ever be beaten in
battle, so today, however wildly the Bank Rate fluctuates or the
trade gap widens, somehow she never seems likely to go bankrupt.

This is the principle of London, and the generality of this city,
the broad sweep and the instant impression, still rings true and
traditional. To most foreigners, the Londonness of London is
apparently still overwhelming. Even her fogs, from time to time,
still fulfil all Hollywood preconceptions. The variety of her everyday
life is still unexcelled in the Western world—the marvellous range
of her faces, for instance, stimulated rather than stifled by the
pressures of a class society, not so typed as those of the Parisians,
nor fused by circumstance and central heating, like those of the New
Yorkers, nor uniformly comfortable, educated and ordinary, like
those of the plump Scandinavians. The London pub is still a friendly,
fuggy place, even when its plush and whirligigs are swamped in
chrome modernity. The London railway terminus is still marvellously evocative, with its echoes, its snorting tank engines, its high
glass roof and its smells of steam, damp, mackintoshes and draught
beer. The Thames still looks like liquid 'istory, as old John Burns
described it, when the sun goes down over Westminster, or some
bright-lit warship anchors in the Pool. The parks of London are still
like lovely estates, the Georgian squares of London still suggest dry
sherry and lean intelligent women, the Rolls-Royces still stand
pensive and lordly in Harley Street, the taxis are still recognizably
cabs—with little windows to tap upon, when you want to speak to
the driver, and an air of brown dalliance inside. It is still a fine thing
to turn the bottom corner of Whitehall and find yourself face to face
with Westminster, the Abbey gaunt and pinnacled before you, the

London

flag brave as ever above Parliament, and all around you the shades of great men, the evocations of responsibility.

London is still a city of profound if stoical emotions—impersonal emotions mainly, concerned less with people than with ideas, less with love than with history, ambition, principle: and he is a dull traveller still who will not feel a tremor of pride or respect, to stand in a city that was for so long beloved, admired and obeyed.

Pride, respect—but also, a little later, perhaps, pity: for there is much pathos to London today, and when you descend from the general to the particular, from the hazed allure of the railway station to the punctuality of your own train, you will find that much of this city's life is seedy, frayed, threadbare. London may have kept her style, but she has lost her urbanity. Her breastplates may be burnished still, but her trousers are ill pressed. In the middle layers of her existence, between the royal splendours and the public instincts, she feels, just at the moment, disagreeably vacuous.

Fings, as the song says, ain't wot they used to be: and though this is perhaps true of most cities of the West, nowhere is it so forlornly apparent as it is in London, whose occupation's gone. A city is a reflection of history, and in London today history is taking a breather, or perhaps changing gear for the next hill. The spirit of London, that massive, grey, granite abstraction, has been supported for a century or more by the responsibilities of strength. This is a city made for command, an imperial city, too big for its islands, too big for its people, but built to stand at the centre of a vast structure of authority. The very look of London is the look of the law-giver, the arbiter or the governor-general. Now all is gone, you no longer see the sunburnt men of Empire uncomfortably pacing these streets, in floppy hats and thick-soled shoes, and Downing Street is no longer the world's supreme repository of power. It sometimes seems to me, as the moods of London infect me one by one, that the core or kernel of this city is accordingly rotted, like the shrivelled old ghost of a walnut that you sometimes find, beneath the wrinkled armour of its shell.

Not so long ago the essential characteristic of London, the thing that every foreign observer remarked, was her unshakable self-assurance. She did not give a damn. If she listened to alien criticisms at all, she dismissed them as frivolous or irrelevant, and her attitude to the world at large was one of unassailable, but not usually

London

arrogant, superiority. The world, rather grudgingly, respected this confidence, as a whole library of foreigners' books has demonstrated, and only twenty years ago indeed it stood to the nations as an earnest of all that was true, sane and decent, the tremendous opposite to Hitler's vulgar and maniac Berlin. Today, though, the certainty has gone with the responsibility. London can no longer govern the affairs of the earth, and like many an executive retired from business, she feels demoralized out of office. Her newspapers are streaked with self-doubt, grievance, puffed-up patriotism, delusions of pomp or persecution. Her businessmen are often to be seen lunching in sickly subservience with their American superiors, or looking ill at ease and slightly dishevelled with suave visitors from Zurich. Her patricians, once to be observed strolling down St. James's in marvellously leisured serenity, now look a little harassed, a little worn, even —that last betrayal of gentlemanly values—a little cross. Her policemen are testier and more hectoring than they used to be, her cockneys less uninhibited, her drivers worse-tempered, her green places more hideously littered with cigarette packages and old newspapers, making a mockery of the Englishman's legendary respect for the proprieties. London feels at odds and ends. She has lost the unity of assurance.

For once you break through that haze of nostalgic fulfilment, that glitter of Horse Guards in the morning, you will find that nearly everything that is unique to London seems somehow on the defensive, if it has not already been humiliated. The oligarchy that ruled this city so long, the polished ruling class of London, has gone to seed, surviving floridly in board rooms and interior decorators' *salons*, but no longer powerful or determined enough to set the tone of the city. So far no new cohesive social force has emerged to succeed it, and London is left groping between a variety of values and cultures, some American, some European, some Afro-Asian— some ennobling and inspiriting, some merely dingy. London elegance, once the cynosure of fashion, has lost its pre-eminence to Milan or New York, and now has to be jazzed up, as often as not, with Italian lapels or Ivy League trouser-bottoms. London comfort, essentially a full-blooded, cold-climate, insular affair, has been tarnished by false brightness and pastel shades—epitomized above all by the ubiquitous espresso bars of the city, peeling and fading a little now, but still emblazoned with Polynesian fabrics and Sicilian basketware, or unaccountably hung about with fishing nets. The old

234

London

London glories of Lords and the Oval have a dated ring to them, and through the thoroughfares of this traditionally phlegmatic place there now rush, in a perpetual game of cops and robbers, the armoured cars of the security companies, their drivers got up like Chicago policemen, their shotguns ready for action, their tyres screaming as they skid in perpetual frenzy from office to bank vault. The tessellations and elaborate conceits essential to the flavour of this pre-eminently *fin de siècle* city are disappearing one by one, and in their places rise the mock-skyscrapers, the half-way buildings, which do not look like proper buildings at all, but only like pallid plastic imitations of architecture.

Today London feels a superficially Latinized capital, partly because she has been flooded with immigrants from warmer climes, Italians, Cypriots or Jamaicans, but mostly because her temperament has changed. Deprived of the satisfactions of power, disillusioned with the benefits of puritanism, dominated no longer by a masterful gentry, saddled with all the disappointments of lost dominion, she has burst out in gaudy pleasure and opportunism. She is vividly, almost hysterically, alive, exuding push, excitement, colour and life —but life, it seems to me, of an essentially unvirile or infertile kind. She feels as though she no longer gets gloriously plastered on ale or Scotch whisky, but only lascivious on champagne cocktails—as though her young men have forgotten how to swear, but learnt how to slander. She feels at last what Napoleon thought she was, a retail city: no longer—or so it seems—pondering immense decisions of trade, industry and statesmanship, but bound on the never-never to the chain stores and the mail-order houses, fed on tinned cream cheeses, beautified with home perms, stuffed with sickly chocolates and packed in cellophane. London has lost her sense of privacy, and she feels, perhaps for the first time in her often rumbustious and generally warlike history, more female than male.

Nothing wrong with that: many of the most formidable Londoners have been women, as every Dickensian knows. London's leathery atmosphere, compounded of brief-cases and club legends, has long been outworn anyway, and she has badly needed some blither upholstery. What is sad is not the undeniable new zing and sparkle of London today, but the strain of bitterness which seems to be curdling the temper of this city—a frustrated, mocking, envious feeling, suggestive partly of that soured haven, New York, and

London

partly, I fear, of Berlin under the Weimar Republic. An inescapable sense of pique or bile is coarsening the temper of this capital, and it springs out of envious uncertainty.

The old citadels of London life have not been stormed, but only discredited—not replaced by something better, but only cast aside with a sneer. The new London is not evolving in fulfilment or consolidation, or even in pride. She is rising rather upon foundations of envy and disillusion. Hardly anything London does nowadays is really big, or altogether new, or quite the best, or even entirely hers. Almost everything is derivative, second-class, tongue-in-cheek. She has lost the touch of greatness. Satire is the watchword of this new and meaner London—satire being, in the new definition, the practice of being unpleasant about everything, and respectful towards nothing at all (not what Dr. Johnson had in mind, when he defined it as 'a poem in which wickedness and folly are censured'). Scepticism has always been an agreeable London trait, but now it is being distorted into cynicism, into the belief that nothing, however loved, however honoured, however well tried, is really sacred or worth while. A newly vicious element has entered the political exchanges of this generous old city—not the traditionally boisterous give-and-take of parliamentary politics, but something more querulous and bitchy. A new petulant superiority informs the conversations of its intellectuals, as they find themselves ever more influential in a community that has lost the taste for action. Almost the only original social phenomenon contemporary London has fostered has been the hang-dog running protest of the nuclear disarmers, whose ideal is noble indeed, but who have made it all squalid with their grotesque and grubby accoutrements, the limp strumming of their guitars, and their manner of faintly narcotic self-righteousness— living symbols, as they lie flat on their backs in Trafalgar Square, of a capital that has lost the power of active decision.

Poor London, whose lion regnant once decreed the destinies of the world, now reduced to a yapping dog-in-manger!

Or is she? Were we right the first time? Is it the idea of London that is true, or the appearance, the atmosphere or the detail, the glorious hissing murk of Paddington or the dirty little electric train, ten minutes late from Esher? Sometimes you may feel, when she seems almost beyond hope, that in fact you have grasped the wrong end of a slippery stick, and that away at the other end of it, peering over

London

its antique silver knob, this venerable city is grinning slyly back at you, with a finger on the side of her nose. She is a city of deceptions and double-takes. Generations of observers have pronounced her melancholy obituary, only to be disconcerted by her virility in the end, and it may be that even now, behind her gaudy new exterior, the principle of London is undaunted after all. She is so old, so secretive, so swamp-like in her appetites, like some vast and imperceptibly gurgling quicksand—could it be that even now she is, once again, absorbing and digesting all her diverse new elements, her foreign energies and her domestic uncertainties, only to fertilize yet another flowering of her glory? Is she, like some huge grinding mechanism, only churning up the ore, to yield it at last in ingots or taconite?

Today she seems the most tentative of all the great capitals, the least confident of purpose or function, the least true to herself: but it is hard to believe that a city of such tremendous character can really have lost its spirit in two short decades. There is something about her decline that rings false—perhaps its very abruptness, for cities are like people, and do not easily rot. London feels as she does, I think, because she is a city that moves in cycles. She is an island capital, an offshore meeting-place or conduit, through which ideas and influences pour in successive waves. She is a city of merchant venturers, whose fortunes depend upon the enterprises of England—now in America, now in India, now in Africa, now in Europe itself. She is also a city of actors, governed by a profound sense of timing—and just at the moment, restrained by caution, exhaustion, and a sort of historical aestheticism, she is marking time. If she feels eclipsed today, it is partly by choice, or instinct. She could still cut a flaming figure in the world, if she chose to throw her weight about, refused to co-operate, beat a big irresponsible drum, blazoned her intention of going it haughtily alone. She is not, however, that kind of capital. She knows when to stay in bed, even when to bend the knee—it was the Duke of Wellington himself, whose mansion at Hyde Park Corner is called No. 1 London, who fell on his knees before some minor Spanish grandee from whom he wanted a military favour. ('I wanted the thing done,' said the Duke afterwards, 'so *down I plumped*.') London's malaise is not, I think, senility, but only menopause. She is biding her time. She has lost one kind of authority, and is waiting to assume another, has emerged from one cycle, and will presently enter the next. If she seems neurotic today, bitter,

London

catty, light-headed, lascivious, it is because her horizons have momentarily contracted, and she is left all alone at home. *Wait and see!* she is murmuring still, as she slips a penny preoccupied into the juke box, and consults her brass-bound almanacs.

But there, I am only speculating. London is never explicit. What is really happening behind her shifting façade, which way her mighty intuitions are turning, whether she is declining once and for all into gaudy mediocrity, or permanently curdling at the soul, or only gathering her strength for yet another assault upon history—whether we should laugh, cheer, or cry when the Queen rides by, London's foggy genius does not reveal to us.

MADRID

There is an abstraction, I am told, called *casticismo*, a kind of universal Spanishness, a mode, a tone of thought, that combines all Spaniards in its atmosphere, and makes of them, for all their regional differences, an instantly distinctive people. I had never heard of this substance when I first arrived in Madrid, but though I did not know its name, nevertheless I felt it all about me, from the very first moment I drove down from the Escorial, through the exquisite flowers of the Castilian spring, into the elegant boulevards of the capital.

It was something not quite tangible, but nearly: something very old, and fine, and stubborn, and complex, like the melancholy grandeur that infuses the paintings of Velázquez, or the pall of sacrifice that still hangs, twenty-five years later, over the legend of the Spanish Civil War. Madrid is a city unique to herself, lapped as she always is, in the heart of her arid plateau, by this eerie but beautiful feeling: in Europe, but not of her, a sort of island capital, aloof behind the rampart of the Pyrenees and the surrounding moat of the sea. She feels extraordinarily alone and lofty, in that harsh and magnificent landscape. She feels very proud, and very courteous, and somehow never far from tragedy.

For though one thinks of her as a sunshine city, she is infused with sadness. A suggestion of sickness hangs over her, like the indefinable oppression of an English winter, or perhaps the weight of altitude that makes Bogotá so grey and moody. This is partly the legacy of that fearful civil war, in which the opposing armies faced each other at the very gates of this city. It is partly the familiar heavy mediocrity of despotism, that second-class ideology, within whose iron grasp the Spaniards have been clasped through three decades. Madrid is a southern city, but she does not feel Mediterranean, like Barcelona, alive with colours and flamboyances. She flaunts none of the excitements of the castanets, none of the flounce of the gipsy skirts, none of the flash or fire of the textbook Latins. She is a tall and

Madrid

aristocratic sort of place, her streets spacious and carefully tended, her monuments mostly of the reproachful kind, which you inspect more as a duty than an actual pleasure. There is nothing sweaty or hugger-mugger about Madrid, except in her pitiful slums. She is not a large metropolis, and very often down her side streets you may see the blank tawny ridges of her countryside, like a desert at her threshold.

It is the isolation of this city that sets her style. She is like old Quixote, himself a child of Madrid, proudly defying the humdrum truth outside. In the thirties the image of Spain had a symbolic and universal quality. She stood as a microcosm of a divided world, and men everywhere, looking at her passions, saw themselves and their societies reflected in the conflict. Today her future offers us no such pattern of hope and despair, and Madrid is no longer one of the archetypal capitals. On the contrary, she seems to stand apart from history now, and feels frozen in the attitudes of an earlier generation. You may sense this superficially in the male fashions that pass you on the street: Madrid is one of the last cities on earth where the standards of English upper-class elegance still survive the assaults of Ivy League and Milano. You may feel it in the formality and convention of public manners, which tend to silence the whistle on one's careless lips, and make one blush for many an unsuspected solecism. You may hear it in the conversations of the angry suppressed liberals, with their open-necked shirts and their well-cut sports jackets, their Bohemian postures and air of reluctant gentlemanliness, their fondness for words like 'intellectual' and 'autarchy', their lingering echoes of those Faber yellow-covered poets I used to read at school. This is a city out of the Orwellian past, inflamed by the issues of another decade, and queerly immune to all the hopes and horrors that animate our own. No ban-the-bomb marchers demonstrate here. If ever there is a protest in Madrid, it is a protest of the old kind—liberty against oppression, Left against Right, Liberals against Fascists, agnostics against the Church, even Spaniards against Foreigners.

Magnificently old-school are the church services of Madrid, so elaborate but austere, so mysterious in their dark and gilded ornaments, so powerful in the stooped grey postures of their priests, so grand with the music of the distant organ, high in its eyrie-loft beneath the roof. Gorgeously nostalgic are the royal memories of Madrid, the palaces and the picture galleries, the echoes of sonorous

Madrid

titles and gilded grandees, from Philip II brooding in his Escorial to the doomed Alfonso of our childhood stamp albums, whose successors still hopefully await the return of their throne. Almost pathetically traditional are the bullfights, with the tootings of their tinsel trumpets, the stylized swank of the toreadors, the foreign *aficionados* glued to their binoculars, the theatrical gestures of a more stately past—and the mass of the citizenry happily up the road at the football match. Disagreeably out of date are the symptoms of Madrid's despotism—the gigantic new Air Ministry, which is said to have more doors than the air force has aircraft, or the foolish headlines which announce, day after day, year after year, the Caudillo's latest unparalleled triumph. There is very little new architecture in Madrid, for all the immense new suburbs that now surround the city. There are very few new ideas. Half the conceptions of the fermenting West, let alone the reviving East, never penetrate this haughty bastion, and Madrid stands all alone in her glory, like a mother superior on a hilltop.

Much that is admirable, too, stems from this condition of virgin insulation. The people of Madrid retain a dignity, a humanity even, that is rare in the modern world, and has been generously sustained throughout these long cold years of autocracy. To this handsome people there feels nothing tarnished or half-cock. Here the human spirit seems to have reached some apogee, if not of cultivation, dash or even decency, at least of self-respect. Here the human creature, soul and flesh alike, seems to have achieved an equilibrium of fulfilment, and even the prosaic occupations are somehow elevated into a perhaps specious dignity, so that there is pride to the very movements of the garbage men, and satisfaction to the flick of a housemaid's duster. A quarter of a century ago, when Spain lay at the heart of the world's preoccupations, it was the power of political conviction that took the young idealists 'to this plateau beneath the night's grave manifold of stars'. Today the *casticismo* of Madrid reinforces no political dogma, confirms no ideological faith, but only serves to remind us how noble a thing, beneath it all, is Man.

And yet there is always a melancholy to the place, if only because she no longer feels among us, but seems to gaze back at us out of some cloister or mausoleum, as a lovely nun might smile silently through the grille. Madrid is a fearfully noisy city, yet she still feels hushed, almost numb, as though she is still half cloaked in tragedy—like one of those ravaged cities that are hollow at the heart, Hiroshima

Madrid

beneath the neon lights, Berlin behind the bluster. I once made a pilgrimage to the Giorgione that hangs in the Prado, one of the half-dozen paintings that are to my mind unmistakably the work of that elusive genius. It brought the tears to my eyes, for I love the fellow so: but as I stood there before the Virgin, St. Roch and St. Anthony of Padua, and stole once more into Giorgione's bewitched silent world of unanswered inquiry, where something portentous and mysterious is perpetually on the brink of happening—as I stood there with those holy people in the half-light of that peculiar vision, I felt that the painting was a proper paradigm of the city outside the gallery, a capital full of lofty magic, where for a third of a lifetime history has held its breath.

MARIENBAD

' A nd this morning, Mr. Morris,' said my guide briskly, rearrang-
ing a businesslike bun in her blonde hair, 'we shall visit
Marianske Lazne, in the western area of our country.'
My heart neither leapt nor sank, for it was numb with cold and
scepticism. I was enduring one of those officially sponsored visits to
a Communist country to which members of my profession are,
stifling their instincts and muffling their better judgements, from
time to time subjected: and I was, after a week of it all, deep in
disbelief. The country was Czechoslovakia. The time was the very
depth and nadir of a grim Central European winter. The car into
whose back seat I lowered myself, with a rather frigid smile of
acceptance, was a bow-legged green Skoda. The driver was a
friendly but cautious soul, who looked as though he would enjoy
nothing more than an afternoon with Mum and the kids at the
Palladium. And as she settled herself beside me, giving me a sweet
but not altogether convincing smile, my guide added as an after-
thought: 'Under the old régime, you know, they used to call it
Marienbad!'
Marienbad! Instantly a bell rang in my mind, jangled but golden,
cracked but still rich, oddly familiar after my peeling baroque
evenings in Prague, my icy folk-customs in the High Tatra Mountains, my long shuddering drives through the snow-enshrouded,
fir-blackened, heartless and cheerless Czech countryside. Marienbad!
It was like an echo of a golden age, just to hear the name, and many a
discredited vision crossed my mind, as my guide kindly explained
to me the new medicinal treatments for dispirited Workers' Families
—visions of lace and stiff white collars, of clip-clopping greys and
fawning courtiers, here a plumed Imperial hat, here a fluttering
embroidered fan: little lap dogs, hurrying servants, coffee on spindly
tables, the orchestra tuning its fiddles among the roses and the hotel
manager, moustaches pomaded, hurrying to greet His Excellency.
They were pictures of an age that was rightly ended, of a society

Marienbad

justly abolished, of unfair privileges and outdated protocol; but they retained an old lavender charm in the imagination, as of faded holiday postcards.

And for me they offered more: for through them all, through the strolling old-fashioned crowds and the string bands, there glared boldly into my mind the eyes of a particular face. One of the divinities of my personal pantheon is old Jackie Fisher, Admiral of the Fleet, creator of the *Dreadnought*, iconoclast, egocentric, flatterer, failure and humorist, who died six years before I was born, but who is still marvellously alive in my affections. This old great-heart was an habitué of Marienbad in her palmy bays. There he consorted proudly with the Imperial potentates, and danced bliss-fully with the Imperial ladies (for he had a sycophantic streak in him, like many ruthless men), and picked the brains of foreign generals, and cocked a gay eyebrow at many a Continental beauty. Many a letter had I read in Fisher's huge-scrawled hand on the browning writing-paper of forgotten Marienbad hotels, with elaborate flowery letter-heads, and engravings of the winter gardens.

So we were going to Marienbad! As we laboured through that grim landscape, a place for wolves and Slavs, Fisher's wrinkled cynical face peered at me constantly through the firs. He had an extraordinary face, so oddly striking that legend had him the illegitimate son of a Ceylonese prince, so unforgettable that the Sultan of Morocco, once inspecting Fisher's Mediterranean Fleet, was asked what had struck him most, among all the gleaming lines of battleships, the great barbettes and the impeccable gun drills, and replied without a second's hesitation: 'The Admiral's face!' Never was a face so congealed with self-esteem, so glorious with gaiety, so proud, so contemptuous, so flirtatious and so compelling! I could see its heavy-lidded eye winking, all but imperceptibly, through the damp fog that lay like a shroud upon the fields.

But we were there, and driving through the fine avenues of the place towards the graceful squares and colonnades that surround the baths. Marienbad was stately still, for all her dismal Communist miasma. The old hotels (now occupied, as I remember, chiefly by Workers' Groups) were still stylish beneath their peeling paint. The covered promenade (along which, as I recall the morning, the girls of a Youth Association were sauntering in frumpish crocodile) was still sadly elegant. The fountains were still delicate. The gardens were still fresh. The charming houses, all official or institutional, still

Marienbad

possessed a faint scented allure of satin and window-boxes. It was a ghost with shreds of colour.

We looked around the place conscientiously; and inspected the free treatment in the baths; and examined institutions of one kind or another; and strolled a little forlornly among the pallid splendours of the spa; and presently found ourselves, marshalled by a huge Comrade of the coarsest kind, looking at the civic museum. This queer collection of souvenirs, mostly about the bad old days of the Empire, was housed in a small pretty villa in the centre of the town; and sometimes, as we wandered from room to room, from glass case to glass case, while the Comrade Curator leered at the Archdukes, and the guide attended intermittently to her hair—sometimes, as we looked at this sad exhibition my eye wandered through an open window, to the curve of the esplanade below. How easy it was to imagine those old grandees of the eighties, wicked perhaps, often selfish, generally heedless, sometimes cruel, but alive with a vanished panache and glitter! How easy to see the whiskered potentates, and the willowy English peers, and the doll-like Austrian ladies, and Fisher himself, the boldest of paladins, like a laughing mandarin among the feather boas!

I tapped the Curator, rather gingerly, upon the shoulder. The museum was fine, said I, but was there no one in the town who actually remembered those old times, when the plutocrats and warmongers battened themselves so shamelessly upon the spa? The churl thought long and deep before replying, and then told us with a grin that there was somebody, in that very house—none other than the woman who had owned the place and occupied it in greedy ease and luxury, until the advent of the people's Government. Like a huge shambling bear he led the way, down the steep staircase among the prints, until we stood again in the hall of the house, beside the entrance. This woman, explained the Curator, was permitted to live in a room in the basement, in return for keeping the place clean: and opening a door he shouted hoarsely down the basement stairs. At first there was only silence. The Curator bellowed again, in a harsh imperative, and presently there was a sound of movement below. A cough, a rustle, laboured footsteps up the stairs; and there emerged into the hall beside us an old woman, dressed almost in rags, wiping her hands on her skirt. Her face was blank and quite impassive. Her movements were oddly stiff, as though she had had a stroke. Her skin was dirty and her hands were rough and crooked.

Marienbad

She looked like some spiritless old animal, a broken pit pony, a lame and useless sheepdog. 'Here she is,' said the Curator, gesturing her roughly into the hall. 'Ask her what you want.'

I was embarrassed, and angry with the man, and wished I had never summoned the old lady into this cruel limelight: but the guide smiled at her with sudden unexpected kindness, and I asked her my one question. Did she happen to remember, out of all the foreign visitors to Marienbad, all the eminent men and dazzling women who must have crossed the corridors of her life—did she happen to remember Admiral Jack Fisher of Her Majesty's Navy?

A glimmer entered her eye, and warmed, and flourished, and very nearly sparkled: and turning her head stiffly to look at me, and straightening her drab-cottoned back, she answered in a perfect, clear-cut Edwardian English. 'Ah!' she said. 'Jackie Fisher! Jackie Fisher! *What a face that man had!*'

So I shook her limp soap-coarsened hand, walked out of the museum into the cold fog, thought how lasting was the glow of a good man's fun, and ended my visit to Marianske Lazne.

MELBOURNE

Love, they say, prefers the back alleys, but history rolls down the great streets of the world: down Wall Street through the ticker-tape, down the Mall between the bearskins, sabled in sledges along the Nevsky Prospekt, proud or poignant towards the Place de l'Etoile. In Australia history has not been long in esplanade, but already one street possesses this swagger of consequence, and reflects block by block, church by shop-front, the parade of Australian events and the pattern of Australian society. Collins Street in Melbourne is *not* the finest thoroughfare in the southern hemisphere—even an Australian might concede that accolade to the superb Avenida 9 de Julio in Buenos Aires. It is nevertheless recognizably one of the great streets, and a morning walk along it is a conversation with the continent.

They call this part of Melbourne the Golden Mile, and Collins Street begins sumptuously, beautifully planted with shade trees, and exuding at its eastern end all the elegance that has been fostered in these parts by the sheep stations and the mines. Here the great families of Victoria, the bankers, the graziers and the magnates, come to be fed, clothed or cured, and here you may inspect almost in its entirety the small layer of grace that ornaments Australian city life. There is nothing like this in Sydney, let alone in Adelaide, Perth or Brisbane. Three or four blocks down Collins Street—such is the sum of Australian urbanity.

Here are the *boutiques*, gay with the unsurpassed sports clothes of Australia. Here is Henri Gomo, for Chic Coiffures, and Madame Tija Favicki's opera school, and here is a window bilious with tinted wedding photographs, and here the glittering mosaic portal of Caper's Gold Door Bistro. Grand curtainless windows peer from the façade of the Melbourne Club, and a splendid anthology of Australian names welcomes you to the medical consulting rooms— Dr. F. X. Dooley, Dr. Adelaide Gault, Dr. Euan I. Littlejohn, and many a scholarly Central European tongue-twister. In the coffee-

Melbourne

shops the exquisitely dressed young women of the city, incessantly smoking, chatter rather too loud over their elevenses. On the pavement outside fine old ladies talk to each other in clipped near-County accents about tweeds, horse shows and eligible young men.

Then quite suddenly, at the spot where the Independent Church glowers Gothically at the Scots Church across the way, the character of Collins Street shifts, and you find yourself in the hurly-burly of the shopping district, expressing all the brash but somehow fusty commercial life of this contradictory state. Life down here is less delicate. There is a touch of the honky-tonk to it all, a suggestion of beer and Barbary Coast. Drunken men with Irish brogues stagger singing out of pubs, an old woman in a felt hat sits outside the Ladies' Amenities selling oranges, and there seem to be policemen everywhere, big men in white-topped caps who look like overgrown bus conductors. Collins Street has always been respectable (to every other Melbourne Street, wrote Clara Aspinall in the eighteen-fifties, 'there is an American, go-ahead spirit, very objectionable to the well-regulated minds of our sex'): even so, these pavements have seen some boisterous fun in their time, and heard many a chime at midnight.

Lola Montez frequented these parts, when she had broken with the royal court of Bavaria, and had not yet taken San Francisco by storm. Here Mr. Henry Baker established the celebrated Imperial Hotel, of which a sincere if homespun bard once wrote:

> *Here you may quaff your draughts secure from harm,*
> *No noxious drugs within the goblet lurk,*
> *For Baker's spirits, however strong their charm,*
> *Deal not in any hocus-pocus work.*

In the eighteen-nineties this was *the* place to be seen, and no person of fashion could afford not to 'do the Block' each morning between Elizabeth and Swanston Streets, where 'beaux of the most elegant description', so Miss Aspinall tells us, 'contemplated the fair promenaders', and the young Phil May looked on with an amused but always kindly eye. To this day it remains an observant and opportunist part of town. One morning I dropped a copy of the *Melbourne Age* into a waste-paper basket down here: within seconds a man who looked like a senior oil executive had rescued it, swiftly refolded its pages, slipped it neatly under his arm, and continued his unruffled way towards the board room.

Melbourne

There is a sort of majestic homeliness to this part of the street. Above you the rooftops are marvellously embellished with minarets, pinnacles, arches, fretted towers and gargoyled balustrades. Away to your left, down the side streets, you may glimpse the sprawling railway yards of Melbourne, the derricks of the docks, the heliport upon the Yarra River, the big roads running away south to St. Kilda and Hobson's Bay. The cinemas are prodigies of bombast, plush and chandelier, and not far from the Town Hall there is a 'player roll library', a collection of two thousand mixed melodies for all the beloved pianolas which, to this hard-boiled day, still tinkle happily away in the purlieus of this city.

Past the jazzy Australia Hotel, past the heavy enticements of the Manchester Unity Arcade, and presently Collins Street changes step again, and becomes the financial capital of this Commonwealth. 'My word, yes!' say the taxi-drivers, in a favourite Australianism, if you extol the wealth of these buildings, for this is where the staggering resources of this continent are converted into hard cash. Up to the right is the Menzies Hotel, which Melba's father built, which MacArthur used as his headquarters, where Mark Twain once stoked the furnaces, and where Dot, a queen among barmaids, still presides over the fortunes of the tap: but mostly it is money that rules down here, and this part of the street retains, like the snootier reaches of Wall Street and the inner enclaves of Johannesburg, a cool touch of the English Establishment.

What could be more heftily discreet than the façade of No. 260, where the mining kings live in a radiance of magical names— Kalgoorlie, Broken Hill, Rum Jungle or Mount Isa? What could be more blandly alluring than the nameplate across the road—The Christmas Island Phosphate Commission? What Saarinen or Niemeyer could improve upon the headquarters of the English, Scottish and Australian Bank, a prodigious flourish of Venetian Gothic, all striped and pinnacled sandstone, and looking as though Ruskin himself must surely be in charge? British investment still dominates Australia, the ultimate link between the two countries, and in this part of Collins Street, though you may sometimes see slinky foreign-looking men in cars of blazing opulence, still nobody looks more at home than the occasional true-blue Briton, rolled umbrella, bowler, upper lip and all.

From this gilded climax our street now gently descends, through the offices of the wool brokers and the estate men, the grain and

Melbourne

chaff merchants, past the great warehouses beyond the Rialto Post Office, past the stock agents with their portraits of champion merinos or legendary shorthorns, past shop displays of tractors and well-borers and milkers, past Sabrina's Sandwich Bar and the Salvation Army's People's Palace, into the world of the shabbier saloons, the butchers and the oyster cafés, until at last the thoroughfare is blocked by the hulk of Spencer Street Station, where the great trains leave in a shudder of diesels for Sydney, Adelaide and the west.

And here, properly enough, history too stops short, for it was on this very spot, less than a hundred and fifty years ago, that Mr. John Batman built the very first white man's house in Melbourne, after signing an agreement with the indigenous bigwigs of the place—the three brothers Jagajaga, that is, plus Cooloolock, Bungarie, Yanyan, Moowhip and Mommarmalar. Fifth Avenue leads you to the Bronx, the Nevsky Prospekt ends at the golden stupa of the Admiralty, but not many streets can usher you so generously back to the thumbprints of the primitives.

MONTREAL

O God, cried Samuel Butler (several times, as I remember), O God, O God, O God, O Montreal!

I thought the same myself when I first visited this city, and had no doubt that the finest road in Quebec was the one that led to Manhattan. Now I am not so sure. This may not be Canada's century, as the Ottawa orators have it, but it is a moment in history when Canada stands in the world as a haven for the homeless, an arena for the ambitious, a kitchen for the hungry. It is to Canada that today's masses, yearning to be free or rich, most often turn their anxious eyes: and it is to Canada that the young man goes, when Mr. Greeley's succinct advice speeds him expectantly westward. All this excitement of newness and hope, this bustle of aspirations, this sense of relief and greed and variety, you can experience most potently in Montreal. The feeling has faded in New York, as that old refuge ages and hardens, and has never quite bloomed in Sydney: but here in Jacques Cartier's city, where the noble St. Lawrence strikes for the heart of the continent, and the great expresses pound away to Winnipeg and Vancouver and the wildernesses of the north-west—here in Montreal you can still understand what it means to stand on the edge of a new world.

In Montreal you cannot escape the new Canadians, or fail to respond to their emotions. 'Yes, sir,' said the young taxi-driver who took me one day to the top of Mount Royal, the green hill that stands miraculously at Montreal's back door. 'Yes, sirree,' said he, surveying the grandeur of the prospect before us and slightly amplifying the music which came from a transistor radio in the pocket of his leather jerkin, 'I certainly am proud, as proud as hell of Montreal!' When I questioned him closer, though, I found that he was born in Rumania, and had known the city for a slightly shorter time than I had myself; such is the promise of the place, and such its benediction.

It is, of course, primarily a French-speaking city—the second largest on earth, they like to tell you—but an astonishing babel of

Montreal

accents and tongues now greets you in its streets: accents Balkan and
Slav, Teutonic and Scandinavian, Chinese and Irish—even accents
unmistakably English, for you still meet a multitude of English
adventurers and go-getters if you wander across this continent of
chance. In Montreal there are churches of every shade of orthodoxy
or dissent. There is the largest synagogue in the British Commonwealth. There is a substantial community of Confucianists, and a
growing colony of Mormons. There are restaurants of every cuisine,
faces of every bone structure. It is a little world of its own, fermenting a ferment, I imagine, rather like Chicago's in the twenties and
thirties, which produced a minor Middle West renaissance.

Montreal has always been, since her French days, a place of
schools, colleges, and other improving institutions, from an infinity of
nunneries to the splendid McGill University, couched in green below
the city mountain. But she has now become, under the stimuli of the
post-war years, something like an eastern San Francisco, with a
touch of the beat to it, plus a streak of the Barbary Coast. There are
beards everywhere, and espresso bars, and highbrow bookshops
selling the editions of the Foreign Languages Publishing House in
Moscow; and there is a fine open-air art gallery in a square, where
the loafers doze in the glare of the abstracts: and you can buy *Le
Monde, Epoca,* or even *Pravda* on the news-stands. You need never
be short of conversation in Montreal: stop any citizen and he will
tell you the story of civilization, and quite likely invite you, if you are
in the right part of town, to sign a petition of protest. Nobody, not
even the angriest of young men, could call Montreal dull. She may
not produce much great art or quivering philosophy, but at least
she tries.

This is, though, just the froth. More fundamentally the melting-
pot function of Montreal makes for pace, commercial push, acquisitive gusto. I am told that economically she is dominated by her
American neighbours, but she feels, all the same, a very paragon of
capitalist zest. The whole place is exuberantly on the make—far
more vividly, it seems to me, than its sister cities across the frontier.
Here you can still see in a man's eye the glow and gleam of 'making
good', such as illuminated Detroit or Cleveland, I suppose, half a
century ago. Huge new buildings are springing up everywhere,
dwarfing the old French stolidity of Place D'Armes and Notre-Dame.
The immense Queen Elizabeth Hotel, sprawling above the Canadian
National Railway Station, is a conundrum of escalators and dim-lit

Montreal

cocktail bars and flamboyant commissionaires. A splendid new airport stands on the outskirts of town, and the monumental St. Lawrence Seaway begins just down the road, over the Victoria Bridge.

A slight suggestion of violence hangs on the air, as it does in all such thrusting towns, from mid-Victorian Huddersfield to contemporary Hong Kong. Montreal, one feels, for all her innumerable priests and nuns, her scholars and her admirable *Star*, is essentially a place where few holds are barred. It was here that the mad idealists of the Quebec Libeiation Front planted many of their bombs. There has also been a spate of unsolved gang murders in recent years, and it is odd how often you find yourself short-changed or overcharged. ('Quebec Province,' one man said to me almost with pride when I pointed out to him that he had cheated me of a quarter, 'is noted for its petty larcenies.') Montreal people, though charming to the stranger, seem to be awfully rude to each other, pushing about on sidewalks and snubbing one another in incomprehensible dialects in the back rooms of snack bars. It is a city where most things go, not a place for puritans or sobersides. It is one of the few places in North America where you cannot be fined for jaywalking—though it would be, so one citizen told me quaintly, 'a damned good stunt if you could'.

Nor is it, in superficials anyway, an efficient city. In Montreal shoes get lost and bags get broken. Service in her hotels and restaurants, though always courteous and usually most disarming, is of a slowness almost Russian. Some of her projected complexes of fly-overs and underpasses are of staggering complexity and ingenuity, but the general standard of driving today, and some of the traffic control, appears to me distinctly slipshod. There seems little tautness of discipline to Montreal. Her character is expansive, generous, easy-going, like the shape of the city itself, thrown along the bank of the great river like one immeasurable wharf.

And indeed this unbelted affluence is part of the power of the place. Montreal still feels like a pioneer. She is a young city still, and in many ways a simple one, for all her self-conscious elegance. Her social pretensions still feel endearingly provincial, if you spend an hour or two in the lobby of the Ritz-Carlton Hotel. Her smart ladies of Sherbrooke Street, though not so baked or leathery-looking as their opposite numbers in New York, are often pitiably overdressed. She still seems to cluster around her docks and her railway lines: and

253

Montreal

for me it is the bigness and rawness and brawniness of the place, far more than its beards or its charity balls, that save it from diligent mediocrity.

Samuel Butler remembered best, of all the citizens of Montreal, the man who claimed to be brother-in-law to Mr. Spurgeon's haberdasher. I have memories more robust. If I were writing a poem about this city, I would commemorate a pair of dockers, both prickly and unkempt, one from Poland, one from Ireland, whom I met taking their lunch break down by the quayside. They had been poor immigrants both, ten years before: but now they had taken their sandwiches out to their cars, and they sat there side by side in their metal helmets, prosperously munching, while the radio blared a baseball game and the big trucks lumbered by towards the docks. Such sights—of poor men redeemed, exiles rescued—used to represent the meaning of America, and they are still the glory of Montreal.

Several times Sam Butler cried: and God, looking down upon that irascible and irreverent poet, and contemplating the haberdasher's putative brother-in-law, evidently took notice.

MOSCOW

Through an ambuscade of aircraft the traveller stumbles—more aircraft, it seems, than he has ever set eyes on before, with their fierce noses and high tails shining dully in the snow, hulking and unfamiliar, like great predatory pike: but inside the stuffy, ill-lit reception hall a line of prickly porters, in brown quilted jackets and fur hats, lounges and slouches on benches, while an official in a blue cap peers myopically at documents, turning them this way and that for a better grasp of their purport, like a country policeman in a farce.

A fusty crowd of passengers, muffled in wrappings, hangs about the Customs desk: a fat, broad-faced woman in tears, her child tugging at the strap of her handbag; a sallow man in a velvet hat, arguing over a suitcase of brocades; a covey of Chinese, dignified and double-breasted; a welter of thick-set, sweaty, colourless men with badges in their lapels and elaborate medals dangling from their chests. Among them all the traveller warily passes, a shuffling, heavy-breathing porter carrying his bags behind, and into the car that waits outside; and so down the dank, snow-muffled road, through a landscape numb with cold, he is driven towards the city.

Thin flurries of snow are chased by the wind across the road. The windows of the car are thick with ice, frost, and condensation. Blurred in a haze of winter, as if seen through a toper's eyes, are the places along the route. There are shambled lines of shacks and shanties, painted an ancient peeling blue, with rickety verandas and precarious porches, knee-deep in snow, invested by old outhouses, fences, dog-houses, bits of masonry. There are clusters of small houses, tightly huddled together for warmth and comfort, as if they had heard the howling of wolves. There are wide, desolate acres of snow-encompassed land, cruel and grubby, supervised by brooding firs, and crossed perhaps by a solitary old woman in a trailing tattered coat and a green kerchief, bundled with packages and

Moscow

buckets, and pushing her way like a lemming towards some unseen homestead in the wood.

Sometimes a gaunt old horse hauls a sledge lop-sidedly down the road, piled high with baskets and packing-cases; or a car ploughs past with a puff of oily exhaust and a whiff of crude petrol; or a great rough-hewn lorry, painted a sombre green and wrapped around the bonnet with quilted fabric, rumbles darkly through the trees; and presently there appear through the misted windscreen the first tokens of the city. A suburban trolley-bus slides alongside, painted a bright blue and yellow, its windows so steamy that only a blur of head-scarves and wrinkled faces can dimly be seen, or the pink tip of a child's nose pressed against the glass. The traffic thickens, the empty countryside falls away, and soon there looms out of the fitful snowfall a monstrous parade of buildings. Huge, square, and forbidding they appear, of no definable style or period, like so many vast eight-storey breeding-houses. They look shuttered and deserted, but for a bleak light here and there, and they rise sheer and stern on each side of the road, window after window, block after block, mile after mile, like enormous piles of ammunition boxes in some remote and secret dump. Only a few squat women move in and out of their vault-like doors, and the television aerials, standing awry on their roofs, seem sad but lovable impertinences.

Immensely wide is the street that strikes through this gloomy cavalcade, and presently the rhythm of the buildings shifts, like a train crossing the points. Dreadful symmetry gives way to a jumble of old and new and indeterminate: a sagging, classical portico behind high walls; a rickety cul-de-sac of single-storey chalets, the plaster and lath peeling to show the criss-cross wood beneath; a bridge across a frozen river, its ornamental urns stacked with sculptured rifles, swords, trumpets and machine guns. The traveller rubs his window with his fur hat, and sees that the city has closed in upon him.

Not a drop, not a hint, not a memory of colour enlivens its frozen outskirts. All is brown and grey and stacked with snow. The stocky pedestrians of the place are swathed in greatcoats, furs and high boots, and move stuffed and bundled along the pavements, their children so encased in hoods and sheepskin that only their eyes

---

The photographs following are of: Kyoto, Leningrad, Lima, London, Moscow, Naples, New York.

Moscow

appear like gems among the wrappings. Machines bustle everywhere, clearing away the sludge—jolly little motor-sweepers, like benign weasels, and huge clanking devices with spindly arms, like lobsters, and suction chutes, and tall, frowning snow-ploughs; and among them, wearing padded jackets over white aprons, an army of rugged women sweeps, shovels, and picks, leaving an intricate meshed pattern of brushes on the pavement, and an obbligato of swishing and chipping constantly on the air.

From an iron grille in the ground a plume of steam arises, and in its vapour crouches a flock of birds—half a dozen proud but shabby pigeons, a few rapscallion sparrows. A line of small boys paces on skis through the trees of a garden, and an old philosopher with flaps over his ears sits defiantly on a bench reading a book, the snow like white fur upon his coat collar. Across the vast crossroads a stream of huddled figures endlessly plods, hurried along by the chivvying of whistles and the testy gestures of belted, padded, high-booted, fur-hatted policemen. The city feels at once curiously empty and claustrophobically crowded: empty because its buildings are pallid and aloof, like monuments to dead scientists; crowded because to the movements of the scurrying citizenry there is something dark and inexorable, as though nothing could ever staunch its sheer weight of numbers, as though it is impelled not by pleasure, industry, ambition, or even duty, but by irresistible physical instincts—like birds migrating, or small black salmon fighting their way upstream.

But now there appear, in glimpses among the office blocks, weird and spectral skyscrapers, solitary above the rooftops, ornamented strangely with spikes and pinnacles, like the pavilions of Eastern satraps; and just as the dusk begins to fall the traveller sees before him, raised upon an eminence, a huge and haunting fortress. Ancient turreted walls protect it, and a wide, icy river lies beneath its gates; and within it there shine clusters and globules of gold, complicated bell-towers, citadels, palaces, weathervanes, emblems of power and politics, a mound of cathedrals and barracks and florid watch-towers, an immense straggling tessellated rampart, a dome with a gigantic flag streaming arrogantly in the wind.

In the square beneath this chill marvel he steps from his car; and joining a silent queue of citizens, he passes between a pair of sentries, rigid as idols, their collars turned up around their cheeks, their boots glistening, their small eyes hard and unshifting. Slowly, meditatively, like mutes, the queue shuffles between granite portals

Moscow

into a bare and massive building. Officers in long grey greatcoats peer watchfully from its shadows, and only the cries of a heedless baby break the silence as the crowd, bareheaded and awe-struck, presses clumsily down the granite steps into the stomach of the edifice. Silently, silently it lumbers on, with a pulse of breathing and a swish of thick clothes and an awkward clatter of boots on stone: until at last the traveller, hemmed in willy-nilly among the pilgrims, finds himself within an inner chamber, like a dungeon. Four silent soldiers stand there with their rifles, and the endless queue winds its way around the room like a fascinated viper, button to button, breath to breath, gazing always at the crystal box that stands in the centre.

A dead man lies embalmed there among the bayonets, bathed in an unearthly light, waxen and preternaturally clean, with a short beard and a high-domed head. Not a word, not a sigh, not a cough escapes the crowd as it passes this cosmetic relic. An occult sense of ritual pervades the place, as in the eerie tomb-heart of a pyramid. The traveller, caught in the fustian momentum of the queue, is carried as in a dream out of the chamber and up the broad steps into the evening light: and already he feels clinging to his person, trapped in the folds of his coat and the turn-ups of his trousers, impregnating his hair like tobacco in a railway carriage, creeping beneath his finger-nails, smarting in his eyes, the odour and essence of Moscow.

Moscow in winter is hardly a dream, and not exactly a nightmare, but has more the quality of a hangover: blurred, dry-mouthed, and baleful, but pierced by moments of almost painful clarity, in which words, ideas, or recollections roll about in the mind metallically, like balls on a pin-table.

It is a graceless but obsessive city, the capital of an alien Asiatic world. Among its avenues of ugly buildings, stamped with the inexpressible emptiness of Stalinist taste, the muffled multitudes shove their way with hungry gusto: not indeed mindlessly, as myth would have it, but with a special technique of ill manners, a kind of self-induced trance in which the existence of anybody else on the pavement is erased from the consciousness, as a yogi dismisses the blistered crowd around him. Nobody can push more effectively than a Muscovite: but drab and docile are the queues, all the same, that trail away from the milk counter in the central market, or wait in

Moscow

suffocating proximity, each man breathing stertorously down his neighbour's neck, for their hats and galoshes after the opera. No elegance or style is left twitching in the streets of Moscow. This is the metropolis of the common man, and he eats his bortsch with a proud snuffle.

Through the dreary proletarian pall, though, crooked mysteries gleam. Some are the mysteries of Communism: mummied philosophies and deifications, medallions of Lenin as a baby, a dead physicist lying in state upon his bier, a wilderness of pamphlets and slogans and Five-Year Plans, the shifting mosaic of strange faces that makes this an imperial city—Mongols and Kazakhs and bland Chinese, scarred Africans, wide-eyed Indians, lean men from Central Asia, with knobbly sticks and crinkled lambskin hats.

Some are the mysteries of ancient State: the spiked mediaeval helmets of the Kremlin Treasury, the gorgeous saddle trappings and the royal sledges, gold in piled elaborate formality, splendid silver from England, jewellery of minute ingenuity, thrones of ivory, sceptres, golden cocks, owls, pheasants, railway trains, ships in golden eggs, galleries of armour, all shining and glinting in their cases while the tourists, their feet muffled in felt overshoes, as in a mosque, pad in obedient groups behind their guide.

Some are the mysteries of religion—the religion of Leninism, which has already etherealized that eminent political scientist, or the religion of Tsarist Russia, still ornately surviving beneath its onion domes. Church service on Sunday morning is still veiled in strangeness and suffering. Outside the door an old man with a forked beard feeds a gaggle of mangy pigeons: inside a million Muscovites seem to occupy the nave, crammed so tightly that a sudden genuflection sends a ripple across the church. Far, far away the vestments of a priest sometimes flicker in the candlelight, and always drifting around the pillars and the ikons loiters a cadence of hidden choirs. Near the door the corpses of two old ladies, pale but peaceful, lie encouched in flowers. In a side chapel a bespectacled priest with long golden hair, sitting on a kitchen chair beside the altar, accepts a stream of murmured confessions and entreaties, the women pressing round him like dwarfs around a magician.

Strange are the encounters of Moscow, like incidents in a fevered fancy. A man in clumping boots and huge leather gloves will introduce himself in a champagne bar as a Brigadier of Communist Labour, and ask after the welfare of the comrade plasterers in

Moscow

England. A gay girl in the Lenin Library will slip you an irreverent witticism about Socialist realism. A female judge in a divorce court will burst into tears at the memory of her orphaned childhood. Two youths in slinky coats will solicit you for pound notes, fountain pens, *Life* magazine, chewing gum, nylon shirts or gramophone records. A charming renegade, springing out of the night, will eat caviar in your hotel room, talk for an hour or two about Proust, Evelyn Waugh and Wiltshire, and vanish again like a perfumed phantom. Moscow is full of innuendoes, hints of espionage, suspicions, the threat of imminent portentous confidences.

Sometimes a sense of suffocation overcomes you, and you feel yourself so far from the sea, in the heart of something so swollen and incalculable, that the blood throbs in your head and your mind sags. In the immaculate subterranean halls of the underground you may feel like this, stifled by gigantic symbolisms and frescoes of dancing milkmaids; or lost among the myriad textbooks, tracts, collected works of Lenin, portraits of bemedalled demi-gods, economic treatises and inspirational posters of a bookshop; or wandering among the awful symmetries of Moscow University, Big Brother's *alma mater*, a brain factory, a production line where 25,000 students labour like so many ants in a 32-storey heap (33 reading rooms, 5,754 sleeping chambers, 80 Members of the Academy of Sciences, 20 Merited Sciences, a million books, 50,000 trees, an assembly hall with 1,500 seats and 11 floors of storage space—'The best university in the world,' as an Intourist pamphlet puts it, 'can only be seen in Moscow').

Sometimes you may feel frightened: not simply by the suggestion of hidden microphones and secret police, or the strained isolation of the foreign residents, herded into their ghettoes, or even by the sense of stark power that emanates from this dismal but impressive city; but by a profound sense of alienation, as though you belonged to some unrelated visiting species. Your conversations, however cordial, never really bridge the gulf of ideology. Your informant, kindly and hospitable, will suddenly assume a tone of quite unexpected arrogance. Behind the inquiries of the Brigadier of Communist Labour there lurks not hostility exactly, but a sense of inescapable misunderstanding, as though at some predestined point both your languages and your conceptions will diverge, never to be reconciled. You can never get to grips with the truth in Moscow. It slithers away from you into the snow, and even its tracks are obliterated by armies of passing footfalls.

Moscow

But sometimes you may, nevertheless, catch a glimpse of the very heart, the core of this city's mysteries, as the man with the hangover analyses with cheerless clarity the exact mixture of drinks that was his undoing. It may well be at the Bolshoi, while some gigantic Russian epic is being ferociously enacted, with rolls of kettle-drums and clashes of armour, a mammoth chorus open-throated, a clutch of heroes swelling in the foreground, with a passage and repassage of knights, horses, serfs, a frenzy of conical helmets and chain mail, banners dramatically waving, flames issuing from a backcloth, smoke, flashing beacons, the orchestra in a quivering *fortissimo*, the conductor wiping his sweating bald head, the enormous audience gripping its seats or craning from the high gilded balconies above the chandelier—then, in the middle of it all, you will glance across your neighbour's shoulder to the great State box in the centre: and there will be sitting the most powerful man on earth, looking bored and rather glazed, a slight sad smile playing around the corners of his mouth, his wife, in a bun and a brown sagging dress, demure and attentive at his elbow.

You need not wait for the last act. Go home and sleep it off.

MUNICH

'Well,' said I to the German at the dinner table, a little on the defensive perhaps, 'well, that may very well be true, and I admit you've done miracles: but all the same, it does seem to me that though we may be poorer than you are in Germany, nevertheless we do produce more ideas and creative people—you know, writers, poets, actors, Bertrand Russell, all that sort of thing.'

The German clasped the upper part of my arm with a beringed hand. 'My dear friend,' he replied, 'I was in Indonesia a month or two ago, and they said *precisely the same thing there.*'

I could have clonked him on the head with the salt-cellar, were it not for the susceptibilities of my hostess: and few Englishmen of a certain age would deny that there is something about the middle-aged Germans, with their revived complacency, their suggestion of hidden contempt, their absolute blank disregard of the evil their nation has done to the world—there is something about the middle-ageing German that rubs us in the raw, emphasizes the divine injustice of history, and makes one reach, if only in vicious fancy, for the pepper-pot. Nowhere will you feel this sensation more insistently than in Munich: for though this fine city has none of the baleful power of Berlin, and stands indeed in a setting of exquisite charm in the approaches to the Bavarian Alps, nevertheless it was here that the Nazi philosophy was born, it was here that many a Gestapo infamy was contrived, it was here that Hitler found his first disciples, and it is here in the Munich beer-cellars, among the boisterous burghers and their always smiling wives, that the solitary Englishman feels most clearly the gregarious uncertainties of this clever, terrible and unfulfilled people.

For me it is the queerness of the Germans that is most apparent in Munich, and this arcane quality stems chiefly, I suspect, from their lack of homogeneity—often patched up, never sealed. This is not,

Munich

like ours, an old, tight-knit family people, weathered and matured by centuries of common experience. It lacks continuity, suppleness, assurance. Half of Germany is Catholic, for one thing, and half is Protestant—and if you wander through the nobly restored Cathedral of Munich, with its cool tall pillars and its breath of chastity, you may feel that even German Catholicism has to it something of self-doubt, so that it seems to lack the warmth and homeliness of that supremely homely faith. Then everywhere in Munich you will find reminders that not so long ago, in our great-grandfathers' time, there was no such thing as a German nation, only a hodge-podge of four kingdoms, thirteen duchies and principalities, and three free cities. They are Bavarian kings that are still remembered here, in the vast baroque arcades of the Residenz, or the gallery of royal favourites at Nymphenburg (the naughty Scotswoman Lola Montez, who died penniless in New York, or the formidable Archduchess Sophie, whose sons became Emperors of Austria and Mexico). They are Bavarian generals whose thoughtful classical figures stand, like saints in Florence, beneath the arches of the Feldherrenhalle. They are Bavarian soldiers, perished in Russia under Napoleon, who are remembered in the Karolinenplatz obelisk, and it is a Bavarian Army museum that still stands, shattered and despondent in its ruins, above the Residenz garden.

What is universally German about Munich, indeed, is often circumvented or disguised, for this city's principal contribution to political history has been the fostering of National Socialism. Everywhere, if you care to look, there are relics of that fearful phenomenon. Here beside the elegant Königplatz still stands the old party headquarters, a centre of culture nowadays, but still instinct with the whip and the black list. Here is the house where Hitler, Chamberlain, Daladier and Mussolini signed away the Sudetenland, and gave the name of this city a new meaning. Here is the square where Hitler mounted his first attempted *Putsch*, and here the beer-cellar where his party was formally reconstituted when he came out of prison. The wicked men of the Nazi hierarchy were the familiars of this place, and it is only eleven miles through the pine woods to Dachau ('a favourite resort of landscape painters,' as the guide-book remarks). 'We prefer to forget all that,' Munich people are inclined to say, almost patronizingly: but the traveller must be blithe indeed if he, too, can disregard these dreadful memories.

For beneath the lacquered surface of Munich there remains, I

Munich

cannot help fancying, some hint of strut, arrogance, or dangerous gullibility. This does not feel either a gentle or a sceptical city. Its smiles, though ubiquitous, do not seem heartfelt. It has no wry humour like Berlin, and no sense of liberal ease, like Hamburg. In Munich I do not often catch an eye, as I do every day in Damascus or La Paz, New York or Warsaw, into whose passing glance there steals some instant glow of sympathy, the natural collusion of one human being with another. Among the myriad tables of the Hofbrauhaus, the very place where Hitler first proclaimed his principles, where the thousands of jolly German families swill their beer from enormous earthenware tankards to the thump of a Bavarian band—among that seething, genial, healthy, back-slapping, belly-laughing gathering of citizens I do not seem to see one single face, one single smile, with which I feel quite at home or really at ease. To me this remains the most alien of all peoples: the most enigmatic, the most evasive, the most frightening.

And also, in many ways, the most admirable. One can only admire the tremendous resilience of the Germans, unthinking or misdirected though it may be. It is a moving thing to ask a series of Munich working-men what happened to them during the last war, and to envisage the immense sequence of battles, from the gates of Moscow to the English Channel, in which these formidable men fought for their squalid cause—nearly always bravely, nearly always skilfully, against odds that seem in retrospect to have been impossible, and with a spirit that seems, from this distance of time, quite incomprehensible. One can only enjoy the taste and decorum of Munich, its lingering air of market-place and country town, the shepherd who stands, with his dog and his flock, on the grass beside the airport runways. One can only wonder at the general sense of deep-rooted education, so much more universal and pervasive than it is at home, so that the taxi-driver consults his map in the manner of a cultivated man, the concert audiences are dauntingly knowledgeable, and almost nobody seems altogether oafish. One can only marvel at the great Deutsches Museum, that supreme exhibition of the scientific age, which reminds us how pre-eminent these people remain in matters of invention and research, how imperturbably they have rebounded from their misfortunes, and how whole-heartedly they have entered into the spirit of our times. Even the Zoo is the only one in Europe where the birth rate exceeds the death rate.

There is nothing fusty about Munich. It is all glitter and go, and

Munich

indeed the more you talk to the young people of the city, the more you may begin to wonder whether your instincts have not been unfair: for so far the incipient arrogance of their elders has not infected them, and though they look precisely as I have always imagined the Hitler Youth to look, with their blond blank faces and their passion for the more grotesque outdoor accoutrements, nevertheless they do seem to have outgrown the old cankers of nationalism and despair. With their resolute internationalism, their disregard of politics, their reluctance to look over their shoulders into the unhappy past, they remind me sometimes of sensitive Jews in the Diaspora, half ashamed of their origins, half intensely proud. I do not know what gave birth to the Nazi ideals in this city, whether it was a combination of history that might have happened to any people, or whether it sprang from something cruel in the German soul alone: but to any young German born too late for those horrors, we must surely offer the benefit of the doubt.

For if you come to Munich hostile, you cannot leave her without at least a flicker of esteem. The Germans have done us much harm, but they have brought us much noble pleasure, too. They are a people to be treated with always watchful care, but they are also a people of genius, and in the towers and magical clocks and brave new buildings of Munich, in the music always flowing from her halls and the books always streaming from her famous publishing houses, in the ineffable green parks beside her river, in her great libraries and galleries and cultured drawing-rooms—in all these things and places you may recognize the latent good of Germany, the radiant side of the pfennig, so often overlaid with belligerence, slyness or humourless bonhomie. There is something very peculiar about the Germans, and there is something niggling and uncomfortable about the character of Munich: but this is a great and gifted city still, and demands if not exactly our trust, at least our wary respect.

So I took another mouthful of my pudding instead, and turning to my companion with a magnanimous English smile, 'What a curious coincidence!' said I. 'The very same words indeed! I suppose you sell a good many cars in Djakarta?'

NAPLES

In Venice the East begins, in China (so they say) the West; but Naples is a paradigm of the South. The South means one thing to an American, another to an Ulsterman, another again to the hawk-nosed Khartoum gentleman, fresh-descended from the slavers. It means warm beakers to the English poets, inefficiency to the Milan industrialists. It shares, though, nearly everywhere, a mystique and a set of values, scented, pathetic, lofty, deplorable, seductive, easy-going; and its pride and its pinnacle, the emblem of its manners, is unquestionably the city of Naples.

Everyone knows the splendour and the shame of this sensual metropolis. Everyone has sat, if only in imagination, above the sweep of its incomparable bay, with its destroyers firing their salutes as they slide into port, and Vesuvius grimly watchful across the water, and the dim hogback of Capri hazed in sea mist, and the monastery of San Martino high and grand above the tangled streets, and the great water-front promenade sweeping away to Posillipo and the Phlegraean Fields. Everyone has stumbled, if only in fiction, among the degradations of its poverty: the stony stinking alleys strung with shirts and stockings, the dim peeling hovels and toppling shacks, the sleepless street corners, streaked with urination, where the skinny wide-eyed children play.

Yet Naples is not really one of your cities of contrast, for she has a character so powerful, a history so complex, that her disparate parts are fused irrevocably into an ironic unity. No boundary divides the squalid from the ostentatious. This is a city of many subtle layers—the glittering tourist sea-front; the great port; the old patrician heart of the place, now crumbled into the plebeian; the handsome new suburbs, sprawling away over Vomero; the drab industrial accretions round the bay. There is the warren of narrow, geometrical streets that was built to house the Spanish garrison, and is now the popular exemplar of the Naples slum; there is the Città Americana, a huge American military enclave

Naples

on the outskirts of the city; there are the horrible refuse heaps beside the harbour that house the very poorest of the Naples poor; there is the elegant mesh of shopping streets, frequented by hawk-nosed princesses, surrounding the old piazza where Lady Hamilton received her little admiral. All spill into each other and merge, so that there is often an aristocratic splendour to the darkest of the slums, and a nagging suggestion of shabbiness to the boudoir boulevards.

For the character of this southern city stands beyond poverty and wealth, away in the heady realms of faith, heritage and custom. Queer and introspective are many of its manifestations, candle-lit and aloof to our cold northern certainties. Deep in the crypt of Sant'Agostino, for example, lies its famous ossuary, where the bones of the departed are prettied up with ribbons and paper flowers, arranged like shop displays in glass cases, and illuminated with electric bulbs—to complete a votive circuit you buy a small two-pronged plug from the priest on duty upstairs. Treasured in the Cathedral is the miraculous blood of the martyred St. Gennaro, which turns to liquid three times a year to the sighs and loud prayers of the assembled multitude and the ritual curses, vituperations, and insults of the old women entitled to be called 'relatives of the saint'. Tucked away in a mouldering little square is a strange figure of a bearded sage, clutching a cornucopia which is popularly supposed to symbolize the spirit of Naples, but which is really an Alexandrian representation of the Nile, with a new head on it; and in many a house you may still come across a *presepe*, one of those exquisite and elaborate Christmas cribs, encrusted with cherubs, that are the most beguiling manifestation of Neapolitan art.

Every corner of Naples, the most threadbare and the most pretentious, cherishes such unique and beloved curiosities, some ghoulish, some comic, some altogether lovely, from the steam whistles by which the vegetable-sellers draw custom to their carts (tiny donkeys with pom-poms on their heads waiting thoughtfully through the din) to Mazzoni's breath-taking *Pietà* in the Church of Monte Oliveto, whose eight terracotta figures have stood there down the centuries in the twilight of their chapel in attitudes so heart-rending that it seems the agony cannot last much longer. Naples is a palimpsest: each generation has left its signature upon the city, whether it be a slum, a catacomb or a Gothic apse. She is also a treasure-house: the National Museum is one of the greatest of

Naples

archaeological museums, and the Capodimonte art gallery must surely be the most beautifully housed of all picture collections.

Pride, too, is a tough strand in the fabric of the place, as it is in all these southern cities, battered as they are by alien notions. The Neapolitan aristocrat is proud—all too proud, very often; but even the ramshackle poor parts are sometimes informed by a sharp sense of self-sufficiency. Certainly the citizens are living five to a room, cooking their macaroni in the streets outside, sharing their every snore with their neighbours, urged sometimes to thieving and prostitution, ill fed and unschooled; but over the generations they have made a way of life out of it, have accepted its hardships if only because they know no better, and have infused their squalor with a curious dignity. Absolutely they are pitiful; on the spot, with no horizon in sight, with all their attitudes of intimacy and wry comradeship, they sometimes seem to me almost enviable. 'It is not a problem,' my Neapolitan host kept saying to me as we wandered the old city. No lavatories? It is not a problem. No schools? It is not a problem. No privacy? It is not a problem. Not enough food for the children? Well . . .

Of course there are problems, vicious and apparently insoluble, however assiduously we case-hardened romantics sublimate the character of Naples. There are the problems of utter ignorance in a city where no small ragamuffin need go to school if he can earn something on the streets instead. There are the problems of ill health and terrible congestion, of too many babies and no free medicine. There are the problems of crime and corruption, in a place where extortion is a commonplace, violence a way of thought, dishonesty almost a necessity. And there are above all the plain problems of poverty: not just the lack of comforts, but the absolute lack of enough money to buy the necessary food. This is something the most high-flown Neapolitan traditionalist, with his mind on the whims of national character, the glories of national history, the philosophical quandaries of poverty and possession, cannot honestly circumvent; and for myself the most striking thing in Naples, beyond even the marvels of her setting and the fascination of her spirit, is the frightening pallor of her children.

This is a very poor city, one of the poorest of its calibre. It is less poor than it was a decade ago, and something has been done to relieve its miseries—new roads, new houses, a new aqueduct, some brave initiatives like Father Borelli's celebrated home for urchins. Ask any

Naples

poor Neapolitan, and he will agree that things have undeniably improved since his childhood. Ask him again, though, and he will probably concede with a laugh that for all the good intentions—*plus ça change*. Naples is not going to change much, I suspect, in our lifetimes. The horrible shanty settlements, we may hope, will be demolished; but the archetypal shambles, the old, slovenly, smelly, sleazy quarters of the city's centre will still be there, I swear it, when we poor compassionates stagger sere and disillusioned towards our last ossuary. Naples is Naples is Naples. She may be a disgrace, but her character seems to be stubborn and not awfully ashamed, just as the decadent South, for all its hedonism, irresponsibility and primitivism, has a way of outlasting our clean-cut energies of the North.

And let us be honest: which one of us, for all our instincts of reform, would really wish Naples to change? We would like to see the very worst of her abolished—only a sadist or a mad theorist would wish otherwise. We would like to see her children plump and happy, and her vices tempered by prosperity. But for the rest of her, the rowdy, crowded, unwashed, hugger-mugger southern soul of Naples may not please the sociologists and the planners, but at least it feels real, and human, and unexpectedly cheerful. Shelley called her the heart of the world, and that's exactly it. She may beat erratically by electronic specifications, but in the Frankenstein world we logicians have created, it is nice to find a heart at all.

NEW YORK

Through the drab flatlands of New Jersey sweeps the turnpike, eight lanes wide and fearfully busy: past oil refineries spouting smoke and flame, ships in dock and aircraft on the tarmac, railway lines and incinerators and dismal urban marshes, until it plunges into the tunnel under the Hudson River. All is ordered and regimented. Your speed is regulated, and your route, and the traffic moves nose to tail through the tunnel in a glare of harsh lights, a rumble of engines and a stink of impatient exhausts. You feel like a machine yourself, urged in jerks along a conveyor belt, and behind you the mass of America seems to extend in a wasteland of automation, tranquillizers and winking lights.

The moment you emerge from that tunnel, though, and drive blinking into Manhattan on the other side, all the old dream of America comes to life again. Instantly, as the skyscrapers greet you with a sheen of glass, a miracle occurs—a sort of daily renaissance, a flowering of the commuter's spirit. The cars and trucks and buses, no longer confined to their lanes, suddenly spring away in all directions like animals off a leash. At once, instead of conformity, all is profusion. Policemen irritably chivvy you on. Men push racks of summer frocks along the sidewalk. Trains rumble through blackened cuttings. Great liners tower above the street. There are shops with unpronounceable Central European names, and racks of strange newspapers, and black-eyed dowdy-haired women with shopping bags, and drivers hurling imprecations out of taxi windows, and bright colours everywhere, and spiced smells, skinny cats on window sills, bus-drivers with weary, patient faces, and always above you, shiny of flank and sharp of outline, the tremendous meditative shapes of the skyscrapers. You are in New York, the noblest of the American symbols, the most exciting of the cities of the earth, and in some ways the nastiest.

New York is the richest of mixtures—rich in sheer wealth, rich

New York

figuratively. A fusion of races contributes to this cornucopia, and a restless disregard for things past or permanent, and a spirit of hope and open-heartedness that still survives, if only just, from the days of free immigration, when America was the haven of the earth. The Statue of Liberty, graphically described in one reference book as 'a substantial figure of a lady', is dwarfed by the magnificence of the harbour skyline, and from the deck of a ship it is easy to miss it: but in New York, more than anywhere else in the United States, there is still dignity to the lines carved upon its plinth, and reproduced a century later at the airport of Idlewild:

> *Give me your tired, your poor,*
> *Your huddled masses yearning to breathe free,*
> *The wretched refuse of your teeming shore.*

Even today New York is not the all-American city, and perhaps reflects the state of the nation less faithfully than Chicago, say, or even Boston: but here the idea of America is still at its bold best, enlivening every situation, ennobling every squalor. To comprehend the magic of New York, and her very real glory, bear in mind that London had been in existence for fifteen centuries before the first settler built his shack on Manhattan.

Everyone has read of the magical glitter of this place, but until you have set foot in New York it is difficult to conceive of a city so sparkling that at any moment Mr. Fred Astaire might quite reasonably come dancing his urbane way down Fifth Avenue. It is a marvellously exuberant place, even when the bitter winds of the fall howl through its canyons. The taxi-drivers talk long and fluently—sometimes with a tiresome affectation of home-spun philosophy, often in pungent recollection of Russia, old Naples, wartime England or derelict Ireland. The waiters are sometimes brusque but often jolly. ('Ask for anything in the world,' one dear old boy at the Waldorf likes to tell the wondering provincial, 'and if we ain't got it, we'll get it.') Down at the Rockefeller Center skating rink, one of the very nicest places in America, there is always something pleasant to see—pretty girls showing off, children doubled up in hilarity, brave old ladies determined to succeed or wild-eyed eccentrics of diabolical skill.

For boundless vivacity and verve are the inspiration of Manhattan. The thrill of America is fading a little, as the haven matures into the greatest of Powers, but in the downtown streets of this city, away

New York

from the slums and dingy suburbs, you are still in a world of ever-spirited astonishment. The best of the new buildings are glass eyries, gay and delicate. The stores breathe a most cultivated kind of opulence—not the seductive allure of the French shops, nor the masculine distinction of London's, but something more homely without being less sophisticated. Clouds of steam from the central heating systems periodically issue from the streets, like small urban geysers, and sometimes if you look through a grille in the sidewalk you may see the gleaming metal of a great express on the underground tracks beneath. Wander up to Central Park, and you will find a row of hansom cabs, heated in the winter with little charcoal stoves, tended by elderly gentlemen in top hats, and much in demand by susceptible romantics for bumpy dalliances in the park. Potter down to the water-front, and you may stand in the shadows of the Atlantic liners, the ultimate ships, or watch a tall Yankee tug steam insolently beneath the girders of Brooklyn Bridge, her captain chewing his gum with splendid nonchalance on his high curved bridge.

This is a beautiful city—beautiful of silhouette, of colour, of dramatic impact. Nor is it a vulgar one, as long-outdated European slander has it. There are palaces of great pictures in New York, and millions go each year to see them. Each week a whole page of the *New York Times* is filled with concert announcements. There are incomparable museums, scores of theatres, famous publishing houses, a great university, private art galleries beyond number, every conceivable variety of antique dealer, bookseller, bric-a-brac merchant, jade carver, chinoiserie expert, clock-dealer, specialist in mediaeval mosaics or esoteric philately. Two or three of the New York restaurants are, by common consent of the most demanding gourmets, among the best in the world. New York is no longer the gauche *nouvelle-riche* of her lingering reputation; she has achieved a civilization if not as mellow, at least as close-knit and complete as the cultures of the old European capitals.

But somewhere behind the glitter, I sometimes feel, there is embedded a kernel of disappointment, as though all this wealth and celebrity is not quite what the city originally intended for itself. New York is an entertaining city indeed, but she is often sour to the taste: a spinster sourness, unfulfilled. Power weighs heavily upon her shoulders nowadays, and makes her sometimes a rather terrifying

New York

place. This is the seat of the United Nations, where the grandees stride and the mediocrities bicker, and it is also the prime bastion of the capitalist system, the Moscow of the West. The newest buildings of Manhattan are dreadful in their size and grandeur, and there is something eerie to the pace and frequency with which the New Yorkers tear their city down and build it up again—ever bigger, ever grander, ever more domineering. It is an almost Pharaonic zeal that inspires these mighty structures: and though it sometimes seems the result of some unbearable frustration, some unrevealed disappointment, nevertheless, as a sensitive New Yorker recently observed (himself a little frightened, I think, by the scale and savagery of the process), only a great people could erect such buildings—or demolish them with such an absolute lack of ritual or superstition.

So New York, though always stimulating, is not always happy. Beggars abound in these streets of endless promise, litter flaps depressingly through the side streets, and all around the fiery-coloured centre stretch drab sandstone suburbs, pallid housing estates, slums or sordid tenements. The inner perimeters of New York are frayed, down-at-heel and testy, full of squabbling racial conglomerations, Negroes, Puerto Ricans, Poles or Italians. The Jewish genius of the city, at its best witty and imaginative to a degree, curdles at its worst into a cruel grumpiness. The crime rate is appalling. The greed and endless rivalry of the place become depressing after a day or two. The pervasive suggestion of sham and false intention sometimes becomes so overpowering that no face value seems acceptable, and even your dearest friend appears to have an ulterior motive, as he grips you by the arm and leads you off to a martini. This is a selfish city, in some ways a vicious one, where it is exceedingly foolish to walk across the park after dusk, and where even the nursing recruitment authorities can think of no more altruistic slogan than 'Learn to take care of others, and you will know how to take care of yourself.'

But what can you expect? New York is, *par excellence*, the city acquisitive, and though marvellous incidentals have sprung from the aspiration, nevertheless most of her citizens came here in the first place to get rich—to be free too, of course, but preferably rich as well. Whatever her discontents complain about, they do not often reject the system that raised these skyscrapers with such lovely arrogance into the clouds. Even the poorest layabout likes to boast

New York

of the wealth of New York, and even the laziest striking longshore-man seldom seems to reject the proposition that if ya don't wanta get on, move over, and make way for a guy who does.

New York is a hard city perhaps, but always extraordinary, like the Jews who have made her what she is, and leaving her is like retreating from a snow summit. When you drive back along that turnpike the very air seems to relax about you, as you re-acclimatize yourself to a lower plane. The electric atmosphere softens, the noise stills, the colours blur and fade, the pressure eases, the traffic reluctantly thins. Soon you are out of the city's spell, only pausing to look behind, over the tenements and marshes, to see the lights of the skyscrapers riding the night.

ODESSA

The most dramatic, as well as the most diligent, conductor in the world is to be seen in action at the Theatre of Opera and Ballet in Odessa. He is an elderly man, but passionate. All around him as he works peculiar things are happening. Behind, in the half-empty auditorium, a constant buzz of homely conversation underlies the score, and three ill-shaven Levantines in the second row seem to be in the throes of opium dreams, squirming and sighing in their seats. In front, the stage is alive with minor mishaps —trapdoors mysteriously closing and opening, fans being dropped, iron accessories clattering, while the cast of *La Traviata*, none apparently more than five feet high, smile resolutely across the footlights with a treasury of gold teeth.

The conductor is unperturbed. Majestically he sails through the confusions of the evening, impervious to them all, sometimes grunting emotionally, sometimes joining in an aria in a powerful baritone, throwing his fine head back, bending double, conspiratorially withdrawing, pugnaciously advancing, with infinite variations of mood and facial expression, and frequent hissed injunctions to the wood-wind. Nobody in the Socialist bloc fulfils a norm more devotedly, and nobody does more credit to the Hero City of Odessa.

It is not often easy, in Moscow or Kiev, to respond to the simplicities of the Russian Revolution. In such great cities the deliberate vulgarity of Communist life, the perpetual aura of baggy trousers, hair-cream and Saturday-night hop, is more depressing than endearing, and you begin to pine, however egalitarian your convictions, for a really snooty upper-crust restaurant, or the high-pitched gossip of débutantes. In a smaller provincial centre like Odessa, though, it is different. Here, far away from the dreadful workings of State, there still feels some faint suggestion of idealism to the People's Dictatorship, a sense of simple pride and purpose: and in such a setting it is difficult not to warm to the conscientiousness of the modern urban

Odessa

Russians, whether it is directed towards a mastery of English vowels or the correction of a wandering contralto.

A century ago Odessa was an urbane seaport of Francophile tendencies, raised into eminence by a French satrap of the Tsar, the Comte de Richelieu. Though long stripped of her boudoir fripperies, she retains a certain faded elegance. A fine wide boulevard runs above the harbour, and from it descend the broad steps that figured in *The Battleship Potemkin*—forming a striking parallel, in art as in topography, with the celebrated staircase, tumbling out of the Kasbah in Algiers, that provided a climax for *Pépé le Moko*. There is an ornate old Bourse in Odessa, and the ghost of an English Club, and the shell of a Crédit Lyonnais, and an Opera House of lofty traditional opulence, muse-haunted and nymph-scrolled. There is even the old building of the local Duma, dishonestly identified by Intourist as 'yet another former Stock Exchange under the old system'. Wide, straight, and Parisian are the avenues of the city, and embedded in the thigh of a statue of de Richelieu is a cannon-ball from H.M.S. *Tiger,* a ferocious visitor to these waters during the Crimean War.

Odessa was built by the Tsars as a southern outlet for Russia, and remains the second port of the Soviet Union. She faces south and east, and her quaysides are embellished with vast welcoming slogans in Arabic, Chinese, French and English—'Long Live Peace and Friendship,' they proclaim, 'among the Peoples of the Whole World.' A smell of tar hangs agreeably on the Odessa air, and a fine jumble of shipping lies always inside the moles: a pair of lovely three-masters manned by cadets; two or three smart Black Sea liners, running down to Georgia or Istanbul; freighters from Latakia or Alexandria; a squat Russian warship with sloping bulbous funnels. In the summer British and Greek cruising liners, flecked with the Aegean, put in here for brief inquisitive visits: in the winter a fringe of ice loiters around the harbour, and most of the ships seem to lie there supine and deserted.

The docks are shut off by high walls and policemen, and you can only peer at their quaysides from an eminence, or skulk about their gateways pretending to meet a comrade: but Odessa anyway feels unmistakably a port—a peeling, rather regretful port, a Russian Tangiers. It is a cosmopolitan city still, full of Greeks, Jews, Armenians, Georgians, Egyptian seamen, Chinese delegations. The jolliest of old sacristans will conduct you around the decaying synagogue, lending you a white peaked cap for your head, and sallow

Odessa

Mediterranean faces will greet you solemnly in the Greek church. Odessa is a languid southern seaside city, snowless and sunlit, and even the pantheon of Communist deities, even the Workers' Honours Boards, even the blaring loudspeaker from the Central Committee's headquarters, even the tinny new carillon, even the nagging suspicion that somebody is following you cannot altogether stifle the relaxed and easy-going nature of the town, like a soft warm breeze across the Bosporus.

She is on the regular Intourist circuit, but is scarcely a show-place of the régime. She has busy industries, a large university, and a celebrated eye hospital: but thanks to the occurrence of a soft subsoil she has none of your towering tomb-like blocks of flats, and you have only to step through an archway off almost any boulevard to find yourself back in pre-revolutionary Russia, with tumble-down apartments around a shambled courtyard, and women with buckets collecting their water from the communal outdoor tap in the middle. All feels small, friendly and unpretentious. In the new railway station, dedicated to Odessa's heroic resistance during the war, there is a large notice-board which, upon the pressure of a button, illustrates in illuminated signs the route to any Western Russian city; and there is something very appealing to the pleasure this simple toy gives the concourse of people constantly consulting it, the air of wondering merriment that hangs about its buttons, like country festivity at a fairground.

There is also something paradoxically old-fashioned about Odessa. Her restaurants, though sprawling with greasy young men and loud with brassy jazz, are marvellously nineteenth century in appointment. Her public buildings still preserve, beneath their threadbare sloganry, shreds of old decorum. And if you observe a pair of young women sauntering together down the promenade, you will be struck by niggling sensations of *déjà vu*. What is so familiar about them? Where have you seen them before? And then, in a revealing flash, you have a vision of old newspapers lining attic drawers, full of the cloche hats, long coats, and elaborate buckled corsetry of the thirties: and you realize that these young ladies of Odessa take you back mysteriously to your childhood, like snapshots in an album, like a recollection of those devoted parents you used to see, shivering loyally beside the touch line, as you self-consciously prepared to tackle Richardson Minor.

Odessa

Just think! Odessa is the second port of Russia, the gateway of the Ukraine, the pearl of the Black Sea; yet it all boils down in my mind, such is the indivisibility of time and experience, to the memory of a prep-school soccer match, dormant for twenty years and more, and only revived by a glimpse of forgotten fashions above the Potemkin Steps.

OXFORD

Suddenly you see Oxford, a grey blur in the valley, as you drive over the hill from Newbury and the south. A haze of smoke, age and legend veils her, a locomotive snorts in her railway sidings, and all around her lie the moist green hills of the English Midlands, like open lettuce leaves. Visionary and beckoning stand her spires and domes, as Jude the Obscure glimpsed them long ago, for Oxford possesses always the quality of an idea. She is more than a city, more than a railway station, more than a road junction, more even than a University. She epitomizes a remarkable kingdom, here in the belly of England; she is a kind of shrine, where many a lofty soul has worshipped; she is a paradigm of the human conflict, between the right and the wrong, the spiritual and the material, the ugly and the beautiful; and most of all she is an aspiration, a sad reminder of what the world might be, the turn of a phrase and the joy of a discovery and the smile of a pretty girl in a punt. Her comprehension transcends classes and races, and grasps the whole range of human experience, from the sublime to the rock-bottom. She has been fouled by time and degradation. She has been fortified by centuries of controversy, rivalry and anguish. She stands beyond everyday logic, crooked, deep and contradictory. She is not a large place—from your bump in the road you may see the whole of her, and inspect her suburbs in a sweep from Headington to Hinksey: but she is one of those few cities that are more than cities, that reflect the meaning of a civilization, and thus belong not to a nation, but to the world.

The trappings of Oxford are hideous. Around her core of pinnacled beauty the modern suburbs lie faceless and blighted, genteel mock-Tudor or heedless functional, tired housing estates in awful symmetry, cheap red brick and chromium plate, miles of mess and acres of apathy. On her eastern fringes sprawl the great car factories and steel works of Cowley. On her southern flank a little wilderness of

Oxford

railway tracks, gasometers, huts and reservoirs stands like a drab no man's land beyond the canal. Through her heart a stifling stream of traffic clogs her ancient arteries, rattles her mullioned windows, and keeps her celebrated structures always trembling.

All this is because she lies in the very middle of England. Oxford was born, before the first universities were conceived, as the guardian of fords across the two rivers, Thames and Cherwell, which meet at this place, and which make this wide sedgy valley a place of vapours, water-meadows, swans and reeds. Through this fulcrum the traffic of trade began to pass in Saxon times, some by river, some by road: from London westward to Bristol, from Southampton and Winchester to the remote cities of the north. Bridges were built, with a protective fortress. Guilds of merchants came into being. Famous trading fairs were established. At the end of the eleventh century this was one of the busiest and most prosperous of English cities, with a strong sense of community and a keen eye to the main chance—it had, as the historian J. R. Green has claimed, 'five centuries of borough life before a student appeared in its streets'. Romantic myth, speculating among the quadrangles, attributes the foundation of Oxford variously to the Trojans, to the Druids, to King Mempric, who lived a millennium before Christ, or to the indistinct St. Frideswide, saved at this spot by divine intervention from being ravished on the banks of the Thames. In fact, though, the place was almost certainly founded not by saints, kings or scholars, but by hard-headed Saxon merchants, marketmen and transport contractors, with their feet on the ground and their minds on their money-bags.

By the twelfth century the University had sprung fitfully into being, and for several hundred years imposed a severe academic autocracy upon the old city, reducing it, as Green observes, from a 'busy prosperous borough . . . to a cluster of lodging-houses'. Today the pendulum has swung again, and the supremacy of Town over Gown, of matter over mind, is forcibly reasserted. Some one hundred thousand people live in Oxford, but scarcely a tenth of them have any connection with the University, and today there are many people in the civic suburbs who hardly realize that the institution exists, except for its quaint buildings and its comical traditions. The big Cowley factories cast their shadow across the flavour of the place. To their generous pay-rolls the workers have flocked from half England, and any morning in Cornmarket, the

Oxford

city's central shopping street, you may see them in their hundreds: plain but patently prosperous people, raw of accent and homely of manner, with a margin of spindly greased youths lounging around the coffee-shops, and a nub of stolid, jolly, down-to-earth Midlands housewives carrying tins of cat food in shopping baskets. Many a shiny store has erupted to serve them, overwhelming the old-school watchmakers, bespoke tailors and booksellers who used to represent the commerce of the street. Many a tattered tabloid flutters past the libraries, and many a whiff of Woolworth's scent seeps down the cloistered lanes. The common man has invaded Oxford again, and he comes to town in such numbers, with so much money to spend, that this has become one of the most cruelly congested cities in Europe.

Everywhere in the public streets there is relentless noisy movement. The wide by-passes that ring Oxford are never empty, never silent, and the apex of the place, the ancient cross-roads called Carfax, is so inundated with converging traffic that at dusk the policemen assume refulgent white coats, and are illuminated by spotlights above the crush. Stand for half an hour at the top of the High, one of the world's loveliest thoroughfares, and you may observe a cross-section of England on the move, a mirror of her functions, a gauge of her activity. Here is a double-deck trailer of gleaming new cars, bound for Lagos or New Orleans. Here is a coach-load of tourists, goggle-eyed at tinted windows. Here is a consignment of steel rods, pounding down from Birmingham to Southampton Docks, and here a glittering expense-account Rolls-Royce, whisking some padded London magnate from board-room to boudoir. You can tell by the names on the tailboards how crucial is this vortex to the motion of England: London and Bristol, Portsmouth and Newcastle, Sheffield and Chester and Newcastle-on-Tyne. Oxford is a hub, and her two old road bridges are nozzles through which, like a reluctant dentifrice, the impetus of the Midlands must be squeezed.

In a way it is historically right. The commercial life of Oxford is marked by a resilient consistency, so that we may recognize many of its patterns far back in the Middle Ages. The Freemen of the city still meet in council. The Sheriff of Oxford, once a year, still mounts his horse to impound the Commoners' horses grazing on Port Meadow. And for a perfect image of the continuity of the place you should visit Oxford during the annual St. Giles Fair, successor to the great trade fairs of mediaeval England. Today it is only a jollification, a spree, but its atmosphere remains paradoxically and piquantly antique. The whole of St. Giles, the widest street in Oxford, is cluttered with its stalls, tents, roundabouts and generators, the barking of its buskers and the popping of its airguns, and sauntering among its sideshows you may catch the people of Oxford off guard, all pretence discarded. There they stroll still, the immemorial characters of England, every type and degree of mortal, from the exquisite patrician to the grubbiest slut in carpet slippers, from the sheepish parson to the pinch-faced, leather-jerkined, weedy but raucous motor-cycle lout—all old English archetypes, and direct descendants, every one, from predecessors of the distant past, when the Cotswold hill farmers brought their wool on the hoof to Oxford market, and the city thugs cherished so violent an antipathy to the academic aesthetes that not an inch between Carfax and St. Mary's, it was said, had not been at one time or another soaked in student blood.

For always, through any Oxford scene, there stalks the scholar. The skin of Oxford is pocked and scarred, but the heart of the place remains ineffably beautiful: and this is because for eight centuries the old market-town has sheltered one of Europe's noblest universities. It is not the car factories, the bridges or the cross-roads that make Oxford one of the absolute cities: it is *Universitas Oxoniensis*. Miraculously the charm of this institution, if not the prestige, has survived the battering of the years. The population of Oxford has doubled in this century, and increased twelvefold in the past two hundred years, so that when you reach this legendary place at last, your head awhirl with madrigals, all the horror of hasty growth greets you with a sneer. But poke about a bit, give it time, reserve your judgements and restrain your resentment, and presently you will realize that Oxford's essential character has survived it all. It does not show at first. It does not flaunt itself. Oxford is a private kind of entity, and if you wish to understand the place you must look through the keyhole.

Clean across the city, stretching away into the country with playing-fields and boathouses, libraries and laboratories, sprawls the University. No central campus gives rigidity to this puzzling organism, no plan, no uniformity, no rule or universal authority clamps it into docility. Oxford University is its own master—since

Oxford

1919 the State has paid the piper handsomely, but it still dare not call the tune; and the University itself consists of some thirty autonomous colleges, each a corporation sanctified by Royal Charter, each a thing of individual character, method and style. This means that the inner texture of Oxford is unbelievably rich and varied. A warren of venerable societies straddles Carfax and the High, each with its own mellow quadrangles, its lawns and fine old lodgings, its cherished cedars or beeches, its trim porters' lodges, its old portraits glimpsed through leaded windows, its bells heard bland but insistent across the tumbled rooftops. Turn any corner in the centre of Oxford, step down any side lane from the nightmare of the traffic, and you will discover some alcove of seduction. Look through any half-closed college gateway, and you will glimpse some quaint surprise. Oxford is suggestive rather than imperative, which is why the tourists, hastily cancelling their hotel bookings, so often take one look at Carfax and hasten on to Stratford.

Nobody quite knows when this University was born, though only the most determined romantics now attribute its foundation to King Alfred. Some say it began with monastic schools, some think its first students were scholars expelled from Paris in a wave of xenophobia in 1167. Certainly by the end of the twelfth century there was a guild of teachers in the city, loosely coalesced in a *Studium Generale* on the French model; and a century later there were probably about fifteen hundred Oxford students, living in lodgings, inns, and communal societies known as 'halls'. As early as 1214 the *Studium Generale* received the first of its charters, giving it immunity from lay jurisdiction: the people of Oxford then agreed to pay an annual symbolic tribute to the University authorities, and have been paying it ever since. The University expanded inexorably, often in controversy and sometimes in violence. There were riots against the Papal Legate, fights against the Jews, quarrels between northerners and southerners, constant bloody battles between Town and Gown. Through it all learning flourished. Roger Bacon, Duns Scotus, Wyclif, Colet, More and Erasmus were all Oxford men, and under the influence of the Schoolmen and the Renaissance scholars the University so strengthened its links with Europe that it became one of the three or four greatest centres of learning on earth— rivalled only, at least in the west, by Paris, Bologna and Salamanca. By the time of the Reformation Oxford had developed its system of independent colleges, to one of which every undergraduate must belong,

Oxford

only loosely subject to the authority of the University itself. A great deal has happened to Oxford since then: the English Civil War, when King Charles moved his court to Christ Church; the Anglican religious ferments of the nineteenth century, which gave birth to the Oxford Movement; the foundation of the women's colleges; two world wars; the English social revolution; the irresistible advance of science as a fit subject for scholarship; the decline of Britain herself, and hence of nearly all her institutions. Nevertheless the University system today, with its jealously preserved college autonomies, would be easily recognizable to any wandering scholar out of the Restoration.

It is true that in recent years the University authorities, the central but amorphous governing body, have been impelled into a livelier rôle: the immense cost of new laboratories, in particular, is beyond the means of individual colleges. Nevertheless the Oxford colleges remain proudly, resolutely, sometimes rather absurdly individual. They have their own incomes, often sizeable, derived from landownership, skilful investment, and endowments of diverse kinds. They decide their own curricula, and need accept no academic edicts from the University itself. They appoint their own instructors, and choose their own students, so that each college still has a distinctive style and type of its own, from the socially glittering (Christ Church or New College) to the academically daunting (Balliol or Magdalen). They have their own traditions, customs, ranks and honorifics—Christ Church is presided over by a Dean, Magdalen by a President, All Souls by a Warden, Worcester by a Provost, St. Edmund Hall by a Principal, Pembroke by a Master, Lincoln by a Rector. They are often shamefully selfish, notably uninterested in each other's anxieties, and they are sometimes pitifully short-sighted, cheerfully yielding to the pressures of big business for the sake of a quick profit or a promising endowment. Many critics think the system outmoded, and demand the centralization of authority, administrative and academic: but it is the survival of the colleges, their persistent complexity, their hauteur and stubbornness, that has maintained the constancy of Oxford, and kept the place unique.

In their glorious buildings you can best sense its meaning and its character. In the old Benedictine cottages of Worcester College, for instance, you may recognize the original lodging-houses of mediaeval Oxford, narrow, gabled, mullioned places, with dark

Oxford

narrow staircases and gimcrack chimneys. In St. Edmund Hall, with its delectable flower-fragrant quadrangle, you may see the very last of the old residential halls. In the fifteenth-century Divinity Schools you may see reflected the growing power and prestige of the *Studium Generale,* and in Wolsey's magnificent Christ Church you may sense the new social consciousness of the University, supplementing its poor scholars and earnest clerics with dazzling noblemen, fops and playboys. The Age of Reason is epitomized in Magdalen's lovely New Buildings, set among the deer groves; the very essence of the Tractarian Movement infuses the Victorian red-brick of Keble; all the rising prestige of science gleams in the new laboratories beside the University parks. Above all, everywhere, among the colourful boathouses on the river, in the vaulted reading rooms of the Bodleian, among the aromatic splendours of Christ Church Hall, in the great Ashmolean Museum or the spanking Playhouse—above all you may sense, everywhere among these structures, the endless variety, the breadth of idiosyncrasy, the pride and the pragmatism that give this institution its character.

It is an old, gnarled, evocative thing, *Universitas Oxoniensis.* Its buildings are not usually spectacular, but are mostly gentle and kindly, from the delicate little quadrangle of Corpus Christi to the benign classical rotunda, portly but dignified, called the Radcliffe Camera. Its corridors echo the tread of a thousand great men: Erasmus or Sir Walter Raleigh, Gladstone or Sir Philip Sidney, Gibbon, Shelley, John Wesley, William Penn, Pitt, Swinburne, Lewis Carroll, Chatham and Lord North, Inigo Jones and Christopher Wren, Max Beerbohm, Peel, Hakluyt the geographer, Rhodes the imperialist, Foxe the martyrologist, Richard Burton the Arabist, Sydney Smith and Charles James Fox and John Galsworthy and T. E. Lawrence and De Quincey. Its splendid libraries boast no electronic catalogues, but are stained with learning and scholarly delight. Its doorsteps are worn deep with age, and here and there among the colleges you may stumble across a remnant of the city ramparts, long since integrated into the academic life, and looking so shaggy, pebbly and eroded that it seems less like a wall than a geological formation. The clocks of the University move with ancient whirrs and ticks, the doors of the University open with creaks and wheezes, and the gardens of the University, with their sensual abundance of design, their treasured creepers and their pampered

Oxford

lawns—the gardens of Oxford, for all their conceits and elaborations, seem inevitable and immemorial, as though they have sprung ready-clipped and weeded from the spongy subsoil of the Thames marshes.

Most of all, perhaps, it is these gardens that keep the heart of Oxford, for all the ravages of time and progress, still a place of inexhaustible allure. One of the classic English experiences is to stand in the gardens of Merton College, say, on an afternoon of high summer, when the valley air hangs warm and heavy, and the trees preside over a heavenly shade. The thud and roar of the traffic is only a suggestion beyond the college gateway. The four golden weathervanes of the chapel tower loiter above you in idle parallel. Before you Christ Church meadows lie damp and virginal, like a slab of open wet country, and away to the east the famous tower of Magdalen stands sentinel above its bridge. Merrily on the afternoon hang the sounds of the river beyond the meadows—the shouts of a towing coach, a ripple of badinage, a girl's laugh, a snatch of song. From the shadowy staircases behind you emanate suggestions of donnish activity—a slow rustle of pages, the clink of a glass, arguments testily exchanged, the hint of a snore. The bumble-bees potter benevolently from blossom to blossom. A lawn-mower is busy somewhere beyond the wall. Somebody is knocking a ball about with a cricket bat, to the magical hollow thud of well-oiled wood on leather. There is a smell of cut grass, books, old wood, flowers, linseed oil and stone. There is a soft rustle of leaves, and a squeak from the weathervanes above, when a breeze springs off the river.

Some will call it an outmoded world, that these sensations represent. Some will call it doomed anyway, as Oxford reluctantly tacks to the winds of time. But for some it is a glimpse of the world as it might have been, of England as her lovers used to see her, before disillusionment set in.

For Town or Gown, divine or unspeakable, old or new, vital or fuddy-duddy—whichever face she presents, Oxford is always a mirror of England. She draws her inspiration from the genius of the nation, and all her faults and virtues, all her scars and splendours, are but microcosms of a greater model. Hundreds of thousands of foreigners have lived in Oxford down the centuries, contributing marvellously to her glories, and there are always hundreds of foreigners about today, from eminent visiting professors to the blonde German girls with bicycles and airline bags who have come to help with the children and learn the language. Yet no city in England remains more English, and no institution remains more faithful to its origins than this remarkable University.

In Oxford you may encounter the whole range of the English species, *homo anglicus*, from the highest type of civilized and sagacious animal to the lowest humped and furtive degenerate. At any one moment you may find here twenty or thirty of the cleverest men in England, ten or twelve of the most distinguished, half a dozen who have become nationally famous as television performers or writers of detective novels: but you may also bump into as primitive a type of urbanized peasant as survives anywhere in western Europe. The climate of Oxford is dank, and the Oxfordshire native often has mould in his soul. There is eccentricity in the air of the place, and bloody-mindedness, the defiance of swart bucolics, the supreme indifference of dons. Nowhere in Oxford is altogether prosaic. The drab old railway station has its own glamour, for did not Zuleika Dobson arrive there on the train from Paddington? Even the grubby Trill Mill stream, emerging sluggishly into the daylight from its subterranean channels—even that gloomy waterway has romance, for did not Lawrence of Arabia once sail down it in a punt? In Christ Church meadows Dr. Johnson slid on the ice. In Alice's Shop in St. Aldate's the White Queen turned into the old sheep knitting behind her counter. You may find Oxford disappointing at first, as Hilaire Belloc's stranger did—

> *Is it from here the people come,*
> *Who talk so loud, and roll their eyes,*
> *And stammer? How extremely odd!*
> *How curious! What a great surprise!*

You may not sense her enchantment from your first sniff on the Newbury road, your first glimpse of her gasworks and frowsty tobacconists. Give her a week or two, though, and her old slow magic may enthrall you too, as it has generations of addicts before you. She is no paragon, no virgin Paradise, no Shangri-la. She is beloved, by the truest of her admirers, in a special, wry kind of way: because she is beautiful but blotched, wise but fallible, proud but also pitiful: because she is, more than most cities in a steely world, incurably, gloriously human.

PARIS

Gingerly the middle-aged Englishman, tilting his trilby, emerges out of the Gare du Nord into the streets of Paris. He has a couple of hours to spend before he rejoins his train at the Gare de Lyon, but he views the prospect with no wild abandon, for deep inside him, however hard he tries, however polished his French or cosmopolitan his past—deep inside him there stirs, like a rustle of bones in a dark cavern, an old English antipathy to the place. It stems from centuries of bloodshed and rivalry; from the bitterness of tragic alliance; from the puritan strain that still runs through the English character, and long ago stigmatized this incomparable capital as an anteroom of Purgatory; from envy, perhaps, and a sense of provincial origins; from the robust self-assertion of sea-going islanders, and the blinkered vision of history. Americans adore Paris, hasten there to write their novels or paint their violent abstracts, love her in the spring-time, hire her same old taxi-cabs, set themselves up with slinky blondes in desperately expensive garrets. The middle-aged English approach, however, is altogether more wary and restrained, and the visitor looks sharply right and left, tucking his wallet more securely into his pocket, as he walks briskly through the maniacal taxis and settles at the corner café for what, he thinks with a wry smile, the French comically call a cup of tea. He knows he is in the wrong. He knows he ought to have coffee. But there is something about Paris that inflames his insularity, and makes the Channel behind his back feel very deep, wide and important.

It is partly the confounded foreignness of the place. To this Englishman nowhere in the world is more irrevocably abroad than Paris, which is a good deal nearer London than Newcastle is. If she felt a little closer before the war, four years incommunicado sealed her off, once and for all, as a city beyond the divide. Danger and ignominy have hardened her arteries of pride, and spared as she is the burden of a common language, she remains today, in a world of

Paris

fading frontiers, overwhelmingly and magnificently French. She is the fulcrum of Europe, but she is emblazoned with all the splendours of old-school patriotism. She is the headquarters of N.A.T.O., but no vacuous Allied soldiery slouches through her streets. She shelters, as always, a vast foreign community, but her guests are clothed in the fabric of France. Hardly anybody in the Paris streets seems to speak English. Hardly anybody looks Americanized, or Anglicized, or Italianized, let alone Germanized. Paris is French all through, from *pissoir* to Academy, and the middle-aged Englishman, with all his inherited instincts of patronage, feels himself at an unfair disadvantage. Like the poet before him, he loves Humanity with a love that's pure and pringlish: but he feels an obscure resentment towards the French, who never will be English.

Then, says he to himself, Paris is so damned pompous. A Mall or two is all right in its way, of course, and comes in useful for royal processions or emergency car parks: but a whole city drawn geometrically, in circles, arcs and right angles, offends the English taste for studied informality. Paris has, it is perfectly true, her vast rambling filigree of back streets, climbing over Montparnasse and through the warrens of Montmartre, but as the Englishman pays his bill and sets off through the city, he feels himself to be transiting endless acres of formality. The Champs-Elysées goes on and on. The Place de l'Etoile goes round and round. It feels a mile from one corner of the Place de la Concorde to another, and retreating through the Tuileries from the gorgeous severity of the Louvre is like retiring backwards, with frequent obsequious bows, down the interminable audience chamber of some royal presence. The very river of Paris feels artificial, like a long water-folly in an elaborate belvedere, and the Eiffel Tower looks as though it has been placed there by a divine landscape gardener, as a lesser practitioner might erect a wicker pagoda behind the rose-beds. All this upsets our Chestertonian, who, reflecting that Britannia needs no boulevards, no spaces wide and gay, feels it somehow irritating that the French should need them either.

He supposes, as he broods down the Rue de Rivoli, that it's all part of the Frenchman's *cleverness*. Everyone knows the Parisians are as clever as so many monkeys, and in this city nothing feels simple or unsophisticated. Everything is scented. Even the crusty door-keepers inspect you with a knowing air, and the fat market ladies of Les Halles do not look like proper working women at all, but rather like enormous eccentric dowagers slumming it for fun, or honouring some cracked family conviction. The worldly Parisiennes are not only unattainably elegant, but also dauntingly well read, and have a maddening habit of being good with horses, too. The suave young men are rubbed smooth as almonds with the unguent of *savoir-faire*. The students at the Sorbonne blaze with politics and weird philosophical speculation, but never seem to ladder a stocking. Even the dustmen sip modish drinks, like pernod, and eat fancy cheeses, like Camembert or Brie, and smoke strong tart cigarettes, and generally behave with an urbanity that seems to the middle-aged Englishman, recalling his visits to the sergeants' mess, just a little presumptuous. He stifles the thought at once, of course, for he is a liberal sort of fellow: but it is there, it is there, as it was when the heads rolled.

He distrusts them, too. Yes, he does. He knows all about the English crime wave, but he cannot restrain the sensation that he has fallen among thieves. There is something sly and underhand to the careful indolence of the little shops, those lovely clothes tossed into the windows like nightdresses in a bottom drawer, that calculated clutter of exquisite frivolities, that scalpel juxtaposition of the gay cheap and the ruinously extravagant. There is something very suspicious about the sullen brusqueness of the taxi-driver, as though he is swiftly summing his customer up with a view to disembowelling him. There is something horribly ingratiating to the waiter's smile, as though he is secretly chuckling over false additions. Nothing feels quite straightforward to the middle-aged Englishman: and what's more, he tells himself, as though this really were the last straw—'what's more, I wouldn't be surprised if these blighters *actually cheat each other!*'

For long ago, far back in his origins, he was taught to look twice at a Frenchman's credentials, and in his own lifetime, he feels, the Parisian record has scarcely been impeccable. Philip Sidney could write of 'that sweet enemy, France', but later the feeling wore off. Who knows, the Englishman asks himself with a sniff, whether the French will be any better next time? Who knows when the next coup will occur? Who has not seen the gendarmes, in the land of Fraternity, bashing the poor students with batons, or spraying them with tear-gas? What about the O.A.S., and the water torture, and Algeria? What about this fellow de Gaulle, and Laval, and Fashoda, and Old Bony, and the burning of Rye, and Agincourt? Who (says the middle-aged Englishman to himself, getting quite hot under his

Paris

collar, which is made of the same heavy Sea Island cotton that his father always had)—who, says he bitterly, are the Parisians to talk?

And so, disturbed but undeniably stimulated by his visit to Paris, he makes his way towards the station—a little apprehensively, for he feels pretty certain that they gave him the wrong departure time, and anyway he has never been very adept with the twenty-four-hour clock. He is, you see, a man of habit, and he is also middle-aged. He is expressing all the prejudices of an imperial generation, reared to grandeur, fostered on the last fragments of splendid isolation. He can just remember, dimly in childhood, an England that was still the world's arbiter, grandly correcting imbalances of power—here crossly checking a potentate, there patting a suitable revolutionary kindly on the head. He does not realize how fast they are draining his beloved Channel. He is not, I think, a married man, but if he had children of his own he would know that every thought that crossed his mind in Paris stamped him a child of his age. His is the last generation into whose silly old eye, when the white English cliffs appear at last above the blurred horizon, a hot atavistic tear embarrassingly insists upon rising. He is well the right side of fifty still, but he is almost the last of the islanders.

We should not blame him, or scoff at his ideas. His way was singularly successful in its time, and honourable too, and enabled the English, entrenched behind their moat, to evolve a national genius that has enriched, astonished and amused us all. The cycle of history has turned, though, and one of the excitements of our time is the thought that the old European comity is awakening again, recalling its estranged children, stretching itself like Rip Van Winkle and massaging its mighty muscles. Never again, I prophesy, will an English generation step so cautiously into Paris, with so many prickly reservations, for it is the inescapable destiny of this city to be the capital of Europe. Who would seriously begrudge it her? Who could long be jealous of such a place? If the younger English go to her as supplicants, it is only like asking a goddess for a dance, and need not make us blush.

And even our friend in the trilby, startled to find his train at the right platform at the advertised time, has to admit, grudgingly, that the Parisians seem to be making some progress at last.

PORT OF SPAIN

If you walk across the Savannah in the dying heat of evening, you may sometimes hear the strains of unaccompanied music, and know that young Mr. Morgan is practising his violin. The Savannah is a wide green common on the northern side of Port of Spain, in Trinidad, where the tropical hills come sidling down to the sea, and around its perimeter there stands a company of legendary Trinidadian mansions. One is gorgeously Gothic, one exotically Moorish, one predominantly blue: but the most stylish of them all is No. 25 Maraval Road, where Mr. Morgan lives. It is a big white house surrounded with balconies, like an eccentric gunboat on the China Station, and it is encrusted with every kind of ornament, towers and turrets and filigree and wrought iron and balustrades and flagstaffs and weathercocks and all possible fractions of elaboration.

In the Moorish house there lives an archbishop, in the Gothic castle an old plantation family; but it is characteristic of Trinidad that among the inhabitants of No. 25 should be young Mr. Morgan, who came from England only a few years ago and who loves to play his violin in a cool vaulted upstairs chamber. Port of Spain is a city of endless tumbling variety, mingled races, haphazard collusions, surprises and incongruities; gilded with the histories of the Western world, with a past of piracy, slavery, and war, and a present ranging from razzle-dazzle politics to the British Council. Mr. Morgan may sound an improbable figure, up there with his music-stand, but he is only an agreeable chip in a gaudy and multitudinous mosaic.

As you wander on through the Savannah, with his music faintly in your ears, you may sense some of the gusto and exuberance of this heterogeneous society. Here is the piazza of Trinidad. In the empty grandstand of the race-course a big Negro in a straw hat sprawls across the seats in indolent splendour, but below him on the grass all is movement, bustle and vivacity. Wherever you look, from the hills to the city, they are playing cricket. To be sure, they are playing the game all over the island, in numberless unmapped clearings in

Port of Spain

the bush, overhung by lugubrious banana trees or gorgeous flamboyants: but this is the very heart of Trinidadian cricket, where the game is played today with more dash and delight than anywhere else on earth. There may be thirty or forty games, all at the same time. The thud of the balls echoes like muffled fireworks across the green, and wherever you look there are the crouching fielding figures, the big stylish black batsmen, a game suddenly collapsing in hilarious laughter, or the poised theatrical expectancy, all white eyes and quivering arms, that follows the magical cry of '*Howzat?*'

Some of these sportsmen are grand and mannered, with spotless whites and rolled wickets; but they trail away through immeasurable gradations of clubmanship to the raggety small boys on the edge of the field, with an old bit of wood for a bat, and a stone for a ball, and the wicket-keeper peering with breathless expectancy over a petrol can. Whatever the style, the game is pursued with panache. Balls, stones, and fieldsmen hurl themselves indiscriminately across your path. Wild cries of scorn or enthusiasm punctuate your progress. 'Him's out! Him's out!' shout the small boys in delight, and the young man with the pipe murmurs 'Pretty, very pretty shot.' Many a strand of culture or tradition contributes to the texture of Port of Spain, and one of the strongest is that tough old umbilical, cricket.

Not all the cricketers are black. Many of these citizens are Indian by origin, and many are a *mélange* in themselves, part European, part African, with a touch of Chinese and a Hindu grandparent on the mother's side. Racial rivalries are still potent, especially between brown and black, and sometimes you may catch a hint of them on the Savannah. An Indian father, for example, shoos away a small black boy anxious to play kites with his son. 'Go away, sonny,' he says crossly, 'this is a private game we are playing, you see, we do not want other people coming and playing here.' The black boy gazes stubbornly into the middle distance. He is wearing an old Army forage cap, much too big for him. 'I'se not playing with you anyway,' he says. 'I'se playing here all by myself. This ain't no private garden. I'se just flying my kite right here where I belong.' And you can see a spasm of annoyance cross that Hindu's smooth face, a spasm that runs through the society of Trinidad, and gives an extra vicious animation to the politics of the city.

There are white people on the Savannah, too. The girls playing hockey on the south side, watched by an audience ranging from the maternal to the frankly salacious, well represent the shades of allure

Port of Spain

once conceived by a local competition promoter: 'Miss Ebony and
Miss Mahogany, Miss Satinwood and Miss Allspice, Miss Sandalwood,
Miss Golden Apple, Miss Jasmine, Miss Pomegranate, Miss Lotus
and Miss Appleblossom.' Here and there a weathered white West
Indian plays long-stop or lounges in the grass, and sometimes you
may even see an elderly imperial couple, in khaki shorts and linen
skirt, exercising themselves doggedly across the green. Beside the
botanical gardens the Governor-General's house still looks exceedingly British, but only very rarely do you hear the strident voice
of anti-white nationalism. There seems no public resentment against
so diffident a pigment as ours, and the loiterers will grin at you
pleasantly as you pursue your watchful navigations between the
pitches.

Often they will do more than merely grin, for the Trinidadian is a
great talker. He may want to talk about religion. 'You have to understand that we are Sunnis; it's all a matter of orthodoxy, we do not
agree about the succession, you see.' Or: 'My friend, I come here not
to play games but to meditate. I come to think, to try to understand,
you get me?' Or they want to talk politics. 'It's all a matter of race,
man. This man's a dictator, that's quite clear. He's got no experience.
A man like Bertie, he's got politics in his blood. That's the truth,
man.' Or: 'Where do you belong? England? I've got two brothers
and an aunt and a cousin in Birmingham. They live 102 Middens
Lane, Birmingham 2. Sure, they like it fine, making plenty money!'
Or here, as everywhere in the Western world, you may hear the
time-honoured cry of the taxi-man, leaning across the railings beside
the road. 'You want a car, sir? I take you all round the island, Pitch
Lake, Benedictine Monastery, Airport, Calypso, Limbo Dance,
Night Clubs? Here's my card, sir! That's my name, Cuthbert B.
Harrison!'

And finally, a climax to your wanderings, you may find yourself
embroiled in the counter-marchings of an embryo steel band, twenty
boys in home-made uniforms beating on cans and tin plates and
chanting rhythmically. On their sailor jackets the words 'Brass
Boys' are hazily embroidered, and they prance there in the evening
sunshine like black leprechauns, banging away at their plates,
singing their boisterous but monotonous ditty, round and round in a
vigorous long-legged barefoot circle. The cricketers play their
ancient game; the kites stream above the Savannah; an English lady
waits patiently for her dog beside the race track; the Negro in the

Port of Spain

grandstand stirs, tilts his hat over his eyes and goes to sleep again; and in the middle of it all this noisy rite exuberates, the shining lithe legs kick to its clattering rhythms, and the white teeth flash in the sunshine.

Port of Spain is a tolerant, cosmopolitan, relatively well-educated city; but one sometimes feels that for all the stroke-play and the intelligence the real essence of the place is contained in these raw and raucous celebrations. Certainly there are moments when the music of Mr. Morgan's violin, still riding the breeze uncertainly, seems the melody of a retreating world, just as the intoxicating turrets and baubles of his house are memorials to a Trinidad of long ago.

PRAGUE

When President Nasser of Egypt first decided to buy weapons from the Communist bloc, he told the British Ambassador that he had reached an agreement with the authorities in a place called, or so it seemed, Praygew. This baffled the diplomat for a moment or two, but running his quick mind through the roster of Communist capitals, Peking to Sofia, he realized that the President could only mean that chill but lovely paragon, that evocation of baroque and Bren gun, Prague.

The Egyptian's pronunciation was perfectly understandable, for when you fly into Prague, even if you are a European yourself, you find yourself at once in several simultaneous unfamiliar worlds. You stand, for a start, in one of the westernmost capitals of the Russian Empire, stretching away portentously from Berlin to the Aleutians. You enter the ornate historical world of the Hapsburgs and the old Empire, dignified by a multitude of hazy half-remembered monarchs and graced by the attendance of the great musicians, poets, artists and architects of a vanished Europe. And you step from your aircraft into the very cockpit of the Continent, land-locked and mountain-bred, embedded between the Germanies and the Balkans. No wonder Colonel Nasser stumbled. Prague is not very far as the bomber flies, from Cairo or from London, but when you get there she does feel a little remote and inexplicable, like a very foreign lady in a bus.

Her Communism will strike you first, exercise your imagination most strenuously, and provide an inescapable sombre background to your visit. A huge red star dominates the airport, and on the tarmac there may be a sleek jet from Moscow, a burly transport up from Bucharest, or a squadron of eager fighters. You are plunged at once, all eyes and scepticism, into the milieu of the People's Republics. Poor Prague welcomes you beautiful but servile, with the slogans of party piety nagging you from her hoardings, and the drab emblems of State management on every corner tobacconist's. There are

Prague

Afghans or Syrians in the hotel lounges, come to buy arms, cars or steel rods, and ubiquitous coveys of Poles, Rumanians, Hungarians and East Germans. The London *Daily Worker* lies about in unfamiliar and flattering profusion. There are pictures of party dignitaries upon the walls, and now and then a group of square-shouldered Russians marches through, in baggy trousers or school-marm hats, here a thoughtful Mongolian student, there a genial bald Muscovite endearingly bawling for vodka. The people of Prague will treat you only with kindness, and even the policemen do their best to help, when they hear you come from the capitalist West: but though Czechoslovakia is scarcely the most lovable of Moscow's acolytes, and is indeed far from morose or moribund, still there is great pathos to the subservience of this ancient capital, and a trace of degradation too. Prague is not, like Warsaw, always crackling with irreverent independence, glittering though her night-clubs are, and well-stocked her shops; she feels, as was said of the Chevalier d'Eon after his metamorphosis, 'sensibly adjusted to her new condition'.

One of the perpetual solaces of the more sensitive Czechs, though, must be the florid grandeur of their history, just as the pageantry of London comforts those Englishmen who feel themselves misused by contemporary history. A dim but gorgeous succession of kings strides across the chronicles of Prague, and the air is elaborate with the complications of her past. You may look out across the capital with good King Wenceslas, who stands in effigy beneath the National Museum, or you may follow the coronation route of the Bohemian kings through the tortuous cobbled streets that led them to the Cathedral. Here, says your guide, with an historical flourish, occurred the Defenestration of Prague, in which, as the reference books graphically observe, 'the Bohemian Diet emphasized its position by throwing two imperial councillors out of the castle windows'. You perhaps have no intimate recollection of Ottocar I or the Emperor Sigismund, and your vision of the Taborites and Utraquists may be blurred: but in Prague the stately figures of history remain startlingly alive, parading stylishly outside your window, or whispering hoarsely in your tourist's ear.

Glorious is the culture that survives from their unregenerate times. Prague herself is a masterpiece of Gothic and baroque, still serenely regal for all her dingy patina. The window-frames may need a lick of paint, the five-pointed stars do become a little tedious,

Prague

and I have not myself visited the Lenin Museum: but Prague Castle still sprawls gloriously above the river, a township of squares, vaulted halls and lofty gateways, rising like a symphony to its climax, through successions of palace roofs, turrets and flagpoles to the tall defiant pinnacles of St. Vitus's Cathedral. Below the castle hill the celebrated ranks of saints and symbols still stand, lumpishly ornate, upon the balustrades of Charles Bridge. They are blackened by the centuries, but still lavish with scrolls and flowery architectural grace-notes: here St. Christopher conveys the infant Christ with infinite stylized tenderness across the stream, and here a company of poor Christians, immured in their cramped stone cells, peer wanly out at the pedestrians beneath the portly stomach of their Turkish gaoler.

Prague is full of such elaborate embellishments, giving her a rich heavy flavour, like a Tokay. Many a romantic palace, impregnated with legend, meditates behind its towering leaf-clad walls. Enormous semi-nude figures, entwined with vines, scrolls or tridents, support the doorways of houses or sustain the assurance of numberless allegories. Everywhere Gothic towers and gateways stand in cheerless magnificence, everywhere splendid spires or castellations ornament the skyline, and on the old Town Hall a glorious mediaeval clock strikes the hours with a courteous procession of bowing apostles, the clanging of a deathly bell and the hopeful blast of a trumpet (and there is always a little crowd of sight-seers—tourists, untidy soldiers or merely proud citizens of the place—standing in the square to applaud this hoary marvel).

There is grace and delicacy, too, to the heritage of Prague. On the outskirts of the city is the house where Mozart lived, now a delightful museum, rich in autographs, instruments and curiosities: outside in the yard there stands a big stone table beneath the trees, at which, in the sunny Bohemian summer, he worked upon *Don Giovanni*. Smetana and Dvořák were natives of this place, Wagner and Chopin frequented it, and Prague remains a metropolis of music. There are two resident opera companies in the city, and at least four symphony orchestras. An eager, if scarcely experimental, intelligentsia survives, fortified by State encouragement, and if you would like a reminder of the old artistic Prague (a little coarsened and tattered, to be sure, a little weary and threadbare at the corners) go and eat roast goose at the restaurant that still flourishes, like an irrepressible family steward, actually within the castle gates—the very sign and summit of Bohemianism.

Prague

So Prague is a city of overlapping ambiances, some sociable, some hostile, some heavy-going to a degree. You may not respond to her at first, weighed down as she is by the leaden burden of Communism, but her beauty is undeniable, and she has a sort of bitter fascination to her, a taste of gall and honey. For myself, when I was wandering one winter evening through Wenceslas Square whistling a jolly melody, I was suddenly overcome by the melancholy of this Christian capital, bound by an alien creed: and entering a nearby gloomy buffet I engaged in halting conversation the very first old man I saw, and brought him a cup of coffee. For Praygew can feel, at such a moment, a long, cold, friendless, unpronounceable way from home.

RAWALPINDI

I was woken in Rawalpindi, my first night there, by a bugle-call played with such flawless perfection that for a moment I thought it might, like those improbably impeccable peals you sometimes hear from English village steeples, all be done on tape recorders.

I should have known better. Rawalpindi is the interim capital of Pakistan, and since that Republic's chosen public image is nothing if not well tailored, I ought to have known that anything so cheap as a taped reveille, like an immoderately padded shoulder, would be anathema to the place. This is a city dedicated to the straight eye and the steady trigger, upper lips stiff and thumbs down the seams of the trousers. It feels as though its affairs have been taken over by the adjutant, abetted by the padre, of some smartish regiment of the line—nothing so irreverent as the cavalry, nothing quite so posh as the Brigade—and it has paradoxical overtones of Henty, Tom Brown and Maud Diver. Officially the ideology of Pakistan is all Islamic, but to me the contemporary aspirations of Rawalpindi seem perfectly expressed in a well-known poem by a local journalist: '*If*.'

To anyone with a taste for the military virtues, this is not at all disagreeable. What could be nicer, in the whole blighted context of modern travel, than to awake to the bugle in the tall chill room of your Rawalpindi hotel? Outside the first spanking tongas of the day, all shining woodwork and polished brass, are clip-clopping down the Mall, and presently your bearer arrives, in his plumed white turban and blue tunic, to poke up the embers of last night's fire, and stack it high with crinkled logs. Tea is there, in a glittering pot. Your shoes stand beside the door gleaming like wax. 'Bath running, Sahib,' says the bearer, and Lord! what a lost loved world is re-created all around you, with that sting of the Punjab morning outside your door, and the smell of burning wood, and the first steam issuing from the bathroom door, and that fine old fellow hobbling out to chivvy up the breakfast!

The new Pakistani capital, Islamabad, stands on the outskirts of

Rawalpindi

Rawalpindi, beneath the first foothills of the Himalayas: and to this choice of a national fulcrum there is a point scarcely less forceful than the exhausting symbolisms of Brasília. The military autocracy that chose the place came to power because the old Pakistan was riddled and demoralized with corruption, and the very emblem of that degradation was Karachi, the former capital. She remains, to my mind, a singularly nasty town, grasping and characterless, and the move to these northern reaches of West Pakistan, for a traveller as for a Government, is like switching from stale beer to iced pineapple juice. The winters are cold and stimulating up here; the traditions of the land are warlike and inspiring; and always up the road stand the mystic mountains of the Karakoram and the Hindu Kush, icy and all-seeing. When the bugle calls in Rawalpindi it is almost a pleasure, and certainly a sort of nagging obligation, to get out of bed.

Like Alex, Valpo, Pompey, Jo'burg, B. A. and L. A., this is a city known by its nickname. Everybody calls it Pindi, and even this in a curious way reflects the spirit of regimental bonhomie that permeates the place. 'Old man,' I read in a handbook for officers of the Pakistan Army, 'is an affectionate way of referring to one's C.O. only in his absence. The epithet is never used in his presence.' So one feels about Pindi. She is not an old town, nor a large one—the British plucked her from obscurity, and she is still not much more than a swollen cantonment; but she has a manner of genial, if not romantic, authority.

Kashmir is over the hills there, and the roads from the mountains rumble with military convoys, or are haunted by shaggy Kashmiri, men as supple as willow-wands, beautiful girls with nose-clips, driving their silky goat-herds to lower pastures. To the south stands old Lahore, to the west is Attock, Alexander's gateway to India, and Peshawar of the marvellous bazaars, and the old Khyber itself, still frowning with forts and Lee-Enfields. The Grand Trunk Road marches through Rawalpindi, Calcutta-bound, and a breath of Central Asia ruffles her avenues. She stands on the edge of the North-West Frontier, half-way to Bokhara and Tashkent, and she seems to smell of sheepskin and horse-leather. The incomparable soldiers of the Pakistan Army give her streets style and swagger. Camberley tastes dominate her bookshops, stocked partly with such works as *First Steps in A. A. Gunnery* and *Lewis Gun Mechanism Made Easy*, partly with those mysterious memsahib's novels, always

Rawalpindi

in their Eleventh Thousand, that have titles like *Time Is Whispering*, *Radiant and Reckless*, or *Such Is Life*, by Dorothy B. Upson, author of *Yesterday*. The principal palmist of Rawalpindi, the celebrated Professor Khudabux, boasts the highest testimonials from 'Viceroys, Governors, Commanders-in-Chief, Judges of High Courts, Prime Ministers, Lords, Ladies and Ruling Chiefs.' Many of her craftsmen are still 'by appointment' to forgotten paladins of the Raj, and Mrs. Davies's Hotel still bears that lady's plump and reassuring name. Pindi is not a mean or vindictive city. Her discipline is always magnanimous. 'It is advisable,' says my handbook, 'to take a reasonable interest even in the prisoners locked up in the quarterguard.'

All this is scarcely representative of Pakistan as a whole, but it does fairly epitomize the flavour of Government in this Republic. The chaplain is always present, for Pakistan uncertainly revolves around the notion of a true Islamic State, but the adjutant is distinctly in command. This is not a bullying or a hectoring kind of State, but it has an instinct for paternal autocracy. The values of contemporary Rawalpindi are those of an officer and gentleman, inherited through generations of Indian Army men and civil servants, out of Arnold's Rugby and Victorian family prayers. They have almost been sniggered out of court in England, overtly at least, but here they survive regnant and unembarrassed. No beatniks will sneer at the principles of Pindi. No disgruntled corporal will write to his M.P. No Flash Alfs or barrack-room lawyers will quibble about the rules. Pindi is a fair city, but strict; genial, but strait-laced: her orders impeccably typed, her stores correct to the last wing-nut, the pebbles of her regimental mottoes dazzlingly whitewashed. 'Be a man, my son!' she seems to say, brusquely advising Gunga Din, as he loiters through the cantonment, to get himself a haircut.

You might not call her Pindi to her face: but only because it would be, as the book says about officers carrying umbrellas, 'unsoldierly.'

REYKJAVIK

'Those Algerians!' an elderly politician once expostulated to me in Reykjavik, putting down his newspaper and wagging his beard in irritation. 'They're nothing but trouble-makers. They were up here, you know, with their pillaging and their carnage—Einar Arnarson, I think it was, put paid to them, he and Jon Olafsson, and one or two others'—and suddenly it dawned upon me, as his sharp affronted eyes blazed into mine, that he was not talking about contemporary politics, but about the savage Barbary pirates of old, who sailed as far north as Iceland itself in search of bloodshed and booty. To such an old man of Reykjavik the Dark Ages are still alive, Einar and Jon are familiar comrades, and all the centuries of Icelandic history are truncated and compressed: for there is no more self-centred capital on earth than this proud, colourless little metropolis on the fringe of the Arctic Ocean.

Nearly half the Icelanders live in Reykjavik, but she remains an unpretentious place, crouched about her harbour without much pomp or dazzle. Her buildings are dull and mostly modern, only a gaunt cathedral, a sober Parliament and a neat little Presidential lodging giving her any architectural distinction: but she is never without a certain dour excitement. In her streets you are always aware of Iceland's peculiar presence, stretching away into the mist behind your back: a desert island, a volcanic lump in the ocean, warmed only by the Gulf Stream and by its own subterranean energies. Due southward there is nothing but sea between Iceland and the Antarctic. Northward only water and ice separates the island from the Pole. Iceland is technically in Europe, but she is nearer to Greenland than she is to Scotland, poised frigidly between the Old World and the New. Her terrain is mostly uninhabited—a grim dream of lava plains and high mountains, with glaciers sweeping in grand desolation to the sea, and a haze of smoke shimmering about the summit of Mount Hekla (a volcano which, in the eyes of the ancient travellers, provided irrefutable evidence of the existence

Reykjavik

of Hell). Splendid glacial streams water this gloomy landscape, and scattered everywhere across the island, down to the purlieus of Reykjavik herself, are the celebrated Icelandic geysers, spouting, fuming, bubbling and hissing like gigantic sulphureous kettles constantly on the boil. Only the hardiest of animals inhabit this country, enchanting ponies and wiry sheep, and few of the delicacies of nature soften its awful grandeur. 'Concerning Owls in Iceland' is the title of Chapter 12 in one eighteenth-century guide to the island, but the chapter itself is brief. 'There are,' it says, 'no Owls in Iceland.'

Such is the hinterland of Reykjavik, and the cruelty and hauteur of this magnificent country makes the capital feel bleak and wary still, like an exposed beachhead on a hostile shore. The wilderness is always near, and the citizenry is still bound by the fraternity of isolation—it is 750 miles from Reykjavik to Inverness, the nearest town of comparable size. The people are homogeneous, self-assured and self-reliant, considering themselves, not without reason, a people apart. Nobody lived in Iceland until the Vikings came, to be followed by the early Celtic immigrants from Scotland and Ireland, and nobody in particular has gone to live there since. Even the Americans, who maintain a base outside Reykjavik, do not mix very freely with the indigenes, and the British soldiers stationed here during the war did not, if they could help it, mix with them at all.

The inhabitants of Reykjavik all come from common stock, and are emblazoned with all the tokens of Nordic exclusivity: blue-eyed, fair-haired, long-limbed, with a taste for things like folk costume and national art, and a fierce unreasoned patriotism. There are only a few hundred Catholics in this city, and hardly any Jews, and the place is infused with Lutheran diligence—more books are written, printed, bought and read in Reykjavik, per head of population, than anywhere else on earth. She is an exceedingly introspective city, much concerned with matters of self-respect and self-improvement, and enmeshed in blood relationships. Sometimes she feels like one immense and earnest family gathering, for there is no such thing as a surname in Iceland, and people merely call themselves 'Eggert the son of Skuli', or 'Gudrun the daughter of Larus', so that you half expect to be introduced to Grettir the Strong or Thorfinnur, or share a card table with Beowulf. (And since the Icelandic language has hardly changed since the Middle Ages, anyone in Reykjavik can read the sagas as easily as he reads the fishing regulations.)

Reykjavik

All this gives the city a tingling air of unity, strength and defiance. Its people believe in the morality of self-defence and the sanctity of survival, and they display obvious kinships with the irrepressible Israelis, the unshakable Afrikaners, and all the brave company of last-ditchers and never-say-diers. This has only been an independent capital, in fact, since 1944, when it threw off the yoke of the otherwise preoccupied Danes, but it has kept its cultural identity marvellously intact for centuries, and it is rightly proud of the fact that twenty-five miles out of town, on the wind-swept plain of Thingvellir, the first of all proper parliaments assembled more than a thousand years ago.

But if the tight and honourable pedigree of Reykjavik gives her a special cohesive force, she has her weaknesses of breeding too. The people of this city look splendidly manly, healthy and upright, but this is no northern Elysium, where the blessed walk in righteousness among the arctic lotus blossoms. There is a pervasive under-the-counter feeling to the commerce of Reykjavik. There is a suggestion of slyness to her politics. The city's illegitimacy rate is said to be the highest in Europe, and among the clapboard saloons around the harbour you may bump into more old-fashioned drunks in a week than you will evade in a London year. Reykjavik is not in the least Americanized—she has strong Communist leanings—but she is a great place, nevertheless, for the lounging youth, the wolf-whistle and other such non-Nordic phenomena.

Inbreeding sometimes gives her, too, a distinctly Eistedffod atmosphere. That old politician would make a convincing chief Druid at Stonehenge, and not infrequently you will find bent over an office typewriter, or choosing a box of chocolates, a woman dressed in the full blowsy regalia of eighteenth-century Iceland, braided blonde hair, apron, embroidered bodice, sickly smile and all. In Reykjavik some crank or other is quite likely to assure you that Lief the Lucky, the discoverer of America, was born in the house next door, and sooner or later, as an intemperate American once remarked, you will probably find a citizen with infallible proof that an ancestor of his wrote the Song of Solomon. The people of this city sometimes seem astonishingly insulated against the mundanities of the outside world, like Pyramidical enthusiasts, or widowers who believe themselves to be Napoleon. This can be exasperating. An eminent Western diplomat in this capital once told me, quite casually, that the night before he had thrown a whisky bottle at the Icelandic Foreign Minister.

Reykjavik

Nor in fact is this citizenry so tough and hard-living as you might suppose. Like many go-it-aloners, oddly enough, they prefer their last ditches to be well drained, and like to have their backs against a nicely whitewashed wall. The standard of living is very high. The last shanty-slums have been cleared away, and most citizens live in solid new apartment blocks, with a car in the garage and a washing-machine in the kitchen alcove. The best-dressed women of Reykjavik are enviably elegant—they often pop down to Edinburgh for their mid-week shopping. Winter in this wind-swept place is still dark, cold and snowbound: but central heating, constant hot water from the natural geysers, tinned foods and hothouse vegetables all help the population to withstand its severities rather more easily than did the turf huts and curdled milk of their rugged forebears. When I once sailed out of Reykjavik on a small Icelandic coasting steamer, most of my Viking fellow passengers cowered miserably beneath the forecastle, and even the ship's cook, in an unguarded moment, confessed to some pangs of queasiness.

But there, Reykjavik is a city tempered more than most by a harsh environment and a challenging history. If her citizens sometimes seem complacent, comic or petulant, we must remember the circumstances of their extraordinary little country, high in the immensities of the Atlantic, sunk in sagas, rigid in isolation, plagued by volcanoes, Grimsby trawlers and impertinent Algerians. This is a city with reason to be testy. If you shared a horse trough with Grimur Goat-beard, wouldn't you be bloody-minded sometimes?

RIO DE JANEIRO

When I was once hanging around an airfield in Patagonia, hoping to thumb a lift to the north, I noticed a small group of people, dressed apparently for *après-ski*, who seemed to dominate the waiting-room with a kind of steely radiance. They looked very rich, and very brassy, and very thrusting. Their children were ill-mannered but intensely vivacious, their women were gimlet-eyed but seductive, their men had a feline Italian elegance to them: and unexpectedly, when I offered a smile in their glittering direction, one and all suddenly, brilliantly, delightfully smiled back. I asked where these magical creatures were making for, and was answered in one short tingling word: 'Rio!'

Angels they are not, the people of Rio, but instantly I felt like an old Pope in a slave market, for to me there seemed something remote and romantic about their manner of effervescent, if not reckless, audacity. It is this spirit of excitement, this animal crackling of the spirits, that sets their city apart from its South American peers, and makes it such a shot in the arm, such a haunting tune in the head. Rio is not, as legend has her, one perpetual Mardi Gras, thumping and blaring in false noses all night long. She is a place of deep and humane variety, full of fun indeed, but tinged also with a high-strung melancholy. Here you may well be deafened by the sambas blazing down Copacabana Beach, but you may also stumble across some elderly grey Negro, in dungarees paled by many a scrub, plucking upon his guitar melodies of a very different kind, half African, half Portuguese, part New World, part Old, sad as an east wind, soft as any courtier's lyric, and played with such grave and sophisticated intellectualism that you may feel yourself, down there by the harbour-front, in the presence of some remarkable inheritance, some old and unassailable attitude of mind.

For Rio is a manner of thought: not just a spectacle, not just a song and dance, but a particular approach to the problems of human progress. In this city you suck your milk out of the coconut with an

Rio de Janeiro

impeccably hygienic straw: and whether you are discussing economic philosophy with some whiskered academic, or holding hands with a mulatto courtesan in the dim of a night-club dawn—whether you are twanging your guitar in the Dorian or the Lydian mode, you will find that here, by some happy freak of the time mechanism, the clock always stops at midnight.

Everything they say about her, all the same, is factually true. Never did a city better live up to her reputation, or more handsomely justify the picture-postcard flattery. In her splendour of situation, encouched among bays and humped hills, she has only half a dozen rivals on earth—Hong Kong perhaps, Venice, Wellington, San Francisco, Naples, Sydney if you happen to be Australian, possibly Beirut, Cape Town at a pinch. Her brilliant beaches, lined with parades of skyscraper hotels and patrolled by gaudy bird-shaped kites, have become the very emblem of sunshine hedonism—to my own taste ineffably boring, but to those who enjoy the salacious torpor of a rich sandy foreshore, incomparable in their kind. Her climate, sometimes desperately hot but often softened by sea mist, gives her a sensual, heavy-lidded, perfumed temperament. Her old culture, inherited equally from Portuguese gentlemen and Muslim slaves out of Africa, makes her much more than just a pleasure-drome. The miserable hovels of her slums, perched in sad incongruity above the waterside highways, or crouched hang-dog among the apartment blocks, remind us that she is a city in the round, where every kind of man lives and makes love, and women in rags can look across a pavement to see the ripple of Balenciaga. The squalid indigence of her countryside, only twenty miles from Copacabana, rams home the truth that she is only the beautiful pinnacle of a vast, half-ignorant, disease-ridden, mostly empty, partly unexplored hinterland. Rio is all things to everyone. She fulfils every preconception.

She is an urgent, overcrowded city, invested in the rear by the Brazilian jungle, still creeping gloomily down her hillsides, and giving to some imaginative visitors a spectral impression of impending doom. Her topography is cramped and awkward. She is sprawled about the big bay of Guanabara, big enough to shelter half the navies of the world, and all around her stand mountains, some in massive forested ridges, some in sudden bumps and protrusions at the water's edge. If you stand beneath the gigantic hilltop figure of Christ, where the tourists buy their pictorial crockery or their cases of pickled

Rio de Janeiro

Brazilian beetles—if you stand up there on the peak called Corcovado beneath the outstretched arms of the statue, you may see how sinuously Rio weaves her purlieus among the contours, sometimes slinking behind a mountain, sometimes huddling beneath a ridge, sometimes charging clean through a hillside in a pair of masterly tunnels. The water-front of Rio is all curves, all unexpected coves, lined with trees and tall white buildings, cut off one part from another by high ground or inlets. The roads of Rio are a congested clamour. The waters of Rio stream with shipping, from the chugging Niterói ferry-boats to the big Brazilian carrier lying like a grandee beyond Flamengo. Even the skies of Rio are full of animation, for never did a city plunge so enthusiastically into the air age, so that the municipal airport lies slap in the middle of town, beside the water, and there are four hundred services a week to São Paulo alone.

But if she is sometimes frantic, she is also handsome, in a curled and burnished taste. São Paulo to the south is genially plebeian, a haven, a labour market and a gold mine. Brasília across the mountains is doggedly futuristic, airily above class or controversy. But in Rio it is easy to accept the unlikely fact that Brazil was once an Empire of her own, and that up the road in Petropolis a pretender to the imperial throne still sits hopefully in a florid palace. We call her Rio indeed, but her proper name is São Sebastião do Rio de Janeiro, and her origins are nothing if not high-flown. She does not feel an old city, though in fact she was founded in 1560. Her impatient gusto has torn down most of the old structures, and long ago discarded the old design, leaving only an occasional gilded church among the office blocks, or a splendid theatre high and dry among the traffic jams. Her manner, though, is seldom blatant, and more than most cities she feels organic to her setting. This is a place naturally clothed, as the Scottish wanderer John Robertson said in the early eighteen-hundreds, 'with richness and beauty altogether marvellous'. The modern architecture of Rio is not often ugly, and is sometimes magnificent. Her elderly suburbs do not feel unwanted or humiliated, but are allowed to age there quietly among their palms, like rather cantankerous, but still affectionately regarded relatives. The famous mosaic pavements of the city blend as happily with glass and concrete as they did with sculptured stone and whirligigs. Almost nothing feels intrusive, from the incomprehensibly abstract war memorial on the water-front to the famous cable car swinging hungrily across the bay to the restaurant on top of the Sugar Loaf.

Rio de Janeiro

For the spirit of this city is tolerant and sanguine to a fault, and makes you feel that nothing is unwelcome, and nothing altogether impossible. In Chicago you are regarded as Negro if you have a drop of black blood in your veins: in Rio you are accepted as European if you have a speckle of white. Here you can be, by and large, what you want to be, behave how you like, wear a frock-coat to dinner or a Jamaica shirt, a mink stole or a bikini. Rio takes you as you are, impelled by the conviction that in a community of such endless and pulsating variety, every little helps. Of course this magnanimity has its seamier concomitants—greed, exploitation, corruption, extravagance, materialism, ostentation. Even the transient visitor to Copacabana, searching desperately for a hotel room, will soon detect the advantages of greasing a Rio palm. Somehow, though, one is not affronted by these weaknesses, for all the fiddlings and coarser ambitions of the place are blunted, softened and made innocent by the warm tropical air of Brazil, which brings to this city's affairs a faint languorous suggestion of *dolce far niente*—not enervating enough to prevent the making of fortunes or the beating of drums, but sufficiently soothing to make you feel that here, more than in places of more rigid principle, humanity still lingers on. For Rio is, as a hard-boiled oil-man once observed to me, a very benediction among cities, like a morning of English summer among days of the year, or an apple pie among puddings.

The sceptics will scoff, and of course this is the romantic's view of Rio. It is true that there is to this city a certain never-never feeling, just as there is to Brazil as a whole a certain naïveté or childish enthusiasm. It is not exactly power that you feel in Rio, immense though the resources of this city are, but a sense of heady appetite— a looking-glass appetite, where you may shrink or grow by a nibble or a sip, sing wild songs or consort with strange knights. Brazil has been the Country of the Future for several centuries now, and Rio is her mirror. The overwhelming impact of the place is one of always impending euphoria, as though things are just about to be all for the best in practically the best of all possible worlds. Some people liken her to a supremely talented dilettante, perpetually about to fulfil the promise of youth, mincing down the years with a novel always at the back of his mind.

But Rio cares not what they say. She is never put out, never discouraged, always hopeful, always sure. She has far more faults

Rio de Janeiro

than I have cared to enumerate, but I loved her from the start, and I think her carping critics, sniffing at her over-drafts and deploring her excesses, cannot see the oaks for the nettles. Perhaps, like Brazil itself, she lacks some niggling virtues of common sense, but she glories in that grandest of historical qualities, style. Whatever she does is big, whatever she thinks is generous. Great God! I will swap you a dozen prim and thrifty boroughs for one such lovely greatheart!

ROME

Thoughts in Rome are easy to come by, as any half-baked philosopher knows: thoughts overwhelming in St. Peter's, thoughts sententious in the Forum, thoughts deliciously extravagant in the Via Condotti, thoughts frankly frivolous on the beach at Ostia. I once did a little thinking, patronizingly, perhaps, but affectionately, in the Piazza del Quirinale, where the President of Italy has his palace, for a reason that may not have been lofty, but at least was harmless: not because that Piazza is particularly beautiful, or because the flag of the Republic streams above the palace, or because I could see the dome of St. Peter's always gravely in the distance, or because Castor and Pollux stand in gigantic effigy in the middle of the square, but because when I was strolling through the Piazza del Quirinale that morning, kicking my heels and looking about me, a band began to play.

It was a police band, and it was celebrating the changing of the guard at the Presidential Palace. The guard itself had not emerged yet from the recesses of the building, but the band had struck up in lively expectation, and a little crowd soon gathered there to share its enthusiasms. Two sentries stood beside the gateway, poised in that posture of noble insouciance peculiar to the Italian Army. A beadle in a cockaded top hat hovered about the entrance. Two gorgeously cloaked carabinieri sauntered around the square, and half a dozen motor-cycle policemen sat astride their machines waiting for the parade. The sun shone, the flag billowed, and the band played lustily.

It was dressed in grey, with feathered hats and greatcoats that looked too big for it. Its faces were cheerfully bucolic. The bass drummer wore thick horn-rimmed spectacles. The conductor, standing to attention with his back to the instrumentalists, kept them in time with convulsive jerks and spasms of his white-gloved hand. It was a wheezy, thumpy kind of performance, but if it lacked finesse or Sandhurst swank, it was never short of gusto. Bravely and

Rome

genially blew the euphonia; furiously twitched the bandmaster; all around the Romans stood, as at a zoo or a waxworks, the children marking time with spirit, the adults smiling a smile that was part poignant, part content, part wishful, part affectionate.

It was the smile that set me thinking. It was sixteen years since I had first set foot in Italy, and during that time a marvellous transformation had overcome the reputation of the Italians. Then, they were an international joke: their armies discredited, their navies shattered, their currency worthless, their foolish Fascists strung up or skulking. All the good will of art and history was in abeyance, tucked away in memory or intention, and when a friend of mine bought an Olivetti typewriter people thought he had done a very silly thing ('It may look smart, but it'll never last!'). The music-hall ice-cream man, with his greasy hair and comic accent, was the world's image of the Italian. The evil buffoonery of the dictators had done its work, and in my regiment we used to say that the ordinary Eyties were very nice, but *absolutely* hopeless.

We would think differently now, for the arts of war are in discredit, the Italians have been freed from the shackles of sham and pomp, and Rome has come into her own again. Now all the world admires the Olivetti and the standards of design it has pioneered, and the absolutely hopeless Eyties have amassed for themselves one of the greatest gold reserves in Europe. The shape of our cars, the allure of our actresses, the swing of our skirts, the tunes we whistle, the curtains we hang—all stem indirectly, as likely as not, from the revived Italian genius, which has stamped its ideas indelibly upon the taste of the world. Today the archetypal Italian is not Mario the Soho grocer, but Perry Como, the most elegant of crooners, relaxed but not indolent, smooth but not greasy, flirtatious but never flashy. The able and sophisticated North has replaced the archaic South as symbolic of the nation, the bumble-head bureaucracy is put out of mind, and once again there are few peoples on earth more genuinely beloved than the Italians.

How on earth did it happen, I wondered, as the melodies lurched about me in the Piazza del Quirinale; and the first explanatory word that came to my mind was—innocence. The great strength of the Italians is their resilient simplicity, their unworldliness. Cynics will retort that Rome is the least innocent of all the capitals, that vices and perversions of every kind were festering there beneath my very nose, that Italy writhes with fiddles, evasions and half-truths.

Rome

Nevertheless this remains, at heart and in essentials, a people of innocence. What an air of childlike goodwill pervaded the Piazza at that moment! How delighted were the children, beyond the cravings of our blasé juveniles at home! How transparently pleased were the grown-ups, tapping their toes to the big drum! With what an air of unanswerable logic, as though they were explaining the laws of gravity, the policemen kept the crowd away from the trombones! The motor-scooters roared down the Via Milano, and sometimes a razzle-dazzle sports car streaked by with a glimpse of dark glasses and nylon knees: but up there beside the Presidential Palace we were lost in simplicity, lost to the fustian magic of the band.

And from this simplicity springs the elegance of the city Italians, which is their stock-in-trade. They were poorish people mostly up in the Piazza, but they bore themselves with style. Nobody looked messy. Nobody needed a shampoo or a hitch to her petticoat. Even the vagrants lounged lithely upon the steps, and the children merrily hopping about us were hauntingly impeccable—not a hair out of place, not a single sticky thumb mark upon a laundered blouse. Many a half-slum survives in Rome, and only fifty miles away the South begins, that backward Ireland of Italy: but there in the centre of the metropolis all seemed prosperous, plump, well dressed, manicured. Are there beggars in Rome? There are. Do people care too much about appearances? They do. Are the upper classes degenerate, amoral, and antisocial? So they say. Is snobbery both rampant and absurd? It is. But stand with me at the Quirinale, just out of the tuba's range, and you will sense how admirable, all the same, has been the contemporary renaissance of the Italians.

It has brought them a new assurance, for everywhere their national values are storming into significance. More than most peoples they have always seemed beyond chauvinism and petty pride, just as Rome herself stands beyond nation, race, and language: partly because of their glorious religion, partly because of their fluctuating past, which has taught them (sporadically, to be sure) how ephemeral is power. They have watched the armies and the emperors pass, from one sad century to another, and they know, if anyone does, that only the good things last, only the honourable things. The Italians seldom ask you what your nationality is, unless they are thinking of putting the price up, and they seldom brag about their accomplishments, unless they are salesmen or politicians.

How healthy, I thought, are the lessons they can teach us, we

Rome

atavistic patriots in the grey barbaric North! How crazy was the
twist of history that made these friendly people, only a decade or two
ago, our mortal enemies, to be bombed and derided and kicked
about! How pleasant to make up for it now, to the beat of a drum and
the laughter of children! How extraordinary—but just then, with a
climactic blare of the trumpets, the guard came swinging out of the
palace and marched splendidly away down the hill, flag aflutter: and
somehow the fun and swagger and sunshine of it all, and the twirl of
the drum-major's stick, dispersed the last of these thoughts in Rome,
and guided me hungrily towards my spaghetti.

ROTTERDAM

Lord Bryce, that most prescient of reporters, once described New York as 'a European city, but of no particular country'. The phrase came back to me one day as I wandered through the burgeoning new centre of Rotterdam, for never did a city feel less parochial than this great port of the Dutch, less circumscribed by local tastes and affinities. The people of Holland are immensely proud of Rotterdam, second only to New York as a port, second to none as an example of modern urban planning: but they have created something bigger than themselves, a long-limbed well-heeled genie, at the command not of a nation, but of a continent.

The centre of Rotterdam was almost entirely destroyed in the unspeakable German attack of 1940, and its reconstruction is a monument of pride and diligence. It is also a symptom of our times: for though the citizens of Rotterdam are stout and loyal Netherlanders, though the flag flies everywhere and the wind blows chill off the polders, nevertheless they have built themselves a city that does not feel Dutch at all. It is a supra-national city, 'of no particular country,' and if you close your ears and half close your eyes, sniff the air of the mighty docks and imagine the distant clanging of the money-bags, then you might think, paradoxically enough, that you were somewhere in West Germany.

One reason is the architecture of the rebuilt city. The new Rotterdam is not a soaring, head-in-air, aluminium place. She does not blaze with colour and vivacity, like the flamboyant masterpieces of Mexico and Brazil. Nor does she spring frankly from her own mercantile roots, like the new City of London. *Au fond* she is, I suppose, a Bauhaus city, a square, solid, knife-edged, intensely functional entity. Her new suburbs are endless, handsome expanses of rectangular blocks; her heart is rich and imposing and admirably organized; but she feels queerly unsympathetic. It is as though someone were to bake a plum pie of exquisite flavour and fragility, but forget to put in the plums. The key building of the place, the

Rotterdam

one that contributes most forcibly to this sense of frigid splendour, is the magnificent department store called De Bijenkorf—The Beehive. The external design of this great structure is by Marcel Breuer, one of the most eminent of the Euro-American architects, and it might just as well be in Winnipeg, Sydney or Singapore. It is a building of immense power and distinction, but rootless. Like its peers in America, it is huge, square, largely windowless, and gives the impression of a sumptous fortress, or perhaps a converted Doges' Palace. Its manner of affluent but soulless internationalism sets the tone of the new Rotterdam, and the other buildings seem to squat around it in silent respect—some of them bigger, some of them more resplendent, but none with quite the same steely assurance.

Of course, in aesthetics as in gastronomics, one man's caviar is another's soggy dumpling. Even among Rotterdam people opinion upon the new city is divided. But De Bijenkorf and its companions, whether or not you respond to their style, do undeniably reflect the meaning of Rotterdam today. They are hard, cosmopolitan, vaguely German buildings: and Rotterdam is a hard-headed international city, dependent for its prosperity upon the trade and industry of inner Europe. If this feels like Germany to you, in a way you are right: the body may be Dutch, but the life-blood flows down the Rhine from the steel mills of the Ruhr. Rotterdam rose to prominence with the rise of industrial Germany, and though she now has great industries of her own, and immense oil refineries, still she is pre-eminently the Ruhr's gateway to the sea. She is not just Holland, she is Europe—and in this context at least, Europe means Germany. Here the iron ore arrives for Germany's car factories. Here the oil pipeline begins its march towards Düsseldorf. Here the German barges trans-ship their cargoes to the ocean freighters, and the German steel magnates come to hammer out prices with shipowners and agents. As Beirut is to the world of the Arabs, so Rotterdam is to the Ruhr.

And like Beirut she is never tranquil. She must be one of the most endlessly energetic places on earth. Her immense complex of docks and quays, one of the great industrial sights of the world, stretches away into an infinity of cranes, masts, chimneys and refineries, as far as the eye can see—a mesh of moving boats, swinging bridges, smoke, trucks and trains, and far, far away towards the sea the distant flaming beacons of the oil refineries. They handle more ships here, and refine more oil, than anywhere else in Europe, and they are

Rotterdam

always expanding. There are two hundred tugs in Rotterdam, and twenty-four dry docks. The size and impetus of this seaport take one's breath away.

But it lives upon Germany, and this truth makes Rotterdam an oddly twisted place. She is not exactly a satellite city, for Holland herself forms a sizeable and productive hinterland of her own. There are seers in the city, indeed, who wish to free the place as far as possible from the strings of the German economy, and who view the prospect of united Europe with more distrust than elation (they feel that the more European trade is satisfied by internal exchanges, the less their port will be needed). Nevertheless, as Germany goes, so goes Rotterdam, and this is a sad paradox for the Dutch, a proud people with long memories. There seems, at least to the imaginative visitor, something ill at ease to the grand new Rotterdam, as of a man who accepts a job from his mother's murderer. In the centre of the city is Zadkine's brilliant, haunting, and indeed frightening statue symbolizing the destruction of Rotterdam in 1940—a single tortured and terrified figure, its arms raised to the sky in hopeless self-defence, with a gaping torn hole where its heart should be. 'We can forgive, but we must not forget,' observed a citizen to me of this fearful image: and even as he spoke the long strings of barges ploughed down the Rhine to Rotterdam, the great bridges smoothly opened and closed, the myriad winches clanked, the big ships lay in the shine of the oil-tanks, and the iron tide of Germany flowed past us to the sea.

SAN FRANCISCO

Not long ago they opened a new bar in Geary Street, San Francisco, and named it in honour of the Emperor Norton I. 'All loyal San Franciscans,' it was announced, 'will be required to LUXURIATE in *Lavish Gilded Era Surroundings*, IMBIBE *Ambrosial and Healthful Refreshments*, FRATERNIZE with *Ladies and Gents of Fashion*, and TOAST THE MEMORY of EMPEROR NORTON, the Late and Glorious Protector of our Fair City.'

Thus, with the wry and tangy whimsy that is peculiar to the place, San Francisco saluted herself, for there is not another city in the world that would have treated the Emperor Norton, self-styled monarch of Mexico and the United States, with quite such affectionate good humour. It was in 1859 that Joshua Norton declared his imperial status, and from then until his death in 1880 San Francisco handsomely humoured his pretensions, publishing his royal proclamations in her newspapers, humbly soliciting his patronage at her restaurants, ushering him to the platform on all her grand occasions, rising to her feet when he strode into the Opera with the royal dogs, even accepting, with a kindly tongue in a sceptical cheek, his ornate but nonsensical currency. What other city, asked Robert Louis Stevenson, would cherish a harmless madman thus? And where else, we may wonder nearly a century later, would they still be drinking Ambrosial and Healthful Refreshments in his memory?

San Francisco is the most tantalizing of cities, simply because she is unique. She represents the civilization of North America at its most subtle and imaginative. She proves how gracefully Western man might have learnt to live, were it not for the preoccupations of war and power. She was born into all the gusto of Gold Rush and Barbary Coast, but in one short century she evolved a culture all her own, bold but also mellow, altogether distinct from the philosophies, simultaneously developing to the east, that were to

San Francisco

dictate the image of the United States. She has never been emulated, scarcely even copied. She was fashioned by her isolation, away across the Rockies on the Pacific coast, and as the world shrinks and the cultures merge, so she must lose a little of her individuality at last, and become a little more like the rest of America. As Venice is to Italy, as England to Europe, so San Francisco stands to the United States: for we live in a rookery, and phoenixes are out of date.

We may see her plumage fading a little already, and there is something rather wistful and will-o'-the-wisp to her allure: but she remains the most lyrical city of the New World, one of the half-dozen loveliest on earth, one of the very few where a benevolent and entertaining crank may, with a toss of his plumed hat and a whistle to his dogs, still persuade an accountant to cash him a dud cheque.

Some people think that Drake entered San Francisco Bay, swinging his little ship through the heads of the Golden Gate, and keeping his discovery secret to spite the King of Spain. Certainly the Spaniards built a fishing village on these shores, and called it Yerba Buena—'Good Herb,' after the wild mint that abounded there. The magic of San Francisco is still largely the gift of the sea—the misty and illimitable Pacific, which often seems a disenchanted sort of ocean, and which inspired the visiting Chicagoan of legend, gazing out from the San Francisco water-front, to observe after a moment's contemplation that it wasn't as big as he expected it to be. It is the pale vapours of this sea, creeping always around the hills of the metropolis, veiling the skyscrapers and so swirling around the Golden Gate that only the great bronze towers of the bridge protrude above the whiteness—it is the gentle dank mists off the Pacific that govern the temperament of the place, softening many an angularity, calming many a bigot. The climate of this city is essentially moderate, never unbearably hot, seldom fearfully cold, and the lap of the waters all around, like ice packed around a bottle, keeps its temper too always cool and unflustered.

For all around the waters lie, tumbling in great breakers along the ocean highways, blue and placid along the Bay shore, and at the end of almost every street you may see the glint of the sea, the high flank of a bridge, the distant shimmer of yachts, a great carrier sweeping past Treasure Island or a freighter chugging sturdily into the Pacific. Without the sea and the almost land-locked Bay, San Francisco would not be much to look at: it is the waters that make

San Francisco

her beautiful, and the ships, and the green hills sloping delectably to her water-fronts, and her fortress-like posture upon her peninsula, and the islands of her Bay, and above all the celestial span of the Golden Gate Bridge, the most airy and ethereal of human artifacts, and a work of art to be revered in the same breath as the Acropolis.

San Francisco always responds to the sea, and has absorbed some of its restless fascination. This was a beachhead long before the railways crossed the continent, and everyone who made the original legend of San Francisco, from the whores to the Emperor Norton, came here off a ship. She is still a beachcombers' haven, still a place of quays, longshoremen and wharfside bars, where the sea birds goggle at you loftily from their posts, and the tourist restaurants look down at the boats of the crab fleet—*Pik Nik* and *Cindy Lu, Belle of Dixie* and *Gioconda*, weathered sun-bleached craft, slung around with tackle, whose skippers came from Sicily long ago, and brought with them a blistered blue suggestion of the Mediterranean. San Francisco does not feel like a *seaside* city, for all her multitudinous tourists, for all her esplanades: her relationship with the sea remains something much more robust and mercantile, an affair of engine-rooms and cork floats, flotsam and waybills.

Thus she is still full-blooded, as a seaport should be. She is rich in earthy, muscular qualities still. The sea brought her into being, the gold of the hills enriched her, she was half destroyed by the earthquake and fire of 1906, and she has always been familiar with violence. In 1855, so the municipal records say, there were 583 deaths by violence in this city, and even today skullduggery lies not very far below the surface, and the stains of bloodshed linger. The prison island of Alcatraz, stocked with the most dreadful of America's criminals, lies squat and formidable offshore, like a gunboat, peered at by morbid tourists through binoculars, and suggesting to the over-sensitive visitor an almost mediaeval sense of brooding retribution. Tales of old brutalities haunt many a street corner, and the chronicles of the city are flamboyant with bold men and loose women—the railroad barons, the bonanza kings, the great madams of the Barbary Coast, the vigilantes, the Sydney Ducks, the shanghaiers, all the rip-roaring trigger-happy adventurers who built San Francisco out of a shanty town, and made her name a legend. Architecturally not much remains of the plush and bloody old days, for the houses of wealth and vice have been swept away by fire, earthquake, aesthetics and morality: metaphysically, though, the gusto of the

San Francisco

frontier survives tenaciously in San Francisco, illuminates many a sequestered alley, and sets the doors swinging in many a dim-lit saloon.

Of course it is partly tourism. The honky-tonk flavour of this city has long been dedicated to the tourist trade, and the wilder glories of the Barbary Coast have long been suppressed. Even so, this is a city of hedonism, where most of the human appetites can be pleasantly satisfied. The law must be respected nowadays, but the spirit of this port is still cheerfully uninhibited. Here the prima donnas of the Bocce Ball Bar lace your martinis with their arias, while in the yard outside elderly unsophisticated gentlemen still play the antique game for which the place is named. Here the clever young men of the hungry i, astutely adapting for a plainer audience whatever is currently fashionable among the *avant-garde*, moan their sick ditties or strum their lugubrious guitars. Here the female impersonators of Finnochio's, gloriously ambivalent, send the Gray Line sight-seers dizzy to their nightcaps. You may eat handsomely in San Francisco (abalone, crab's legs, sea bass or Peking duck) and drink well (the fresh white wines of California, the exotic alcoholic coffees of the North Beach dives, the huge expensive martinis of the swank hotels). You may indulge, without much fear of public censure, whatever tastes your libido demands. San Francisco is still the least puritan of American cities. She is a Pacific port, looking towards Hawaii, Tahiti and Hong Kong, and the Pilgrim Fathers never heard of her.

Yet of all the cities of the United States, by one of history's happier paradoxes, she is the most genuinely cultivated—which is to say that the taste for everyday beauty, the hunger for knowledge, the feeling for empiricism, seems to run deeper here than it does in Boston, New York or Chicago. This is the American city where Jefferson would most feel at home: not only because it shares his notions of liberty and tolerance, but also because San Francisco loves the crooked ways of culture, the quirks of the civilized life, the innuendo rather than the declamation, the entertaining gadget more than the chromium façade. She was raised boisterously indeed, but subtlety has broken in.

In herself she is not very beautiful. Deposited in prairie or painted desert, far from the embroidery of the sea, her hilly silhouette would scarcely be distinguished. Even her rich residential areas, though exceedingly comfortable, look drab beside the intoxications of Lima or Hollywood, and her downtown shopping streets are

San Francisco

mostly shabby, even hang-dog. As an urban pattern she is a sorry mess, plodding onward in abject rectangles, with a total disregard of contours, mile after mile into the hinterland or down to the water's edge. The colours of her buildings are oddly pallid, the shapes of her skyscrapers are generally lumpish, and she possesses only half a dozen buildings that stamp their personality upon one's memory.

Nevertheless she gives you, somehow or other, an instant impression of urbanity. The seams of her stockings are always straight, her manners are invariably polished, and there is nothing sour or curmudgeonly to her tone of voice. She is, in the best and most generous sense of the adjective, an aristocratic city. Flower stalls ornament her street corners, huge and splendid parks adorn her, her gardens are delectable and her ostentation is discreet. Her women display an agreeable weakness for well-cut suits and good woollens. Her clubs are both suave and original: the Pacific Union, which has only one hundred tremendously grand members, the Bohemian Club, which goes in for campfire sing-songs and dominoes, or the Sierra Club, which was founded with the specific purpose of 'doing something for wildness'. This is where the California Academy of Sciences built, with its own resources, the first of the American planetariums. This is where Yehudi Menuhin grew up, and Isaac Stern, where Gelett Burgess wrote 'I never saw a purple cow,' where Saroyan and Kerouac have lived and worked, and Steinbeck too. San Francisco has one of the world's best museums of modern art, one of the three resident opera companies in the United States, the only resident ballet company outside New York. She is a city of fine bookshops, from the long-haired City Lights, where the poets go to collect their mail, to the exquisitely polished and panelled antiquarian shops that deal in the more esoteric Americana. An almost Victorian avidity informs the intellectual life of this city, a cultivation very thorough and precise, and she is graced by the presence of a lively American gentry—by which I mean a class of citizens genuinely interested in the arts, who really enjoy Milhaud or Proust, and are not simply content to prop books about primitive sculpture on the music-stands of grand pianos.

All this means that she is, like Kyoto, Florence or Oxford, interesting in depth. She is a provincial city still, and cannot boast the endless proliferating talent that brings such ironic distinction to the nightmare purlieus of Los Angeles: but she is a joyously cosmopolitan community, full of surprises, stimulations and asymmetries.

San Francisco

She is a great city of the Chinese, who call her Dia Fow—Big Town —and who still precariously sustain, in the regions around Portsmouth Square, some semblance of their noble civilization. She is a city of many Italians—fishermen, night-club proprietors, the legendary Gianninis, who founded the Bank of America as a savings-house for the urban peasantry, and turned it into the largest bank on earth. There are thousands of Japanese in San Francisco, and thousands of Filipinos, and Hawaiians, and every shade of white, pink, yellow, tanned or tawny skin. North Beach is one of the few proper foreign quarters in the United States that is not, at the same time, a slum. Years ago there used to be race riots in this city, when the Chinese in particular were hunted down and tormented, but San Francisco was founded by spacious adventurers, and has never been one of your petty chauvinist towns: Jews have always been prominent in her affairs, the temples of the Confucianists still rather pallidly survive, and now as always this is a haven for those good men who believe in the infallibility of the Pyramids, the end of all things next Saturday morning, or the divinity of the Emperor of Ethiopia.

Nothing is altogether banal in San Francisco. An alley like Maiden Lane turns out to shelter one of the most beautiful stores on earth, the little masterpiece designed for V. C. Morris by Frank Lloyd Wright. An ordinary shopping street like Grant Avenue is transformed, after a block or two, into a teeming Chinese thorough-fare, with a Bank of Canton on the corner, a Chinese newspaper on the news-stands, smart Chinese typists hurrying to their morning coffee, a smell of joss-sticks and bric-a-brac, and sometimes a window full of musty herbal remedies—Lion's Paw Universal Linament, or Aeroplane Oil, 'a secret prescription of a German professor'. An all too businesslike bank bears that name of magical evocation, Wells Fargo. A prosaic corner lot once housed the agents of the Pony Express.

'Presented by H. D. Cogswell to our boys and girls,' says a chill inscription on the drinking fountain in Washington Square, 'who will soon take our places and pass on'—and the three spigots placed there by Cogswell, a millionaire dentist, are labelled California Seltzer, Vichy and Congress Water, but all emit precisely the same fluid. The flower garden in Golden Gate Park proves to contain, if you inquire, every single variety of plant mentioned in Shakespeare's plays. Cost Plus, down by the water-front, is I suspect the only self-service store anywhere that sells painted peacocks from India,

San Francisco

boomerangs, African figurines and Mexican money-pigs. Even the tourist stalls of Fishermen's Wharf, so crammed in summer that you can hardly hear the cries of the restaurant doormen for the slow chattering shuffle of the crowd, sell odd things like bags of Pacific Ocean water, boxes of sea-shells, kits for junior beachcombers, horned toads, Japanese paper flowers, and live turtles, to be shipped by the North Western Turtle Co., to any address you please, in neat cardboard turtle boxes.

This is where the beatniks came from, broody in their darkened pads, for in San Francisco, more than anywhere else in America, you may be what you like, dress how you please, say more or less what you think. Even the commerce of this city retains some strains of bubble and old-school extravagance: the Sit'n'Chat Shoe Shine Shop, for instance, the Wee Wee Café, the Cut'n'Curl Beauty Shop, and the Carnation Milk Company, whose telephone operators used, in less urbane times, to greet callers with the formula 'Moo to you!' And emblematic above all of this lovable profusion and waywardness are the cable cars of San Francisco, still labouring their way, ninety years after their inception, up the precipitous streets of the place. With a marvellous swaying, lurching and tilting motion they proceed, with a clang of the bell and a hissing of the cable beneath the street, the young men clinging carelessly to the outside steps, the ladies demurely inside—with an earnest, determined, but undeniably comical mien, like very small ponies approaching a ditch: and when, for one short thrilling moment, something seems to be slipping, there is a perceptible backward motion of the vehicle, the cars behind hoot their horns with alarm, and the conductor leaps to the rear platform to do distinctly dramatic things with the brass brake handle at the back—then, for a moment, all the excitement of old San Francisco is recaptured, and you almost expect to see the side-whiskers twitching around you, or hear the clatter of the Volunteer Fire Brigade galloping down from Nob Hill.

But it is fading a little, just a trace of the old fragrance is lost, and the cable cars feel each year, as they approach their centenary, just a little more self-conscious. I think we are watching the last years of San Francisco's prime. Hers has been a brief but enthralling eminence, a style of life uniquely her own, which cannot I think survive the shrinking of the world and the terrible new responsibilities of the American nation. Indeed, she has made her point already

325

San Francisco

—has demonstrated that the ideals of liberty, sympathy and fun that inspired the Founding Fathers need not be enforced by flag-wagging or admonition, but can sturdily fend for themselves. Nobody of our generation can leave San Francisco altogether unaffected, for she is an exemplar of all that America meant to the world in her happy days of independence, before supreme power overtook her—a reminder of the essential kindliness of the Great Republic, and of all the human happiness it has fostered.

Today, willy-nilly, the American image has changed, and so has San Francisco's. She is a little more tawdry than she used to be, as the conformity of capitalism begins to swamp her, as the tourists pour in more refulgently each year, and even the Bohemians find themselves gawked at like pelicans or modern art. She is a little harder, perhaps, a little more pompous, a little more subservient to the palaces of Montgomery Street, the Wall Street of the West. The crucible is working, even here: the Italians are less Italian than they used to be, the Mexicans are blending, and the old culture of the Chinese is distinctly tarnished. Ugly but efficient motorways block some of the city's favourite vistas, and there is a Nike missile station on one of the islands in the Bay.

But there, if she has changed a little in manner and appurtenance, she has stayed the same at heart. It sounds sententious to say so, but what makes this middle-sized metropolis one of the great cities of the earth is not really its rip-roaring past, nor its incomparable setting, nor even its intimate association with the sea, but essentially its *goodness*. It is a kind and understanding place. Half a century after Josiah Norton's death they transferred his body to a handsome new tomb in the Masonic Cemetery, paid for by the rich old bigwigs of the Pacific Union Club. There you may see it still, once you have found the right burial-ground among the Eternal Homes, Halls of Peace and Portals of Eternity that cling like so many premonitions to the southern flank of the city. It is four-square, simple and dignified, and its inscription is majestic indeed: NORTON I, EMPEROR OF THE UNITED STATES AND PROTECTOR OF MEXICO, 1819–1880.

Just across the road, such is the fullness of this vivacious city, is buried Wyatt Earp.

SANTIAGO

Santiago is different. Everyone tells the traveller so, and it is true. When you wander down the western coast of South America, through the chill hauteur of Lima and the turmoils of La Paz, Santiago greets you sensibly and urbanely, with tickets awaiting you for *Swan Lake* that evening, and a friend from Oxford expecting you in the bar downstairs. Gone are the pretensions of the conquistadors and the aboriginal uncertainties. Santiago is almost, all but, very nearly, just not quite Europe. 'The Argentinians are like a lot of Texans,' say the Chileans, 'and Lima's full of Chinese and niggers, but here in Santiago we flatter ourselves we're civilized.'

So they are, on the level that chiefly shows. Chile has her problems, Heaven knows, menacing enough to keep her constantly on the brink of Communism, but they do not much intrude upon Santiago. The rain-sodden south feels far away, the destitute share-croppers of the countryside are nowhere to be seen, and all the disease and degradation scarcely scars the surface of the place. Santiago is a proper cultivated city, by almost any standards, and gives an immediate comforting impression of order and efficiency. This is not one of your tear-gas capitals, addled by riots and politics. Here the democratic processes are firmly established, and there are few vicious contrasts of violently rich and abysmally poor. The suburbs of Santiago are not all posh, the worst of the slums have vanished, and a substantial urban middle class gives the city a sense of solid purpose. Church congregations are mostly well dressed and sober, and there is none of that flickering, tinsel sense of awe-struck superstition that haunts the dark churches of Peru. Restaurants are full. Clothes are not exquisite, but adequate. The President of the Chilean Republic lives in a small bachelor flat in the middle of the city, drives his own car and walks each morning to his office in the Presidential Palace. Santiago is a steady, middling kind of capital. They call Chile the Prussia, or sometimes the Scotland, of South America, and certainly this capital does not often feel Latin.

Santiago

She is not a striking place. Her setting is splendid indeed, with the great wall of the Andes standing like a rampart beyond the city, the delectable Pacific coast only a morning's journey away, and all around the suburbs the gentle, green, vine-rich fields of the Chilean heartland. Her buildings, though, are mostly ordinary; it is not her appearance, but her temperament that distinguishes her, and makes her second only to San Francisco as cultural capital of the American Pacific. She is a city Indian and Spanish in origins, but with strong Nordic overtones. There are thirty-five Smiths in the Santiago telephone book, and thirty-six Schmidts, and though most of them have long been absorbed into the Chilean bloodstream, their eyes subtly elongated and their attitudes indefinably shifted, nevertheless their presence here colours the very texture of the city, sprinkles the streets with blond hair and burly shoulders, and helps to modify the natural insularity of this remote and mountain-barred metropolis. Twelve live theatres flourish in Santiago. There are two symphony orchestras, two big universities, two observatories, newspapers of first-class technique, satirical magazines of mordant bite, revues of happy impertinence, art galleries, excellent bookshops, the biggest library in South America and one of the few botanical gardens south of New Orleans. Santiago is a city of eminent poets— some of the best lyrics in the Spanish language, I am told, were written there. She is a city half dotty about ballet: when I first arrived there, a company from Moscow was dancing at one theatre, a company from Copenhagen had just been dancing at another, and a film of the Covent Garden company was showing at several cinemas. She is a city of absolute feminine emancipation, and her women display an altogether delightful sparkle and assurance, without seeming in the least mannish or bluestocking. She is, as cities go, a little on the stodgy side—it is against the law to ride side-saddle behind your boy friend on his motor-scooter: but she offers most of the things a European demands of urban life, from race-courses to *boutiques*, from last week's London papers to a seat in the public gallery at a Congressional debate.

With it all goes a degree of self-discipline unexampled along the Andean coast. Chile is a country of luscious profusion, a land such as pioneers dream of, her countryside so beautiful, her ski-slopes such fun, her lakes so magnificent, her distant archipelago so strangely exciting, that an air of perpetual promise hangs over her, and makes you think that in such a varied paradise some golden mean of life is

Santiago

surely attainable. In Santiago, however, you do not feel this riotous fecundity. Instead, the capital conducts itself with a rigid, sometimes lofty concern for the order and appearance of things. Every other morning they change the guard outside the Presidential Palace, in the very centre of the city. This is a ceremony of impressive precision, and it well sums up Santiago's flair for the correct procedure. An enormous military band plays in the Plaza de la Constitucion, and the two guard companies, in uniforms of vaguely German cut, with high boots, swords and resplendent spurs, moving to a rhythm impeccable and purposeful, march and counter-march with an almost ominous certainty. It is not a toy-soldier parade, like the Cochrane pageantries of Buckingham Palace. It feels all too real, as though the participating soldiery, dropping to the firing position at the flick of a command, might easily exterminate each other by numbers, or decimate the bystanders with text-book bayonetings: but it ends happily enough, for when the ceremony is over the two young subalterns of the guard, marvellously slim and elegant, salute each other with brisk respect, shake hands like brothers, and stride off together into the palace.

There is a moment or two of silence, and then, when they have disappeared into the great gateway, one, two, three, one, two, three, the band strikes up a Viennese waltz, and even the undemonstrative Chileans, standing woodenly all about, tap an occasional tight-laced toe.

SINGAPORE

Singapore! The very name is an evocation, melodious, Kiplingesque, obscurely melancholy, the sort of name you find on frayed leather trunks in English attics, half obliterated by antique instructions—'Rear Carriage At Suez,' or 'For Collection in Cantonment.' When you think of Singapore, you think of Empire. You see in your mind's blurred eye the pride and pomposity of the dying Raj, the doomed forts among the mangroves, limp duck suits in Raffles' bar, tall grey warships meditating offshore, the flags and the flourishes, the saints and the snobs.

The British created modern Singapore in the flush of their early Victorian vigour, transforming a rotting fishing village into a great port, a celebrated stronghold, a rich and vital city. They founded their settlement, on a swampy island at the southern tip of Malaya, partly to thwart their rivals the Dutch, partly to serve as a way-station on the Eastern trade routes, partly to be a trade centre in its own right—a funnel of commerce for all south-east Asia. Nothing, however, is more ephemeral than power. Yesterday Singapore epitomized the *Pax Britannica*. Today she expresses the very essence of lost dominion, the pathos of faded supremacy, the muffled anxiety that has, all down the ages, inevitably succeeded the certainty of conquest.

You must come to Singapore by sea, for this is a city of the ocean highways, built upon navigation. Like Gibraltar, Malta and Aden, it owes its significance to the fact that the British are islanders, that their master-weapon was control of the sea, and that the great merchant fleets of their prime, deep with the burnished products of the steam age, must pass in a constant puffing stream down the arteries of the East. Sir Stamford Raffles, the creator of Singapore, saw her as 'an emporium, to secure to the British flag the maritime supremacy of the Eastern seas': and even today, if you approach the city out of the Malacca Strait, you may still taste the flavour of the

Singapore

British heyday, as you may pace the Appian Way in the purlieus of Rome, or hear the winds of legend whispering through the Parthenon.

A litter of low green islands, steamy and tangled, speckles the sea approaches to Singapore. The air is fiery, the sea seems thick and vegetable, and down every channel among the islets you can see the ships, shimmering on a blue horizon, pounding grandly down the archipelago, chugging inshore in a mesh of nets. A fort on a headland is the first you see of the city: tall, gaunt and deserted, haunted by snakes and lizards, ignominiously choked with brambles, like some discredited but still imposing old general, rigid in his Bath chair on the promenade. A line of big freighters lies at anchor in the roads, the sampans flurrying around them; an armada of battered coasters shelters beyond the breakwater, from Borneo or Sarawak, Bangkok or Djakarta; and presently a breath of hazed and humid air, a jabber of small boats, a whiff of oil, pepper, sweat and dried fish, welcomes you to the wharfs of Singapore.

All the mystique of the place instantly assaults you. High upon the water-front stand the old merchant houses: some quaintly arabesque, with tumbled balconies and preposterous ornaments, some massively functional, all brass plates and air-conditioning. Encouched in green lie the structures of Government, gracefully colonnaded, transplanted here by the hopeful English from the soil of their classical education: elegant, symmetrical buildings, peeling and fretted with age and damp, but still gentlemanly and self-assured. Evangelically among the palm trees stand the churches of the place, from the episcopal splendour of the Anglican Cathedral to the adorable little Armenian church, demure, precise, reverent and complete, like something white and impeccable out of Jefferson's Virginia. And there beneath the bridge runs away the Singapore River, the hub of the emporium, where a thousand rafts and sampans, day and night, shift the teak and the rubber, the spice and the skins, the steel bolts and the machinery from ship to shore, from dim-lit cluttered godown to deep and greasy hold.

A spirit of tenacious nostalgia still emanates from this vast and vivid water-front, the façade of Singapore. On the green *padang*, outside the City Hall, they still play cricket in the imperial manner—Europeans at one end, Eurasians at the other. Through Empress Place, down Mountbatten Road, along Connaught Drive, the double-decker buses still lurch with a rumble quintessentially English.

Singapore

Down at the yacht club they still sip their sundowners in their blazers; from the wicker chairs of Raffles' they still keep an eye open for old-school friends or unexpected cousins; in a thousand spruce and chintzy bungalows they still pin on their regimental brooches for the rites of English hospitality. Singapore is independent nowadays, but the British are still familiar there. Down on these waterside boulevards, between the banks and the patient ships, you may still sometimes fancy the throaty echoes of old commands, 'Colonel Bogey' on the morning breeze, the tap of a dead drum or the last silver note of an English bugle, exquisitely sad, infinitely homesick, from a warship in the roads.

When Raffles set up his ensigns here, a dense and soggy jungle rolled down the island to the mouth of the river, where a few fishermen's homes stood decrepit and malarial in the mud. Singapore was a beachhead, a clearing on the sea-shore: and to this day, though the island has long been tamed and suburbanized, the clinging, cloying presence of tropic vegetation pervades the city, as though the landing-stage is still temporary, and the jungle is only waiting to reclaim her own.

Forbidding and predatory foliage sprawls over the small islands of the harbour. Brilliantly sensuous plants ornament the city gardens —orchids and gorgeous frangipani, travellers' palms like powdered dowagers, dazzling gladioli, flaming creepers and curious cacti. Patches of dark woodland penetrate the very core of the place, settling in gullies among the houses, and when the rainy season comes, and the whole place drips, gurgles and eddies with wet, then you may sometimes see, sweeping down the deep monsoon gutters, the writhing forms of hapless pythons, or drowned curdles of cobras. Bulbuls thrive here, and scorpions, and flying-foxes. At night the bellow of frogs rings from the mangrove swamps behind the city, and sometimes the chicken-runs of the outskirts are raided by huge monitor lizards out of the night. Singapore is a city on the edge—on the edge of an island, on the edge of a jungle, on the edge of a continent.

She was always a labour-camp more than a community. To her clanging water-fronts, impelled by the magnetism of imperial power, men thronged from half Asia, just as goods from the whole Malay Peninsula, from all the islands of Indonesia, from Siam and Burma and China herself, erupted through these quays like water gushed

Singapore

through a tap. All the tradesmen of Empire set up shop in Singapore, and you may meet their descendants still—the speculators and the entrepreneurs, the aldermanic merchants, the coolies and the snivelling middle-men, the pimps and the domestics. A medley of picturesque money-changers accosts you, as you wander along Collyer Quay, or step from your juddering taxi in Raffles Place. A host of industrious gardeners attends the lush lawns of Tanglin. In Singapore there are still tri-shaw men, pedalling their cycle-cabs merrily among the buses, and down by the piers the jolly boatmen lie bobbing offshore, waiting to take a captain to his command, or bring the liberty-men to town. In many a dim bar the hostesses, their skirts split exuberantly to the thigh, bring you your whisky with an authentic period allure, as though you were a Swedish skipper out of Conrad, or a roistering younger son: and at many a roadside food stall you may still see, deftly chop-sticking his abalone, one of those threadbare but irrepressible philosophers, those chunks of flotsam washed up from Europe, who have wandered these equatorial outposts since the days of the paddle-steamers.

The faith of power and money brought armies of pilgrims to Singapore, and now that the Raj has disintegrated, the shrine remains. Around the surviving monuments of Englishry—houses of Government, of commerce, of God—a mass of miscellaneous humanity clusters like supplicants about a derelict totem. Singapore is one of the most tolerant and cosmopolitan of cities. There are Arabs here and Javanese, Burmese and Indians, men from the Celebes and the Moluccas, from Borneo, Sumatra and Brunei, from Ceylon and the Coromandel coast, from America, Australia and every corner of Europe. There are Buddhists, Confucianists, Muslims, Taoists, Jews, Hindus, Parsees, Christians of diverse ritual. There are nearly two hundred thousand Malays, blithest of people, who often live in thatched urban villages, tucked away among shrubbery in the heart of the city, and who bring to the place a leavening of nimble, easy-going, rather ingratiating charm. There are still several thousand Britons, more broad-minded than they used to be, but still unmistakable, with the neat hats and tweedy suits, the white gloves and head-scarves, the scrubbed children and the pink-cheeked ladies of their unquenchable tradition.

Singapore accepts and absorbs them all. Every tongue is spoken in this city, every kind of costume is familiar, every creed is avowed, every loyalty is honoured, from the true-blue to the rebel-red. At one

333

festival you may see the ascetic Hindus piercing themselves with mystic spikes, at another the grave Confucians, in skull-caps and silken bloomers, prostrate themselves in slow ceremony to the wheezing of a Chinese band. Here is a glittering super-market, all corn flakes and detergents, but around the corner a queer wise woman, still in occult trance, laboriously foretells the future in animal grunts and spasms. Every kind of face, every nuance of manner, gives variety to Singapore. Every sort of custom gives tang to her ambiance. She is like a soup: one of those rich and viscous French broths that bubble perpetually in the stock-pot, brown and clogged with nutrition, with a marvellous grafting and blending of ingredients, and a bone or two protruding through the stew.

In Singapore, the ligaments are now Chinese. More than anything, this is a Chinese city, one of the greatest of them all. From the beginning Chinese labourers flocked to Singapore's docks and warehouses, sometimes with families, sometimes alone: and they have worked so hard, flourished so spectacularly, agitated so successfully, conducted themselves so ably, expanded their activities so greatly, multiplied so fast, that today they are the masters of Singapore. In a population of one and a half million, more than a million are Chinese. The Government of Singapore is almost entirely Chinese. Chinese money gives Singapore her sense of wealth in depth. Chinese gusto keeps the city ever restlessly on the move. Every day, every hour Singapore becomes more Chinese, and already this old British stronghold, this jewel in Victoria's diadem, has become the southernmost great outpost of the Chinese culture, half-way to Sydney.

Behind the brass-bound commercial façades, filling in the ordered British streets like a feverish filigree, all the meshed activity of the Chinese way pulses and proliferates. All is noise, energy, movement, cheerfulness, a forest of washing hung across the lanes, a babel of stalls and outdoor markets, a puzzle of Chinese signs, a cauldron of Chinese smells. The pressure and intensity of life is indescribable. The congestion is unbearable, from the cluttered higgledy-piggledy slum apartments, four beds to a room, to the tottering death-houses in which a multitude of wrinkled but uncomplaining ancients awaits the last joss-stick. The sense of sleepless, tireless purpose would be nightmarish, were it not for the Chinese talents for fun, tolerance

Singapore

and easy living. Singapore has the highest birth-rate on earth, and the youngest population, and if you stand in Sago Lane, Chin Chew Street, or Keeong Saik Road, amid all the ramshackle but exhilarating confusion of Chinatown, you may feel that no city in the world lives life more to its *papier-mâché* hilt.

Overwhelmingly Chinese is the din and dazzle of modern Singapore, the blinding glare of the Great World Fun Fair, the gaudiness and twinkle of the back streets. Delectably Chinese is the exquisite food of the open-fronted restaurants or the gourmet's market stalls—marvellously garnished with sea things, spices and exotica, delicately laid in fronds of glistening green, placed before you, no matter how humble the *restaurateur*, with all the pride of artistry. Ominously Chinese is Singapore's suggestion of conspiracy, her underground politics and her hundreds of secret societies—the Hung Min Society, the 329 Gang, the Little Heroes, or the 13 Dots, dedicated, as one reference work blandly phrases it, to 'Murder, Extortion, Protection Rackets, Kidnapping, Opium Smuggling, Gang Fights, Assaults, Gaming Promotion, Armed Robbery and Political Activities'. Splendidly Chinese are the Singapore millionaires, with their private bodyguards and their legendary possessions, their interests ranging from the eminently respectable to the distinctly dubious, their tastes from the orgiastic to the supremely cultivated. All Chinese is the bold abstract art of Singapore, the jauntiness of the wayside theatres (flickering candles and clashing cymbals), the hint of cloistered connoisseurship, the slithery temple ritual, the hollow clapping of stick on wooden board, knocked together by the strolling urchins of the city as the Western schoolboy whistles his way to the milk-bar. Always scheming, always loving, always working, always awake, Raffles' clearing on the jungle island has become a great city of the Chinese, graced with the fascination of their ever-noble civilization—'China 'crost the bay!'

It is a wide bay, though, and a long haul from Singapore to Peking. Though this is still one of the busiest of ports, nevertheless the City of the Lion, now that the British have given her up, feels oddly isolated and neglected. In general, far more than in particular, she feels stifled and seedy, frayed, stained, fretted, for all her boundless Chinese vitality. She badly needs a lick of paint. The flagstones of her grand waterside boulevards are buckled and bent. She feels as some distant frontier town of Rome must have felt, when the legions

Singapore

had gone, but the Goths had not arrived yet.

For she is an orphan of Empire, designed as a strut in a collapsed construction. Trade followed the flag to Singapore, and commerce still thrives there, but history has left her, for the moment, high and dry. She remains a workshop, an assembly plant, a floating dock, a hospital, a warehouse, a service station, but she still does not feel a home. Her tall buildings, towering above the water-front, look always restlessly out to sea, as though they are expecting a mail-boat that will never come again, bringing dispatches from Whitehall and order-books from Manchester. She feels a lonely sort of place, sustained no longer by the warm if unwelcome bonds of the imperial ideal. If you stand on the knoll of Fort Canning (where the old British grandees lie at peace in crumbling Grecian mausoleums) and survey the wide panorama of the port before you, from the big Empire Dock to the cluster of schooner masts beside the Kallong River, you will sense how harsh has been the destiny of Singapore, and how unkindly fortune has jilted her. Her old imperial purpose is lost, and for all those vast docks and derricks, those memorials of success, she feels all on her own, out on a limb, rootless on the fringe of Asia.

One of these days, no doubt, some new comity of peoples will claim her, some rising federation, some Motherland, fitting her once more into a grander pattern of authority: but for the moment Singapore stands like an uncertain giant, an Asian in an old-school tie, down the line from China.

STOCKHOLM

I did not want to be rude, but I could not help eyeing my neighbour with interest, for she seemed to me to have the makings of a Microcosm. More than most cities, Stockholm projects two images—the one you have been led to expect, the one you discover for yourself: and this plump but not unalluring citizen, wearing a pink linen dress and a white straw, her eyes bluish but somehow glazed, her hands well kept but a little stubby, her mastication rhythmic and her bosom calmly heaving to the flow of the salad—this lady of Stockholm, evocative partly of Chanel and partly of Dettol, slipped into my preconceptions like a slug into a socket.

She was eating alone, with a bottle of Niersteiner and what appeared to be the financial page of *Svenska Dagbladet*. Her lunch was large but looked obscurely colourless, as though it had been bleached in some anti-fattening lotion. Her gaze now and then wandered from her victuals and paraded the room, in a slow and undeniably bovine motion, resting at last without excitement upon somebody else's pudding. Her expression was content without being joyous, and beneath her loose blonde curls, I told myself with satisfaction, all kinds of Swedish neuroses surely festered: anxieties of opulence and ill-faith, of spinsterhood or free love, occupational frustrations and suicidal impulses. She seemed to express all that I expected of Stockholm, and when at last I engaged her in conversation, and boldly asked her what she did for a living, I could almost have hugged her in gratitude. 'I am a Juvenile Social Welfare Worker,' she replied with a sweet smile, taking a delicate last sip of the hock.

It is the easiest thing in the world to confirm your previsions in Stockholm. Just as you expect, the city gives you an instant impression of hygienic pallor. Everything is tidy, everything is clean. Every girl is delectable, every child is immaculate, every car is washed, every Juvenile Social Welfare Worker eats impeccable salads off spotless tablecloths. The faces of Stockholm are rarely

Stockholm

craggy, twinkling or eccentric, but seem moulded to a pale and unarresting norm, and even the patricians of the place are stolidly Germanesque in style, with spats and fur collars. This is essentially a middle-class commercial city. Stockholm has long abandoned the high roads of glory, and looks out across our heart-rent Powers and dying empires with a compassion that is strongly fortified by self-congratulation. She feels, to the outsider, too rich by half, too introspective, too pleased with herself. The businessman shows you his graphs, his adding machines and his polished daughters with maddening superiority. The pundit dismisses with a polite but airy sniff any possible criticism of Swedish foreign policy. The Swedish court, behind the vast enigmatic façade of the Royal Palace, is said to be the stickiest in Europe.

Keep an eye cocked for neurosis, too, and you will find it soon enough. Fourth husbands, abandoned wives, step-sons and half-sisters seem to abound at every party. Dissolute youths and heedless girls scream by on motor-bikes, wearing black leather jackets and shiny jeans, and breathing the spirit of delinquent rebellion as fretfully as ever they do in Liverpool or the Bronx. The retired cavalry officer, clicking his heels at you and bowing with a comical but pathetic insistence, pungently reflects the nostalgia of an egalitarian society. The irreverent young intellectual, scoffing at the pretensions of the royal house, wittily lampoons the paradox of a Socialist monarchy. When the sun shines on Stockholm, and coveys of young women are to be found propped against doorposts or dreaming on benches, their eyes closed and their faces radiant in trance-like repose, like lemmings out of hibernation—when the sun shines down on Stockholm you may feel beneath the surface of the city strange old forest energies, stifled mysticisms and atavistic instincts. Stockholm is a frankly provincial city, Americanized and strictly conformist, immune to dauntless rebels, careless visionaries, moth-eaten dukes, misogynists or disagreeable hermits. She is not, however, all sweet smiles and serenity. She is perhaps the most comfortable of all the capitals, but she does not feel at ease.

She is, however, exceedingly lovely. It cannot be denied. It is all too easy, as you survey this upholstered place, to pine for something more harum-scarum, a dingy back street in Marseilles, a grubby London courtyard, the sour ebullience of New York or the frowning pathos of Moscow. Nevertheless, there is to the physical appearance

Stockholm

of Stockholm something at once elegant, homely and reassuring. She is no dazzling long-legged debutante, no sophisticate of urbane sensibility, nor even a handsome powdered dowager: but she suggests to me one of those well-built, perfectly manicured, tightly curled, pink-cheeked and neatly corseted matrons sometimes to be found running, with brisk courtesy and unfailing efficiency, expensive private nursing homes of snobbish predilections. She is seductive, but in a faintly medicinal way.

This scrubbed allure is partly the fascination of the northern climate—so dark but icy in the winter, so magically sparkling in the spring. Stockholm is a city of water, of fountains, harbours, inlets and canals, built at the spot where the little river Ström connects Lake Malaren with the island-speckled Salt Sea. There is fresh water behind her, salt water in front, and you are always walking at the water's edge. The City Hall overlooks the water, and so does the Opera House, and so does the Royal Palace. There are ferry-boats everywhere, and big white liners, and bridges, and the sails of yachts, and in the very heart of the capital you may see the destroyers of the Royal Swedish Navy, hulking and dark grey at their moorings. The light of Stockholm is water light, limpid and lucent. The legends of Stockholm are sea legends, full of dolphins and mermaids. The symbolisms of Stockholm are salt-fresh and glittering, like the gay and graceful nymph, naked but unblushing, who dances perpetually beside the water on the terrace of the City Hall. Stockholm stands up at the top of the world, as far north as Alaska, and she always feels near the snow-maidens and the northern lights.

In their heyday the Swedes responded to this lucency with a florid dignity of their own. They were not always a nation of burghers, and in their fighting years, when the Baltic was virtually a Swedish lake, and Stockholm lurked in ambush behind the screen of her archipelago, this must have been an exciting and exotic city. You may still sense its gaiety and power in the old part of the capital, compactly assembled on the island that stands between the fresh water and the salt. Here at last your preconceptions will be happily belied. There is nothing pallid or monotonous about this quarter of town, carefully though most of its buildings have been restored. Everything here is elaborate, higgledy-piggledy and unexpected, washed vividly in pinks, reds and yellows, the tall merchant houses looming above the quays, the rooftops crowned with towers, spires, high gables and jumbled gimcrack chimney-pots. There are huge

Stockholm

carved inn signs, and smoky basement taverns, and gilded clocks, and woodcarvings of exquisite detail, and memories of poets, adventurers and courtesans: and summing it all up, a paradigm of Stockholm's old martial individualism, is a magnificent fifteenth-century figure of St. George in the church called Storkyrkan, his wooden armour formidably studded, his wooden horse triumphantly rearing, his wooden sword-arm raised for the kill, his wooden maiden demure in prayer beside the battle, and his poor wooden dragon, writhing on its haunches, boasting that unique monstrous appendage, a pair of wooden elk's horns.

And when you explore a little further, get to know the lady better, you will begin to see new beauties in modern Stockholm too. There are the obvious physical beauties of space and contrast, clean line and uncluttered vista, but there is also a less obtrusive grace of style. This is never a vulgar city, because it is rich in depth. I do not mean simply the ubiquity of cars and washing machines, gleaming shops and lovely clothes. I mean that the attitudes of sufficiency are universal, giving to this bourgeois capital something of the ease of a mid-Victorian mansion. The habit of assurance runs deep and strong. The taste for quality is rooted. You do not feel, when you take a bus, that anyone is travelling without a ticket. You are not afraid, when you buy a toy or a cardigan, that they have forgotten to put the key in, or left a button off. Everything *works* in Stockholm, and in prosaic everyday things, in eating and telephoning and ordering the morning paper, this city feels like a well-ordered old-fashioned household, where money really is no object.

And though life in Stockholm is scarcely a shot in the arm, it is hardly soporific, either. At first sight this looks a sated and stodgy society, where the old men of the Nobel Committee meet stertorously to distribute the profits of death to politically suitable geniuses: but in fact Stockholm is still a creative city, still enlivened now and then by true intellectual controversy, still sometimes rejuvenated by the clash of public opinion. Stockholm can still produce men like Dag Hammarskjöld and Ingmar Bergman, the very antitheses of the archetypal Swede (whom we usually envisage as a velvety ball-bearings magnate eating underdone steaks in wartime). Good modern painters are hard at work in this city, and a multitude of small art galleries displays their work. Stockholm novelists are lively and productive, Stockholm publishers produce some of the most handsome of books. Sometimes you may even see, across the munch-

Stockholm

ing commuters at the café tables, the distant jogging placards of a protest march—nuclear disarmers, perhaps, anti-vaccinationists, or people who feel violently that women should not be priests. This is no Paris or seething Warsaw, but it is no Geneva, either. There is more to Stockholm than salad forks and pension funds. If I were a citizen of the place, I confess with a trace of reluctance, I would be exceedingly proud of it, snigger who may. I would be proud of its social order, expressed in a city without slums, beggars or rickety children. I would be proud of my always clean streets, my invariably beautiful women, the groaning smorgasbord of my restaurants and the absolute equality of my schools. I would be proud of the integrity of my city, its sense of justice and fair play, its decency if not its high jinks, its diligence if not its derring-do.

And if, one fine Scandinavian morning, I found myself with a carping Londoner beside the Riddarfjärden, with the Royal Palace aflutter with flags before us, and the jumble of the old city dreaming in the haze across the water, the lean grey warships throbbing beside their quays, the sharp skyscrapers piercing the skyline like axe-blades—if ever I found myself in such a situation, by Heaven, how complacent I would be, how infuriatingly smug and Socialist, how neutral and pampered and overfed! 'We can't complain, my dear fellow,' I would say with a smirk, 'we can't complain'—and if that goaded Englishman pushed me into the water with a sharp jerk in the back of the neck, well, it would almost be worth it.

SYDNEY

Sydney is a harbour, with a bridge across it that everyone knows by sight, and a city around it that nobody can quite envisage. The origins of Sydney are unsavoury, her history is disagreeable to read, her temper is coarse, her organization seems to be slipshod, her suburbs are hideous and her politics often crooked, her buildings are mostly plain, her voices rasp on the ear, her trumpeted Art Movement is, I suspect, half spurious, her newspapers are either dull or distasteful, and in the end, when you hunger for beauty or consolation in this famous place, you return willy-nilly to the harbour-front, where the ships tread with graceful care towards their moorings, and the great humped bridge stands like an arbiter above the quays.

Harsh words for a stranger to utter, but then there was never a harsher contrast than the disparity between Sydney and her setting. This harbour is not, to my mind, so beautiful as its popularly nominated peers, Rio, Hong Kong and San Francisco, but it is still exceedingly lovely, and to stand upon North Head on a crisp sunshine afternoon, with a swell rolling in from the South Pacific and an idle flurry of yachts beyond Bradley's Head—to stand at the gateway of Sydney on such an afternoon is among the classic experiences of travel: such an ineffable antipodean blue is the sky above you, so unexpected and inviting are the countless coves and fjords of the harbour, so imperturbably do the tankers sweep out to sea, so silent and lordly are the warships in Athol Bay, so grand but monstrous does the crook-back of the bridge protrude above the promontories.

It is a San Francisco that such an environment deserves, and sometimes indeed the anxious traveller will find himself reminded of that celestial seaport. He will see affinities in the winter mists, the lap of the water at the end of every vista, the cool green gardens of The Domain above Wooloomooloo, the villas poised so delectably on their cliffsides above the harbour. He will taste, if he meets the right

Sydney

people, the same careful but seldom humourless diligence, the same
meticulous interest in a brief past, comparable cheerful clubs, and,
among the cramped espresso bars of King's Cross, similar wayward
but resolute Bohemians. Pinchgut Island, with its stone fortress and
its dismal recollections, will remind him of Alcatraz, and the bustle
of the boats at the Circular Quay, as the Manly Ferry sails away to a
tinkle of its resident piano and a quaver of its mendicant violin, may
seem a distant homespun echo of Fishermen's Wharf.

This is, though, a San Francisco sadly *manqué*, just as Dorman
Long's fine bridge, however sensible and sturdy, is a lumpish
substitute for the Golden Gate. Sydney is not one of your absolute
cities, and in nothing that I have detected, except perhaps the racing
commentaries, is she quite in the first class. She is almost as old as
San Francisco, indeed, and bigger than all but a handful of European
capitals, but there is something cold and vacuous at her core, something that makes the stranger, however hospitable his acquaintances,
feel obscurely lonely in her streets. For most Sydney citizens the
purpose of life may perhaps be summarized in the parade of the life-
savers on Manly Beach, all bronzed open-air fun on Saturday afternoons, and perhaps it is this paucity of purpose, this lack of lofty
memories or intentions, that makes this metropolis feel so pallid or
frigid at the soul.

This, and what seems to be a shortage of kindness. The people of
Sydney will usually greet you warmly enough, even heartily, but
compared with the great immigrant cities of the New World,
Montreal, New York or São Paulo, this place feels cruelly aloof.
Perhaps it is the origins of Sydney that invoke this sensation—for
despite the sophistries of her society ladies, she was founded by the
scum of England, only six generations ago. Perhaps it is the expressions on the faces of those ladies themselves, so steely, scornful and
accusatory, as though they are expecting you (which Heaven forbid)
to offer them an improper suggestion. Perhaps it is the intolerance of
one citizen to another, sour bus conductor to irritable passenger,
cross-patch waitress to graceless customer. Sydney does not feel like
a haven. She does not reach out, as New York once did, to receive
'your tired, your poor, your huddled masses yearning to breathe
free'. No great ideals of politics or humanity animate her, no visions
of nobility, but only starker impulses of self-advancement or survival.

Nor does she even feel content. She seems full of reproach, sneer
and grumble. The immigrant from Europe or England all too often

Sydney

feels resented. The dinkum Aussie all too often seems to cherish racial prejudices of the nastiest kind. The sleazy bars of the place, looking like public lavatories and smelling of slopped beer, exude no genial good cheer, but only a mindless and sometimes rather frightening sense of male collusion. A proud new bridge collapsed in Melbourne while I was in Australia, but the Sydney *Daily Telegraph*, in its editorial on the matter, offered not a breath of sympathy, nor even a kindly joke, but only a column of crude and spiteful mockery. The people of Sydney like to think of themselves as a 'weird mob', but they strike me as weird not in any free-and-easy gallivanting way, but only in a sort of twisted uncertainty and isolation.

I blush even to consider the numberless exceptions to these hasty generalizations: all the kind and cultivated people who do live in Sydney, all the patient Dutch waiters and gay Italian stevedores, all the charming dons up at the University, all the scholarly attendants at the Public Library, many a jolly taxi-driver and many a thoughtful bookseller, the courteous attendants at the State Parliament, the splendid ferry-captains who stride so grandly, like admirals on a quarter-deck, from one wheelhouse to the other when their boat turns round. The brave new Opera House is perhaps a foretaste of more stylish things to come, and each year the influx of Europeans rubs a little elegance into this raw city, and a little gentleness too. Some of the new skyscrapers, though scarcely breath-taking, are handsome enough. Some of the new highways breathe the dash and dazzle one expects of such a young and explosive port.

Even so, Sydney does not yet feel a great city—not a generous, confident, serene city, not a city of any warmth and splendour. Turn your back on the bridge and you will travel through a wilderness of peevish suburbs, a labyrinth of unlovely boulevards, a humdrum desolation, until at last you reach the outskirts of the place, and there before you, if you persevere, stretches the emptiness of Australia, which is inescapable, which runs like some chill virus through the bloodstream of this country, and so binds the fragile years together that even now you may sense the presence of the chain-gangs in Sydney, and fancy the punishment cutter striking out to Pinchgut.

TEL AVIV

*C*ivis occidentalis sum, and so I do not feel altogether abroad in Tel Aviv. The air is Asian, the sun Oriental, the buildings are white and the trees tropical, the beer of the sidewalk cafés possesses a curiously chemical quality, far removed from the vegetable grandeurs of European ale: but if you feel yourself to be Western man, you will always be half at home in this, the principal city of the Jewish State.

Jerusalem is the official capital of Israel, and Haifa up the coast is a more serene and elegant city, but in the streets of Tel Aviv are enshrined, once and for all, the formidable efforts of the Zionists to achieve a homeland of their own. Here, better than anywhere else in the world, you may consider what it means to be a Jew, ponder the tragic significance of this astonishing people, and wonder whether this smallish seaside town, half resort, half business centre, will ever be a great city in a great nation, or whether the heart of Jewry lies elsewhere still. There was to the energies of Zionism, before the Israeli State became a fact, a mystical, Biblical, tribal force, like the shifting of a season or some enormous celestial truth: but Tel Aviv is one of the deflations of history, for today she feels an essentially provincial, hopefully prosaic town, where the nice young women promenade down Allenby Road with their babies, and the conversation at the next table is generally concerned not with dark fundamentals of truth and cruelty, but only the cost of cucumbers or why little Moshe can't spell.

Tel Aviv, indeed, wants to be an ordinary town, and to any Western visitor nowadays she seems half familiar from the start. The climate is a dream, and all along the city's water-front run heavenly golden sands, with the long slow swell of the Mediterranean curling up to the esplanades: but though the setting is exotic, this is almost a European city, inhabited by people who, though handsomely bronzed by the perpetual sun, are almost Europeans. You hear

Tel Aviv

English, German, Polish or Yiddish almost as often as you hear Hebrew, and time and again you will see someone walking down the street who seems at first sight to be somebody you know, a publisher in Paris or a musician in London, but who turns out to be familiar only because he is a Jew and a man of the West. Just as America was once called, by the poet Philip Bailey, the 'half-brother of the world', so Tel Aviv is distantly related, through the blood-brotherhood of Jewry, to all the greater cities of the West.

She still feels a city of the thirties, as do those London suburbs where the refugees from Hitler's Europe chiefly settled. There is little to show of the British who were her rulers between the wars—a street name here, a police station somewhere else: but her architecture smacks heavily of watered Bauhaus, her undistinguished squares, trim and symmetrical, look like town-planning designs in architectural reviews before the Second World War, and even her sea-front, though it has its glittering new hotels and raucous coffee bars, mostly retains a demure but determined period flavour. Tel Aviv was founded in 1910, but she was really born after Hitler came to power: the refugees who came then stamped her with the mark of their times, and beneath her housewifely exterior you may still detect, if you think long and hard enough about her, some of the sadness of fugitives, and the nostalgia of exiles.

She wants to be an everyday city, but can never quite achieve it, for Israel is not yet an everyday State. She has mellowed since her most defiant days of resentment, lost some of the chips upon her shoulders, but she still lives by the slogan of Ein Brera—'No Alternative'—and she is still precariously isolated among a ring of enemies. Moreover, every now and then the Israelis are halted in their tracks by a declamation out of the past, a reminder from State or history that they are no ordinary people, but a nation still apart, a nation of awful suffering genius, beyond the normal processes of time. They are still confronted by a unique dilemma, apparent enough to the thoughful stranger in the streets of Tel Aviv: either they can abandon their Jewishness, their separateness, and become ordinary healthy citizens of a second Lebanon, or they can deliberately preserve their sense of persecution, superiority and detachment, and attach their new State to the dark and splendid centuries of the Jewish past. They can contract out of genius, if they please, and live as a small but gifted Levantine republic: or they can remain within the prison-palace of their magnificent heritage, and

Tel Aviv

make this place not simply a city of the Israelis, but a city of the Jews.

In Tel Aviv you may feel that they have already made their choice, for there is nothing very gilded or terrible about this city, and here all feels plump and satisfied. Watch them closely as they saunter down to the beach, so tall and fit and laughing, with their gay sunhats and brief shorts, their picnics and their plump babies —watch them with a detached Gentile eye, and you will see that Tel Aviv is already moulding, as Crèvecoeur said of America long ago, a new kind of man. A generation is maturing that was born in Israel, and never knew the horrors of the ghettos or the lesser humiliations of Jewishness: and it is both the triumph and the tragedy of Tel Aviv that though her younger citizens are unmistakably Israeli, they do not feel like Jews.

Is this a worthy function for such a city, born out of the genius of such a people? Many Jews think not, and for myself I cannot suppose that Tel Aviv properly represents the Jewish future, faithfully though she may reflect the prospects of the Jewish State. Such an end to a supreme story does not ring true to history, to prophecy, to art, or to Judaism itself. The longer I spend among the cosy comforts of Tel Aviv, the more it seems to me that the Jews are, in a towering and inexplicable sense, some kind of Chosen People. So often, if you pursue a human activity to its source or its conclusion, you end up among the Jews. They will never be quite the same as us, however happily humdrum they manage to make this city, and will perhaps never be restful, serene or ordinary for long. They are a nation doomed but exalted, lapped perpetually in the divine twilight.

Tel Aviv will fructify, I have no doubt, and play her worthy part in the affairs of the lesser States: but the only proper conclusion to the tale of the Jews is the victory of the selfless over the selfish—and sure enough, in the heart of that conception too every Christian finds a Jew.

347

TOKYO

At the bottom of the escalators in the big Tokyo department stores two girls usually stand in attendance, one at each side. They wear uniforms, like air hostesses, and between them there passes a constant and fairly ordinary stream of shoppers, tweed-skirted or mackintoshed, rich with packages and babies. The duty of those two girls is this: all day long, in dignified unison, they must offer obeisance to the passing customers, bowing low and stiffly from the waist, up and down, up and down, their tiny porcelain faces impassive but respectful, like neat blue puppets bobbing against a backcloth, in a world of war-lords and cherry-blossom.

In many another capital city, from Lima to Katmandu, such a situation would offer one of those contrasts of period or custom so dear to the travel writer (the best-flogged horse in the whole stable of travel imagery is the Sheikh-and-Cadillac piebald). In Tokyo, however, it provides no such easy symbolism, for this is a city with its own conventions. Here the traditional and the modern neither clash raucously nor unite sententiously: they merely progress in a condition of habitual but uneasy coexistence. You can wear a kimono or an Empire line, whichever you like. You can sleep austerely on a straw mat, or squashily in an expensive bed. You can go to a symphony concert or a Noh play—or even, according to the entertainments guide of my newspaper one day, to a function described beguilingly as a Nude Immoral Lecture. Tokyo is a hodge-podge capital, her rhythm hovering between the antique and the honky-tonk, but she is plagued by no sense of violent cultural conflict.

By now, indeed, the new is more intrusive in Tokyo than the old. A century of industrialization has made of this a spectacularly ugly city, far removed from the watercolour hygiene of the Japanese legend. Vast, teeming, and gloomy are the factory suburbs which, like a wide blighted wilderness, surround the capital on every side

Tokyo

and straggle away to Yokohama. Driving into Tokyo from the south is like traversing some interminable Slough or Jersey City, a morass of low wooden houses, chimneys, power pylons, messy back yards and bumpy, noisy, ill-lit roads. Nor do the people, in their dull workaday clothes, add much gaiety to the scene: old women shrouded in sacks and wrappings wave you on at the innumerable road obstacles, and often you will see men stalking moodily through the streets with cotton pads over their faces (they look eerily suggestive, but in fact have colds in their noses). You can travel for a couple of hours without seeing one single beautiful thing, unless, through a break in the drizzle, the white summit of Fujiyama appears momentarily above the mills.

The centre of the city is Westernized in another way. Not only are there the great unbeautiful offices of the banks and Government departments: there is also the fizz and glitter of modern commerce. Scores of advertising balloons bob gaily in the sky above the Ginza, and a turmoil of traffic bumps its way down that celebrated boulevard with a Parisian intensity of purpose. There are few more splendid stores in the world than the shops that command this district: stores so complete that you can buy anything from an oil painting to a razor blade, glittering with bright lights and shining silks, thick with recorded music, packed tight with the pearls and cameras and toys and brocades and telescopes and ivories and prints that are among the most delectable of the Japanese specialities. Upstairs you may eat the raw fish and seaweed of tradition. Downstairs a crowd of young people, in postures and gestures of Existentialist genesis, clamour around the old Moores of a contemporary Japanese sculptor (and on the third floor they will run you up a Dior dress, from the original *toile,* for the price of a plastic raincoat at home).

These are aspects of the New Japan that instantly strike the unsuspecting visitor: but he need not dig deep for the old, either, even in Tokyo. There is the huge rambling palace, walled and moated, in which the Emperor still lives, shorn of his godhead but not his monarchy. There are the numberless kimonos that still flutter and totter through the streets, with their silken butterfly bows and their high-soled shoes. There are the students in their dark blue uniforms, and the businessmen bowing to each other so earnestly on the pavement, and the coy subservience of the middle-aged women, and the occasional lordly magnate stepping from his car with all the old hauteur of the shoguns, as though he carries an

349

embossed scimitar beneath his overcoat, or is about to obliterate a faithless general.

Or you can spend an hour or two at a Kabuki theatre, still among the great popular attractions of Tokyo. The audience will consist mostly of women in kimonos, following the drama with an informed avidity I have only seen paralleled among Rugby crowds in South Africa; and you will sit there wedged between the brocades, baffled by the tortuosities of the plot, swathed in the sickly perfumes of Japan. High above you in his balcony the narrator, shaking his head about with movements of infinite import, declaims his lines erratically but majestically from his tasselled lectern; and the man beside him plucks dreamily at his ancient instrument; and on the magnificent stage the grotesque mediaeval figures sit and strut and gesticulate, with falsetto voices and grand flamboyant costumes; and down the elevated walk above the audience there prance or stride the criminals and heroes and high-flown dancers, with a beat of drums or a black silence, a soft twanging of strings, a swish of fabrics and an emanation of passion. All that is grand or awful or ablaze in the old Japan lives on, twitching and quivering, in the theatre of the Kabuki.

So the new and the old, the silken and the smoky, pursue their courses distinctly if not defiantly: but the travelled stranger may sense, after a day or two in Tokyo, the existence of a kind of no man's land between the two. At the heart of many a conversation he will come across an emptiness, just as in the blaring razzle-dazzle quarters off the Ginza you may see the Tokyo teddy-boys, neither one thing nor the other, lounging or sidling down their alleyways. They wear their hair long and their trousers tight, but their high-boned Eastern faces are startlingly reminiscent of the old Japanese pictures, from which the slit eyes and pointed noses of evil peer out with such horrific potency. These frightening young men and their painted courtesans are the children of uncertainty, bred by progress out of tradition, but not in holy wedlock.

Who can be surprised? The old Japan was a country of deep accepted loyalties, based on feudal honour, on religion, on respect for family and ancestry, on pride in arms and unreasoning patriotism. One by one, by fortune and by war, these concepts have been laid low: first by the deliberate industrialization of the country, eagerly accepted by a people of great industry and ability; then by the abject humiliations of a defeat which punctured once and for all the legend of divine superiority. The two cultures do not squabble in Japan, but

350

Tokyo

one gets the impression that the new (so vigorous, so glittering, so easy of discipline and demand) is slowly corroding the old by its very proximity.

Is there something familiar about this process, by which the mores and manners and certainties of an ancient society are gradually whittled away, by which old rituals are gradually abandoned, and inherited beliefs lose their lustre, and great truths degenerate into baubles, and history itself turns sour? Certainly there is. Towards the end of the day, when closing time is near, those two smart girls by the escalator begin to giggle at each other as they bow, and neglect the formality of their courtesies: and this may insidiously remind you of another old island, where the guardsmen on parade do not seem to be quite so rigid as they used to be, and the honest men appear to be not quite so honest, and the gilded traditions of pomp and circumstance occasionally crumble into quaintness. 'This, to me, is truly educational,' says the American lady with a kind but patronizing smile, as some demoniac villain of Kabuki storms on-stage: and she says precisely the same, in just the same tone of voice, of the State opening of Parliament in London.

(There, so there was a symbol in it, after all. Trust the travel writer!)

TRIESTE

'**W**hat's become of Waring?' you may well ask of Trieste (where in fact he was): for never a city slipped so adroitly out of the world's headlines, or vanished so utterly into the limbo of forgotten crises. Sometimes a traveller returns with a glimpse of the place—a forlorn and demoralized city, he says, without a purpose in life. Sometimes a wandering diplomatist, passing through from Egypt or the East, thinks he recognizes a demarcation line or hears the echo of a Slovene demonstration. For the rest of us, Trieste has simply faded from our acquaintance, and most of us have even forgotten what all the fuss was about.

For fuss there was, for several years after the Second World War, when both Italy and Yugoslavia laid claim to this port, and squabbled so fiercely over it that time and again some sort of half-cock conflict seemed imminent. The dispute fizzled out gradually, inconclusively, point by point, and the *de facto* result is that, while the neighbouring peninsula of Istria has dropped into the maw of Yugoslavia, Trieste is now, in an anonymous and muffled sort of way, part of Italy again. There is still a testy Slovene minority in the city, and there are Slovene schools and cultural centres, but in effect this is an Italian port. Bright little Fiats scurry along the water-front, smart Italian liners laze beside the quays, and the girls who stroll by arm in arm, high-bosomed and languid-eyed, look like so many aspirant Sophia Lorens. The flavour of Trieste today is unmistakably Italianate, and high in the grand old Governor's Palace sits the Commissioner-General, every inch a Roman Consul.

There is a slight legal haziness to it all, though, owing to the fact that the United Nations never really made up its mind what to do with the place, and this blurred status perhaps contributes to the torpor of Trieste. She is a dissatisfied, rather petulant city. It is

The photographs following are of: Port of Spain, Rio de Janeiro, Rome, San Francisco, Singapore, Stockholm, Sydney.

Trieste

nearly half a century since she lost her old function as the chief outlet of the Austro-Hungarian Empire, but to this day she is always looking over her shoulder to the palmy days of old, the lavish imperial days, when the floodtide of the Empire's prosperity poured into her coffers, and all the urbanity of Vienna spilled over into her salons. Trieste is now the easternmost protrusion of Italy, but she looks Central European still, four-square and brooding, and feels like one of those impoverished gentlewomen, addicted to piquet and von Hofmannsthal, who are still to be found in stuffy drawing-rooms bewailing the decline of the Hapsburgs. 'Of course,' this city seems to say, 'we were used to better things, my boy, but there, ha! the world has changed! And how's your poor dear mother?'

For those few years of contention, after the war, Trieste was, if not happy, at least alive and crossly kicking. Her hinterland had been lost, and her position as a great entrepôt centre: but the eyes of the world were upon her, happily boosting her ego, and the Powers argued over her future, gently buttressing her id. Perhaps it was only whistling in the dark, but there was foreign money about in those days, and a well-paid occupying soldiery. They were effervescent, speculative, exciting times, with a riot on Saturday night and a hey-ho for Tito! Today, however, Trieste has subsided into lassitude. By slow stages the Italian Government has integrated the port into the affairs of the Republic, and there is nothing special about her any more. She has been domesticated, and lost her fizz. Once she was the seventh port of the world. Now she is only the third port of Italy.

Of course chance and history have dealt harshly with Trieste. 'Our city is built in a very uncomfortable position,' a Trieste lawyer once remarked to me: and so it undeniably is. Those bleak hills over the ridge are in Communist territory. Those waters beyond the headland are the Adriatic, bounded by Marxist shores. Most of the hinterland that should cherish these wharves has been bundled behind the Iron Curtain, and it is many a long uneconomic mile to the factories and markets of Italy. Things are certainly easing, as the monolothic façade of Communism cracks before our eyes, but look at the map of Europe, even so, and you will see why nobody wants to invest capital or enthusiasm in Trieste, poised so precariously between the ideologies.

To be sure, she is still the seaport of Austria—the trains that clank industriously along the promenade have usually come from

Trieste

Graz or Vienna. A reasonable amount of traffic still flows through Trieste. The shipbuilding yards are, when they are not on strike, fairly busy. There are several new local industries. Unemployment is no worse here than it is anywhere else in Italy. The tourists still come in season. People are quite well dressed, and adequately fed. This is still an important insurance centre, and the name of Lloyd Triestino is still familiar on the high seas. Nothing very tragic is happening to Trieste. She is simply pottering. 'Look at Genoa,' say the Triestinos angrily, 'and Bologna, and all the Italian boom towns! Look at Fiume! Look what the Italians promised us! Look at this bumble-head bureaucracy they've given us! I'll tell you, my friend' (here a flick of cigarette ash, a drooping of eyelids, an intricate change of inflection), 'there are times, loyal Italian though I am, when I wish our problems had never been solved!'

For it is lack of gusto that mostly strikes you in Trieste today. Neither time nor toil, said Browning's eye-witness, could mar the features of Waring; but Trieste has not been so resilient in her exile from celebrity. Her talented young people are leaving her, her old liberal tradition is neglected, her brave commercial instincts are blunted or frustrated. Depressed and half-hearted, she meanders on in disillusionment: not drunk, indeed, or crippled by war, or oppressed, or even destitute; just bored, that's all, just bored.

VENICE

At 45° 14′ N., 12° 18′ E., the navigator, sailing up the Adriatic coast of Italy, discovers an opening in the long low line of the shore: and turning westward, with the race of the tide, he enters a lagoon. Instantly the boisterous sting of the sea is lost. The water around him is shallow and opaque, the atmosphere is curiously translucent, the colours are pallid, and over the whole wide bowl of mud-bank and water there hangs a suggestion of melancholy. It is like an albino lagoon.

It is encircled with illusory reflections, like mirages in the desert —wavering trees and blurred hillocks, ships without hulls, imaginary marshes: and among these hallucinations the water lies in a kind of trance. Along the reef strings of straggling fishing villages lie deserted and unkempt. Away in the wastes there stand the sails of fishing boats, orange, yellow and magenta, with cabalistic signs or heraldic symbols, a rampant red horse, an all-seeing eye. The shallows are littered with intricate shambling structures of sticks and basketwork, and among them silent solitary men, knee-deep in sludge, prod in the mud for shellfish. A motor-boat chugs by with a stench of fish or oil. A man on the shore shouts to his friend, and his voice rolls away muffled and distorted across the flats.

Small islands lie all about, lapped in mud and marsh. Here is a glowering octagonal fort, here an abandoned lighthouse. A mesh of nets patterns the walls of a fishermen's islet, and a restless covey of boats muzzles its water-gate. From the ramparts of an island barracks a listless soldier with his cap over his eyes waves half-heartedly out of his sentry-box. Two savage dogs bark and rage from a broken villa. There is a flicker of lizards on a wall. Sometimes a country smell steals across the water, of cows or hay or fertilizer: and sometimes there flutters in the wake of the boat, not an albatross, but a butterfly.

Presently this desolate place quickens, and smart white villas appear on the eastern reef. The hump of a great hotel protrudes

Venice

above the trees, gay parasols ornament a café. A trim passenger steamer flurries southwards, loaded deep. A fishing flotilla streams workmanlike towards the open sea. Away to the east, beneath a smudge of mountains, there is a thin silver gleam of oil drums, a suggestion of smoke. A yellow barge, piled high with pop bottles, springs from a landing-stage like a cheerful dove from an ark. A white yacht sidles by. Three small boys have grounded their boat on a sand-bank, and are boisterously bathing. There is a flicker of welding from a dark shed, and a barge stands on stilts outside a boatyard. A hooter sounds; a bell booms nobly; a big white sea bird settles heavily on a post; and thus the navigator, rounding a promontory, sees before him a city.

It is very old, and very grand, and bent-backed. Its towers survey the lagoon in crotchety splendour, some leaning one way, some another. Its skyline is elaborate with campaniles, domes, pinnacles, cranes, riggings, television aerials, machicolations, eccentric chimneys and a big red grain elevator. There are glimpses of flags and gilded rooftops, marble pillars, cavernous canals. An incessant bustle of boats passes before the quays of the place; a great white liner slips towards its port, from Athens, the Levant or the Hudson River; a multitude of tottering palaces, brooding and monstrous, presses towards its water-front like so many invalid aristocrats jostling for fresh air. It is a gnarled but gorgeous city: and as the boat approaches through the last church-crowned islands, and a solitary jet fighter screams splendidly out of the sun, so the whole scene seems to shimmer—with pinkness, with age, with self-satisfaction, with sadness, with delight.

The navigator stows away his charts and puts on a gay straw hat: for he has reached that paragon among landfalls, Venice.

Venice is like a rock in that lagoon, encrusted with limpets, winkles and a multitude of infinitesimal brittle crustaceans. She sprang out of the mud fifteen hundred years ago, built by men who had fled from the mainland of Italy into the fastnesses of these waters—driven by barbarism or by heresy, according to your historical fancy. Her beginnings are blurred, and her history is always strange. A small isolated city with canals for streets, she became the greatest naval power of her day, mistress of the Oriental commerce, banker to half the world. For a thousand years a patrician oligarchy governed her, merciless but impersonal, and she stood grandly apart from the

Venice

ordinary currents of history, religious and political, that repeatedly convulsed the rest of Europe. She was decked with treasures of the Orient, decorated by the noblest artists of the day, courted and hated by East and West, derided, respected, feared, attacked, envied as few other nations have ever been. And when at last she grew too old and weak for greatness, she spun towards her fall in a dizzy whirl of merry-making, a daze of perpetual masked carnival, when even the Papal Nuncio wore a domino, when 'women were men, men were women, and all were monkeys'. Through all her years of splendour and decline, from her dim foundation to her conquest by Napoleon, Venice remained something unique among the nations and the cities: half-way between a freak and a fable, like a gryphon among beasts, or St. Simeon Stylites upon his pillar, in the days when Popes and Emperors sent their envoys to consult him.

She remains the strangest of the world's great cities. The forces of uniformity plod inexorably across Europe, but she remains a city apart, peopled by islanders. The true-born Venetian is still different from other Italians. His manners are different, his outlook is different, he even has his own language—a dialect so strong and resilient that for a century and more it has been defying prophecies of its imminent extinction (and dazed are the faces of visiting linguists, confronted by this hairy hybrid, for its derivation is partly French, partly Greek, partly Arabic and partly German, and it specializes in inexplicable slurrings and contractions). You can tell a Venetian by his face. Morose but calculating is the look in his limpid eye, and his mouth is enigmatic. His nose is very prominent, like the noses of Renaissance grandees, and there is to his profile an air of home-spun guile and complacency, as of a man who has made a large fortune out of slightly shady dealings in artichokes. Occasionally his glance contains a glint of contempt, and his smile is distant: usually he is a man of gentle reserve, courteous, ceremonious, his jacket neatly buttoned and his itchy palm discreetly gloved.

He is often bow-legged, but not from too much riding. For a century Venice has been linked to the mainland by a causeway, but she remains a city without roads. '*Streets Full Of Water*,' Robert Benchley cabled home, when he first set eyes on Venice. '*Please Advise*.' Venice remains a labyrinth of canals and narrow alleyways, dark, cramped and tortuous, in which all sense of direction is lost, the points of the compass are inextricably confused, and you never know whether you are going to see the back of the Basilica, when

Venice

you emerge from your alley, or the front of the Doges' Palace. This
fretted intricacy contributes to the Venetian's sense of wry fatalism,
something almost Oriental. 'Which way to the Basilica?' you will
ask him: and summoning a wise and helpful look, he will take you
kindly by the arm, usher you to the nearest vantage point, consider
the situation carefully, and pointing a finger through the maze of
lanes that lies before you, entangled in canals, archways, dead ends,
unexpected squares and hidden passages, '*Sempre diritto!*' that
Venetian will say courteously—'Straight ahead!'

Into this queer mediaeval framework all the paraphernalia of modern
urban life must be fitted. The only wheels in the city are on porters'
trolleys, perambulators, children's toys, and on the ramshackle
bicycles used by a few taciturn knife-grinders as the motive force
for their calling. Down the great artery of the Grand Canal, and
along the web of connecting canals, all the raw material of modern
civilization must pass, in barges and motor-boats, on trolleys, and
sometimes in big wicker baskets on the backs of men. Thousands of
boats are always on the move in Venice, and sometimes her canals
feel positively clogged with traffic. Two hundred thousand people
live in this city, with not a single delivery truck among the lot of them.

All the civic services, too, must be distorted to suit the Venetians.
Electricity strides in on pylons over the lagoon. Fresh water arrives,
paradoxically, in subaqueous aqueducts. The telephone company
lives in a seventeenth-century cloister, the municipal broadcasting
station in the house where Wagner died. The policemen chug about
in little speedboats, or are sometimes to be seen, muffled in double-
breasted greatcoats, laboriously rowing skiffs up the Grand Canal.
The garbage is taken away in splendid grey motor-barges. The
magnificent water-bus system sold fifty-three million tickets in one
recent year. The postmen walk briskly through their allotted sections
of the labyrinth, calling out names in a vibrant baritone, and popping
letters into the baskets that are lowered on strings from upstairs
windows. The drains of Venice empty into her canals, fostering her
celebrated *essence de Venise*, part rotting masonry, part excrement:
and every few years each canal is drained, and the workmen of the
Magistracy of the Waters are to be seen, deep down below the palace
steps, shovelling the filth into trolleys and barges. There is a set of
traffic lights in Venice, above an awkward intersection of canals;
there is a fine modern railway station; there is one of the biggest

Venice

garages on earth, at the head of the causeway; and on the neighbouring mainland a big new airport is named, for the greatest of the Venetian adventurers, Marco Polo. Yet for all the advance of modernism she remains unique, a city all on her own, like a very old golden monster in a pond.

She is very beautiful. What else can one say? There have been many scoffers at the Venetian legend, rationalists, sceptics, anti-Romantics, habitual debunkers: but most of them have fallen to her spell in the end. An endless procession of the gifted and the celebrated has come in pilgrimage to Venice, from Petrarch and Dante to Napoleon, Byron and George Eliot, whose husband, leaning in ecstasy over the balcony of their hotel room, once fell with an ignominious plop into the Grand Canal. 'A most incomparable and decantated city,' one sixteenth-century Englishman said of it: and though we may not quite know what the words mean, most of us know what he felt.

Her peculiar allure, though, is difficult to analyse. It is partly the light of the place, always shifting and flickering, always lucid, often delusive, etching the skylines in uncanny precision, foreshortening bridges and distorting distances. It is partly the shape of the city— neat, self-contained and functional, bisected by the greatest of waterways, surrounded by a crescent lagoon. It is partly its texture, rich, lush, exotic, enriched with porphyry, damask, diamonds and alabaster. It is partly its architecture, from the dazzling carbuncled Basilica of St. Mark's to the grim ponderous palaces of the Grand Canal. It is partly its feeling of theatrical delusion, as though it were all some brilliant stage set, so skilfully exploited by the Venetian artists that their mock-marbles, hovering angels, tricks of perspective and proportion sometimes leave you staggering around their masterpieces in a state of dizzy disbelief. It is partly the ever-present sense of Venetian history, so powerful and pungent that you almost expect to see the great beak-prowed galleons beside the Customs House, or hear the clink of the money-changers upon Rialto. It is partly the languorous, seductive movement of Venice: the dappled flickers of her water reflections, the grand lop-sided passage of her gondolas, the liquefaction of cassocks and wimples, the slow ponderous shaking of the beadle's head as, pointing his wand severely towards a short-sleeved dress or a plunging neckline, he dismisses some blushing tourist from the portals of St. Mark's.

Venice

Most of all the beauty of Venice is sensual, if not actually sexual. 'Other cities have admirers,' one nineteenth-century visitor put it. 'Venice alone has lovers.' When you lean from your Venetian window in the early morning, when the air is sea-fresh and the sun unsullied, when there is a soft splash of oars beneath your window, and the distant hum of a boat-engine, when the first sun glitters on the golden angel of the campanile, and the shadows slowly stir along the dark line of the palaces, when there is a smell of salt, age, velvet, fish, mud and incense in the air—then a strange delicious yearning will overcome you, as though some creature of unattainable desirability were passing by outside.

But her beauty has always been tinged with sadness—the sadness of refugees, the sadness of isolation, the sadness of decline, and now the sadness of nostalgia. The Victorian celebrants of Venice mourned her lost power, and saw in her either a vindication of their own political systems, or an awful portent of things to come. 'Men are we,' wrote Wordsworth, 'and must grieve, when even the shade of that which once was great has passed away.' Today the world has forgotten the mighty fleets of Venice, her formidable merchant-Doges and her pitiless Inquisitions. We no longer think of her as humiliated: but when the summer comes round each year, and the tourist machine swings into action again, then she feels a great city degraded.

She is a museum. In the winter her gates are closed and her life is private and pleasurable: in the summer she rings to the clang of the cash-register, the squeak of the turnstile, the complaints of those hundreds of tourists who understandably feel themselves to have been overcharged. This is the modern function of Venice—part art gallery, part burlesque. She is the greatest tourist attraction on earth. Her monuments of power are mere spectacles. Her wide suzerainties are reduced to the sing-song banalities of the guides. Venice is like some old general who has gone on the music-halls, displaying his gallantry medals to a tinny fanfare of cornets from the pit.

They talk of reviving her trade and industry, of making her the prime oil port for Central Europe, of linking her with the markets of Germany with vast highways and fleets of trucks: but though the nearby mainland is burgeoning with docks and factories, the city of Venice remains no more than a marvellous anachronism. She poses an insoluble dilemma. If they modernize her, fill in her canals and

Venice

take the cars to the Piazza, then they wreck her absolutely. If they leave her alone, she potters down the years as a honeymoon city, where film stars cross their legs revealingly in gondolas, and the annual army of tourists swirls and sways in sun-glasses and polychromatic cotton among the sorrowing edifices of the Republic. Poor Venice! Roll up for the freak show! A dime to see the dodo!

Sometimes, though, if you shut your eyes hard and forget the price of the coffee, you may see a vision of a new Venice. She became great as a market-city, poised between East and West, between Christianity and Islam, between Crusader and Saracen: and if you try very hard, allowing a glimmer of gold from the Basilica to seep beneath your eyelids, and a fragrance of cream cakes to enter your nostrils, and the distant thump of a café orchestra to orchestrate your thoughts—if you really try, you can imagine her a market-place again. In these incomparable palaces East and West could meet once more, to fuse their philosophies and settle their bickerings. There would be Turks in the Piazza again, and Chinese, thick-set Russians and earnest Americans, Englishmen feeling (as always) obscurely proprietorial, and Frenchwomen in blue lipstick. In the Doges' Palace the senate of the world would meet, and in the dim cavernous recesses of the Basilica, thick with incense, glimmering with faint lamps, all the gods would meet in reconciliation.

Venice is made for greatness, a God-built city, and her obvious destiny is mediation: here, as nowhere else, the arts, talents and tastes of the whole world coincide. And if you are not the visionary kind—well, pay the man, don't argue, take a gondola into the lagoon and watch her magical silhouette sink into the sunset: still, after a thousand years, one of the supreme sights of civilization.

WARSAW

Seen across the hours from a hotel window in the depths of winter, Warsaw could only be Warsaw, for nowhere else on the face of the earth breathes quite the same fusion of atmospheres. Room 221 in the Bristol Hotel is heavily but quite cosily Victorian, with a wicker mat hung in incongruous ornamentation on one wall and a bright if unadventurous abstract on another. Outside the door two dear old pudgy housemaids sit habitually on the floor in white caps, aprons, and carpet slippers, sibilantly gossiping, and down the corridor the immense glass lift, like a cage for a phoenix, slides in magnificent lurches to the foyer, its voyagers slipping a few zlotys to the operator as they leave. There is a violent smell of cooking on the landing, and downstairs you may just hear the tapping of a progressive American playwright's typewriter—he spent last evening with a group of eminent sociologists, and is busy working up his notes.

It is a fusty, old-fashioned, plush but mournful hostelry: but outside the window Warsaw is nothing if not spacious. The sky is grey, immense, and unmistakably Central European. The snow lies thick and sullen on the broad streets. Down the hill only a thin winding stream of water forces a way through the frozen Vistula. The air, to a visitor from England, seems slightly perfumed with petrol and boiled potatoes, but feels nevertheless like country air, blown out of forests and endless plains and Carpathian ravines; and when you first lean from your window in the icy morning you will hear the clatter of horses' hooves and the triumphant crow of a cold but irrepressible cock. Below you then the first citizens of the morning intermittently appear: an elderly lady with a jolly black dog, a covey of merry school-children, entrancing high-boned faces peering through their fur hoods like fox cubs through the bushes. Long carts full of snow go by, with a column of big lorries, and even an antique barouche trundles with creaks and squeaks towards its cab-rank; and presently Warsaw is wide awake, the sun is wanly

Warsaw

shining, and the observer in Room 221 can watch the world of the Poles pass by.

It is not altogether a drab world, for the Poles have forced many concessions out of their Communist masters. The citizenry that now pours down the pavement is not badly dressed—colourlessly, perhaps, by Western standards, but well shod and warmly coated. Sometimes a young beauty steps by almost ludicrously glamourized, slinking skilfully in the Bardot manner, in the finest nylons and the most preposterously frivolous of fur hats. Sometimes a peasant stumps down the street in thick but threadbare serge and mighty boots. Mostly the people look less arresting than workmanlike, as though they are more concerned with keeping warm and getting to the butcher's first than with turning heads or charming the boss's daughter.

The shops across the way might not win prizes in Fifth Avenue or Regent Street, but have more sparkle to them than you might expect (weary though the queue may be at the grocer's, and tiresome the shortage of meat). A surprising variety of inessential imports glitters bravely among their displays—American cigarettes, French sardines, Hawaiian pineapples, Florida fruit juice, tinned coffee from England, tea from Madras, olives from Argentina, things that look like bottled gooseberries from Bulgaria, Chinese jams (in bottles shaped like illustrious mandarins of the eighth degree). A bright parade of foreign books shines in the bookshop down the road, from a picture book of Oxford that almost breaks the homesick heart to an empirical range of American paper-backs. You can even buy French perfumes in Warsaw, if you happen to prefer them to the local product, and have an indulgent husband.

The cars that pass in increasing but still moderate profusion mostly look beetle-backed and froward, but now and then one of the smart new Russian limousines appears, not a bit Socialist-realist, and sometimes an opulent Mercedes-Benz slides by, or a delicate Fiat. Agatha Christie is probably on at one of the theatres. You can read the Manchester *Guardian* at the Grand Hotel. The buses are made in France. Just down the road is the headquarters of the British and Foreign Bible Society. Nostalgic you may be for Tom Quad or Times Square, but in Warsaw there are still tenuous links with home.

And even from Room 221 you can see something of the character of the Poles, for they move with a special kind of vigour, almost jaunty, and they have strong and interesting faces. Warsaw is

Warsaw

haunted always by sad memories, but there is nevertheless a liveliness, a jollity, a gaiety in the air that springs only from the hearts of the Poles. A gleam of wrinkled humour lightens the eye of the elderly chambermaid when she arrives, some hours after lunch, to make your bed. Polish conversation, for a visiting Englishman anyway, is infinitely easy, entertaining and somehow familiar. Sometimes in the street below a rip-roaring jovial drunk will stagger through the snow, bawling witticisms and singing bawdy songs. They are not an aloof, remote or inscrutable people, the Poles; they might do well, I sometimes feel, in Ireland.

At other moments, though, Warsaw feels a long, long way from Galway; and as the evening draws on, and the progressive playwright closes his typewriter and leaves for a séance with seven eminent philosophers, you may notice a stream of citizens moving intently towards the church which, with its twin angels sustaining the cross on its golden ball, stands in ornate confidence beyond the park. They walk with an air of functional resolution, very different from Ballycommon on Sunday morning, and slip into the church hurriedly, as though they have work to do there, crossing themselves for all the world as a worker clocks himself in at the factory; and if you are patient you will see them emerging again a few moments later, buttoning up their coats, putting on their thick gloves, and hastening away towards the trolley-bus. They look as though they have stopped at a petrol station to get fuel for the evening; and they even remind me—not with irreverence, only sympathy—of addicts on a lost weekend, stocking up at Joe's Bar on Fourth Avenue.

Then the night falls on Warsaw, chill and early, and the dim lights of eastern Europe reluctantly awake. The view from your balcony grows grim and depressing, with the presence of the harsh frozen Vistula always behind your back and only a trickle of prepossessed traffic enlivening the streets. The coffee-shops and restaurants hide their identities behind curtains and closed doors, and few bright lights entice you towards the theatres. The thump of a jazz band may reach you across the snow, but the city feels obscurely muffled and padded, and the gaunt square buildings of the new Warsaw lie there unsmiling in the cold.

Raise your eyes above the rooftops, though, above the chimneys, above the angels with their golden ball, and there you will see the big red light on the Palace of Culture and Science, presented to Poland by the Soviet Union, and towering above this grey city like a vast

Warsaw

watchman in the dark. And perhaps at the same time if you listen hard enough, closing your ears to the clang of the trams and the rumble of the passing cars, you may hear from some distant student attic the thin thrilling strains of a Chopin polonaise, riding the cold night air like an invocation.

But probably not. I must not romanticize. 'Room service? A cup of coffee, please, two aspirins, and a cable form. That's it, bless you, Room 221.'

WASHINGTON

A little of the allure of the Old South, the scent of river mud and magnolia, seeps into the purlieus of Washington, the capital of the United States; for this symbolic metropolis lies on the shore of the Potomac River, and if you scratch very hard, explore very thoroughly, evade as many hostesses as possible and skip all possible functions, you may still find a boatyard or two beside the water, see the blunt tugs nosing their way through the winter ice, or listen to the badinage of longshoremen down among the derricks.

It would be wild to suggest, though, that Washington is in any way a brawny capital. She ought to be, Heaven knows, when you think of the power exuding from her offices, the hulking frontier energies she represents, the vast resources she commands, or the generations of burly go-getters who have made Capitol Hill what it is. But in fact, like all artificial cities, she is ham-strung by self-consciousness. She is one of your planned capitals, and they are nearly always depressing (unless, as in Paris, the immensities of style are relieved by a filigree of ancient tumble). The boulevards of Washington seem endless indeed. The cherry trees of Washington would afforest an exotic mountain chain. The monuments of Washington, each two or three miles from the next, are luminous but seldom comforting. The venerable little suburb called George-town, the Chelsea of this city, is charming but dauntingly impeccable, its neat unpretentious façades masking, as often as not, air-conditioning units of breathless expense, and the kind of housewives who prop enormous books about Aztec sculpture on the open music-stands of grand pianos. Washington is not a large place: from any of her vantage points you may see how bravely the surrounding countryside resists her urban pressures. She has, however, under-standable pretensions to grandeur, and with all her flags and crests and emblems, her slogans and her statuary, her busts of dead heroes, her vast Government buildings and her Presidential presence, she

Washington

sometimes reminds me of a more gracious but scarcely less ritualistic Moscow.

With this difference, in particular: that while Moscow has to her an air of limitless continuity, stretching back far beyond the commissars to the dread gilded Tsars of old, the character of Washington recognizably shifts each time a new administration takes office. There is an eighteenth-century quality to this facet of the American political system. In comes the new President, and with him arrives an entirely new ruling caste, a Holland House coterie, complete with all its experts and advisers, its fashionable hostesses and modish mistresses, its favoured court jesters, its hair styles, dogmas and transient taboos. Eisenhower's Washington was full of amiable bumble-heads, staunch double-chinned chapel-goers, self-made company presidents with Germanic heads and Principles. Mamie Eisenhower's comfortable dresses and motherly manners somehow set the tone of the place, and there was a benign unsubtle flavour to the city's affairs, like a Norman Rockwell painting. Into this ambiance, which grew vaguer and unhappier each year, and more harried by criticisms, Jack Kennedy, his wife and his young men swept like a keen cold wind out of the prairie. The new President spoke of New Frontiers, and somehow in the first months of his administration there was a real sense of the fire, fun and purpose that must have characterized the great days of the West. Not long after the inauguration I met a Washington acquaintance of mine looking distinctly pallid, and asked him what the trouble was. 'I guess it's these New Frontiers,' he said. 'I'm getting too old for the Injun country.'

For this is almost exclusively a city of Government, and it is the Executive, not the Legislature, that dictates its style. Just outside the city stands the gaunt grim Pentagon, secretive and mammoth, and less awful bureaux of authority, from the Mint to the National Geographical Society, dominate every quarter of the place. Nearly every citizen works for the Establishment, and very often his wife does too. Ask the taxi-drivers, and half of them will tell you that they are studying for the Civil Service examination. Even the hotel chambermaid often works part-time at the U.S. Treasury. Washington is not a complete, full-blooded city. Her theatre is vestigial, her university crouches out of sight, her music is mostly amateur. Her galleries and museums are splendid, but her shops are feeble. Her waxworks is a pale imitation of Madame Tussaud's, her

Washington

Episcopal Cathedral is decorous in contemporary Gothic. She has virtually no industry, and even her tourism, though it must attract millions of visitors each year, seems wan and half-hearted. When the winter blizzards hit the Atlantic cities, Washington is much the slowest to clear the snow from her streets. She does not feel a city in the round. She is more gently mannered than most American towns, and by the nature of things she accepts eccentrics and outsiders with aplomb: but she is short of earthiness, open-throated humour, boisterous local pride, the clanging of engines or the blaring of night clubs. Her tastes are caustic rather than genial. When the design was published of a monolithic national memorial to Roosevelt, all jagged slabs and angles, it was a Washington wit who dubbed it 'Instant Stonehenge'.

She also has a skeleton in her cupboard, which perhaps helps to mute her manner. The District of Columbia, which is in effect Washington, is constitutionally voteless, except only in Presidential elections. It is not only unrepresented in Congress; its own municipal affairs are governed not by an elected council, but by a Congressional committee. This is, as everyone agrees, an anachronism, and from time to time measures are introduced to Congress to abolish it. There is, however, one tricky stumbling-block. Washington now has a Negro majority, and giving the city the vote would not only increase black power in the Republic at large, but would probably give the national capital a Negro mayor and administration. The very notion sends a shudder down the Southern spine, and seems only a step towards that ultimate degradation, a Negro in the White House. Washington, largely for diplomatic reasons, has no colour bar in her restaurants, hotels and theatres: but if you think racial prejudice is dead in this apex of the democracies, talk to the estate agents, and see to what lengths they will go to keep the more exclusive suburbs free of blacks, Jews or indeterminate aliens (even the British Embassy, I am told, was recently unable to buy property in one area because of the racial company the Queen keeps). It is one of the more awkward facts of American life, and of American diplomacy, that the capital of the United States stands in black man's country, invested, at the end of every boulevard, by the shades of bigotry. The Nigerian Ambassador may go where he wishes in Washington: but if he drives his Cadillac a few miles to the south, down the Virginia highway, he may be unable to buy a cup of coffee in the roadside coffee-shop. What is more, each year Washington becomes

Washington

more Negroid, further complicating a labyrinthine issue. Each year the white people retreat further into the embattled suburbs. Each year the downtown stores seem to cater more exclusively for Negro ladies. Each year, as the poor black people move in, so the crime rate goes up—in 1962 the incidence of assault was the highest in the nation. Each year the black fringes of the city, the drab brownstone houses and shambled stores, corrode still further the pompous city centre, rotting away many an old precept and many a rooted conviction. Before many decades have passed Washington will find that she has, to borrow a prognosis for the world's future given me by a cheerful Jamaican novelist, 'bred out brown'.

But paradoxically there is the glory of the place, the grand old truth that still seeps through the squalor, the prejudice and the snobbery: that if one city in the world really does hold out a promise of ultimate decency, of fraternity among all peoples, it is still this dull old entity upon the Potomac. Here you may still feel, when the wind is right, the faith of the Founding Fathers, and may still sometimes glimpse, reflected in classical colonnade or florid portrait, the incomparable dignity of America. In Washington the Supreme Court of the United States still reassures you that, for all the petty graft of American life, this remains a fief of the Law. In Washington you may still see the President of the United States personally questioned, at his weekly press conference, by the representatives of his people. In Washington, if ever you escape the awful parties and the dreary social arbiters, you may still feel this great Republic groping for the good, and somehow still pursuing, come slump come rocketry, the honourable mean between arrogance and irresponsibility.

And if, one summer night, you stroll alone through the city after a mellowing dinner, and see its famous monuments all about, the great floodlit dome of the Capitol, the gleaming obelisk of Washington's memorial, the White House demure and domestic behind its railings, craggy old Lincoln dim-lit in his marble chair—if ever you wander through the capital in such a mood, Jefferson in your head and Chesapeake prawns in your belly, then I defy you to resist the magic of the American experiment, or evade its ever-noble pathos.

WELLINGTON

Carefully and kindly the keeper placed the creature in my arms, and I felt its feathers rustling against my hands so sharp and metallic that they almost felt like scales. The beady little eyes were blind and filmed, the strong wire-like legs scratched and struggled against my chest, and the long tube of a beak, nostrils at the end of it, prodded its way crossly under my arm. It was about the size of a hen. The rain was dripping through the trees above us, the puddles had leaked into my shoes, on the ornamental lake along the path I could see, of all things, the broken hulk of a gondola, and as I stood there with the kiwi in my embrace I recalled my misty preconceptions of Wellington, and decided that the truth far surpassed the fancy.

The capital of New Zealand offers no instantly symbolic tokens, no harbour bridges or Table Mountains or pyramids or clumps of skyscrapers, and cuts no recognizable figure on the travel posters and airline brochures. Not many foreigners, asked for a speculative description of this place, could offer more than an abstract conjecture of sea and dullness. Most Englishmen have been told, and may now remember with a wry chuckle, that the entire Royal Navy could be accommodated in Wellington Harbour. Many Americans vaguely suppose that geysers spout in Wellington's suburbs, while Maoris in grass aprons frequent her outskirts. More than that, most of us do not even pretend to imagine, and we are quite likely to be uncertain whether Wellington is in the South Island of New Zealand, or the North.

But there is one proper symbol for this city: wind. Wellington is nicknamed, like Chicago, the Windy City, and if I wished to represent her on a decorative map, I would inscribe there a zephyr-kiwi, perpetually puffing out its snout. This is a city of the south—much further south than Cape Town, say, or Tristan da Cunha—and it stands in a situation of rugged if spectacular exposure, at the very tip of the North Island. Outside its almost circular bay run the

Wellington

tumultuous seas of Cook Strait, some of the choppiest and queasiest on earth: and through this narrow water-canyon, connecting the Tasman Sea with the open Pacific, the winds of the south perpetually bluster. In the summer, I am told, they blow from the north, jolly recreational winds: but in the winter they spring rasping out of the Antarctic, scurry and scour through the hilly streets of the capital, and so shake the frames of the suburban houses that you feel yourself to be actually at sea, in some stout old wooden-waller plugging down to Lyttelton.

For woodenness, salt-tempered, is another quality of Wellington. This is a modest capital, with only one or two of your glass-and-concrete ostentations, and the pleasant prevalence of wood gives it a pioneer manner still, and puts me in mind of the little seaports of southern Chile, on the other side of the Pacific. In winter at least this is a planked and creaking sort of city, a city of toasted sandwiches and steaming tea in shamelessly stuffy cafés, washed by the driving rains, dappled by splendid bursts of sun and cloud, always quaint and fragrant with wood. Thick dark scrub crawls down the hillsides. Clapboard and verandas grace the older suburbs. The old Government offices in the centre of the place are said to be the largest wooden structures on earth, and look like those innumerable British military edifices that were first condemned to demolition before the First World War, but are still struggling gamely on.

Indeed Wellington, like New Zealand, like England herself, breathes an endearing but mystifying air of gameness. We can manage, she seems to be saying, we'll get by somehow, it's being so cheerful that keeps us going—as if she is constantly undergoing, Heaven knows why, some awful test of civic stamina. Perhaps it is because, although she is peopled by very ordinary workaday British folk, decent, plain, and possibly rather idle, she stands in a position of princely splendour. The winds and the woodenness, and the pluckiness too, are only incidental to the grand fact of Wellington's harbour—which, just as it must form the climax of any essay about the place, is also the very point and purpose of the city.

It is more tremendous by far than Sydney's overvaunted harbour, if only because it is uncluttered by islets and fjords, but stands there like a noble bowl among its surrounding mountains. It looks symmetrical, purposeful, altogether functional. On a spit of land at one end, between bay and sea, run the new runways of Wellington Airport. Further north, towards Kaiwharawhara, ships stand high and dry in the floating dock. Along the western shore run the quays and warehouses of the port, and neatly protected by the promontory of Seatoun runs the narrow outlet to the open sea. It might have been scooped out by a million bull-dozers, so exactly does it fulfil the functions of a port, but for the grand bare highlands that surround it.

For tall and wild they stand there, Orongorongos and Tararuas, towering above the homely suburbs like sardonic reminders of a geographic truth. At night time, when you survey Wellington and her harbour from some high vantage point, the balcony of some friendly white villa or the blustery summit of Mount Victoria, then the sweep of the water-front, the glimmering lights of Hutt across the bay, the flare of the airport and the tumble of lamps and riggings along the docks may suggest to you, improbably, Monte Carlo: but the presence of the mountains there, unseen in the dark but always evident to the senses, gives Wellington her proper touch of the exotic, and tells us how far off we are in the remote South Seas, away beyond Fiji and Samoa, on the way to the ice.

Turn your back on this spectacle, the finest sight in the Antipodes, and inevitably you descend into anticlimax. It is true that the sea pervades Wellington, so that the ships tie up a stone's throw from the General Post Office, the Marine Department issues licenses for lifts, and even inland streets, built on reclaimed land, are sometimes still called Quays. It is true that when one of the big liners sails for England, with a streaming of pennants, a forest of waving arms and a general sniffing into small sad handkerchiefs, then you may feel, as you do when the Union Castle liners sweep out of Durban Bay, at the far end of a long and tenuous lifeline. Away from the water-front, though, Wellington is essentially a homely, family city, where women wearing trim inexpensive hats eat extraordinary quantities of sticky cakes, where there is a Floral Clock and a Centennial Fountain and a road called Wigan Street, and where vagabond birds out of the surrounding green fly happily into the zoo to get the aviary pickings.

It is mostly a late Victorian city, merrily built on ledges and inclines, and confused by the numberless hills that interrupt its pattern, so that driving down from the surrounding islands is a testing topographical exercise. A triumphantly Victorian cable car, all brass handles and garden seats, labours diligently upwards from Salamanca Road, through the intriguing *mélange* of bush and back garden that clothes the purlieus of the city. A fine Victorian university building stands in didactic sentinel above the business

Wellington

section. Inside Parliament House the affairs of the nation are conducted with a bucolic bonhomie and simplicity, and your cicerones at the uncompleted Anglican Cathedral may, with their acolyte attitudes and frequent references to the Bishop, strongly recall to you some of Trollope's lesser ecclesiasts.

It is an old-fashioned, genial provincial city. Nobody, you feel, is going to let you down or cheat you, slow though they may be in completing your commissions, and second-rate though the finished job may be. Some people find Wellington prim and stodgy, and prefer the sour ebullience of Sydney, or even Auckland's semi-American bustle. I much liked the taste of this little capital, though, and found its character much more tart and stimulating than I expected—more varied in colour and more dramatic in posture, windier, woodener, more comically stiff of upper lip, and un-expectedly ennobled, like San Francisco, by that queen of the tram-lines, the cable car.

And more idiosyncratic, too. If I began with a kiwi pecking my buttons, I will end with a reminder of Wellington's founding genius. They call this a prissy capital, but it was created by the vision of William Gibbon Wakefield, who eloped with an orphan heiress when he was twenty years old, abducted a second one by enticing her from school with a forged letter and whisking her up to Gretna Green, and spent three years in Newgate gaol before deciding, none too soon, to reform the economic practices of the Antipodes. He is buried in the Bolton Street cemetery in Wellington, up the road from Stout Street, and is rightly revered by the citizens of this capital as a very remarkable fellow.

ENVOI

You will perhaps excuse me Zagazig and Zermatt, and I never did
get to Zapadnaya Dvina—nor, for that matter, to Peking, whose
representatives courteously acknowledged my applications for visas,
but never wrote twice. In any case, one morning in 1963 I caught
myself, when preparing for a trip to Spain, packing a pair of bedroom
slippers: and I realized then that my footloose wandering days
were over. You can skim the world for just so long, but when you
get to the fluffy slipper stage, then you must dig deeper.

So I put this book together, as a souvenir: a souvenir of ten years'
unsurpassable enjoyment, and a souvenir of the particular transient
world that nurtured me. If nobody else reads the thing, at least
I will.